HOPE FOR THE CITY

A CATHOLIC PRIEST, A SUBURBAN HOUSEWIFE AND THEIR DESPERATE EFFORT TO SAVE DETROIT

Jack Kresnak

Cass Community Publishing House

For more information and further discussion, visit
ccpublishinghouse.org

ISBN: 978-1-942011-15-6

Version 1.0

Cover photo: Ira Rosenberg
Cover design: James Denk
Back cover design: Rick Nease
Author photo: Deutsch Photography

Published by Cass Community Publishing House
Copyediting and layout by Front Edge Publishing, LLC.

For information about customized editions, bulk purchases or permis-
sions, contact Cass Community Publishing House at 11745 Rosa Parks,
Detroit, MI 48206 or ffowler@casscommunity.org.

To Diane Kresnak, Mary Ellen Kresnak and Eleanor Josaitis—
three inspiring women who guided my life.

Contents

PREFACE

"Hope is necessary for life. Hope is necessary for freedom. It is necessary for creativity and for spirituality. Hope is one of the basic structures for an adequate life." —Dr. Martin Luther King Jr., Detroit, March 15, 1968, nine days after the founding of Focus: HOPE and less than three weeks before he was assassinated in Memphis.

ANSWERING THE CITY desk phone at the *Detroit Free Press* late morning on May 26, 1997, I heard Neal Shine's familiar voice tell me our friend, Father Bill Cunningham, had died. I had known Cunningham as my English literature and drama teacher at Sacred Heart Seminary High School in the 1960s. Indeed, Cunningham had urged Shine to hire me back in 1969, leading to a long career in journalism, so it was appropriate for me to write the obituary that would top the newspaper's front page the next morning.

Eleanor Josaitis, composed and collected a few hours after her mentor's death, met me as I entered Cunningham's suite at Harper Hospital to get her quote for the story I had to write. She led me to visit the priest's corpse first and left me alone to contemplate what Cunningham had done for me, personally, and what he'd accomplished in the City of Detroit. I returned to Eleanor, notebook in hand and started to ask for her comment. She stopped me, held my right hand and stared into my eyes. She said she had something to tell me first. One of Cunningham's dying directives to her, she said, was that I write the book about him and Focus: HOPE.

Why the priest thought I could write any book was a mystery to me—the longest piece I'd ever written was for the newspaper's

Sunday magazine, maybe 1,500 words. But I was in debt to Cunningham (and Eleanor, too) for making my career possible. I said yes immediately without having a clue to the challenges that lay ahead. Why, I asked myself, hadn't Cunningham told me this months earlier so I could interview him about his family and other events in his life? How and why had he become such an advocate for civil rights and for black people struggling in Detroit?

For more than 18 years I chased Cunningham's ghost, even as I held two high-pressure jobs (at the *Free Press* as children's issues reporter, and then at Michigan's Children, an advocacy organization for kids in Lansing). And I'm not sure I have answered the questions about Cunningham's inspiration and motives. What I think I have done is piece together a remarkable story about a charismatic mega-leader and his unlikely partner who inspired many and improved the lives of thousands of people. They helped people find a way to make a difference in the world, and I count myself among them.

Hope, as Dr. King said, is vital to human life. Without a belief in a better future, people lose the reasonable expectation that they can better their lives. When hope is absent, mental health issues arise, physical health deteriorates and impoverished families dissolve in despair. And when hope for an entire city seems to disappear—as it did in the months after Detroit's disastrous 1967 civil disturbance that left 43 dead and millions in property damage—someone needs to stop cursing the dark and light a candle. In Detroit, that someone was Father Bill Cunningham, a visionary leader whose energy, passion and powers of persuasion drove initiatives that fed the under-nourished, engaged teenagers in ways to overcome racial distrust in their schools, and trained the under-educated for higher-wage skilled trades jobs.

Cunningham's ordination vow to be obedient to his bishop was in conflict with his need to get something done—and quickly—to confront white racism and to make the Church more welcoming to black folks. He judged the Archdiocese of Detroit's response to the riot to be inadequate and talked for months about finding ways to take action without waiting for approval from some Archdiocesan bureaucrat.

I was among a group of seminarians who answered Cunningham's call to volunteer for a movement he named Focus: HOPE. With the help of one other priest on the seminary faculty, a handful of seminarians and a couple of female volunteers, Cunningham began to organize a response to racism in the city. Among the first Focus: HOPE volunteers was Eleanor, whose work ethic and loyalty to Cunningham were never equaled. With Eleanor at his side, Cunningham's little project became a uniquely creative, multi-million dollar non-profit behemoth on the edge of an industrial neighborhood in Detroit that wowed thousands of visitors, including two U.S. Presidents.

Cunningham and Josaitis used hard work, political savvy and a talent for inspiring volunteers to grow their movement into an organization that became a beacon of hope in Detroit's darkest years, shining a light on a path toward economic and social justice.

As close as a man and woman can be without sexual intimacy, Bill Cunningham and Eleanor Josaitis ran the enterprise like married business partners would. He and she worked together, prayed together and ate countless dishes of chicken at banquets together. They lobbied Congress together, with Bill bringing his passion and Eleanor handling details of planning and follow-up. They made decisions jointly. And they weren't shy about loudly disagreeing with each other in front of the staff. Bill's Roman collar didn't stop her from speaking her mind or correcting the priest when he was wrong.

Their work and their lives were rich in action and accomplishment. So many things were happening at once—especially in the 1980s, when they struggled to open a training center for machinists, while simultaneously building a first-class childcare center and a "Star Trekkian" manufacturing center that featured cutting-edge technology. Just keeping the story lines straight was mind-bending.

The book you are reading is my best effort to recount their complicated efforts to fight racism in the city they loved, Detroit, and its suburbs, in a way that makes sense and is readable. Daunted by the priest's challenge at first, I came to trust Cunningham's judgment that I'd figure it out. It was his voice I heard in my head as I tracked down records, interviewed those who knew him in spiritual and secular worlds, and reflected on how he influenced the lives of thousands of people with the force of his vision and the partnership he shared with Eleanor and their feisty Focus: HOPE colleagues.

Like other seminarians who had Cunningham as a teacher, I strove to not disappoint him. I hope—there is that important word again—he and Eleanor would be pleased with this narrative. More importantly, I would like their story to inspire others looking for ways to help Detroit and America's other urban centers by engendering a spirit of service to others and hope for a better future.

—*Jack Kresnak*

Father William T. Cunningham, 1968

Credit: Ira Rosenberg

1

A Guy With Guts

THE PRIEST NOTICED nothing unusual that hot, humid Sunday morning in July 1967 as he straddled his new Harley-Davidson in the parking lot of Detroit's Sacred Heart Seminary. He stomped twice on the ignition lever and the white-and-chrome bike coughed into a deep rumble. He released the clutch, twisted his right hand on the accelerator and pulled onto Linwood Avenue heading to the Ford freeway. He was unaware that his route skirted the epicenter of a full-blown riot that had been brewing for the past few hours just a few blocks from the seminary.

Father Bill Cunningham was late, as usual, so he gunned the Harley as he headed west on I-94 to St. Alfred Catholic Church in Detroit's suburb of Taylor. Twenty minutes later, the congregation patiently waiting in the church heard the rumble of the Harley as he parked outside the entrance near the sacristy. Most had grown accustomed to Cunningham's tardiness. He quickly dressed in green vestments, and Mass began. The all-white congregation at St. Alfred, including Don and Eleanor Josaitis and their five small children, loved the way Cunningham celebrated the Catholic liturgy with enthusiasm, passion and an excellent singing voice. He was charming, friendly, genuine and, oh, so good-looking. The Dominican nuns at St. Alfred often whispered to each other how charismatic and, yes, sexy Father Cunningham was. A brilliant homilist, his sermons were anecdote-laden gems, filled with knowledge, love and hope.

He was memorably different from other priests the St. Alfred community had seen. He seemed to be unique in the Archdiocese of Detroit for his ability to weave themes of racism and injustice into his homilies. It was an unpopular message for many white parishioners. But this young progressive priest's words caused many to rethink their prejudices.

Cunningham spoke about hope for Detroit, where a suffering and restive black population had been unjustly blocked from the economic and social mainstream for decades. African-Americans who held jobs in factories across Metropolitan Detroit were unfairly assigned the worst, most dangerous tasks. And they were denied training and apprenticeships that led to better jobs and could have helped them become middle class.

But many blacks were making it, and looking for homes outside of the run-down ghetto areas African-Americans had been confined to for years. More blacks were trying to buy homes in Detroit's white neighborhoods, but they were steered away by real estate agents. Those who persisted were met with cross-burnings, racist graffiti, vandalism, violence and public protests by whites. By 1960, black Detroiters had endured decades of harassment from hostile Caucasians, especially police officers. Some vigilantes, many transplants from southern states, terrorized blacks who quietly moved into white areas. In just one month—April 1965—25 crosses were burned in front of black homes in the city's handful of integrated neighborhoods. Detroit in the 1960s was rife with racial distrust, anger and fear. Tensions between Detroit's blacks and its overwhelmingly white police force had reached a boiling point in July 1967.

Although he worked hard as a high school English lit teacher at the seminary, Cunningham had energy to engage in St. Alfred's activities wholeheartedly. Parishioners enjoyed his company and invited him home for Sunday dinner or for drinks, conversation and music. A witty conversationalist and debater, Cunningham would take unexpected positions on issues, challenging assumptions. During Friday night hootenannies, he'd sing along with gusto. Wine was poured, but Cunningham preferred scotch—never the cheap stuff. Dewar's White Label was a favorite. On weekends, he led dozens of married couples on weekend retreats organized with the help of Eleanor Josaitis, the beginning of a partnership that would last decades.

After Mass at St. Alfred that Sunday, Cunningham learned from parishioners that something was going on in Detroit, where many of them had relatives.[1] He phoned his dad, William T. Cunningham, Sr., who lived on upscale Boston Boulevard, within blocks of the riot area and the seminary. His dad knew nothing of a riot. Both he and Father Cunningham's elderly aunt Rose Marie were fine, but on the way back to Sacred Heart the priest stopped to check on them anyway.

By then, news had gotten out that a civil disturbance had broken out overnight at an illegal bar, called a "blind pig" in Detroit. Reports said Detroit police were unable to control it. Some seminary faculty stayed where they were, safe in rectories. Those who remained at the seminary, including Cunningham, prayed in the chapel then gathered in the priests' lounge on the second floor to watch the news on television, discuss events and make phone calls.

The rioting rattled Cunningham, who had been among a small group of Catholic priests in Detroit preaching about the sin of white racism. He and several other seminary faculty had gone to Selma in 1965 to march with Dr. Martin Luther King Jr., across the Edmund Pettus Bridge two days after "Bloody Sunday," when mounted cops attacked peaceful marchers. Selma was life changing for Cunningham, although he already was

---

1   *Radio and television news stations had broadcast nothing about growing acts of civil disturbance that morning. Detroit Mayor Jerome P. Cavanagh asked that news about rioting be held back out of fear of creating panic, an embargo that would last until mid-afternoon.*

working with various civil rights and interracial groups since his ordination in 1955.[2]

He continued working with various civil rights groups after being assigned to teach English literature to high school students at Sacred Heart Seminary in 1961. Among the groups was the Human Relations Club at the University of Detroit that was organized by a Jesuit teacher, Father Arthur Lovely. In that program, teams of two or three students, faculty and volunteers of various ethnic backgrounds gave presentations about race. "We used to do speeches in the Catholic schools and groups," said Lucile Watts, an African-American who was then a student at U-D. "Then I started going out making speeches with different priests. Finally, they paired me with Father Cunningham, and he and I became a team. And, I guess, he became a part of my life actually."

Watts said she and Cunningham often faced hostile, even dangerous, crowds in suburban parishes. "We were talking about race relations and civil rights. It wasn't very popular." But Cunningham never showed any fear. He was able to talk through most people's anger. Still, Watts said, "Every now and then you get an idiot" who made threats. Cunningham, she said, "was always a guy with guts. He didn't back down and neither did I."

As the sun set that first evening of the riot, lights in the seminary were switched off so as not to draw sniper fire. Father Cunningham stood observing from the window in his darkened second-floor suite. He watched and listened as flames, smoke, gunshots, sirens from fire trucks and police cars, and carnival-like shouting periodically erupted in the surrounding neighborhoods.

From midnight to 5 a.m., that Monday proved to be the bloodiest period of the five days of rioting. Ten people were hit by sniper fire, including four cops, a National Guardsman and a state trooper. Nineteen suspected looters or arsonists were

---

2   *Father Cunningham had served his first assignment at St. Catherine of Siena – a solidly middle-class parish on Detroit's east side where blacks had just begun moving in – and then for a few years as an assistant at St. Mary of Royal Oak, a white suburb.*

shot. Over the five days of chaos, 43 people died. Indiscriminate shooting by National Guard troops;[3] stores looted and burned by rioters; martial law; whites and blacks arming themselves to protect their neighborhoods; fear and hatred gripping hearts across the metropolitan area—all of it had brought Detroit to its knees.

Of course, Cunningham could not know then how many people were being killed that night, but he was appalled at what he feared was happening. He was angry that years of effort by him and his colleagues to bridge the racial chasm between whites and blacks had failed to prevent a devastating race riot.

That night, as he watched the destruction, Cunningham vowed to work to save African-Americans from white racism. He swore to God that he would not let his allegiance to the Church get in the way of what he believed God wanted him to do. If possible, he would remain a Roman Catholic priest. But he told himself that he wouldn't let Church higher-ups get in his way.

In the morning, Cunningham got a taste of the danger on city streets as he drove the Harley to say Mass at St. Theresa of Avila Church on the city's near west side. It was a short trip, but as he slowly made his way through neighborhoods obscured by smoke, someone fired a gun at him. He told seminary colleagues that whoever it was probably thought he was a cop because he was wearing a white helmet and black leather jacket. His white-and-chrome Harley Electraglide looked like a traffic cop's bike.

The riot in Detroit "uncorked me," Father Cunningham would say later. "At that moment, [the seminary] seemed so completely irrelevant and so awesomely removed from real

---

3   *The Michigan National Guard's reputation as "trigger happy" during the riot was enhanced by two simple statistics. Highly disciplined U.S. Army troops who were authorized by President Lyndon Johnson to help restore order were assigned to the city's east side. Army troops, many of them blacks who had returned from fighting in Vietnam, were more disciplined, firing 202 rounds of ammunition during their tour of duty in Detroit and were not linked to any shootings of civilians. On the other side of town, it was a different story. The National Guard, which was concentrated in the west side, where most of the riot's carnage occurred, fired 155,576 rounds of ammunition that week, killing more than a score of civilians.*

life. Fifty-caliber machine guns taking down sides of apartment buildings! Bloody bodies out in the street, and America's arsenal encamped at Central High School, and choppers overhead! And, here I am looking out of the window of my apartment, a very academic apartment—a book reviewer, I was—and saying to myself, 'How can you go back to what you're doing?'"

Billy Cunningham, age 4; teen-aged Bill with his parents, Will and Alvina Cunningham; unknown artist's rendering of Alvina; Father Cunningham teaching at Sacred Heart Seminary's high school, the Cardinal Mooney Latin School, in 1967.

Credits: Cunningham family photos, Sacred Heart Seminary archives

2

Organizer

A LARGE, ANGRY black man stood in their way.

National Guard and U.S. Army troops still patrolled a city devastated by the five-day orgy of destruction, and Father Bill Cunningham, Eleanor Josaitis and their friend Lorraine Blaty were on foot, surveying the damage surrounding Sacred Heart Seminary that occupied an entire city block, a fortress standing relatively untouched amid the rubble of the neighborhoods.

They were three whites: two young women and a Catholic priest, walking on a Clairmount Avenue sidewalk. A man refused to let them pass, defying them with an angry stare. "I remember there was anger in the people down there," Blaty said. "There was this pretty big guy and he sort of blocked our way. But it wasn't time to fuss about it."

Cunningham calmly led the women around the man and they continued down Clairmount to 12th Street where the riot had started six days earlier. Cunningham "was extremely pensive" as they walked, Josaitis said. "It was not frightening. It was, well, I had seen it all on television. I knew what to expect—the burned-out buildings. We were pensive, trying to figure out, my God, what's happening? How are we going to overcome this?"

Of the 43 riot-related deaths, only three resulted in criminal convictions. At the time, it was the worst civil disturbance of the 20th century in the United States. When it was all added up, damage was estimated at $84 million insured and $50 to $60 million uninsured. The American Insurance Association said 2,509 stores were looted, burned or destroyed, including 611 grocery stores; 537 cleaners and laundries; 326 clothing, department and fur stores; 285 liquor stores and bars; 240 drugstores and 198 furniture stores. Direct costs to the city were more than $11.6 million in overtime pay for police officers and firefighters. Indirect costs to Detroit included canceled downtown conventions; the closing of hundreds of tax-paying businesses; the loss of 1,200 jobs and, for many white Detroiters, a hardening of their negative feelings toward black people. Working-class blacks were discouraged because they felt that police had failed to act early and aggressively to protect their neighborhoods from the violent minority. Blacks who could afford to move began joining the "white flight" out of the city to the suburbs.

Mayor Jerome Cavanagh, a staunch liberal who had thought he'd improved conditions for blacks in Detroit, seemed utterly defeated by the past week. Cavanagh despaired that the city that could have been a shining example of racial peace had instead destroyed itself. "Today," Cavanagh said in 1967, "we stand amidst the ashes of our hopes. We hoped against hope that what we had been doing was enough to prevent a riot. It was not enough."

But after walking the smoky streets of Detroit's riot area, Cunningham and Josaitis knew things could change—indeed, they must change. They pledged to do anything and everything to help heal the wounds caused by racism and injustice. Eleanor's first thought was, "Let's get some food down there. We've got to get some clothing down there. How can we be helpful?"

The daunting task was suited to Eleanor's well-honed traits of organization, hard work and commitment. She was the eldest of four children of George and Helen Reed, and raised in a home near Schaefer Avenue and Plymouth Road on Detroit's west side. George was a carpenter and second cousin to Henry Ford. Their neighborhood was solidly middle class with well-kept homes, leafy lawns and backyard vegetable gardens. The family's only known interactions with African-Americans were with a coworker of George's who would come over every so often to accept the Reed children's hand-me-down clothing for his own kids.

As a girl, Eleanor had thought seriously about joining a convent, and she chose to enroll at St. Theresa of Avila High School.[4] Eleanor "did want to be a nun," said her niece Kathy Young-Griffen. "I guess it was my grandfather that did not want that." She was a leader of the cheerleading squad at St. Theresa and the life of every party. She "taught everyone in the family, all of us, how to dance," said her sister Margaret Kruger. Eleanor was considered a "nurturer" in the family, taking care of her younger siblings and helping their mother when George became ill with Parkinson's disease.

Energetic as she was, Eleanor was unhappy as a teenager. She was stressed due to her strained relationship with her strong-willed mother, Helen, who was critical of virtually everything Eleanor did. A lanky lad across the street, Don Josaitis, saw the worry eating away at Eleanor and he talked her into moving out. He helped her find an apartment. They took a ceramics class together, giving him time to spend with the vulnerable and strikingly beautiful woman. "My mother was so shy, so socially inept, that (Dad) used to drag her to pottery classes. She couldn't come out of her shell," said their daughter Janet Denk. That shyness faded as Eleanor began to assert her independence. "The joke in our family is Don created a monster." Despite the mother-daughter clashes, Helen was Eleanor's model for politeness, manners and hospitality that became hallmarks in her life. Don and Eleanor were married in 1955, then moved into the home in Taylor and started having babies.

---

4   *Father Cunningham also had attended grade school at St. Theresa, but already was enrolled in the Sacred Heart Seminary High School by then.*

In Cunningham, Eleanor found someone to follow on a path that felt right to her—helping vulnerable people. The two of them—the priest and the housewife—worked closely staging the weekend marriage retreats. And despite the five kids in the Josaitis family's three-bedroom ranch, their home became a hotspot for progressive Catholics to meet and discuss the issues of the day, mostly the Vietnam War and racism. Progressive nuns and priests, seminarians and pacifists who were friends of Cunningham, came to enjoy good conversation about Vatican II, folk songs and libations. Eleanor was the consummate host.

Many parishioners wondered about the obviously close relationship between Eleanor and the handsome priest. Don said that he was initially miffed when Cunningham stopped by unannounced and late at night to drink scotch and talk with Eleanor. He owned and operated a hobby store on Wyoming Avenue on the Detroit-Dearborn border, came home late and tired, frequently finding the priest already there. After a time, he would go to bed—without his wife. And then there were the nights Eleanor was out with the priest at meetings all over town. "I think I really felt at that point that he was a man of God and I should forget about any jealousy," Don said. But he still worried and he knew that neighbors were talking about it. Finally, Don confronted the priest.

"Bill and I had that out back in Taylor," Don said in an interview years later. "They were discussing all this shit that was happening—the riots. It went late into the night, so I got into it with him." Don angrily told Cunningham: "I'm not really big about my wife being out, and you're a good-looking guy." Cunningham's response surprised him. "He was like, 'Oh, God! I was hoping this thing would never happen. I get this wherever I go.'" Don said it was obvious that women flirted with the priest. "Apparently, he had run across it at other times. Let's face it, the women really went swoony over him."

Cunningham felt badly, even hurt that some might question his celibacy commitment. He made it perfectly clear that there was nothing romantic or sexual about his relationship with Eleanor—they shared a passion for addressing Detroit's racial and social inequities. Cunningham said he understood that Don "was human and loved (his) wife." Still "there were so many times in our whole relationship that I could've killed that guy," Don said. Satisfied and likewise impressed by Cunningham's sincerity, Don accepted Cunningham as a member of his family.

With their family grown to five kids by the spring of 1969, Eleanor convinced Don to buy a stately home near Seven Mile and Livernois in Detroit. The Tudor-style house had been built in the 1920s with five bedrooms, five baths and a small apartment or carriage house above the garage in an elegant and leafy northwest Detroit neighborhood called Sherwood Forest. At first, Don wasn't keen on the idea but, as he nearly always did, he acceded to his wife. "Eleanor really had to talk me into moving to Detroit," he said.

The idea of living in the city suited Eleanor's ideas of living out a true commitment to the causes of social justice, and the price seemed right to her husband: $28,000. Mortgage rates were high at about 8.5 percent, but the Josaitises learned they could assume the mortgage. The relatively low house payment meant they could afford to send their kids to the Catholic school attached to Gesu Parish, a Jesuit-run church across West McNichols Road from the University of Detroit.

Cunningham had been born at Henry Ford Hospital in Detroit on February 20, 1930, just as the Great Depression was hitting Detroit hard. His father, William Thomas Cunningham, Sr., had made a fortune in real estate, then lost it when the stock market crashed. "Pop" Cunningham and his wife, Alvina Mardian, already had two older daughters when their son was born—Rose Marie, born in 1915, and Elizabeth Cecilia (Betty) who was born in 1918. They were living in an apartment building in Royal Oak then, but moved back to Detroit a few years later.

The senior Cunningham was a salesman who forged deals big and small with a handshake and a round of whiskey. He dressed like a salesman with flashy red-plaid jackets. With a full head of luxuriously silver hair, Pop was gregarious and had an impressive portfolio of Irish tall tales that he'd deliver with gusto. In the 1940s, he bought a red Studebaker convertible to take the family for rides through the expansive farmland in and around Detroit, scouting out real estate opportunities. When he did business, he often brought his son along —then called "Billy" to distinguish him from his dad— often meeting potential clients in bars. Father and son sometimes stopped at a Catholic Church they passed by. They'd walk in, and Mr. Cunningham prayed out loud to God for his family's health and wealth. To young Billy, his dad was bigger than life.

Billy's mother, Alvina, was quite the opposite. She was shy, a homebody and devout Catholic who attended Mass virtually every day but who participated in few parish activities. She preferred to stay home, cooking and caring for her children. Years later, Bill would speak fondly of his mother as "a good, good woman" who liked to recite well-known proverbs to get a point across. "She would say things like, 'You know, you can't make a silk purse out of a sow's ear.' And my dad would hear her in his study just outside the kitchen door around the corner … and he'd call me in and say, 'Let me tell you, son, the only way you are ever going to make a silk purse is out of a sow's ear.' Everything my mother said he would turn around and take the other side of the axiom."

Pop Cunningham had expected his son to follow him into the real estate business. But Billy Cunningham had long felt a calling to serve God as a Roman Catholic priest. At age 6, a Jesuit priest on the faculty of the University of Detroit took him to a football game, let him sit on the players' bench and bought him a hotdog. "I just remember looking up at that priest and thinking, *I want to be one of them*," Bill Cunningham told *The Michigan Catholic* in 1994.

In 1942, Billy begged his mother to call him "Bill" and his dad "Will" because he thought Billy was a "sissy" name. The following year, 13-year-old Bill applied to the seminary, taking the entrance examination on May 15. A report on Bill's application in the seminary archives said the boy had "thought of the priesthood since the first grade." Bill was a "weekly communicant," meaning he received Holy Communion at least once a week, and he had "B-average grades," the priest admissions officer wrote. "Seemed to be very sincere."

The senior Cunningham was against it, but there was no dissuading his son. He told his parents he had prayed about the decision. He told his sister Betty that his parents' opinions on the matter were irrelevant. "Neither Mom nor Dad was an influence on him becoming a priest," she said. Despite that, their parents "questioned him often about whether this was his sincere wish for himself," his sister said.

At Sacred Heart Seminary High School, Bill Cunningham proved to be a popular, if average, student. He soon found a mentor, Father Philemon Merrill, a teacher of English, History and Sociology. Merrill had founded a chapter of the Blessed Martin League at Sacred Heart in response to the 1943 race riot in Detroit in which 34 people—25 of them black and 17 of those shot by white police officers—were killed. The BML was formed in honor of Martin de Porres, a Peruvian mulatto and 16th-century martyr. Its mission was to address the plight of people of color suffering because of white racism.[5] Widely acknowledged by seminarians as a protégé of Father Merrill, Bill Cunningham was elected leader of the group after he matriculated from the seminary high school to its college in 1947.

In late 1946, while Bill was in his senior year at Sacred Heart Seminary High School, his mother's health worsened. Blood clots were detected in her left leg and in her brain, according to her daughter Betty Horning. The medication doctors wanted to use could clear up clots in one area but not both. So doctors amputated the leg, increasing the odds that the medication would destroy the clots in her brain. The operation

---

5   *The Blessed Martin League's weekly meetings were designed to "study the principles and practice of interracial justice and charity," according to the group's constitution. Their purpose was "to form more Christ-like priests, who will solve on the basis of Catholic doctrine and morals the race problems which will inevitably arise during the course of their ministry." Benefits of the League included "the elimination of personal racial prejudice, which is a serious sin against the Mystical Body," and "an understanding of racial problems and their Christian solutions."*

saved Alvina's life and her brain remained sharp, but she was left unable to walk or completely care for herself. Alvina could use crutches to get from room to room, and she rarely left home except for doctor visits or to attend Mass. Will Cunningham, rebuilding his small fortune in the red-hot, post-war Detroit real estate market, hired a live-in housekeeper. Thelma, a black woman with kids of her own, was chatty, funny and friendly to a fault. She must have made a positive impression on young Bill.

In January 1948, Alvina was rushed to Mt. Carmel Hospital in acute distress, and a priest administered last rites. She died the following day of hypoxic encephalopathy or "multiple emboli to brain" and "multiple emboli to right lower leg," her death certificate says. Hypertension was a contributing factor to her relatively early death at age 52.

Cunningham always kept a portrait of Alvina on his dresser, and said hello to her every morning. "He had very tender remembrances of his mother," said Sister Cecilia Begin of the Religious Sisters of Mercy, a longtime associate of Father Cunningham later in his life. "He'd tell us about one time … he was always fighting with his two sisters. According to him, he was running up the stairs. His mother was up ahead and she stopped him, tucked him under the chin with her hand and looked him in the eye. She said, 'You have a very mean disposition and, if you're not careful, you're going to hurt somebody some day.'"

Cunningham was among 47 men ordained Catholic priests by Cardinal Edward Mooney on June 4, 1955, at Blessed Sacrament Cathedral. His classmate and friend Ed Baldwin said that on the bus to the ceremony Cunningham suddenly panicked. He'd have to say Mass for the first time the next day and he wasn't quite sure about a certain part of the liturgy. "Here we are, on the bus going to the Cathedral to be ordained and I'm explaining to him how to say Mass!" Baldwin said with a laugh. For Cunningham, though, celebrating Mass became the most important part of his day. Anthony Tocco, then a high school seminarian and an acolyte at St. Catherine of Siena, closely observed Cunningham celebrate one of his first Masses. "What I remember was during the words of consecration he always wept," said Monsignor Tocco. "The moment brought tears to his eyes. Bill Cunningham was one of the reasons I became a priest."

Cunningham used Father Merrill as his model when he began teaching after ordination—first at St. Catherine of Siena on Detroit's near eastside, then at St. Mary of Royal Oak, and later at the seminary high school where he was assigned to teach English literature. In class, Cunningham would play recordings of Richard Burton interpreting *Hamlet* and *Henry V*, or the poetry of Dylan Thomas. He'd turn out the lights, lower the classroom blinds and set a match to a candle in the darkened room, filling the space with soft light and Burton's rich baritone, or simply let silence envelop the class. In the dark, warmed by the glow of a single candle, Cunningham would say, "Just look at the flame and see where your life is going to lead you; be in presence with the light."

He would point out that the flame doesn't actually touch the wax, appearing to be detached from the candle when it is actually a part of the candle, it's heat melting it down. "The brightest flame is really at the end," Cunningham said. Echoing his dad's habit of turning axioms upside down, Cunningham said, "Maybe it's better to blow out the candle and curse like hell." He had a beautifully expressive voice, similar to Burton's.

At the seminary, Cunningham and Father Jerry Fraser were among several faculty members responding to rising racial tensions in Detroit. They both were involved in the Archbishop's Commission on Human Relations (ACHR) for several years, meeting with parish-based groups to pray for a solution to the racial crisis. Several Sacred Heart faculty members, including Cunningham and Fraser, had flown to Selma in 1965 to march with Dr. King. That shared experience energized them. "There's no going back," Fraser said he told Cunningham then. "We got this far, and it's got to go forward and it's going to go forward." Cunningham sounded out ideas with his friends, including Eleanor, who had made hundreds of phone calls in the days following the 1967 riots, collecting donations of food and clothing for the people whose lives had been devastated.

In February, Eleanor was recovering from a hysterectomy when Cunningham came to visit and to ruminate about ideas that he and Fraser were considering. "I said, 'Why don't you guys do what you do best? Which is go into the pulpits and tell the people. Tell us what I'm supposed to do with my emotions.' And, bingo! He grabbed it," Eleanor said.

Fraser and Cunningham called a meeting of priests, seminarians and lay people already active in civil rights for Wednesday, March 6, at the seminary. "During the year, we had become increasingly concerned about the possibility of further riots that summer and decided that only a full mobilization of people of goodwill would have any hope of changing the atmosphere and attitudes that lingered after the devastating riots of 1967," Fraser said. They called their project Summer Hope, but Cunningham wanted the name to be more distinctive. He added the word Focus with a colon, punctuation that would make anyone who saw it pause for a moment—Focus: Summer Hope.[6] Nearly 300 Catholics—men and women, whites and blacks—crowded into the seminary's Bishop Gallagher Room for a freewheeling discussion of ideas on what the Catholic community could do.

"Focus: HOPE began March 6, 1968, three days after the Kerner Commission published its Report on Civil Disorder," a 1971 Focus: HOPE publication proclaimed. "Focus: HOPE originated from the frustration of two Catholic Priests who felt the need of immediate actions to stem the fear that was mounting in Metropolitan Detroit. People, both Black and White, needed a dramatic and imaginative sign of Hope. ... We must never say that it is too late, for HOPE is our greatest asset when things

---

6   *Mary Stephenson, who had known Cunningham since his days as assistant pastor at St. Mary of Royal Oak parish in the 1950s who later married Focus: HOPE insider Tony Campbell and became Mary Campbell, was typing up the letter and asked Cunningham about the title of his project. He told her, and she suggested they put a colon after "Focus" so the subsequent words would have more impact. Later, when the word "summer" was dropped, Mary Campbell also suggested that they write the word "hope" in all capital letters, making it Focus: HOPE.*

look dark and can be our greatest strength when the prophets of doom offer inaction."

Step one, the group decided under the leadership of Cunningham and Fraser, was to train articulate, committed and courageous priests to preach for three consecutive Sundays in two or three parishes each. The urgency of their mission showed in how quickly Cunningham, Fraser and Eleanor organized a three-day retreat for 55 priests at the Franklin Settlement retreat center in Lake Orion, beginning just five days later on March 11.

At the retreat, Cunningham and Fraser gave their colleagues a "straight talk" on how the Archdiocese's efforts to address race so far was too little and too late. Time was not on their side—hot weather would return to Detroit within weeks. It was urgent to act.

Joseph Hansknecht Jr., who chaired the ACHR for several years, attended the retreat and said Cunningham was "very blunt" with the priests. "He would say every time a white parishioner moves out to the suburbs, how much annual income you lose as a parish," Hansknecht said. "Most of them weren't thinking about that. Every time a family moves out, you have fewer children in your school and what is that doing to the survivability of your parish school? Very practical. Very accurate. Not exaggerating. Some hefty impact."

Recognizing that Archbishop John Dearden would be busy, Cunningham and Fraser composed a letter that they wanted to send to about 10,000 people involved in the ACHR's Project Commitment. They asked Dearden to sign it, as well as a second letter informing pastors about the "crash program" and asking them "to introduce the visiting priests as his own spokesman," Cunningham wrote in a 1971 essay. "Iron John" Dearden, who had come to Detroit from Pittsburgh with the reputation as a staunch conservative, agreed.

The first letter said that the new project, Focus: Summer Hope, was designed "not just to stem riots this summer, but to broaden the foundation of training and education among those of good will so that they can take intelligent and practical steps to root out racism, poverty and injustice." The letter gave the distinct impression that this was a program of the Archdiocese of Detroit.

An estimated 5,000 people, most of them Catholics, showed up at the University of Detroit's Memorial Building on March 17, 1968, for the Focus: Summer Hope meeting. It was like a rally with Scripture readings, folk music and discussions of the Kerner Report findings about the 1967 civil disturbances, the nature of prejudice and Black Power. "We are not here … to dispel fears, but to redirect them to stem the tide of panic," Fraser told the gathering. "People must be given hope. This is an effort to stem the tide of panic. It's an effort to catalyze action."

Newly consecrated Bishop Thomas Gumbleton, representing Dearden, also spoke to the crowd. "That you are ready to go out into your own neighborhoods and suffer if necessary to solve this problem is further evidence of your dedication to eradicating the sin of racism," Gumbleton said. "And today where we find racism in the archdiocese, we oftentimes find the Church in great strength."

Fraser said the role of laypeople was essential. "You can make it easier on these priests who will be coming into unfamiliar parishes to speak on racism if they know you are there as resource people." He asked them to host discussion groups in their homes for their fellow parishioners following the sermons on racism and to choose some action to address white racism. "We are not here tonight to dispel fears, but to redirect them to actions needed," Fraser said. "We must become one people not divided by race. And this is something you can do in your own neighborhood by talking to people just like yourselves."

Over the next three weeks, the 55 priests trained by Cunningham and Fraser spoke to an estimated 300,000 Catholics with messages of hope on March 24 and 31 and on Palm Sunday, April 7. They also planned a second rally for April 14, Easter Sunday.

On the morning of April 4, 1968, Cunningham and Fraser put the finishing touches on a letter to Dearden explaining the first phases of Focus: Summer Hope—"With few exceptions these sixty priests read the congregations well and directed their challenge to the good will of the majority of the parishioners, with the intention of promoting the home meetings. We were happy that these men said what had to be said, but said it with a sensitivity and rapport developed in long hours of serious discussion with professional advisors."

At 6:01 p.m. that same evening, Dr. Martin Luther King Jr. was cut down by an assassin's bullet while standing on the second-floor balcony of the Lorraine Motel in Memphis. He was 39 and had seemingly predicted his own death the night before in a speech to striking sanitation workers: "But it really doesn't matter with me now, because I've been to the mountaintop. And I don't mind. Like anybody, I would like to live a long life—longevity has its place. But I'm not concerned about that now. I just want to do God's will. And He's allowed me to go up to the mountain. And I've looked over, and I've seen the Promised Land. I may not get there with you. But I want you to know tonight, that we, as a people, will get to the Promised Land. And I'm so happy tonight; I'm not worried about anything; I'm not fearing any man. Mine eyes have seen the glory of the coming of the Lord."

The assassin's cowardly act sparked anger and rioting in several American cities, but not in Detroit.

The second "Rally for Hope" was 10 days after King's murder. Nearly 7,000 people came to this rally, again at the University of Detroit. "We first thought this date would be disruptive of family life," Fraser told the gathering on Easter Sunday. "Then we realized that disruption might be a way to point up the need for action and understanding. The senseless, tragic death of Dr. King makes the disruption imperative."

In what was becoming Cunningham's trademark way of operating, it was full speed ahead. In a 1971 essay, Cunningham wrote that Focus: Summer Hope has "grown from the frustration of two men and one woman into an organization of thousands of concerned people. People, both white and black, needed a dramatic and imaginative sign of hope."

Top: The first published photograph of the co-founders of "Focus: Summer Hope" in *The Michigan Catholic* in March 1968. The original caption: "AT A PLANNING session for 'Focus: Summer Hope' were (from left) Mrs. Ernest King of Gesu Parish, Fr. William T. Cunningham of Sacred Heart Seminary, Joseph L. Hansknecht Jr., human relations leader, and Fr. Jerome R. Fraser, also of Sacred Heart Seminary. The educational program is designed to help eliminate racism at the local level."

Bottom: Cunningham and Eleanor Josaitis distribute copies of Focus: HOPE's report on the first survey comparing prices and quality of food from inner-city and suburban grocery stores to survey volunteers.

Credit: *The Michigan Catholic*

3

Chutzpah

BILL AND NORITA Frcka went to bed around 10 p.m. one Sunday in March 1968, disappointed that the priest they'd invited to their home in Troy around 6 p.m. hadn't shown up. At about 11:30 p.m., they were awakened by the rumble of a motorcycle making its way up the driveway of their three-acre lot that was normally country quiet. Someone banged on the door and Bill Frcka got up. "I open the door up and here's this guy in black leather and motorcycle helmet standing in my doorway with a priest collar on," Frcka said. Of course, it was Father Bill Cunningham.

For the next few hours, they sat around the kitchen table discussing racial justice, Focus: Summer Hope and his plan to survey inner-city grocery stores to prove that inner-city blacks were being cheated. Frcka suggested that Cunningham think about a logo for his project. Off the top, Cunningham proposed two hands, one black and one white, clasping in a handshake of friendship. But Frcka, a graphic artist at an architectural firm in downtown Detroit, thought that white and black people weren't yet grasping each other in peace. He came up with the idea of two hands—a black one on a white background and a white one on a black background—reaching towards each other, but barely touching. He worked the logo up at work the next day, tracing the outline of his left hand with the simple word "HOPE" on each side. The logo "was rectangular, like the bumper sticker," Frcka said. It was used for the first time at the April 14 "Rally for Hope."

One of their first projects was coming to the aid of a beleaguered mixed-race couple, Carado and Ruby Bailey, who were being harassed after moving into the white, working-class suburb of Warren in June 1967. Carado Bailey, a black man, his white wife Ruby, her 18-year-old son by a previous marriage, Tom Bridges, and the couple's 7-year-old daughter, Pamela, had been targeted by a white mob. The N-word was spray-painted on the garage door of their rose-colored brick ranch on Buster Street, and Warren police had done virtually nothing to stop protests by loud, angry whites standing in front of their home. Some whites were outraged by the racist vandalism, including members of the Warren Human Relations Council, which held a meeting at nearby St. Anne Catholic Church. That meeting was disrupted by the radical right-wing group Breakthrough led by perpetually angry Catholic Donald Lobsinger. Lobsinger often made loud protests in churches, even during Mass, when a priest spoke about "liberal" concepts such as white racism.

When the Baileys found a burned doll with pins stuck in it like voodoo in their yard, their fear rose. Pamela was the only "colored" child in her school and had been enduring increasing taunts from some schoolmates.[7]

After the Detroit riots, the Baileys considered moving as racial tension increased in Warren. But they stuck it out by keeping their heads down. Cunningham and Fraser thought the Baileys needed a stronger, more public showing of support. It's unclear whether they met with the Baileys. Regardless, the priests and Eleanor Josaitis organized dozens of volunteers, including

---

7   *Today, few people remember that the first race riot of 1967 in Michigan happened not in the black neighborhoods of Detroit, but in a white neighborhood of suburban Warren.*

several seminarians, to go door-to-door in Warren with a petition in support for the Baileys. "We who are citizens of Warren, recognizing that our full support has been lacking, feel that their leaving would be a tragedy for our community," reads the petition written by the two priests. "We will try, as a Christian people, to overcome the prejudice and bigotry shown them on so many occasions."

Some 2,500 Warren residents signed. Focus: Summer Hope spent $5,410—including a $5,000 loan from Father Cunningham's dad—to publish the petition and signatories under the Frcka-designed Focus: HOPE logo in *The Royal Oak Tribune*, *The Macomb Daily* and *The Michigan Catholic* April 30 through May 2.[8]

Some suburban pastors may have complained to chancery officials about what Cunningham and Fraser were doing in their parishes. Dearden, who had announced a campaign to raise $1 million to "ease the plight of inner-city poor and eradicate white racism" through the Archdiocesan Development Fund (ADF), faced a backlash from Catholics who didn't want their donations going to help blacks in Detroit. At the same time, Dearden was perturbed that Focus: Summer Hope was not under his authority. In a letter dated April 15, Dearden wrote the two priests at the seminary: "When I endorsed the Summer Hope Program and asked the parish priests to cooperate fully with it, I did so with the understanding that this program was to be carried out under the direction of the Community Affairs Department. I had received assurance from Bishop Gumbleton that you were working with and under the overall guidance of Father James Sheehan, Director of the Human Relations Division of the Department, and that this program would fit in with the total human relations efforts of the diocese. It was only this understanding that caused me to approve the program as fully as I did despite certain difficulties that its hurried development entailed.

"It is evident that our efforts must be conducted and channeled through one office. ... I am willing to support energetically

---

8   *The Baileys, who apparently stopped talking to reporters in 1968, were still living in the house on Buster in Warren 40 years later. They declined to be interviewed for this book.*

all efforts aimed at easing racial tensions both by confronting the problems of racism, whether of the subtle or more direct type, and by bringing aid to the ghetto areas through self-determination of programs. ... I do not wish to give the impression that I disapprove the ideas you have proposed in your present letter. However, since these are part of the Summer Hope Program, I expect that they will be carried out under Father Sheehan's direction and that reports about the program will come to me and to the community at large from the Community Affairs Department."

Cunningham and Fraser responded in a letter dated April 24 that was masterful in that it seemed to indicate a willingness to cooperate with the Archbishop's directive without actually acceding to his authority: "From the beginning we have shared your conviction for close cooperation of effort and communication with our Community Affairs Office and the ACHR. We have channeled all program suggestions through these offices and have extended our invitations for all meetings to both departments. We thank you once again for your kindness and we reiterate our purpose to serve the whole Church in a cooperative and open manner."

If Focus: Summer Hope had a chance of working for Cunningham and Fraser, it had to be independent. Yet, they still needed the resources of Sacred Heart Seminary where they had commandeered an empty suite of rooms. Didn't matter. They were on a mission to make something out of their new idea. They turned to the problems of hunger and malnutrition that were endemic in low-income neighborhoods of Detroit where fewer grocery stores existed. Anecdotally, advocates for the poor believed that inner-city grocers were gouging their customers, charging higher prices for lower quality food products. Indeed, the Kerner Commission report on the 1967 riots in Detroit, Newark and elsewhere said the suspicion and hostility between shop owners and inner-city customers contributed to the conditions that set the stage for disorder and violence.

The crisis in Detroit demanded swift and decisive actions at all levels. There was no time to run ideas up the chain of

Catholic Church command. They were bolstered by a wave of checks and cash donations for Focus: Summer Hope that arrived unsolicited in the mail—before the priests had thought about nonprofit tax-exempt status. The money went for postage, signs, posters and bumper stickers, and pizzas for volunteers. The seminary tacitly absorbed much of the organization's costs of office space, telephones and copying machines, not to mention the heat and lights in the makeshift office.

They talked late nearly every night and scratched ideas out on legal pads. They turned to volunteer Mary Stephenson to type it all up. Stephenson, who later became Mary Campbell after marrying a former seminarian, had known Cunningham since she was a high school student at Royal Oak St. Mary Church in the 1950s. "They stood over my shoulder and told me what to type," Campbell said.

They worked several days on a 20-page grant request to New Detroit Inc., describing Focus: Summer Hope in grand terms. Their organization, New Detroit was told, was "an education-action program directed at achieving attitudinal change." It described the training of more than 50 priests who reached nearly 600,000 Catholics in three weeks with a message of hope and racial justice. The ranks of lay men and women numbered in the thousands, the proposal said, and the program's "training assembly" of 5,000 ready, willing and able volunteers at the University of Detroit began the process by "concentrating on the Urban Crisis and Black Power."

Focus: Summer Hope was all of six weeks old, but Cunningham and Fraser said it was "a massive program, which from all indications achieved a remarkable attitudinal change and a readiness for action. ... It must be made clear that Focus: Summer Hope intends no programs which parallel existing plans of other organizations." The priests described their accomplishments and plans for action, including the Bailey Support Petition, a Consumer Survey, a Legislative Program, Tutorial Program, Pre-apprentice Program, Clergy Training and "Tea for 10,000," a series of meetings to reach as many people as possible with the HOPE message. They asked for money for an office and staff, a total of $77,460. That would cover expenses for just four months, from May through August when, presumably but unstated, Focus: Summer Hope would fade away. The New Detroit Inc., board approved a grant of $10,000.[9]

The Kerner Commission report placed some blame on the looting of stores on a climate of distrust and racial tensions between inner-city blacks and retailers, particularly grocers and pharmacists. Inner-city merchants denied gouging their customers, saying their security and insurance costs were much higher than their suburban competitors because of robberies and thefts. Cunningham and Fraser believed that a consumer survey would prove that poor people unfairly paid more for the same groceries. But, how to do it?

Help came from Mayor Jerome Cavanagh, who sent a young Vista volunteer from New York, Jerrold Reisman, to work with Focus: Summer Hope. As an alternative to being drafted, Reisman had joined Vista, the domestic version of the Peace Corps. His two-year stint began in June 1967 when he was assigned to work on food co-ops. In March 1968, Cavanagh sent him to Cunningham, who already had a checklist for volunteers to compare the prices of food items like hot dogs, bacon, whole frying chickens, apples, potatoes, green beans and lettuce. But it was Reisman who structured the way the survey was to be conducted and arranged for volunteers to be trained by a federally funded agency coaching anti-poverty workers in Michigan.

"If I was going to be involved in this, I did not want to do something halfway," Reisman said years later. "Bill Cunningham was a real amazing guy. He was able to get things done with his personality and his intelligence. ... The original idea was to have 30 or 40 people and to have sort of a secret survey, just to get the prices, without anybody knowing about it."

Volunteers were schooled on checking for cleanliness of stores, food packaging and service. They were told to note the prices of

9   NDI also gave $10,000 to the Archdiocese of Detroit for expenses related to Dr. King's Poor People's March, in which thousands of people would make their way to Washington, D.C. Several hundred camped overnight at Sacred Heart Seminary on May 13.

specific items and then contact the store manager to try to judge whether he (never a woman) was polite and helpful to them and customers. "Surveyors were given a number to call for legal aid in case of harassment, such as arrest 'on suspicion' of shoplifting," a Focus: HOPE booklet said. "The women were cautioned to always use a basket (it aroused less suspicion), not to carry a large handbag (to avoid suspicion of shoplifting), to keep the survey form folded (a large paper attracts attention), and to leave the store if asked to do so."

Again tapping seminary resources, Cunningham asked two seminary high school student photographers—Patrick Gossman and Bill Sirois—to visually document the issue. They used the seminary's expensive twin-lens reflex camera that made 2.25 inch black and white negatives. Gossman cradled the camera as he rode on the back of Cunningham's Harley for several grocery stores under scrutiny. "I hung on for dear life," Gossman said. "When he first took off on the motorcycle, I damn near fell off. No helmet." He said the spectacle of a priest dressed in leather drew attention. "Here's this priest in white leathers on a Harley, stopping in their neighborhood, and, man, they just came out to see Father Cunningham," Gossman said.[10]

As the survey was nearing completion, Cunningham arrived to teach his high school English class at the seminary one day and, uncharacteristically, said he was nervous. He was scheduled to meet that afternoon with the head of the Farmer Jack supermarket chain, Frank Borman. "We did not do any English that day," said Gossman. "We talked about what he had prepared and what he was going to do, which was to go over and get Borman to pay to publish the book that told the story of the inequalities between inner city and suburban grocery chains. I thought *this is chutzpah*." The meeting actually went better than Cunningham feared. Borman agreed that his company needed to provide better service in the inner city, and he offered to pay the cost of publishing a 120-page large-size paperback.

---

10   *Father Cunningham wore a particular outfit, a blended white and black colored leather jacket. He soon decided that solid black leather jackets were easier to clean and wore them exclusively.*

With the financial support of Farmer Jack, the booklet came out in January 1969. It provided a detailed description of a fast-moving effort: On April 1, 1968—less than a month after Focus: Summer Hope began—there were more than 400 volunteer housewives from the city and its suburbs ready to carry the survey forms into grocery stores. On April 16, Cunningham addressed the women as a group at the seminary and showed the documentary film *The Poor Pay More*. After a lunch provided by the seminary, 22 volunteers were chosen to become trainers and were given their introductory orientation to training that would last three days. "It was in part a get-acquainted session for the black and white housewives who had many misconceptions about one another," the booklet said.

Included were transcripts of question-and-answer conversations between Cunningham, Reisman and Josaitis with the priest acting as the interviewer: "My first task was to set up the assignments of stores," Reisman told Cunningham. "We had the list of some of the stores from the different chains and we color-coded them on maps. Some of my friends from Vista were anxious to do as much as possible, and together we had about a week to assign the stores. We worked till 12 or 1 a.m. picking out the stores. The whole staff generally worked until midnight. We gave our first assignments at the UAW Hall on April 24 and I think we had an immediate success as far as the Vistas were concerned."

Josaitis said they took pains "to determine what both the Negro shopper and white shopper would buy. ... We would determine what quantity we would buy. We formed a list of what we would buy for a whole day. Meals—breakfast, lunch, dinner, and soap powder articles that we would buy. We included, for example, grits and rice."

Despite all of Eleanor's work since the get-go, she was not immediately recognized as a cofounder, but as someone who "initiated Focus: HOPE with Frs. Cunningham and Fraser." The booklet listed Cunningham and Fraser as co-directors and Eleanor as administrative assistant.

Among the suburban women volunteering for the food survey was Rosemary McLaughlin, known in 1968 as Rosemary Lane, who lived on a seven-acre lot in suburban Northville with her physician husband and their five children. She said the Food Survey opened her eyes to urban problems in a personal way. "I had a partner, she was a very, very nice black lady, and we got along so well," said McLaughlin. "We went to 'black' markets around the city and we went to suburban markets. There was a distinct difference in price and quality in the inner city." Another of the suburban volunteers was Margaret Simkins who then lived in Dearborn Heights. She and her husband, Earl, had met Cunningham at meetings of Project Commitment and attended retreats for married couples with him. "In the city, it was stinky and smelly, and not well kept," Simkins said of her visits to inner-city grocery stores. "Everything was in sub-standard condition."

"I participated in the food survey while pregnant," said Joanne Caccavale, who had met Cunningham through her husband, Ross Caccavale, the owner of several art movie houses in the area. "I remember two instances very well. We were in the middle of a second survey and I was assigned to one of the few independent grocery stores up in the Brewster-Douglass Projects area. It was one of the worst. It was absolutely the worst. There were no prices on anything, packages of eight hot dog buns that only had six, frozen food cases that didn't work. You pick up a bag of spinach and you have to wring the water out of it. I remember buying chicken, there was so much grit underneath. It looked like it had been dropped on the floor."

The first phase of Focus: Summer Hope's survey of grocery and pharmacy prices wrapped up and New Detroit released the results on September 4 at Wayne State University. The comprehensive survey of 44 items under 620 brand names in 351 Detroit and suburban stores was undertaken with 403 volunteer shoppers who completed 633 surveys—253 in Detroit and 380 in the suburbs.

Most news reports on the food and pharmacy price survey credited New Detroit and the Archdiocese of Detroit—and not

Focus: Summer Hope. Cunningham and Fraser weren't upset that their project was ignored in the media. Indeed, that may have assuaged archdiocesan higher-ups who still thought Focus: Summer Hope was a diocesan program.

Reactions from surprised, upset and embarrassed grocers and pharmacists were intense. Ed Deeb, executive director of the Associated Food Dealers of Greater Detroit, protested the survey in letters to Dearden and Mayor Cavanagh. Deeb admitted that prices in the inner city were higher, but not because of racism. Higher insurance costs and losses due to theft and burglary in those stores were the real reasons, he said.

Cunningham, in a signal that he was prepared to vigorously defend Focus: Summer Hope's evidence, targeted the stores owned by members of Deeb's association. Some Catholic Chaldeans, many of whom were the owners or managers of the targeted markets, saw Cunningham and Fraser as agents of the Roman Catholic Archdiocese trying to start some sort of schism.[11]

"The independent stores were primarily Chaldean, and this caused a huge ethnic conflict," said Joanne Caccavale. Many storeowners were taking a financial hit because of two Roman [Catholic] priests who, presumably, were under control of the Archbishop. A Chaldean priest "began making a lot of insinuations against Father Cunningham," Caccavale said. A meeting was set between Focus: HOPE and Chaldean leaders. "There were four of us who went to the Chaldean priest's rectory on Seven Mile." Also attending were some Chaldean grocers.

Cunningham apologized for nothing, insisting that the survey reflected the truth. Storeowners should examine their own behavior. "It really became quite vocal, primarily on their side," Caccavale said. The Chaldeans accused Cunningham and the Archdiocese of denigrating the hard-working independent

---

11   *Chaldean families originated in Assyria, now called Iraq, and in antiquity were part of the Eastern Rite of Catholic churches. In the 17th century, the Chaldeans reunited with the Roman Catholic Church, while retaining a certain degree of autonomy to protect cultural customs, including the right of priests to marry. The pope in Rome appoints Chaldean bishops.*

business owners sticking it out in tough neighborhoods of the city. "People had the opinion that Focus: HOPE was part of the Catholic Church," said Caccavale. One of the Chaldeans threatened to go directly to Dearden. Caccavale, the only woman in the room, had heard enough arguing about religious issues: "I finally did my batting-eye routine. 'Wait a minute! I'm not Catholic. What does this have to do with the Archdiocese? This is a non-profit Civil Rights organization. I don't understand why you're trying to make trouble for Father Cunningham.'"

Michael George, the former owner of the dairy company Melody Farms, who was informally known as the "godfather" of Detroit's Chaldean community, said he was not at that meeting.

"I had never heard of him," George said, until Deeb asked him to be at the taping of the *Lou Gordon Show* where Cunningham was scheduled to discuss the food survey. "I went because all of the people represented by the AFD were my customers," George said in a 2013 interview. George, who brought with him industry books with suggested prices for retailers, met Cunningham in "the green room" before the show. "He was very adamant about the fact that people in the city are being overcharged, especially by Chaldean merchants, a majority of the time," George said. "I said, 'Father, how well do you know the grocery business?' He said, 'What's to know?' I showed him an ad for sugar, shortening, soap powder, and asked him to look at the pricing at the sale. 'Now, take a look at what it costs,' and I opened up the book. 'Look, sugar costs a dollar and we're selling it for 69 cents on sale. It's a loss-leader.'"

Cunningham, George said, "looked at me and said, 'are you trying to insult me? Do you think I'm so stupid to believe that anyone would sell anything below cost?'" George said that the priest "didn't understand the grocery business" and the concept of selling something at a loss in order to generate traffic. "His perception guided him, rather than the facts," George said. "Everybody [in the Chaldean community] thought Father Cunningham was causing issues. Being a priest and going out and criticizing independents in urban areas is very damaging to good will and reputation."

And yet, they became friends—the godfather and the priest. George said Cunningham later apologized for being wrong about the grocery business in Detroit, although the priest never publicly acknowledged any mistakes in the surveys or results. They enjoyed fine cigars together and Cunningham often had dinner with the George family. George's wife, Najat, called him a "hippy priest" because of his long hair.

"He was doing all these things priests don't normally do," George said. "My impression was he was very arrogant and lacked humility when he first started going out into the community. But he changed, and I respect a person who respects change. Change is progress. He became one hell of a man."

Harold Weisberg, whose family owned Chatham Supermarkets, agreed that Cunningham didn't know the grocery business. But he was an enthusiastic Cunningham supporter. Weisberg said there was not a huge problem with pilferage by black customers in Chatham stores, although theft by employees was problematic. "What I convinced him with was the different eating habits of Caucasians and African-Americans," said Weisberg. "I was trying to teach him a little about merchandising and marketing in every industry." Cunningham wanted to know why Chatham and other markets had built barriers at store entrances in the city that meant shoppers had to carry bags to their cars. People took the carts home, Weisberg told him, and they cost "one-hundred-some dollars apiece."

Weisberg also became a close friend, smuggling Cuban cigars and expensive scotch from Canada that he shared with Cunningham. It wasn't long before the priest was asking both of them—Weisberg, a Jew, and George, a Chaldean—to help Focus: HOPE with a high school peace initiative. Both readily agreed and appeared together before groups of teenagers from Southfield to talk about diversity.

"Father Cunningham was always so good at sitting with the enemy," Caccavale said. "They began talking in terms of the positives that it would be for that community if they built new stores in certain areas and that it was not bad business, that it was positive business. Certainly, as a result of that I know that several new stores were built. Part of it was to treat the community with dignity."

On October 4—the day before the Detroit Tigers baseball team was to play their first home game and third game of the 1968 World Series against the St. Louis Cardinals—Cunningham, Josaitis and Reisman attended the Southeastern Michigan Consumer Conference in Detroit. Cunningham was invited to speak and he pulled no punches. "The little merchant on the corner is carving the hide out of the poor," Cunningham said. The chain grocery stores had abandoned Detroit and taken their lower prices to their more profitable suburban stores, he said. He showed a slide show of the Focus: Summer Hope survey that proved that the poor pay about 5 percent more in chain stores and at least 15 percent more in independent markets for basic commodities.

Another presenter at the conference wasn't buying what Cunningham was selling. Betty Furness, a former television consumer reporter, a passionate supporter of Vista and then President Lyndon Johnson's assistant for consumer affairs, thought the priest was overdramatizing a "problem" that didn't exist. Furness had a reputation for bluntness and publicly scolded Cunningham, saying his little survey was not scientific.

Smiling broadly, Cunningham asked that Reisman come to the microphone and explain how the survey was done. Reisman went into splendid detail about the survey's methods. "We hit 250 stores all at the exact same time. If we picked 10 a.m., everybody was at the store at 10 a.m." Furness fumed, but Cunningham had won the argument with Reisman's help. "The survey was done properly and it was done without bias," Reisman said later. "We just reported what the women did. ... I had no problem defending the project."

No riot occurred that summer in Detroit, despite the assassination of Dr. King that sparked violence in other cities. That didn't mean Focus: Summer Hope had succeeded itself out of business. The name was quickly simplified to Focus: HOPE.

Cunningham, Fraser and Josaitis, working with determination, energy and boldness, a corps of seminarians, and volunteers, created a hum of activity at the seminary. Visitors who came to visit Focus: HOPE and offer support included white politicians, black leaders and even a famous Olympic gold medalist. "I once met Eleanor at Sacred Heart Seminary, in the original office on the second floor, and Eleanor introduced me to Jesse Owens," Gossman said. Just 18, Gossman didn't realize that Owens was the well-known black American track-and-field star of the 1936 Olympics in Hitler's Berlin. Owens won four gold medals as a runner and long-jumper, and exposed the lie of Aryan or white supremacy.

"Bottom line—I had never heard of him," said Gossman, who later realized whom he actually had met. "Here's this guy, Jesse Owens! I had no clue of the import of it."

Father Bill Cunningham and his 1967
Harley-Davidson Electraglide motorcycle.

Credit: John Collier

4

Easy Rider

JERROLD REISMAN WAS having the time of his life, splashing around a pool during a party celebrating the release of Focus: HOPE's survey on food and prescription prices. Dozens of volunteers were gathered at the Northville estate of Rosemary Lane. The 25-year-old Reisman had just gotten out of the pool when he heard Father Cunningham's motorcycle heading up the long driveway. To Reisman's surprise, the priest cut over on the lawn and drove straight toward him.

"Hop on!" Cunningham shouted over the Harley's rumble. Reisman hopped on. Cunningham swung the big hog around, turned west on Eight Mile Road and gunned it. "I look over his shoulder and I saw that Bill's dial was between 10 and 11. I remember this as if it was five minutes ago. I asked what it meant, he said, 'You idiot! That's the speed.' I won't say what I said, but I sort of cursed. We were going between 100 and 110 miles an hour. He's laughing. ... I was a little bit angry. We're going 100 miles an hour and I have nothing on."

Cunningham was riding high. The food survey had gone well, the archdiocese was off his back for now, Focus: HOPE volunteers were engaged and enthusiastic. He saw blacks and whites coming together and enjoying each other's company. Focus: HOPE was off to a good start, but he saw a long road ahead.

At the seminary, Cunningham still had teaching duties to fulfill. In addition to his classes in English literature, drama and public speaking, Cunningham proposed adding a course on film, particularly foreign and avant-garde movies. Father Arthur Schaffran, principal of the seminary high school, wasn't sure he could get approval.

Cunningham had persuaded his friend Ross Caccavale—Joanne's husband—to loan him films playing at Caccavale's "Studio" theaters. "His whole concept was—with seminary students they needed to know the world at large as well," said Joanne. "He had come up with this idea on his own. ... He said that he thought what we needed to do was to sit down and meet with the higher-ups of the archdiocese."

Joanne couldn't remember who went to the dinner meeting at the seminary, but thought it included a bishop. Cunningham introduced her, praising her work with Focus: HOPE. She whispered to Cunningham that she was a "nervous wreck" because, "I'm not used to being around higher-ups in the Church." He told her she'd be fine, just relax and, "be yourself."

Joanne was afraid her mouth would get her in trouble, but everything went smoothly. She told Cunningham that it was one of the "most nervous moments" of her life, but the priest broke out in "this wonderful, incredible laugh." He said: "You have no idea. You were the first woman to ever be in that dining room. They were so nervous about having you there that they had spent weeks planning what you were going to eat, how they were going to take you to show you the auditorium," according to Joanne.

To her mild surprise, the "Church higher-ups" agreed and Cunningham began showing movies, such as Ingmar Bergman's *The Virgin Spring*, at the seminary once a month. "He had a very good eye for what was considered really quality kind of films," Joanne said.

In November 1968, Cunningham hosted the first public showing in Detroit of *Easy Rider* at the seminary. The story of two motorcycle-riding drug dealers, played by Peter Fonda and Dennis Hopper, on a road trip to Mardi Gras in New Orleans contained depictions of sex and casual drug use, particularly marijuana-smoking and LSD ingestion. Reisman said he watched *Easy Rider* at the seminary and was amazed at Cunningham's ability to lead a discussion about art in film. "It was really fantastic; he was really good at what he did," Reisman said. "He would start pointing out different things you normally wouldn't think of. I looked at movies differently after that."

Somehow, Cunningham was able to pull it off, easing the sensibilities of senior clergy who may have been uncomfortable. In a speech at the seminary many years later, Cunningham admitted that "the films really were a kind of assault on traditional morality at that time."

In a 1972 interview with *Detroit Free Press* staff writer Jim Harper, Cunningham was asked about the motorcycle: "I have a bike and this is part of what keeps me sane, too; even if I just look at it. I know what it means to me. It means going out on the expressway and tooling up to 90, 100 miles an hour at 2 o'clock in the morning and getting rid of some vengeance, violence, frustration."

Film actress Barbara Stanwyck and an exhausted Father
Cunningham at an opening night party for the first Focus:
HOPE festival inside the Oakland Mall in Troy in 1969.

Credit: Carl Bidleman

5

Pastor

THE ELEVATOR IN the Marquette Building in downtown
Detroit was closed due to a small fire in the basement when
Father Bill Cunningham showed up for a meeting on the 10th
floor with Bill Frcka. Nonplussed by the commotion, Cunningham trudged up the stairway in his Italian boots, black leather
jacket, carrying his white motorcycle helmet. At age 39 in 1969,
Cunningham was barely winded due to a regimen of handball
games at the seminary and a newfound interest, jogging.

The priest was there to meet a photographer for the Gif-
fels and Rossetti architectural firm where Frcka—the graphic
artist who had designed the Focus: HOPE logo—worked. Cunningham wanted good pictures for the planned book about the
survey of inner-city grocery stores. The priest was unimpressed
by the photographer, but he was thrilled to meet a young architect at the firm, Dario Bonucchi. "Immediate simpatico!" Frcka
said.

Bonucchi would become an energetic supporter and close
friend of Father Cunningham, Eleanor Josaitis and the rest of
the motley Focus: HOPE crew of unpaid volunteers. Although

an architect by trade, Bonucchi's passion was folk music—also one of Cunningham's musical interests. He managed The Living End, a club on the Lodge Freeway service drive just north of West Grand Boulevard.[12] Cunningham immediately grasped the potential in Bonucchi. When Cunningham asked if Bonucchi could organize a "fun" event that would bring blacks and whites together, he instantly said yes. Bonucchi's idea was a festival with game booths and folk music as entertainment.

Carl Bidleman, then the most active ex-seminarian involved with Focus: HOPE, attended the first planning meeting for the festival at Ross and Joanne Caccavale's home in Detroit's Sherwood Forest neighborhood, a block from the Josaitis family home. "This guy there, named Dario Bonucchi, said maybe he could help get some entertainment for the festival. He could get some performer I never heard of—Odetta," Bidleman said.[13] Besides Odetta Horton, Bonucchi also lined up some local folk musicians who would stay with Cunningham and Focus: HOPE for decades: Phil Marcus Esser, Josh White Jr., Barbara Bredius, Charlie Latimer and Ron Coden.

Bonucchi introduced Cunningham to Coden during a benefit for Focus: HOPE that he had organized at the Raven East folk club in Detroit in September. "We were all looking for causes to sing about at the time," Coden said. After his set, Coden said he and Cunningham talked out in the parking lot. "He commented that my diction was really great, which nobody had ever told me. He's speaking to me like a fan; he loved my voice. I did a poem—'The Highwayman'—he was just crazy about that."

---

12   *Several folk music stars played The Living End before it closed in 1975, including Chuck and Joni Mitchell, Maria Muldaur, Gordon Lightfoot, Odetta Horton, Judy Collins and the Irish Rovers.*

13   *Odetta Horton had been singing folk music since the early 1950s and was becoming a civil rights icon, influencing Bob Dylan, Joan Baez, Janis Joplin and many others. Rosa Parks, who sparked the Montgomery, AL boycott of the city's segregated bus system by refusing to give up her seat to a white male passenger, was once asked which songs meant the most to her. "All of the songs Odetta sings," she said. Parks had moved to Detroit by then and also become a friend of Father Cunningham.*

At the fundraiser, Bonucchi invited Cunningham to take the mic, but to keep it short. True to his nature, Cunningham's speech went on for 25 or 30 minutes—and no one minded. "Everybody was so enthralled, he was like William Jennings Bryan, an oratory that was incredible," Coden said. "He was so dynamic and so good. He would have people on the verge of tears. He was a very hard act to follow." Esser said it was quite a performance, calling Cunningham "a cross between Marlon Brando and Regis Philbin."

"He had quite a program going," Esser said. "There were lots of activists [in the folk clubs], but very few of them on a motorcycle wearing a Roman collar. ... It was him and [Neal] Shine and the Boys of Summer—those seminarians. That was essentially what it was as far as I could tell."[14]

The festival ran one weekend in October at the Oakland Mall in Troy. Cunningham believed that suburbanites needed to see blacks and whites working together joyfully as Focus: HOPE volunteers. Handout materials were designed, fun and games prepared. Someone got the idea of dressing up the Focus: HOPE ladies in red berets and red capes sewn by Joanne Caccavale.

But everything was running late, so Cunningham called John Jabro, then a seminarian at St. John Provincial Seminary in Plymouth, for help. Jabro gathered a group of seminarians and other volunteers, who pulled all-nighters to construct booths, erect a stage and decorate everything with black-and-white balloons, banners and buntings. When they finished after the mall closed late Thursday night, they had a party, even though everybody was tired. Celebrities at the party included legendary *Detroit Free Press* entertainment columnist Shirley Eder, who brought her friend, film actress Barbara Stanwyck. Volunteers, however, were too tired to party heartily. "We were all exhausted from setting up," Bidleman said. "I remember this picture of Bill standing next to Barbara Stanwyck with his eyes half closed."

---

14   *Neal Shine was then city editor of the Free Press, later becoming a columnist, managing editor and publisher.*

Unfortunately for Focus: HOPE, shoppers were not interested in the musicians performing, the game booths or the ladies in their cute red outfits. Still, Charlie Latimer said the musicians had a good time. "We enjoyed it," he said. "You didn't have a sit-down audience; just people walking back and forth. We did it, and they got donations. We were very proud of the fact that we were able to get enough money so they could finally buy stationery."

The three-day festival "was an abysmal failure," said Mary Sullivan, a volunteer and close friend to Eleanor. "There was nobody there but us and our little red hats and little red capes." Receipts from donations, games and the sale of bumper stickers and Focus: HOPE buttons totaled $9,737.87. Expenses, including $2,400 for the construction of booths, were $6,641.28, leaving net proceeds at $3,096.59.[15]

Cunningham gave everyone a break for a couple of weeks, returning to his suite at the seminary to reflect on what he'd do next. His position at the seminary high school was eliminated that semester, although he still taught an English class at the University of Detroit. Enrollment at the seminary high school had dropped sharply, at least partly because white Catholics in the suburbs didn't want to send their sons to a seminary in the inner city. The high school would be closed in June 1970.

Archbishop John Dearden had raised the $1 million for the Archdiocesan Development Fund's effort to improve race relations in Detroit. An obvious move would be to tap the ADF to support Focus: HOPE, but Cunningham knew the cost of that was too high. The archbishop would demand that Focus: HOPE be under his authority. Cunningham would have to fight that notion alone. Father Jerry Fraser, who also lost his position in the high school, said he was open to another assignment.

---

15   *At the end of 1969, Focus: HOPE's revenues, including proceeds from the festival and an $850 grant from New Detroit Inc., totaled just $19,298.49. Eleanor Josaitis had been paid a salary of $350, and a loan from William Cunningham Sr., for $5,000 was repaid. One liability listed was a $700 loan to Focus: HOPE from Father Cunningham. With various other liabilities, Focus: HOPE ended the year with a balance of $4,542.52.*

Cunningham resisted any new assignment, and kept insisting that he'd stay with Focus: HOPE regardless.

Discussions were tense. Bishop Walter Schoenherr, who was in charge of all priest assignments in the archdiocese, summoned him to settle on his future. Cunningham knew this was a critical turning point. Dearden was in the midst of modernizing the bureaucracy, trying to make it more corporate-like with people reporting to people who reported to him. Clearly, the seminary could not continue supporting a project occupying the time of two priests that wasn't under the archbishop's control. Yet, Cunningham was adamant that Focus: HOPE must be independent. His defiance frustrated higher-ups.

Speaking for the cardinal, Schoenherr told Cunningham that he couldn't just work at Focus: HOPE. He had to do something for the archdiocese—perhaps temporarily fill in at an inner-city parish that would probably be shut down anyway. The Catholic Church of the Madonna on Oakman Boulevard and 12th Street in an industrial area of the city's northern corridor was mentioned as a possibility. "The Cardinal said he wanted me to go into Madonna parish to close it down," Cunningham told the *National Catholic Reporter* in 1982. "I said I would not take it on that basis."

He called a meeting of his kitchen cabinet, including ex-seminarian Carl Bidleman and Don and Eleanor Josaitis, at the Green Lantern restaurant in Royal Oak. Cunningham said that Dearden was angry about Focus: HOPE not being part of the archdiocese, and they were forcing him to take a parish assignment. "Bill wanted to know what everyone thought he should do," Bidleman said. "I recall Charlie Grenville saying Madonna was small enough that he could manage both the parish and Focus: HOPE. The group concurred."

Madonna was one of several Catholic churches in inner-city Detroit with dwindling congregations that the archdiocese was considering for closure. White Catholics were moving out of post-riot Detroit, creating a huge need for more parishes in the suburbs, and priests to staff them. The inner-city parishes were left with fewer parishioners, dwindling resources and a smaller pool of priests content to work in "changing" neighborhoods.

One afternoon, lay sacristan Luther Williams was cleaning the Madonna sanctuary when he heard the rumble of a motorcycle as it came to a halt in front of the church. The door was unlocked and as Williams worked he noticed a white man wearing a black motorcycle jacket and pointy black boots walk down the center aisle and kneel in the front pew. After praying for a while, the man with long, wavy dark hair sat and said ... nothing.

Cunningham was secretly checking Madonna out. He wanted to know if the place was worth saving.

"For a couple of Sundays, he sat in the back of the church," said longtime parishioner Max Powell. "Nobody knew who he was. He came twice, then the third time he had the Roman collar on. He didn't talk to anyone here. He just came and he left." Then, Powell said, Cunningham went "to the men's club, the Holy Name Society. He came down to the meeting. Someone found out who he was, so he came down and introduced himself. He said, 'I'm supposed to be your new priest here, but I wanted to make sure that you want me.'" Cunningham told the group that "you fellas' are the pillars of the church and I'd like to know just how you feel," according to Powell. "We all sat there looking at each other. And Bob McSwain said, 'Father, we want you; we're glad to have you,' He said, 'OK, if you want me.'"

Cunningham didn't quite trust the archdiocese to live up to an agreement that left him free to lead Focus: HOPE. He wanted it in writing. He prepared a typed statement for the press about his assignment to Madonna parish while continuing to work for Focus: HOPE that he would present to the archbishop's staff. He later told the *National Catholic Reporter*: "The cardinal made it plain he wasn't going to let me just run Focus: HOPE, which had no connection to the church. So, I said, we can work it out to keep the parish going also, and went with him with a typed-up copy of my appointment to both ministries. The cardinal said, 'That's not my way of doing things'—but I said, 'It's simple; you make it yours.'"

Cunningham told the newspaper that "I was close to checking out of the certified ministry," if he had to, in order to stay with Focus: HOPE.

Negotiations over this point went on for weeks, with Cunningham pushing the boundaries of his loyalty oath to the archbishop. Dearden couldn't understand why Cunningham didn't just agree that Focus: HOPE should come under Church purview. After all, Focus: HOPE was born at the seminary and had received strong financial support from the archdiocese.

"There was something going on with John Dearden, the cardinal," said William X. Kienzle, then a priest and the editor of *The Michigan Catholic* who lived at the seminary. "It seems like they wanted Bill to get out of Focus: HOPE and be a priest. He went down to a meeting with them. He labored with them all morning long about wording of the notice to be put in *The Michigan Catholic*. He wanted to be appointed to Focus: HOPE. They wanted him out of there and doing priestly stuff at a parish."

Cunningham "really dickered to get exact, precise language," Kienzle said. "They were arguing about articles and verbs and adverbs and what could be imputed from language like this. Finally, Bill got what he wanted, but then he was pretty sure that they were going to backslide. And he came as fast as his Harley or whatever he was driving could go to get from the Chancery to *The Michigan Catholic*. He came in and sat down and, in effect, he said, 'I've just entered the most important negotiations of my life and I think they're going to go back on the language.' He wanted me on his team."

Cunningham gave Kienzle a copy of the wording he said had been approved by Dearden's secretary, Monsignor Joseph Imesch, and insisted that it be printed exactly like that in the next issue. Then, they couldn't renege. "Just as he said that, the phone rang and it's Joe Imesch," Kienzle said. "And he's saying, 'Bill Cunningham will be in and he'll probably want to have language for his new appointment that will probably be incorrect—I'll give you the correct language.' Bill is sitting in the chair there … so he knew who I was talking to." Imesch gave Kienzle the new language, which Kienzle said wasn't that much different.

Then, Kienzle told Imesch that Cunningham indeed had been there and that the typesetters in the editorial department already had set the announcement in type. "Really, I think if we change the wording now, all these people know what the original was, I think we could be in some real trouble," Kienzle told him. Imesch folded: "Oh, all right, let it go."

For years, Cunningham showered thanks on Kienzle. "He felt that but for an adverb or something he would be out of Focus: HOPE." The announcement read: "Fr. William T. Cunningham has been appointed pastor of Madonna Parish in Detroit. Formerly an instructor at Sacred Heart Seminary and book review columnist for *The Michigan Catholic*, Fr. Cunningham is currently working with Focus: HOPE, an organization for building racial justice and integration. He will continue working with Focus: HOPE and assume his new responsibilities as pastor effective Mar. 4."[16]

Many Madonna parishioners hadn't heard the news yet, and were startled when they saw a young white man with long hair wandering around. Mitzy Smith said she and her then-fiancé Bill Smith were walking by when she stopped and gawked: "I looked down the street and there's this man, long hair, cowboy boots, walking and swaggering. And he was so handsome! Who was this man? … I just thought, this was a real handsome hippy-type looking man."

An article featuring Cunningham appeared in the March 8 edition of the *Detroit Free Press* Sunday magazine, one in a series of articles about "Handsome Detroiters." In the photo that ran with the article, Cunningham is not smiling, but his face wears a determined look. He stands in the lobby of the seminary near the chapel, wearing his black suit, Roman collar and black-and-white Focus: HOPE pin. The short article called Cunningham "a 39-year-old brown-eyed, silver-tongued Irishman." The priest called Focus: HOPE "a revolving fund of human resources to

---

16   *Cunningham became the seventh pastor of Madonna, which was founded in 1924 by Father Cajetan G. Diana. Several of its pastors were noted for reaching out to African-Americans and converting many of them to Catholicism.*

the poor and depressed. ... Intense, informal (the clerical collar is often worn with a ski sweater and leather jacket), he says of his mission: 'I'm not a priest as such, but a sacramental person. A doctor brings his sacraments to the sick. I bring mine to the poor.'"

Cunningham was embarrassed because he wasn't told about the "Handsome Detroiters" angle. Sister Delores Keller was working at Madonna's elementary school at the time and said the sisters had seen the article. In the picture, "I could see the twinkle in his eye," she said.

On March 5, he asked ex-seminarian Carl Bidleman to move into the rectory with him and to run a youth program. Cunningham wanted to use the school's third-floor gymnasium as a neighborhood recreation center run by Bidleman. There were no paying jobs at Focus: HOPE back then, but Cunningham paid Bidleman $100 a week with church funds, plus room and board at the rectory. Bidleman's "suite" was the attic on the third floor with a low ceiling and bedroom at the back. "I could lie in bed at night and see the 'golden tower of the Fisher Building' way off in the distance," Bidleman said. There was a toilet and a sink up there and a "closet about the size of a phone booth."

Cunningham had decided that the theme of his new ministry would be candlelight, and the script for the formal installation as pastor on March 8 included this prayer: "Father Cunningham, Jesus said, 'I am the Light of the World.' With this candle, the sign of Christ's truth and love, light our lives and the lives of our children, and help us to give truth and love to all who know us."

In the mimeographed church bulletin, Cunningham struck a collegial note as he wrote an initial greeting to his new congregation: "On this first Sunday as your new priest I am excited and happy. As followers of Jesus Christ we are together a people who have good news to share, news of hope and life and love. As your priest-brother I chose the candle to represent the Christ-life for Madonna Parish. I promise to work with you and pray with you that, like a candle flame bright and warm, the faith and love of our parish will be seen and felt by all who know us."

The next day, Cunningham turned to the problem of the parish's troubled finances. Madonna's elementary school was running a deficit, and the parish's older students who attended Blessed Sacrament Grade School or St. Martin DePorres High School were racking up huge tuition debts that Madonna was responsible for. "One week has passed since I moved into the rectory," Cunningham wrote for the next church bulletin. "I've talked to parishioners about the school crisis, a Cabaret Party, a Parish Festival, Holy Week worship, the new form for the Mass which begins next Sunday and on and on. The rectory has been busy with meetings and callers, the phones have been ringing steadily. I am impressed and delighted. This is a parish with life—a parish on the move."

Initially, Sister Delores Keller, a Sister of St. Joseph who taught at the Madonna school, said she worried that Cunningham would be stretched too thin to handle both jobs at Madonna and Focus: HOPE. It wasn't long before she rested easy, she said, because she recognized that Cunningham's leadership skills and warm personality, his energy and his stamina meant that Madonna parishioners would be well served.

"I was very happy because I knew he would make Madonna his place, his parish. He would be a pastor," she said. "They loved him. He kept up the wonderful liturgy, was a marvelous speaker. I think the word 'charismatic' is overused, but I think he was. He could attract people and keep them."

Everyone wore bad clothes in the 1970s, including Father Cunningham, who drew second-looks as he drove around town in black-and-white Focus: HOPE leathers over his Roman collar. Here he arrives late for a party at the home of Madonna parishioner Callie Fulp, circa 1972.

Credit: Don & Eleanor Josaitis family

6

We Will

OVER COFFEE IN the rectory one morning, Father Cunningham told Carl Bidleman that he wanted to spend the last $200 in the parish's bank account on landscaping.

"He was telling me he was going to spend all the money in the church coffers to put sod in front of the school and the rectory," Bidleman said. "I thought this was crazy. With all the needs we had, why pick sod as the thing to sink the last few dollars into?" Cunningham explained to Bidleman that, "you don't plant sod in front of a place that's going to close." Cunningham let that sink in. A moment later, it dawned on Bidleman: "That's right! You don't plant sod in front of a place that's going to close! … It was his way of telling the world that this place is not closing. We're open for business."

The move from Sacred Heart Seminary to the Madonna rectory took little more than an hour. There wasn't that much to haul over: a few boxes of index cards containing names, addresses and phone numbers of volunteers and donors, some records from the food survey, a photograph of the Rev. Martin Luther King Jr., and a new $800 IBM Selectric. Cunningham said they needed the expensive typewriter so that every letter Focus: HOPE sent looked perfect—as good as anything the president of General Motors would mail out. Former seminarian Tim Pilon said that Cunningham carefully scrutinized every letter and "it had to be letter-perfect. It had to be classy, that was the thing."

"We literally have to be better than anybody else," Bidleman explained. "We wanted to be taken seriously for our professionalism. We didn't want anyone to be treating us like a nonprofit organization. We had to compete. We had to be able to walk into the boardroom of General Motors and be accepted on our own terms, and not with a condescending attitude."

They took over all of the rectory space except for a breezeway off the living room that was attached to the church where Madonna's bookkeeper, Thelma Williams, worked. Eleanor Josaitis took the former pastor's office to the right of the door from the enclosed front porch. Inside the office was a giant red leather chair that Dario Bonucchi often used to take "power naps" in the afternoon. Boxes of Focus: HOPE's work over the previous two years was in the dining room where its large table quickly filled up with files, stacks of papers and envelopes. The only open bit of meeting space relatively free of clutter was the table in the breakfast nook behind the kitchen where five or six people could squeeze in together.

On the second floor was the pastor's two-room suite at the front of the building that Cunningham used as his office. He slept in a bedroom at the back, and two other small bedrooms down the hall were turned into offices for Ken Kudek, another ex-seminarian, and Joanne Caccavale who ran a "consumer affairs department." They had telephones and note pads, but just the one typewriter. None of them, except Bidleman, was being paid.

The church had an old addressing machine and Pilon was told to load it with the names and contact information for Focus: HOPE's supporters that were on index cards in shoe boxes. They were about to transfer the information into the machine when Pilon suggested that they first test the accuracy of their collection by sending a letter asking for a response and locking in those who respond favorably, allowing some to opt out. Pilon reasoned the organization would save hundreds of dollars on postage with a cleaner mailing list. It was not to Cunningham's liking. "He had a fit," Pilon said. The priest said: "I spent years developing the names in that box and you're not going to send out a letter giving people an out."

Cunningham told Pilon to find a printing press; Focus: HOPE would come up with the money somehow. The first machine Pilon found was a used model that was delivered and installed in the basement, but then didn't work. "I'll be very honest, we got hoodwinked," Pilon said. "But we made the guy take it back and he did, and then we ended up buying a good one. ... We were a bunch of scrappers. We tried to make something out of nothing. And Bill inspired us to do that. Everything was second-rate equipment, yet he wanted a first-rate product and we were committed to doing that. ... We were going to make a difference."

Mary Stephenson—who had been volunteering at nights when Focus: HOPE was headquartered at the seminary—was laid off from her job at General Motors in 1970 and promptly reported to the Madonna rectory to do whatever Cunningham needed doing. "It was bleak, to say the least," Stephenson said about the shabby, cramped rectory-cum-office. She typed letters, answered the phone, and made funny remarks that kept spirits up.

Yet another ex-seminarian who happened to call the office—Tony Campbell—liked the sound of Stephenson's voice. So he showed up to volunteer and meet her. Soon, after Focus: HOPE got a small grant, Cunningham gave Tony a job, and later the priest would officiate at Tony and Mary's wedding. Cunningham thought he had them both locked into Focus: HOPE, but in 1971 Mary was called back to work by GM. Cunningham did not take it well. "He said, 'Oh, go on! Go back there and make those big bucks.' There was a sneer in his voice and I could tell he wasn't really happy with me," she said. But, "I was one of the ones he really couldn't stay angry at."

Another young woman, Mary Kay Stark met Cunningham and Josaitis at a meeting in Birmingham. Stark participated in the first Focus: HOPE food survey and visited several inner-city markets documenting the poor quality and high prices of food items. Despite her age (19), the priest offered her a job at $50 a month, plus room and board, to work with Bidleman on the youth program. She accepted, living in the Madonna convent with three nuns who worked at St. Francis Home for Boys, less than a mile away.

Always concerned about the proper development of young children, Cunningham decided that Madonna's day care center for the children of parishioners and volunteers needed to be improved. "I had never babysat in my life and he let me start a nursery school!" Stark said. It was called the Sunshine Nursery School and was housed in the basement of the rectory, where there was barely enough room for 10 kids. Stark had to organize her own fundraisers, mostly having kids and families sell candy. "I ate most of my profits, boxes and boxes," she said.

Stark, Pilon, Bidleman, Bonucchi, Kudek, the Campbells—not to mention Bill and Eleanor—were all white. Monica Emerson, who worked upstairs with Kudek, was the only black staffer. The obvious question was how the racial difference between the mostly white Focus: HOPE staff and Madonna's nearly all-black congregation would work out.

"We were conscious of the fact that we were a bunch of white folks coming in and working in a black parish," Pilon said. "We weren't trying to be black and we knew we couldn't be black." The Madonna parish, Pilon said, "had been neglected physically, it had been neglected spiritually and it had been neglected socially." Cunningham, he said, "put a shot of life into the parish."

Cunningham wanted parishioners to know him as a person, so he began inviting them in small groups to dinner at the rectory. The housekeeper, Frances Tribble, was a phenomenal cook. "Frances would fix the dinner and serve as hostess," Pilon said. "She was quite a lady. Frances was in a position way below her abilities. Frances had served as personal secretary for some women of means over the years, had some nice positions, but ended up as a cook. Frances could take any food you wanted—prepackaged, out of a can—and she could doctor that so you would think you were eating the most fantastic new creation. She was a *cook*. It was a joy to eat there."

Parishioners were pleasantly surprised to be invited into the pastor's home. Thom Armstead, a Methodist, agreed to go to the rectory to have dinner with Cunningham because his Catholic fiancée, Henrietta, asked him to. "She says, 'You've got to come and meet this fantastic new priest we have. He's very community oriented and doing some wonderful things down there,'" Armstead said.

"One of the things that struck her the most was that all those years of attending Madonna she never got to see the inside of the rectory. If you had to see the priest, you'd sit outside on the [enclosed] porch. You never got into the convent or rectory, which were off limits." Under Cunningham, however, "the rectory opened up with all these folks running around." Armstead told Cunningham that he was a foreman at Chrysler's Warren Truck Plant. Armstead didn't know it then, but the dinner led to a life-long partnership with the priest. "He asked me if I would like to help Carl out with the youth program, using the gym at Madonna that had been closed for 10 years," Armstead said. He couldn't refuse.

On the inside, Madonna church was dark, old-fashioned, rundown and not very clean. The only apparent attempt at modernization appeared to be a portable table-altar brought into the sanctuary so the priest could say Mass the new way, in the vernacular and facing the congregation. The old stone altar was still on the back wall bearing a heavy crucifix with a lifelike sculpture of Christ at the moment of death. "We rearranged the sanctuary to accommodate the kind of liturgy that he was more comfortable with," Pilon said.

The congregation was accustomed to hearing the unseen choir in the loft sing tired Catholic anthems or Baptist-style hymns. Cunningham brought the choir down to sit in pews he set up in the sanctuary along with a grand piano. And he hired a new choir director, Oriole Taylor, telling Taylor to play music with energy, spirit and meaning to the people. "Bill said, 'You've got some culture here, you've got some heritage here, and I want to hear some soul out of this choir,'" according to Pilon.

Bill and Bea Fenwick and Joe Schroeder, Cunningham's friends from St. Alfred Church in Taylor, began coming to Madonna on Sundays to help out. Bill Fenwick thought the crucifix hanging on the back wall should be hung over the altar by a rope. Cunningham "kind of frowned, and I said, 'Let's try it; if you don't like it, we can take it down.'" Fenwick climbed up into the ceiling space to tie off the rope on one of the building's girders and then hoisted the crucifix up. "I called him over to see if he liked it," Fenwick said. "Man, he fell in love with it."

Whenever the Fenwicks and Cunningham sat down to relax with glasses of scotch, it was in the priest's second floor office. It was the usual gathering spot for Focus: HOPE people to take a late afternoon break, drink some scotch or wine and talk about all manner of things. Cunningham frequently mentioned how he'd like to tear the suite's divider wall out and make it a larger, more comfortable living room. One day, after a scotch or two and yet another lament from the priest about getting rid of the wall, Fenwick decided he'd heard enough. He walked outside to his pickup to get a heavy sledgehammer. "I came back up with it and started smashing the wall," Fenwick said. "He said, 'What are you doing, Fenwick?' I said, 'You want us to smash the walls, don't you?' He never knew how to take me. When he said something, I'd do it."

The refurbishing project took about two months, including an entire day to get a support beam—a pair of 10-foot, 2-by-12 oak boards glued together—put in to brace the ceiling. Then, Cunningham came up with an idea for paneling the entire room, including the ceiling, in weathered barnwood. Fenwick knew about an old farm near Minden City in the thumb area of Michigan where the farmer had recently died. "We traded five gallons of white paint for the wood," Fenwick said. "All good boards. They were going to tear it down anyhow. We brought all that back to the rectory. [Cunningham] and I washed it with hot water to get the bugs and dirt off. We let it all dry and then brushed it down." They had to build a special frame to hang the wood on the ceiling.

Then, Cunningham decided he wanted a door that looked like a barn door that slides back and forth, so Fenwick made it. "We had an awful time getting it upstairs," he said. But the topper was a built-in aquarium.

In April 1970, Cunningham announced a second phase of what had become Focus: HOPE's signature project: another consumer survey in Detroit's inner-city markets. He said Focus: HOPE was doing a second survey because "little has been done to correct these injustices" found in the first survey. Cunningham told *The Michigan Catholic* that he would recruit 10,000 women volunteers to "shop in a poor person's shoes" by living on a low-income food budget for the two-week period of April 20 to May 3.[17] "The major chains refuse to build badly needed food centers and what is worse they have barely moved to rehabilitate ancient stores except to add bars around the doors so that carts cannot be taken to the parking lots," Cunningham said. "This discrimination continues despite ample evidence black people buy more groceries consumable in the home than do suburban whites and that customer pilferage in black ghetto stores is lower than in white suburban stores."

Cunningham was struck by the similarities between the starving children of Biafra, a chronically impoverished country in Africa, and the poor children in Detroit where the infant mortality rate was roughly equal to those in Third World countries. Cunningham said that abject poverty in Detroit's inner city was killing children.

In May, Nick Kotz, a Pulitzer Prize-winning reporter for *The Washington Post* who had written a book on hunger called *Let Them Eat Promises*, came to the Merrill-Palmer Institute in Detroit and gave a talk on "The Politics of Hunger." Cunningham, Josaitis and Armstead attended. "That had a real profound

---

17   *Cunningham often overestimated the number of volunteers and supporters for rallies, marches and other Focus: HOPE events, usually using the figure of 10,000.*

effect on Father," Armstead said. After the lecture, the three of them took Kotz to dinner. "One of the things he indicated was because of greed, because of price supports, the large agri-commercial companies were getting paid not to grow. They were dumping milk down sewers, plowing under crops, when we had hungry people in this country. Kotz just elaborated on that and singled out big food companies like Ralston Purina.

"I think we came out of the meeting with the sense that this is something we have to do on a national level," Armstead said. "The people in the USDA were ambivalent. There was no indication on their part of trying to serve the needs of the poor, and [Cunningham] was going to see to it that his goal that no child in the city of Detroit was going to go without nutritious food during this important stage of his life" would be achieved.

They studied the work of Dr. Don Churchill, a research scientist who "indicated that because a child had not received proper nutrients in the first 14 months—when cells begin to develop at a rapid pace—growth is stunted," Armstead said. "The problem started there—this development is irreversible. Behavioral scientists said a child deprived of nutrition could be hostile toward their environment and saw that as one of the reasons we have a lot of crime and a lot of people striking out at society."

Seeing hunger as a basic violation of human rights, Cunningham committed himself and Focus: HOPE to find ways to attack the malnutrition problem in Detroit as a way to help impoverished blacks. He worked with Wayne State University to bring Dr. Churchill to Detroit to educate city and state leaders about the long-lasting impact of hunger on small children.

The Nixon Administration, Armstead said, became "a little embarrassed by reports of the state of the health of these young people and Nixon called upon the United States Department of Agriculture (USDA) to solve this problem. They came up with Section 32, legislation from decades before that authorized federally funded soup kitchens during the Depression, and tried to put together a USDA commodities food program that would be beneficial to the development of young people."

Black children in Detroit were undernourished because of institutional racism, Cunningham reasoned. A poor diet in the first few years of life inhibited brain development and virtually guaranteed a life of poverty. In March 1971, Cunningham was outraged when he read an editorial in the *Detroit Free Press* that said there were 53,000 poor children and mothers in Detroit and train cars full of high-protein food at Wayne County General Hospital in suburban Wayne meant to be distributed to the needy. "The only problem is that no one in our terribly high-powered and over-bureaucratized society can figure out how to get the two together," the editorial said.

The "surplus" food was paid for by the USDA's price support program that was designed to create stockpiles of food in the event of nuclear war and to protect farmers from price fluctuations caused by overproduction. In effect, the USDA paid for food that was not going to be consumed, but stored in case of national crisis and so farmers could have a guaranteed income. After public pressure, the USDA said local governments or non-profit agencies could distribute some of the stockpiled food to the poor if they wanted to, but the federal government would not provide money to do so. The USDA declined to solicit agencies in Detroit that might be able to distribute free food to the poor. Why not? "It's not our realm of responsibility," William Hairston, administrator of the USDA food distribution office in southeast Michigan, told the *Free Press*.

Local government officials had ignored the problem. "Why can't the mayor pick up a telephone and offer to distribute the food through Human Resources Development field offices?" the *Free Press* asked. "Why can't the city or federal anti-poverty programs pay jobless teenagers to repackage it into manageable units? Why can't the DSR run regular bus service out to it? Why can't it be distributed through existing day care centers, or unemployment offices, or welfare offices, or even the post office? Why can't all those people whose salaries are paid by the taxpayers come up with some better ideas?

"Don't tell us. We already know. Government agencies don't exist to feed the hungry, but to stay inside their realms of responsibility. And don't you 53,000 mothers and children forget it." The *Free Press* editorial's headline was a question: "Who Will Carry the Food to the Poor and Hungry?"

Father Cunningham answered that question: "We will."

Father Roger Morin, who ran a government food distribution program in New Orleans, forged a close relationship with Father Cunningham and Eleanor Josaitis while lobbying Capitol Hill on behalf of the Commodity Supplemental Food Program. Although Morin, later named Bishop of Biloxi, Mississippi, told Congress that he represented the diocese of New Orleans, Cunningham made it clear that Focus: HOPE was independent of the Archdiocese of Detroit. Still, the Roman collar helped, Cunningham often said.

Credit: Courtesy of Bishop Roger Morin

7

Lobbyist

THE WOMEN WAITING for Father Bill Cunningham to show up for a meeting of the Presbyterian Interracial Council (P.I.C.) in April 1970 were growing impatient. Mary Ann Gideon, co-chair of a P.I.C. project to fight hunger in the inner city, had invited Cunningham to the meeting thinking, "that he was some wizened old priest." When she called him, though, "I heard this wonderful beautiful voice on the telephone. He shocked me."

All the women—"typically Presbyterian," Gideon said—had arrived a half-hour early. Now, the priest who was their guest speaker was 40 minutes late. Suddenly, Cunningham arrived. "He came racing in and here was this handsome young man with the long black hair and boots, running around and hugging all the women. He'd been to a family hour at a funeral home." He easily won the women over. "Everybody loved him," Gideon said.

Cunningham spoke for a few minutes about Focus: HOPE's mission to counter the effects of racism. Ann Byrne of the Maternity and Infant Care Project then spoke about "this wonderful new [federal] program that provided food for mothers," according to Gideon. The problem was that people who qualified for the food assistance had no transportation to a distribution center. "It was at that meeting," Gideon said, "that Bill leaned over and said, 'Why don't we get Focus: HOPE volunteers to do it?'"

The United States Department of Agriculture (USDA) had been operating a Supplemental Food Program (SFP) for one year, but the food commodities only were reaching a small percentage of the eligible mothers and children. Hunger in poor communities was a concern of Michigan's senior Democratic senator, Philip A. Hart, who worked with Sen. George McGovern, D-South Dakota, in April 1970 to increase SFP funding by $20 million beginning in fiscal year 1972. But the appropriation did not provide money to administer distribution programs, and Nixon administration officials signaled that it might not spend the money.

Then, the USDA decided that as of April 17, 1970, no new clients of the commodity programs could be enrolled, citing local governmental inefficiencies. Detroit had 53,000 potential recipients, but the city didn't have resources to run a distribution program, so food commodities available under SFP sat uselessly in a warehouse in western Wayne County.

Cunningham traveled to Chicago to lobby the Midwest office of the Office of Economic Opportunity (OEO), a federal agency created by former President Lyndon Johnson as part of his Great Society initiative, to provide funding for an SFP program in Detroit. The OEO authorized a $56,000 grant to Detroit to operate a distribution program from July 1, 1970, through Aug. 31, 1971. Since OEO grants were made through local or state governments, the money for Detroit was sent to the Mayor's Committee on Human Resources Development (MCHRD), which sent out a request for bids to operate the food program.

The only qualified nonprofit willing to take on the distribution program was the Salvation Army. which had delivery trucks that could unload boxcars of food at a "team railroad track" in the Brightmoor neighborhood on the west side. The commodities were then trucked to a warehouse at 5900 Trumbull in

Detroit, space that was donated except for the cost of heat and lighting. A crew of five men was paid to break the bulk shipments down into 30-pound boxes. Poor women certified eligible for the commodity food support by local hospitals could then pick up boxes there or at two Salvation Army centers in Highland Park and in Detroit's Cass Corridor.

The old warehouse was grimy, dark and rat-infested. And despite the Salvation Army's best efforts, only 800 needy women and children—out of the 53,000 people potentially eligible for the food—were participating, primarily due to a lack of transportation. It was impossible for many poor women with small kids to catch city buses to the inconveniently located distribution points, and then carry the heavy boxes back home.

Cunningham gave the task to Eleanor Josaitis who, with Focus: HOPE volunteer Linda Cubbage, organized about 400 volunteers to drive eligible mothers to and from the Salvation Army's warehouse to pick up their allotted boxes of food. By February 1971, the two women had increased the number of people getting food from 800 to 2,400. Their work was done with no funding whatsoever, just through the use of volunteers. Still, that represented less than 4 percent of the 53,000 malnourished Detroit women and children who were going to bed hungry each night.

It cost the Salvation Army nearly $2 to distribute each package that contained seven nutritious foods, including canned meat and vegetables. The monthly food allotment had an estimated retail value of $7 and would be worth nearly $300,000 each month if provided to the maximum 3,500 women and children the Salvation Army said it could handle. But even that meager food program was in danger. Some members of the MCHRD thought it would be better to give $10 directly to the eligible women so they could buy food from local markets, and the agency decided that spring to end its support of the food distribution program by September 1.

Lobbying city officials, Cunningham and Josaitis pointed out the weakness in that plan. "As we all are aware, these little corner markets in the inner city do not supply the supplemental foods that are so critically needed to stem malnutrition, starvation and retardation," Josaitis wrote in a report to the city. "We believe that this year we could reach a quota of 18,000 packages with our volunteers and an extra effort."

Meanwhile, the USDA saw the failures of the SFP system nationwide as justification for its decision to freeze the number of women and children being served, notwithstanding the tens of thousands of hungry children who might have benefited from a more nutritious diet.

Cunningham attacked the problem on multiple fronts. He turned to William J. Horvath, a recent Yale Divinity School graduate who had interviewed the priest in December 1968 for a magazine article, to coordinate efforts to create business opportunities in several inner-city neighborhoods.[18]

Cunningham wanted to develop shopping centers in underserved areas of Detroit. He arranged through Wayne County Clerk Joe B. Sullivan, a well-connected Democrat and neighbor of the Josaitis family, for Horvath to be appointed to the Mayor's Task Force on Inner-City Commercial Development, of which Horvath became chairman. "Focus: HOPE allowed me, as a new staff member, to get to the center of the food store problem immediately," Horvath wrote. "Within two months, I was designated its spokesman on the issue. ... I was allowed the freedom to awake, work and sleep seeking solutions to inner-city food shopping problems. It was awesome to be trusted with domain over an important organizational project."

The entire Focus: HOPE budget for 1970 was just $14,529, not nearly enough to do what Cunningham needed to get done. He went back to New Detroit, writing a letter on January 12,

---

18   *The American Lutheran Church's Coordinating Committee on National Crises made a small grant that allowed Horvath to work for Focus: HOPE. In a later HOPE HAPPENINGS newsletter article, Horvath wrote that he found Focus: HOPE a great place to work for three reasons: "Its dedication to the purpose of relieving the effects of white racism; its impatience with promises lacking performance; and its warmth as a community of people who, while dedicated to serious objectives, also knew the importance of play and festivity."*

1971, to David Chrisco, head of the consumer affairs subcommittee, asking for $22,990 to split about equally for salaries for Horvath and Josaitis. Chrisco offered to provide funding for Horvath, but not Josaitis. Cunningham was all or nothing, even though Focus: HOPE hadn't yet gotten approval for tax-exempt status under Section 501(c)(3) of the Internal Revenue Code. Focus: HOPE got nothing from New Detroit that year.

Focus: HOPE needed a budget of at least $40,000 for 1972, Cunningham figured, so he sent out a letter to supporters appealing for funds: "We are reluctant to admit it, but the time has come, in fact is long overdue, for Focus: HOPE to become more effectively organized and efficiently operated. We are still an organization of volunteers, but as an 'all-volunteer' organization we have found ourselves restricted in maximum utilization of those who want to help. The projects like the food survey, to be followed up by constructive action require a full-time person. We need a full-time person to serve and coordinate the volunteer efforts. We need a secretary—and we must pay these full-time people a modest stipend."

Considering the initiatives Focus: HOPE was undertaking, "the ask" was modest and came in a postscript: "We are suggesting that $12.00 a year, from those of you who can afford it. … Help us with $1.00 if you can."

Focus: HOPE held a rare meeting of its board of directors on February 8, 1971, at Madonna. In deference to Cunningham's busy schedule and propensity for being late, the meeting wasn't called to order until 8:15 p.m. According to the meeting minutes, "The mayor's task force may soon have reached the end of its effectiveness. Focus: HOPE may have to take this project back and move with it on its own." A complete financial report was not available, but the organization had about $2,000 in a checking account, Josaitis reported. Also, Focus: HOPE had borrowed $4,400 at 5.5 percent interest in November to buy a printing press. She then gave a progress report on what she and Cubbage had been doing with the Salvation Army's SFP. Cunningham said the program would not survive unless Focus: HOPE took it over.[19]

Although it's not in the minutes, one board member commented that every Focus: HOPE meeting he attended was disorganized with no written agenda. Instead, Cunningham engaged board members in long-winded discussions about his grandiose ideas. How they'd get the funds for those ideas baffled most of them, but the lack of money never seemed to worry Cunningham. At that meeting, a board member commented that he was "tired of coming to these meetings and muddling through these things," according to Joe B. Sullivan's wife Mary. Miffed at first, Cunningham embraced the critique and began calling the column he wrote for the Focus: HOPE newsletter "Muddling Thru."

Focus: HOPE had taken over much of the Madonna rectory, and some wondered about how Cunningham could do both. "If you were to ask anybody around at that time, we all thought that Focus: HOPE was his primary job and the parish was secondary," Pilon said. "But he brought the parish along by making it the center of Focus: HOPE. He married those two ministries together." Cunningham told parishioner Helen Luckey, though, that "I work at Focus: HOPE, but Madonna Church is my joy."

Despite the Oakland Mall experience, Cunningham wanted to continue doing big festivals with carnival rides, beer tents, live music and games. The "1970 Detroit Hope Happening" was September 10-13 in downtown Detroit—a novel idea at the time. The "festival of rides, boutiques, games, music" was held on the Kern Block and Kennedy Square, despite skeptics who said suburbanites would never come downtown at night. Several thousand came downtown to enjoy music, food and

---

19   *That summer board member John Morpaw, a tall, skinny accountant for a local car dealer, became treasurer of Focus: HOPE, and prepared a financial report for the first quarter of 1971 that showed that the organization recorded $1,085.77 in donations and had gotten $2,764.61 from the benefit hockey game. Total revenues for the quarter—including $3,700 from the Focus: HOPE savings account—were $9,368.39 and expenses were $8,344.34, including $2,416.50 in salaries.*

games. Coeds from Wayne State, the University of Detroit and Marygrove College acted as hostesses, wearing the red berets and ponchos. *The Michigan Catholic* said the Focus: HOPE festival was "the beginning of a really dynamic decade for Detroit and its citizens. The 1970s—the Detroit Decade!"

For the second "Hope Happening" in 1972, Josaitis and Dario Bonucchi asked Common Council to hold the event downtown in late August. The twist this time was that Focus: HOPE wanted to close off Woodward Avenue (except for two lanes for emergency vehicles) for about five blocks from Adams Street to Michigan Avenue for an entire week in order to have "a festival consisting of amusement rides and a tent housing games of skill, a tent housing a boutique sale, and accompanying light food and soft drink and beer concessions." Blocking off car traffic would allow people to stroll the city's major roadway, enjoy the sights and sounds, and give them a chance to shop. They called the festival "a Detroit psychological upper. The expression of a city on the move. A weekend to hear the sounds, see the lights, feel the excitement, sense the enjoyment, appreciate the people that are Detroit."

Focus: HOPE offered to handle security and trash removal, so the city's costs would be close to zero. There was pushback by the Central Business District Association—primarily, the J.L. Hudson Company. CBDA members didn't like the idea of closing a major thoroughfare to their businesses. At a June 22 hearing on the request, the CBDA, Hudson's and the city's Department of Streets and Traffic, opposed closing Woodward. However, the idea was supported by the City Planning Commission, and the Police and Fire Departments.

Bonucchi attended the meeting prepared with a concession to only close Woodward on Saturday and Sunday, as long as Focus: HOPE could use Grand Circus Park, the Kern Block and Campus Martius for the entire week. "The closing of Woodward is an integral part of this revised proposal," Bonucchi said. "Focus: HOPE is not in the carnival business. We are concerned with the people; we are concerned with Detroit." The council voted 7-1 in favor of Focus: HOPE's revised proposal.

Behind the scenes, Cunningham was campaigning to take over the food program from the Salvation Army. He and Josaitis convinced the MCHRD to reverse itself and re-fund the program at a level of $51,000—still barely enough to distribute food to 3,500 but not possibly enough to reach 18,000. They enlisted allies at the Michigan Department of Health, which wanted more malnourished children to get the free food. While frustrated with the city's slow response, Cunningham went back to the OEO in Chicago and got a second authorization for federal funds to run the program, this time for $101,000—but city officials had to show that Detroit could carry off the project and expand it.

The USDA's decision to not enroll any more mothers and young children into the food program still rankled Cunningham. There was only one practical course of action: An appeal to Congress. After a phone call from Cunningham, Senator Hart invited him to come to Washington, D.C., to testify. Cunningham, Josaitis and Dorinda Jones of MCHRD flew to the nation's capital to testify on July 22, 1971, before the Senate Select Committee on Nutrition and Human Needs.

Cunningham's voice broke and his eyes welled with tears several times as he testified. "We maintain that food, like warmth, clothing, housing, medicine and dignity are inalienable rights of all human beings," he said. "If children go hungry at certain critical ages, they may suffer brain damage that can never be repaired. We have already created a culture of hunger." Cunningham told them about Josaitis' work organizing volunteers to get hungry mothers to food centers. In response to a question, Cunningham accused the USDA of having a "mad hatter" mentality for withholding food from impoverished babies and toddlers at the most critical time for brain development.

Cunningham had been working with Father Roger Morin, who was managing several food distribution programs for the poor in New Orleans. They collaborated on a campaign to get the federal government to include canned formula for infants in the surplus food commodities distribution program. There was no "surplus" of baby formula, so there was no government commodity program to give it away. Formula was, in fact, made by corporations in business to sell food, not to give it away. "This was before the Women, Infants and Children program," Morin said. "We had been told to give out 30 cans of evaporated milk and three bottles of corn syrup and that was going to be the consistent formula for babies in the inner city. We wanted vitamin- and iron-enriched formula, just like other families bought.

"It took the longest time, at least three years of battling," Morin said. "In some ways the journey was like a nightmare when you're cut off at the pass every which way you went by people who were in that industry." Finally, the largest manufacturer agreed to make baby formula using a generic label—under contract with the federal government.

The July 22 visit to Capitol Hill was only the first of several lobbying trips that year. In early August, Cunningham, Josaitis, Charlie Grenville and Bidleman flew to Washington for another round. "My recollection is that he was not nervous; he would get charged up," Bidleman said of Cunningham. "There'd be like an energy start blowing through him that had to do with that whole stew mix of outrage, compassion, the senselessness of [hunger]. Basically, he was living the life of a missionary. He could do that kind of thing. You could see it in his eyes. He'd get this edge to him like he was going to go and do the flame-thrower thing for a while."

According to Bidleman, each of them had a specific task. "Eleanor's job was basically to make it all work and build relationships with all the people we were meeting with. Her skills of working the halls of Congress, the staffers, committee staffers, were pretty much legendary. Bill was the center of the circus. Charlie made sure there was substance behind what he was saying and Eleanor was bringing all the pieces together. Actually, they were quite a good, complementary team on all these things."

Grenville was in Senator Hubert Humphrey's office chatting with an aide about getting food to low-income women, infants and pre-school children. He told Focus: HOPE colleagues that the aide was asking how the government could do it. Grenville said he drew out an outline of a program on a napkin or piece of paper. "You could always hand out a coupon," Grenville told the aide, according to colleague Tom Ferguson. "And that is where the WIC program came from," Ferguson said. In September 1972, Congress passed Humphrey's amendment to the Child Nutrition Act creating a two-year pilot in the USDA's supplemental nutrition program for Women, Infants, and Children. By 1974, WIC was operating in 45 states using Grenville's initial model.

More than 90,000 people came downtown for the free Hope Happening on Saturday and more than 100,000 on Sunday. Those numbers were greater than those who paid to get into the Michigan State Fair up Woodward at Eight Mile that same weekend.

By early August, Cunningham had convinced the MCHRD's director, James M. Oliver, to support Focus: HOPE taking over the SFP from the Salvation Army. On August 11, Oliver sent a proposal to that effect to Detroit's Common Council, saying "we would like to contract with Focus: HOPE in an amount not to exceed $101,000." Representatives of the Salvation Army opposed the measure, but at the Council's August 24 meeting it was approved by a vote of 8-0. There was one problem, however: Focus: HOPE had no place to store and distribute food. "We need a larger warehouse, 20,000 square feet, on a railway siding, rent-free to cut costs and give adequate storage and space for our volunteers to package food," Cunningham wrote in *HOPE HAPPENINGS*.

Time was running out because the owners of the warehouse on Trumbull, who had read reports about the OEO grants to run the program, had made it clear that they wanted the organizations to start paying rent as of September 1, the Wednesday after the end of Detroit Hope Happening 2. The hard deadline energized the priest and his colleagues.

It had no suitable building, and Focus: HOPE also had no money to pay anyone to set up a food distribution center. Still, Thom Armstead left a good-paying job as a foreman at a Chrysler plant to help Cunningham pull this off.

On September 1, Common Council "reconsidered" the SFP's issue after the Salvation Army pointed out that Focus: HOPE had not been able to find a warehouse. Further, thousands of dollars worth of food was still sitting in a facility that the Salvation Army would have to begin paying rent for beginning that day. The Army wanted Council to renew its authority to run the program. The Council was sympathetic, but still was impressed enough by Cunningham and Focus: HOPE to give them more time. They adjourned until Friday and then voted 6-0 to give the Salvation Army $3,885 of the $101,000 to operate the program for two more weeks. The understanding was that if Focus: HOPE had not found a suitable warehouse by then, then the entire OEO grant would go to the Army.

Deadline day was September 15. That morning, Cunningham signed a lease with Will Kraus, an entrepreneur who was shutting down his engineering company two blocks west of Madonna on the other side of Oakman Boulevard. Cunningham committed Focus: HOPE to lease the facility for $1,500 a month. "He didn't have any money, but he had signed a lease," Armstead said. "Typical Cunningham." Immediately, a crew of about 30 Focus: HOPE volunteers began cleaning the building. Then Chrysler Corporation agreed to loan Cunningham a half dozen trucks that day so they could quickly begin moving cases of government food into the facility.

On Friday afternoon, Cunningham produced the lease for Common Council and asked again for control of the program. Council voted 6-1 to approve the transfer to Focus: HOPE. Cunningham immediately called the Madonna rectory and asked for Armstead. "Roll the trucks!" he said. About 20 minutes later, a caravan of trucks and volunteers in their cars arrived at 5900 Trumbull and began to load hundreds of boxes of government food. It took several trips and most of the night, but Cunningham had promised that the prescription food program under Focus: HOPE management would be operational the next day. Indeed, it was.

The city's bureaucracy being what it was, the money to operate the program was delayed several weeks. Cunningham was not happy and came downtown for a meeting with James Oliver and aide Robert Brazelton. "It was an interesting meeting because I didn't know anything about Father Cunningham," Brazelton said, chuckling. "The reason I laugh when I think about it is because I remember that Oliver and Father Cunningham got into a kind of pissing contest because Father Cunningham accused Oliver of being dilatory." Brazelton said he had to look the word up later, but Oliver understood that Cunningham was accusing him of unnecessarily holding back money from Focus: HOPE. Oliver, a towering black man and former professional football player, was "normally a mild-mannered guy," but he "got ruffled by being accused of being dilatory," Brazelton said. Cunningham's impact was strong. Oliver moved more quickly to get the check issued for Focus: HOPE.

Cunningham named Grenville as director of the Food Prescription Program and Armstead as manager of the warehouse. The priest made it clear that he expected that the facility would soon look less like a warehouse and more like a regular grocery store. And he told Grenville and Armstead to enroll as many poor women and children in the program that they could—the hell with the USDA limits. He set a goal of 10,000 monthly participants, but the USDA was firm that it would supply only enough food to feed 3,500 women and children each month.

Cunningham took to the pulpit and every available community forum with a simple message: The USDA policy of denying nutritious supplemental food to thousands of needy children in Detroit was condemning those kids to a lifetime of ill health and low achievement. In a letter to Senator Hart he asserted that an additional 13 chain grocery stores had closed in Detroit in 1971, with 11 of those buildings "purchased by independents" whose markup will range from 10 to 30 percent higher than the large chains. "With the variety allowed in the commodity distribution program, we could lend a great deal of human dignity, not to mention better nutrition, to this program. I know you will use the strength of your office to pry the food from the USDA warehouse and budget."

Grenville wrote letters—signed by Cunningham—to USDA Deputy Assistant Secretary Philip C. Olsson criticizing a recent directive that limited the monthly canned juice allotment for needy children from three 46-ounce size cans to one, and the 18-ounce size from nine to three cans. "To say that this two-thirds cutback in juices 'will not significantly diminish the nutritional contribution of the package' is an example of the mad-hatter logic I alluded to before the Senate Select Committee on Health," the letter said. "The package is already critically depleted. Peanut butter was cut on the basis it would not significantly diminish the package, as was chocolate mix, powdered scrambled eggs, and instant potatoes." Appealing to Olsson's "humane and practical judgment," their letter said that, "what is needed, and needed now, is a practical and honest appreciation of the problems of the underfed. We must have a minimum of four cans of meat in a mother's package—peanut butter for the kids, a large can of juice that can be opened each week, some variety to allow the dignity of choice."

Cunningham reminded Olsson that USDA officials had inspected Focus: HOPE distribution center and found it adequate. He said the staff was prepared to handle as many as 18,000 monthly recipients. "May I ask you, Mr. Olsson, to come to Detroit and view personally what we have described: the distribution center, the kinds of grocery stores available in the city and the prices one must pay. We want you to spend some hours talking with the mothers, perhaps visiting homes with volunteer drivers to discover how an underfed mother manages a single can of boned chicken for one month, to hear her response to your directive that one can of juice in place of three per month does not 'significantly diminish the nutritional contribution'."

Among the good advice Hart gave to Cunningham and Josaitis was that they needed to reach out to Republicans, particularly Michigan's other U.S. Senator, Robert Griffin. After speaking to a Griffin aide, Grenville wrote an October 20 letter to the Senator: "We find it both incomprehensible and morally inexcusable that the USDA will not take these actions in light of Detroit's great need."

Cunningham received Olsson's rejection letter on October 29. Olsson said after three years' experience with more than 190,000 participants in 327 projects nationwide, the USDA concluded the program was not efficient. The program in Washington, D.C., for example, was spending $500,000 per year, about half to a third of the cost of the commodities distributed. A Cornell University study showed no "statistically significant" difference between poor people in the food supplement program and those on food stamps. "We are forced to ask ourselves whether or not there may be better uses for such funds."

Cunningham was not about to back down. He and Josaitis flew to Washington again to meet with Griffin, the assistant minority leader in the Senate, in person. After the meeting, Griffin's press secretary assigned a young aide Pete Teeley to help Focus: HOPE in its relations with the USDA. "Griffin had a lot of authority at that point," Teeley said. "I tried to leverage whatever influence Griffin had." Griffin's intercession got Olsson to agree to come to Detroit to see the Focus: HOPE Food Prescription Program.

Noting that President Nixon had nominated Earl Butz, a dean at Purdue University, to be the new Secretary of Agriculture, Cunningham asked Focus: HOPE volunteers to write letters to Butz about the food program even before his nomination was confirmed. Dozens wrote letters to Butz at Purdue. Then, prodded by Griffin, Olsson came to Detroit to see the Focus: HOPE program. Behind the scenes, Teeley had convinced Griffin to withhold his confirmation vote for Butz unless his fellow Republicans in the Nixon administration approved an expansion of the SFP in Detroit.

On December 6, Olsson wrote a letter to Senator Griffin saying he had reversed the decision. "As a result, we at USDA now have a better understanding of your strong support for Focus Hope's application to expand the program," the letter said. "We are pleased to be able to authorize the Detroit Supplemental Feeding Program to expand to serve 15,000 mothers and infants. ... The Department of Agriculture is able to allow this expansion because of the effective volunteer program organized by Focus

Hope which provides transportation for program participants and keeps operating costs at a minimum. Continued operating efficiency is a condition of today's authorized expansion."

Olsson later told *Washington Post* reporter Nick Kotz that he approved expansion of the program in Detroit on its merits, but he still considered the program nationally as inefficient and ineffective. Kotz wrote a story that put the deal-making succinctly: "The Nixon administration last week approved a fourfold expansion of a federal food aid program in Detroit, Mich., to help ensure that a key Republican senator would vote to confirm Earl L. Butz as Secretary of Agriculture." Griffin acknowledged to Kotz that he had used Butz' nomination as leverage to "win a yearlong fight over the Detroit food program."

"It was a curious situation," Olsson said of Focus: HOPE. "Pragmatically, the supplemental feeding program doesn't make much sense. It tends to become a substitute for the food stamp program, and food stamps more adequately meet needs. But the quality of service in the Detroit program is very impressive. It's a tremendous volunteer effort."

"Ironic," Teeley said years later. "We were able to get that through, the increase in the number of women and children receiving food, but Eleanor Josaitis was not happy about it. She came to me and said, 'We don't like this.' I said, 'You got everything you wanted!' 'Yeah, but we didn't get peanut butter,'" Josaitis responded.

A few months later, Cunningham and Josaitis got the USDA to include peanut butter in the commodity food shipments.

Father Cunningham and Eleanor Josaitis, early 1970s.

Credit: Focus: HOPE

8

Call the Woman

MICHIGAN'S REPUBLICAN SENATOR Robert Griffin sat stunned as an angry Father Bill Cunningham poured out a torrent of biting criticism against President Nixon's Secretary of Agriculture, Earl Butz. Cunningham's voice rose in pitch and his eyes widened as he accused Butz of trying to kill Detroit's children.

The reason: Butz was again trying to eliminate the USDA's Supplemental Food Program—the foundation for everything Focus: HOPE wanted to do in Detroit. The priest and his tireless partner, Eleanor Josaitis, had lobbied for months to preserve the SFP. But Butz, like a movie monster that dies only to rise threateningly again, was back at it. Josaitis and a "highly emotional" Cunningham were back on Capitol Hill to save a program the priest believed was essential to saving underserved black children from malnutrition.

Focus: HOPE's food program director Charlie Grenville and his staff had been hard at work. They increased the number of clinics and preschools allowed to certify eligibility in the program from 13 to 31, adding thousands to the distribution roll.

Grenville and warehouse director Thom Armstead also organized volunteers to refurbish the grimy building they were now leasing into a clean, gaily decorated, supermarket-like facility that enhanced the dignity of the individuals who came to pick up the free food. Several grocery store chains—the very companies Father Cunningham had lambasted for abandoning the city—helped out by donating thousands of shopping bags, shelving and grocery carts.[20]

But the heart of Focus: HOPE remained its faithful corps of volunteers, who provided transportation to the women and families eligible for monthly food allotments. Since September 1971, the number of volunteer drivers had increased from 224 to 774. More significantly, an independent evaluation of the Focus: HOPE program in early 1972 found a positive impact on the health of pregnant women.

But Earl Butz still intended to eliminate the SFP from the USDA's 1973 budget. A young aide to Griffin, Gerald Rosen, was at the meeting as Cunningham got emotional about the issue. Josaitis took notes and tried to calm Cunningham. "I love Bill but Bill was not a detail guy," Rosen said. "He talked about the number of people in the program and how the program expanded, but really the details of the program and how it worked with the Agriculture Department were completely missing." Finally, Cunningham quieted down and Josaitis knew what Griffin needed to hear. Josaitis "was much more focused, much more detailed, and Griffin started taking notes," Rosen said. The senator said he'd try to help, everyone shook hands and Cunningham and Josaitis left. "And Griffin said to me, 'Get on this. Let's see if we can help.'"

Rosen said he started with the usual congressional liaison to agriculture but "I literally got nowhere." He told Griffin, saying he couldn't figure out what the problem was at the USDA. Griffin said he had a meeting coming up at the White House that

---

20   *Chatham Complete Food Centers donated 70 feet of supermarket shelving and 30 grocery carts, the A&P Company donated 5,000 grocery bags, Borman Food Stores donated 8,000 bags and Great Scott Supermarkets donated 40,000 grocery bags.*

Butz also would attend, and suggested bringing it up with the secretary there. He asked Rosen to come up with some "talking points" about the SFP to use. As Rosen got up to leave, Griffin stopped him and said, "Call the woman." Rosen called Josaitis and "she gave me some very good talking points, which I put into one page with five or six bullets. Griffin took it, and the next thing I knew the program was reinstated."

The issue of chronic malnutrition among black children always made Cunningham weepy. "I've seen him cry," Josaitis told the *Detroit Free Press* in March 1972. "He's not afraid of the emotional man in him; but the anger he wrestles with. ... I saw him at a Senate hearing and he got so emotional that he had to stop to cry. ... He's in a position to effect change and the biggest frustration in him is he can't make the change fast enough."

For that Sunday magazine story, reporter James Harper asked the priest for his views on blacks in America. "James Baldwin develops the thesis that black people are the salvation of Christianity—that people are coming, like Catholic priests, to save black souls, to save black people—and really what is happening is that the black man, Christian or not, is the saving force not only of the city in the classical sense of the city, and the Church, but the black man is the salvation of society," Cunningham said. "And I believe this. The black man is the major element of honesty and conflict and search in our society today. ...

"Because I'm in the black community. I discovered the problem of mothers and babies. If I were a white priest in a white community then the diocesan directive on abortion would be my main concern. This is the teaching of the Church: the right to life. But instead of me being hung up on the right of a baby to be born, I'm concerned about the black community's right to live. So it's far more important to me to feed babies than whether or not we get an abortion law. ... While the Catholic Church is spinning its wheels about abortion, hundreds of thousands of babies already born are starving to death and nobody apparently gives a damn."

That spring, Don Josaitis reached a breaking point of frustration about his wife working long hours with Cunningham while their children were with friends, relatives and babysitters or just by themselves. Bill and Eleanor lived and breathed Focus: HOPE. Don, focused on running the hobby store, tolerated his wife's commitment, knowing that her time and energy were spent on a just cause. Cunningham's rhetoric, Don thought, was laced with Irish blarney. "Ninety percent of the time, he was right; the other 10 percent, he made you think he was right," Don said.

Instead of trying to rein in his wife, Don found a nice deal on a weeklong trip to Spain—just $202 per person, airfare, hotels and two meals a day included. Without a second thought, he bought four tickets and produced them when Eleanor and Bill were talking late one night in the den. He told them he had tickets—for Eleanor, Bill, Bill's dad and himself—for a trip to Spain. The only condition, Don said, was that he didn't want to hear the words "Focus: HOPE" on the entire trip. They flew to Spain in May. Bill and Eleanor kept their part of the bargain by not mentioning Focus: HOPE, at least when Don was within earshot. But, Eleanor said later with a wink, "We spoke in code."

That summer of 1972, Cunningham got a phone call from an assertive, dedicated and conscientious nun looking for a job. What Eleanor was to Cunningham at Focus: HOPE, Sister Cecilia Begin was to him at the Catholic Church of the Madonna. Sister Cecilia, of the Religious Sisters of Mercy, had grown up in Midland, Michigan, the middle child in a French Canadian family of 13 children, four of whom became nuns. After making her vows, she left for Bay City, a bustling, blue-collar town where many blacks had found opportunities to work. She taught at Visitation parish's school with a progressive pastor, Father Theodore LaMarre, whose preaching highlighted the injustices faced by blacks and other minorities. LaMarre "just taught me so much about the problems; I was very naïve as far as race relations," Cecilia said.

In 1967, she accepted a position at St. Cletus Catholic Church in Warren just in time to witness white "Christians" rioting around a small pink brick home on Buster Street, where the mixed-race Bailey couple and their two children had moved in.

Being a compassionate woman of deep faith, Cecilia reached out to the Baileys without thinking she needed to clear it with her new pastor. She was shocked that the pastor disapproved. "I went over to see the Baileys, much to the dismay of the pastor, and really got scolded for it," Cecilia said. "He was fearful the neighborhood was going to change." The pastor knew his congregation well—many of them had left their older neighborhoods in Detroit for the virtually all-white suburb expressly to get away from blacks. Cecilia, nevertheless, did what she could for the Baileys. "I wanted to bring their little girl into Catechism class," she said.[21]

By 1972, Cecilia decided she'd had enough of the small-minded racism in Detroit's suburbs, and she needed a change. "I knew I could not stay in Warren," she said. "I knew the time had come. I had kind of moved on with the changes in the Church and I just couldn't handle it any more." The Religious Sisters of Mercy allowed their members to find their own ministry and Cecilia was free to find her next position at a Catholic agency of her choice. "I heard Father Cunningham was looking," she said. "I gave him a call. He said to come for dinner, which I did in August 1972."

Although Father Cunningham wanted to hire Sister Cecilia immediately, it really was a decision for the parish council, as the archdiocese had empowered parishioners with many management decisions in the spirit of the reforms of Vatican II. A few days after his dinner with Cecilia, Cunningham left for the vacation in Spain with his dad, Eleanor and Don, leaving the hiring decision in the hands of the parish council. Council members, however, weren't sure about this blunt-talking, no-nonsense sister who usually did not bother wearing a traditional nun's habit. The council couldn't decide—their budget was in deficit—and they did nothing until Cunningham returned. He urged them to take a chance on the outspoken nun, and they offered Cecilia the job. Typically blunt, Cecilia responded: "I'll let you know in a week." A week later, she accepted. Cunningham told Cecilia

---

21   *Sister Cecilia insisted that the author not identify the pastor. She continued to offer the Baileys her support, albeit quietly.*

that her job would be to do "whatever they needed." "What it really ended up with was you did everything—the dog needed to be fed, clean the stove in the basement, sweep the floor when it needed sweeping."

When the archdiocese closed Madonna's school in 1967, it had nothing to do with the parish's finances. The school was solvent and paying its own way. But it was closed to bolster enrollments at two other Catholic schools—Blessed Sacrament Cathedral and St. Martin DePorres. Even though Madonna's school was closed, the archdiocese still expected the parish to cover certain costs for the parish's children who had been involuntarily transferred to the other schools. Tuition charges were higher under the new setup, and by June 1972 the archdiocese figured that Madonna owed a staggering sum, $167,000.

Cunningham refused to pay, and he would not back down. Cardinal Dearden compromised in a deal that he thought Cunningham couldn't refuse, cutting Madonna's debt to $100,000, "interest free for two years." Cunningham didn't blink. He told the chancery that the debt should be canceled in its entirety.

"I personally questioned the psychology of leaving huge debts on parishes much too small in membership to ever hope paying them off," Cunningham wrote to Father Francis Granger, vicar of the Near Westside Vicariate. "This little parish of 200 families, originally supporting its own school without help, directed to close and support two central schools, is now being asked to assume responsibility for $100,000 of the original debt and interest."

While there were 200 families on the parish membership rolls, many had drifted away after the parish school was closed by the archdiocese and were neither attending Mass nor contributing. "Attendance dropped at Madonna after the closing of the school," Cecilia wrote in a letter to the author. "Father Cunningham and I worked very hard to improve membership. I would often ask why we continued with two Sunday Masses when attendance was so low. (The back pews were roped off to get people to sit up front.) Father would always reply, 'Cecilia, we are going to fill Madonna Church.' On Monday morning, I sent bulletins and a summary of the homily to every absent member. (We knew who they were.) In January, we hand delivered all the contribution envelopes and calendars to the homes of the parishioners. Father Cunningham never doubted or changed his mind. I was the one who wavered."

Cunningham's hard-nosed business sense also never wavered. His impassioned arguments about the unfairness of his parish's debt eventually led Dearden to write off the entire amount. On top of that, the chancery granted Madonna $9,572 from the archdiocese's Inter-Parish Sharing Program to cover the parish's operating budget deficit, including $2,800 to pay the diocesan "tax." The archdiocese also gave Madonna $12,000 from its Disadvantaged Schools Fund for the religious education program in the parish.

In the early 1970s, it was difficult to separate Madonna Church from Focus: HOPE. "Focus: HOPE was in every nook and cranny" of the rectory, Cecilia said. Her desk was in the living room next to the fireplace. "I had absolutely no privacy; there was Focus: HOPE all around." The noisy crew was a distraction, but Cecilia's biggest issue was the nonstop profanity. "Everybody used to curse like a sailor," Thom Armstead said. Cecilia's prickly personality also initially annoyed the chronically profane Carl Bidleman. "I did not do anything to make her feel welcome," Bidleman admitted. "I just thought she was this old tight-ass nun. In all fairness, in many ways she was. Being around Cunningham for 20 years did a lot to loosen her up."

Cecilia couldn't quite believe that Cunningham was attempting the impossible: handling two difficult and time-consuming full-time jobs simultaneously. "You had to learn to work with Father," Cecilia said. "We had serious disagreements, but that wasn't how you operate with Father. It began to dawn on me that he didn't need to be in charge. I was in the parish. I took care of stuff in the parish. I could do that and just let him do his thing down the street. When I got that straight in my head, we worked hand in glove."

A young journalist, Tim Kiska, came to work part-time at Focus: HOPE in the summer of 1973, editing the organization's newsletter. "We had to wait until the [church] receptionist left; she had the only typewriter," Kiska said. "I'd show up at 6 at night with a six-pack of beer and start typing away. ... It was kind of cool. Almost like a big clubhouse."

Working for Cunningham was arduous; he demanded effort, long hours, results and loyalty to Focus: HOPE above all else. When Kiska had his first byline in the *Free Press*—a review of a Sha Na Na concert—he was overjoyed. But Cunningham knew he wouldn't have Kiska around much longer. "Bill could see the look on my face and his line was, 'Well, I think I've lost you.' I think he demanded pretty much total loyalty more than anything else," Kiska said. "If you worked for him, it was like signing up for the Army."

In August 1973, it was revealed that Butz's USDA had decided to test the effectiveness of the SFP by drawing blood from the jugular veins of infants and toddlers. Cunningham was the most livid of many critics of the idea, saying the federal government was turning a "so-called feeding program" into a "Frankenstein research program." The government's attitude, Cunningham said, seemed to be "let's get rid of the poor" instead of "let's get rid of poverty." The order requiring the removal of 2 to 3 teaspoons of blood from infants was rescinded, but Butz wasn't giving up. He may not have realized how formidable this wild priest from Detroit was.

"The government has never addressed itself honestly to the hungry people of this nation," Cunningham told *The Detroit News* in December 1973. "Until they do, people like us have to meet the moral obligation. ... The country that doesn't guarantee the right of food to its people is pretty rotten."

Hunger and its sidekick, malnutrition, were the evils that must be addressed in order to help Detroit's poor children, Cunningham said. "The most threatening kind of malnutrition is mental retardation due to early protein deficiency," the priest told *Free Press* reporter Betty DeRamus that year. "Once the damage is done, points of I.Q. are chipped off." A 1970 federal survey of 4,000 mostly low-income people in Wayne County found serious nutritional deficiencies in more than 40 percent of them. Three percent of children showed signs of rickets, a bone deformity caused by deficiencies in Vitamin D and calcium. Statewide, the survey found that low-income children generally were about two inches shorter than kids from higher-income homes.

On January 3, 1974, Cunningham officiated at the wedding of Anne Markley Perron and Wayne County Circuit Judge Peter B. Spivak. Perron, an heiress to part of the Fisher Body fortune, had been divorced in November from businessman Frank J. Perron, whom she had married in a Catholic ceremony. Spivak, a friend of Cunningham's, had been married twice before, both marriages ending in divorce. The couple exchanged vows in the home of Anne's brother. Cunningham presided, then said Mass and distributed Communion to those in attendance.

"He knew it violated the rules" of the Church, his friend Neal Shine of the *Free Press* said. "But it didn't violate his rules. He thought it was the right thing to do. He knew it was going to be a small, private, quiet wedding. But, in fact, there was a *Detroit News* society writer there and she put a little note in the paper about it." Cunningham was summoned to a meeting with Cardinal Dearden's secretary on January 10. At the meeting, Cunningham confessed that he had officiated at the wedding ceremony and that he knew the act was a violation of Church doctrine. His punishment was a month suspension. He was allowed to celebrate Mass at Madonna the following Sunday, January 13, and he broke the news that he had been suspended. "They stood and clapped," Sister Cecilia said of the congregation

In the January 20 Madonna church bulletin, Cunningham explained his mistake in writing: "Several weeks ago I witnessed a marriage of two people, one of whom was a friend. The marriage was in a private home and after the exchange of vows I offered Mass. This couple had been each previously married, and by witnessing this ceremony I was in violation of Canon Law, or Church regulations. I was wrong. ... Starting this week, I will make a retreat at Colombiere and I ask for your prayers. I am sorry for any embarrassment and inconvenience caused the parish. Sister Cecilia will continue her pastoral work and will be available here to serve you. I look forward to seeing you in four weeks."

Even though his suspension did not cover his work at Focus: HOPE, Cunningham didn't believe it was right to continue working out of the Madonna rectory. He told *Free Press* religion writer Tom Fox that he was in the wrong. "I regret the pain and embarrassment I've caused, but I don't regret any kind of personal action. I felt the couple was truly following their consciences," he said. "I believe in the Church and accept its discipline with no bitterness."[22]

He put his suspension to good use. Cunningham spent a week at Colombiere where he prayed with several priests who were thinking of leaving the priesthood. Then he and his dad flew to Bermuda where they spent three weeks relaxing, talking, praying and reflecting. They undoubtedly drank a bit of whiskey, too. Father and son attended Mass at a local church and Cunningham, who did not wear his Roman collar while on suspension, acted as an usher and passed the collection basket.

"About that time, I asked him if he ever thought that he might want to walk away from the priesthood," Shine said. "You're constantly fighting with Church authorities, restricted by rules," Shine observed. "He looked at me as if it was the stupidest thing anybody ever suggested. He said: 'The only reason I am able to do almost all of this is because I am a priest. If I was just another guy in a suit, there'd just be too many obstacles. The fact that I'm a priest [means] I got the full faith and credit of the Catholic Church behind me. If I go to Congress as just another do-gooder from Detroit, that's all I am. If I go to Congress as a Catholic priest representing the conditions of poor people in Detroit, that just opens the door.

"I'm happy being a priest. That's what I always wanted.'"

---

22   *Cunningham's friend, William X. Kienzle, left the priesthood in 1974, married journalist Javan Herman Andrews and began writing novels that featured Detroit and a Catholic priest who solved crimes. His third novel, Mind Over Murder, included a thinly disguised reference to Cunningham's mistake with the Spivak wedding.*

Then Detroit Common Councilman Carl Levin and Father Bill
Cunningham during a Focus: HOPE Walk.

Credit: John Collier

9

Mover and Shaker

OF ALL THE towns in all the state, the Automobile Club of Michigan (AAA) decided in 1972 to move its headquarters west from downtown Detroit to the city of Dearborn where Orville Hubbard, a notoriously segregationist mayor, had long reigned,

Disgust and anger surged through Father Cunningham. The Auto Club was abandoning Detroit—just as hundreds of other businesses had scrambled after the 1967 rioting. It wasn't just the move and investment in a city with a reputation of hostility toward blacks. Cunningham surmised that few black employees working at the Auto Club would be able to keep their jobs with the insurance company because of transportation challenges. Worse, blacks were effectively prevented from buying or renting homes in Dearborn. Cunningham called the city "Hubbard's apartheid reservation." He believed the area's white "shakers and movers" in the corporate world—the white businessmen who ran Detroit's major corporations—were complicit in the destruction of Detroit.

For months, the Auto Club dodged questions about its intentions for a new headquarters building to replace the old structure at 150 Bagley. Detroit Mayor Roman Gribbs identified several seemingly suitable sites in the city and even offered to build a $4 million parking structure at taxpayer expense if the Auto Club stayed. But on February 26, 1972, the company finally announced that it would move to a 30-acre tract owned by the Ford Motor Company near the new Fairlane Town Center mall, taking 1,200 jobs to Dearborn.

Detroit was becoming the poster child of the metaphoric "donut effect" used to describe abandonment of American central cities—an empty core surrounded by rings of wealth. The Detroit metropolitan area became the most segregated region in the United States, with poor and unemployed African-Americans stuck in a deteriorating city with worsening schools and fewer jobs. Add a weak mass transit system that made it a struggle for Detroit residents to get to jobs in the suburbs, and a sense of hopelessness enveloped the inner city.

Cunningham smelled a conspiracy between the Auto Club and Ford Motor Co. President Henry Ford II, notwithstanding the fact that Ford was a leader in Detroit Renaissance and the driving force behind a spectacular new development downtown, the Renaissance Center.

What to do about the Auto Club's apparent duplicity was a question on Cunningham's mind and in Focus: HOPE staff meetings for months. He assigned Ken Kudek to figure out a way to fight the Auto Club. Researching public records on the company, Kudek learned that before 1965 the Auto Club had never hired a single black person for a job other than elevator operator. The insurer did hire more blacks for entry-level jobs after a 1964 sit-in at the Auto Club headquarters building by radicals with the Congress of Racial Equality (CORE). Indeed, it was later determined through the discovery process in a lawsuit that the idea of the Auto Club's getting out of Detroit originated with that sit-in.

Kudek also learned that the nonprofit Auto Club had $55 million in "surplus" funds, meaning the money was not needed to run operations or cover claims. He noted that the Club's bylaws called for regular elections for seats on its board of directors, and that no board election had been held for more than a decade. Further, the Auto Club's original bylaws—apparently never updated at that point—seemed to restrict members of the board of directors to white men.

With that information, Cunningham could turn anger into action. Their new priority would be to take on the Auto Club and stop the move out of Detroit. At Cunningham's direction, Kudek composed a two-page letter signed by the priest and sent by registered mail on May 11 to all members of the Auto Club's board of directors—and not to anyone on the company's management team. "I am writing you in the name of the Board of Directors and 10,000 volunteers who compose Focus: HOPE, an organization dedicated to racial justice in the Greater Detroit Metropolitan area. We are deeply dismayed over your plan to move the administrative headquarters of the Automobile Club of Michigan outside the City of Detroit. ... We cannot see any economic reasons for abandoning the City of Detroit to build these new facilities."

By design, the second page of the letter starts with a paragraph calling the Auto Club's board and management team racists: "If this judgment seems harsh, the facts leading to it are clear. The symbol value of the move to Dearborn is dramatic—a departure from a community which is struggling with the life and death issues of democracy, to an apartheid bastion of self-interest. ... We had thought that the Club had grown wonderfully responsible since the days when officers and members were limited to 'any white male person over the age of 21 years and a good moral character' (Article VII, articles of incorporation of the Detroit Automobile Club, 1916). We fear that open forms of racism have been substituted by covert and more insidious forms."

Calling them racists got their attention. The Club's Executive Vice President Richard Dann invited Cunningham to a meeting. The priest, Dario Bonucchi, Lucile Watts and one or two other Focus: HOPE board members attended. Dann appeared to be going through the motions, making clear that their decision would not be reversed no matter what Cunningham or Focus:

HOPE thought. The priest returned from the meeting fuming. "He had been stonewalled and Bill never liked that," Kudek said. "He was pissed."

For its part, the Auto Club decided to check into who this pest of a priest was. The company hired Kenneth Drake Associates, a consulting and public relations firm, to investigate. A Drake associate even showed up in the *Detroit Free Press* newsroom and spoke with Neal Shine, then the managing editor, apparently not realizing that Shine was a friend of the priest. Shine called Cunningham afterwards and told him that the investigator had concluded that the executive director of Focus: HOPE was a "blowhard."

Focus: HOPE continued expanding its Food Prescription Program and threw another successful Hope Happening August 26-29, this time drawing what police estimated was a crowd of 250,000 over three days. In October, Focus: HOPE launched the first in a series of annual walks, asking people to rally at the State Fairgrounds at Eight Mile Road and Woodward Avenue. Hundreds of energized folks who met at the Fairgrounds seemed to have had a great time. Many of them were young and they welcomed each other enthusiastically, singing "We Shall Overcome" and listening to the charismatic priest with long wavy dark hair speak. "I've read the obituaries, the sad news that Detroit is dead! Are you dead, Detroit?" Cunningham asked. "Noooo!" the crowd shouted back. Hope is what Cunningham was trying to instill in the marchers, but in comparing the city in 1972 with 1967, the priest told a *Free Press* reporter: "Detroit is meaner now."

Behind the scenes, Kudek helped organize the Detroit Action Coalition. Members included the NAACP, Claude Young of the Southern Christian Leadership Conference, the Interfaith Council for Racial Justice and even Ralph Nader and his Center for Study of Responsive Law. They all signed a letter to Dann asking to discuss the move to Dearborn. There was no response.

Kudek said a former priest named Maurice Geary, an investigator for the Michigan Department of Civil Rights, suggested that they go to the cafeteria on the first floor of the Auto Club's headquarters building for coffee and simply start talking to people. "This young lady, a black lady, comes down for coffee in the afternoon, and I said, 'Excuse me, could I talk to you for a minute?' I sat her down, explained who I was, said I was from Focus: HOPE," Kudek said. He asked her if there was someone who had a good idea of who the black employees of the Auto Club were. The woman suggested he talk to a black man in personnel, Carl Edwards. Kudek was invited up to see Edwards. Feeling very much like a spy behind enemy lines, Kudek went upstairs where Edwards told him about a new group of disgruntled black Auto Club workers in Detroit that had just formed, the Afro American Association. With Edwards' help, Kudek identified at least 60 black Auto Club employees and interviewed them. Many later signed sworn affidavits drawn from those interview notes.

The affidavits supported the case that the company was engaged in discriminatory practices. But Kudek said he cautioned Cunningham that any kind of lawsuit was a long shot, given the fact that the Auto Club had $55 million in reserves and Focus: HOPE's annual budget at the time was less than $50,000. "I could not believe that any reasonably intelligent group of people with $55 million would not kill us within two years," Kudek said later. But before long, the Afro American Association joined forces with Focus: HOPE. Together they filed a discrimination complaint with the state's Civil Rights Commission. On December 4, 1972, after a waiting period of at least 60 days, the Afro American Association, Focus: HOPE and a group of 60 black employees filed a class-action suit against the Auto Club in U.S. District Court in Detroit claiming that the proposed relocation of the company to Dearborn "would violate their civil rights under an 1866 law."

The lawsuit claimed that the intent of the Auto Club's move to Dearborn was to discriminate against its black employees and to reduce the number of black people in the pool for future hiring. "This move from Detroit, which has one of the largest black populations in the United States, to a community as segregated as Dearborn, will substantially impede the Auto Club's ability to attract future black employees," said John Green of the Afro American Association. Laurel McKenzie, chairwoman of the Association, said that since the 1964 CORE sit-in "forced the Auto Club to hire black employees, many of our people have been harassed out of jobs by the practices explained within. Others have continued to suffer from these illegal and discriminatory employment practices to this day. The move to Dearborn will insure the removal of those of us who remain."

Father Cunningham called the situation the way he saw it: "The racism of the Auto Club's board of directors and not lawful business reasons account for the Club's decision to abandon Detroit," he said. He told *The Detroit News* that the Auto Club's move would increase the city's already staggering unemployment rate of 33 percent. "We've lost 150,000 jobs in the city because of the removal of industry," Cunningham said. "The parallel economy of people who stay deteriorates also because a person will work for a lot less as a result of the high rate of unemployment. We're creating a locked-in 'other America' of hungry, bitter people."

The facts from the interviews and affidavits supported the lawsuit's claims that white workers in the same job categories were paid more than black workers, that Auto Club policies restricted blacks to jobs in certain departments and that there were virtually no black supervisors. Also, the Auto Club disgracefully honored wishes of white members who didn't want blacks towing their cars. "I do know it was getting pretty tense as people were informed about what Focus: HOPE was doing," said Focus: HOPE team member Monica Emerson. "It wasn't a popular action to be taking. If anything, there was probably more sympathy for AAA's move than there was for Focus: HOPE to keep them there."

Much of the business community in metropolitan Detroit was appalled by Cunningham's audacity. Many firms had left Detroit or were planning to do so. Could they, too, be sued by this small, unreasonable organization claiming to work on behalf of black people? Business leaders were wary and angry. Indeed, the litigation initiated by Focus: HOPE undoubtedly hurt its ability to get corporate grants and sponsorships.

Cunningham was not deterred. He and Eleanor Josaitis made frequent trips to Lansing looking for support from Governor William Milliken's administration and state legislators. On one trip, the pair visited a rookie legislator from a conservative area of northwest Detroit who had defeated a man who would be the last Republican legislator from Detroit in the 20th century. State Representative William Brodhead had joined the Jesuits for more than three years at their Colombiere center in Clarkston, so he was predisposed to be deferential to Catholic priests. Still, Cunningham's passion and intensity left Brodhead agog.

"He wanted me to support their efforts," Brodhead said. "I didn't know anything about AAA. ... He wanted me to support this lawsuit and I kind of tried to follow along." Finally, Cunningham "looked me right in the eye and, of course, he's wearing his collar. And he said, 'Bill, this is a defining issue; this is a civil rights issue. You got to be on one side or the other. Are you with me?' And I said, 'Yes, Father.' I really crossed a line at that time. He inspired me on the spot and I was forced to make a moral choice. Once I had done that, it became easier."

The editorial page of the *Free Press*, typically a cheerleader for anything Father Cunningham did, called the lawsuit "legal nonsense." "For the life of us, we cannot see how a Detroit civil rights group, Focus: HOPE, can reasonably ask an injunction against the move because it would deny black employees of the club their civil rights," one editorial said. "All the arguments made by Focus: HOPE and its director, Fr. William T. Cunningham, are valid on the surface. Most AAA black employees live in Detroit and would find it difficult to get to Dearborn. ... [But] to say that the arguments have surface validity, though, is not the same as saying they make sense. ... We would prefer to see it stay and help solve the city's problems. But to enjoin a business from moving on such grounds as Focus: HOPE has proposed would set a dangerous and ridiculous precedent. ... Lovely sociology. Economic and legal nonsense."

Shine, then managing editor of the *Free Press*, said he remembered being in Josaitis' kitchen for a dinner and telling Cunningham that, "he was going to get his head handed to him in the AAA case." "This is something you can't win," Shine said he told Cunningham. "You've got two or three volunteer lawyers, you're up against a big firm. They're going to kill you. Cut your losses. Get out. Save your energy for a fight you can win. He put his hand on my arm and said, 'We're going to win this. We are.'" Shine asked, "What makes you think so?" "Because we're right," Cunningham said simply.

Cunningham was not intimidated, embarrassed, deterred, rejected, dejected, humbled, shut down, distracted, derailed, overwhelmed, outmaneuvered, silenced or stopped. Indeed, the fight with the Automobile Club of Michigan would last years and was a good example of what Cunningham called "the determination and stubbornness of Focus: HOPE."

"When people ask us why Focus: HOPE is opposed to AAA's move to Dearborn our answer is that the time has come to stop the merry-go-round and the cruel rationalizations," Cunningham wrote in the January 1973 *Hope Happenings*. "Until blacks are as free as whites to live where they please, to receive full educational and job opportunities, to become whatever God has gifted them to be as men and women, then we must use every conscionable resource to gain that equality."

U.S. District Judge Charles Joiner ruled in 1973 that neither Focus: HOPE nor the Afro American Association had any legal standing in the Auto Club case. However, Joiner ruled that five current employees and one former employee could continue on as plaintiffs. Kudek said they expected the ruling: "It was our way to make sure that the public identified the case with Focus: HOPE."

Although it wasn't a party in the lawsuit, Focus: HOPE continued working on behalf of the plaintiffs, with Kudek, Emerson and Gary Faria organizing the case for the attorneys and interviewing witnesses. Using donor contributions, Focus: HOPE hired Ernie Goodman's law firm in Detroit, with lawyer Marijana Relich handling most of the work. After the retainer, though, the lawyers worked on the case on a contingency basis, although they periodically needed money from Focus: HOPE to keep going. Attorneys defending the Auto Club were from Bodman, Longley & Dahling, a silk-stocking firm that had represented the Ford Motor Co. for many years. The Auto Club also retained former Michigan Supreme Court Justice Theodore Souris as the high-powered leader of their defense team.

The defense strategy was delay as much as possible, expecting to wear Cunningham and Focus: HOPE down. In 1974, Judge Joiner ruled in favor of an Auto Club motion to split the case into two distinct actions, one for discrimination based on race, the other for discrimination based on gender. (The Auto Club felt it was more vulnerable.) The ploy seemed designed to force Cunningham and Focus: HOPE, with limited resources to chose which one of two expensive legal battles to pursue. After all, Focus: HOPE was founded to fight racial discrimination, not discrimination against women.

But Cunningham still refused to back down, deciding to fight on both fronts. The cases—*Bell et al v. Automobile Club of Michigan* (race discrimination) and *Greenspan et al v. Automobile Club of Michigan* (sex discrimination) would continue for several years with a second set of Focus: HOPE-backed attorneys handling the sex case. The Auto Club filed subpoenas to take depositions from Focus: HOPE managers and to examine the nonprofit's books, as well as its list of its contributors. Focus: HOPE successfully prevented the release of names of donors, but had to work to create a record of its meager finances since 1968.

Auto Club board members were dragged into this by Cunningham and they became active behind the scenes, asking their high-powered friends to pressure Focus: HOPE to cease. Some served on foundation boards and began claiming that Focus: HOPE was "laundering" grant money to pay for the lawsuit against the Auto Club.

Faria, who later became a lawyer, said he was amazed that "you could actually maintain a case of discrimination based on someone's choice of where they would have their office building. ... We were suing under the Civil Rights Act, which regulated employment policies and practices. Our goal was always to make the choice of office location an employment practice, which is not easy to do. Everybody thought we were nuts."

Cunningham was not nuts, but he was a maverick and somewhat cavalier about fundraising. Kudek said he and Cunningham once met with a Detroit attorney representing several small family foundations that had not complied with regulations to disburse a minimum of five percent to charitable causes every year. They needed to donate money fast, hoping to avoid a regulatory challenge. Joe B. Sullivan told Cunningham that he had worked out a $5,000 donation to Focus: HOPE through the lawyer. All he had to do was go to the law office, chat the attorney up for a few minutes and then collect the check.

At the meeting with the lawyer, Cunningham gave his spiel about Focus: HOPE fighting racism wherever it existed, including suing the Auto Club in federal court. When he finished, the lawyer opened the drawer of his desk, pulled out an unsealed envelope and handed it to the priest. Cunningham already knew it would be made out for $5,000. He opened it, glanced at it, then pushed it back. "I really don't want your $5,000," he said.

Kudek said the lawyer looked confused, then asked why not. "I want $25,000," Cunningham said. But not right then. Cunningham said he was going to raise $25,000 from other sources, and then come back and ask the lawyer to match it dollar for dollar. "When I raise $25,000, I will tell you and you'll give me a check for $25,000," Cunningham said. "I can see that this guy was first confused and then happy," Kudek said. The check went back into the drawer. Cunningham and Kudek walked out of the office to the elevators. "You think I should've taken the $5,000, don't you?" Cunningham asked Kudek. "Yep," Kudek said. Not another word from Cunningham about it. He didn't raise the $25,000, and never spoke to that lawyer again.

Among many motions filed by lawyers for the Auto Club for summary judgment was the question of how the choice of office location could be governed by the Civil Rights Act. "They lost on that issue because our claim was not only would the relocation have the impact of reducing minority employees, but the relocation site was selected with the intent of doing that," Kudek said. Basically, there were two arguments—the impact of the decision and the intent of the decision. Impact required a statistical analysis that may not have held water, since AAA employed over 100 blacks. Intent, then, became the key point in the case, and the Focus: HOPE legal team relying on the 1964 Civil Rights Act and on federal civil rights laws dating back to the 19th century.

In 1976, Kudek and Faria found what they called the case's "smoking gun." They were at the office of the Auto Club's law firm late one night, looking at piles of company documents made available under discovery. "We found this memo that was written by AAA's personnel manager discussing from the personnel department's perspective what these potential office locations meant to them," Faria said. "It talked about the city of Detroit making property available and other locations that were not desirable because we [the Auto Club] would have all these same issues attracting job applicants as we do in downtown Detroit presently."

There was a young attorney at the firm staying late to monitor Kudek and Faria. At the end of the evening they gave her a stack of documents they wanted copied later. But they specifically asked that she make a copy of that one memo that they could take with them. "When she looked at it, her face dropped," Faria said. "We had found this document which was sort of the key to the case. It tied the office location to screening job applicants."

The Auto Club had always told Judge Joiner that it had "no way" to identify the race of its employees prior to 1970. But the previously undisclosed personnel manager's memo said the problem with the downtown office site was it hindered developing a "qualified" labor force because of "crime, parking and unqualified applicants." From the plaintiffs' point of view, the manager was defining "unqualified applicants" as black females who composed 70 percent of applicants and "qualified applicants" as white females.

The "smoking gun" memo led to the discovery of what Focus: HOPE called the "Book of Blacks," documents that the Auto Club had been keeping since 1956 denoting the race of hundreds of job applicants and employees. When the evidence was finally presented in court in October 1977, Judge Joiner's anger almost matched Cunningham's. He sharply criticized the Auto Club, using terms like "inexcusable and unjustified," "misconduct" and "clear misrepresentation."

Over the objections of former Supreme Court Justice Souris, Joiner ordered the Auto Club to pay $52,000 in restitution to Focus: HOPE for denying the existence of the documentation for years and to pay for the cost of re-doing depositions of Auto Club executives and managers in light of the new evidence. Souris told reporters that, "the judge was misled into error in ruling as he did about my clients." Souris said it was "absurd to believe that we were concealing anything." The appeal of Joiner's order, however, was denied.

The Auto Club had been urging Judge Joiner for years to dismiss the lawsuit and had nearly succeeded before the "Book of Blacks" came to light. "On that basis, we kept the suit alive," Faria said. "What I remember of Bill Cunningham, years later, was his optimism that he could accomplish anything."

Father Cunningham and Muhammad Ali during a charity bout. The champ wouldn't box until Cunningham took off the Roman collar, then tagged the priest on the chin before taking a dive to the delight of the crowd at Detroit's Olympia Stadium.

Credit: Focus: HOPE

10

Fighter

ANY DOUBTS THAT Father Cunningham could pull off what seemed impossible were put to rest after Focus: HOPE's fifth "Happening" in 1974. The city had declared that the Kern Block with its new landscaping was off limits, and the civic center area was a mess due to construction of the Renaissance Center.

Cunningham was stuck with a vacant lot, a few acres of riverfront property between Sixth and Eight Streets, about a quarter-mile west of Cobo Hall. It was overrun with weeds; cinders and broken liquor bottles covered the old, broken pavement. It did have a nice view of the city of Windsor, Ontario, on the south side of the Detroit River.

Cunningham, as usual, was enthusiastic about it. Still, nothing was easy for Focus: HOPE stalwarts who turned the nasty spot into a safe place to hold a weeklong festival with game booths, carnival rides, beer and food tents. And, they had to deal with a sudden thunderstorm, as Eleanor Josaitis described during a 50th birthday roast of Cunningham: "I'm standing in this parking lot, and I'm standing in a chuckhole up to my hips, and there's weeds and bottle cans up to my armpits, and the man [Cunningham] says, 'Oh, my God! It's gorgeous. Beautiful spot for a festival!' And I look at him like he's just been released. ... And he says, 'Eleanor, give me four volunteers and two truck loads of dirt and in half a day, we can whip this thing into shape.'"

They pulled strings with Detroit Renaissance, the non-government coalition of business interests led by Ford Motor Company Chairman Henry Ford II developing the RenCen. Some 128 loads of "slag" from the site were trucked to the Hope Happening site, where 87 volunteers spread it smooth then erected fair booths on top of it in time for Detroit Brotherhood 5. Officer Grant Friley, a friend of the Josaitis family, organized a small group of officers dressed in the fashionably wild street clothes of the 1970s. Brotherhood 5 ended the evening of July 1 as fireworks celebrating the American-Canadian International Freedom Festival lit up the night sky over the Detroit River. Cunningham is said to have looked across the river that night and, seeing a brightly lit Holiday Inn sign on the Canadian side, decided it was the perfect place for a Focus: HOPE staff retreat to talk through some ideas on how to improve and grow the organization.

About a week later, the core staff crossed the Ambassador Bridge and holed up in a few rooms at the hotel—Cunningham, Josaitis, Charlie Grenville, Thom Armstead, Dario Bonucchi, Carl Bidleman, Jerry Lemenu and Dave Klapp, another ex-seminarian. "We would grind out the new direction Focus: HOPE was going to take," Klapp said. A major discussion point was how to put more black people into management positions in what basically had been a white-dominated organization. They drew out an organizational chart. Cunningham "said he's going to be executive director, Eleanor's going to be associate director and then have these two other assistant directors," Klapp said. All seemed to agree with Cunningham that the two new positions should be reserved for blacks, and names of potential candidates were discussed.

The usually quiet Klapp, who had spent a year in Washington studying ways to make federal departments more efficient, spoke up. "Looking for an opportunity to contribute and asking a question that occurred to me, I said, 'I'm curious; why is there an executive director and then an associate director and then two assistant directors?' I was asking a question about the organizational tree and Cunningham jumped on me. He basically was saying, 'How dare you? Eleanor helped found this organization and she's going to be associate director and these two are going to be assistant directors.' I was just asking a very simple informational-type question and he jumped all over me like I was slapping Eleanor in the face."

As a boy, Cunningham's mother had cautioned him about his "mean streak," a warning he frequently forgot to heed. Klapp was certainly not the only one to suddenly feel the heat of the priest's ire. Nearly every Focus: HOPE colleague had difficult moments with Cunningham, blowups where he harshly berated them for a mistake, a comment that came out the wrong way, a bad idea or failure to accomplish an assignment. Typically, after an angry burst of withering criticism that would last far longer than was necessary, the priest would move on, acting like nothing had happened. For him, it was over. But those who bore the brunt of Cunningham's fiery temper remembered their humiliation for years.

The new pastor at Madonna was frustrated by criminals who were burglarizing parish buildings, stealing license plates from parishioners cars—and his own. The German Shepherds he'd been using weren't cutting it. So, he turned to Bouvier des Flanders puppies, and fell in love with the breed. Joe Leddy, who raised, trained and sold Bouviers to Cunningham, said the priest's first Bouvier came from a breeder in Kingsville, Ontario. "He had those big, ugly Bouviers," Leddy said. "They had a sure-fire, unbeatable temperament, but not really aesthetic. Rough coated. Big red eyes. People called them devil dogs." Sister Cecilia Begin said Cunningham first bought a Bouvier for his dad, and two others to work parish facilities and one for himself that he named Lobo. Lobo "was just a prince of a dog. How he loved that dog!" Sister Cecilia said.

Bouviers were bred to herd cattle, and Lobo had the habit of head-butting anyone standing in his way. Armstead recalled being in the rectory when Lobo came up behind him and barged into the back of his legs, knocking the large man down. "I looked up and see Lobo and I swear he had a smile on his face," Armstead said.

Bill Shine, a Detroit police sergeant and Neal Shine's brother, often stopped by the rectory to sip scotch and swap stories with Cunningham. Lobo made him nervous, even though he was chained to the radiator in the dining room. "He had a chain on him like you'd put on a boat tied to a tree," Shine said. "I always had to figure which side my gun was on. Every now and then you could hear that chain move and you'd think, 'Oh, oh! Is it going to make a lunge?'"

But Lobo and the other Bouviers were good protection. Leddy said that at about 3 a.m. one summer night, Lobo was on the second-floor porch over the rectory's entrance when a man came running down the street. "The dog didn't think he was innocent," Leddy said. "Lobo jumped off the balcony and pinned the guy to the ground. Those dogs are fabulous."

Cunningham's sister Betty Horning living in Dryden, north of Lapeer, had a lady friend with a Bouvier that had been abused as a puppy by a heroin dealer. The dog Booster was "very dangerous," Sister Cecilia said. Rather than allow the dog to be put down, Cunningham took it in despite its ill temper. "He put it upstairs [in a room] and he shut the door and threatened every one of us—'Don't anybody open that door.' After we all left on a Sunday after Mass, he said he opened the door very slowly and he went out and sat on the front porch of the rectory with the door open and just waited. Pretty soon he could hear the dog crawling down. Father let him come in. He didn't move. He just sat there. This took two or three hours, and that dog, Father said, he just sort of put his hand out very slowly and just touched the dog and the dog came right over. He just waited for that dog to make that move. And [Booster] loved Father ever since." Even so, Booster could not be trusted with other people.

"We had to be very careful around Booster," Cecilia said. "If you went toward Father, watch out."

Since taking over Madonna and expanding Focus: HOPE, Cunningham's exercise regime included a weekly run, usually taking Lobo along. The oldest Josaitis son, Mark, said Cunningham ran a route from Madonna to the Josaitis home in Sherwood Forest, about three miles away. He invited Mark to join his runs and the young man was able to talk to "Uncle Bill" about all aspects of life. "If I was having a bad patch in school or in a funk, he'd say, 'Let's meet at Palmer Park and go for a run,'" Mark said. "He always made me feel better. ...

"I remember jogging with Uncle Bill in Palmer Park with one of the Bouviers, probably Lobo, and Bill lets the dog off the leash. Another runner, a good runner, comes along and the guy picks up this big stick to defend himself." They caught up and, fortunately, the man hadn't hit Lobo with the stick. Cunningham was "upset that this guy almost hit his dog," Mark said. It surprised Mark that Cunningham was more concerned about Lobo's wellbeing than about someone frightened by the dog. "It's almost like not thinking about somebody else," Mark said.

Under Cunningham's tutelage, Eleanor was becoming a skilled public speaker. On December 10, 1974, she appeared before the Detroit City Council.[23] She probably had help from both Cunningham and Charlie Grenville with her speech: "Hunger in Detroit hurts babies' brains, chipping off I.Q.," she said. "Hunger softens bones and puts toddlers on bowed legs. Hunger twists emotions and leaves children hostile, hating, hurt for life. Hunger fills classrooms with tired, listless pupils of the poor. Hunger is anemia, rickets, mental retardation, hostility. Hunger is death by premature birth and infant disease."

Mayor Roman Gribbs appointed Josaitis chair of the city's Task Force on Hunger and Malnutrition. Initially, Cunningham was upset about it. Kudek said Cunningham "thought if she got into the political realm that she would actually leave Focus:

---

23   *The old Common Council's name was changed when voters approved a new City Charter in 1973 during the same election that made Coleman A. Young the city's first black mayor.*

HOPE and get sucked into that environment, get the bug and decide to run for City Council."

Focus: HOPE's Food Prescription Program—now a model for the newly renamed Commodity Supplemental Food Program (CSFP) supervised by the USDA—was feeding more than 23,000 women and preschool children by the end of 1974. Cunningham called it "the largest feeding program of its kind in the universe." The need for a base of operations more suitable than a church rectory was obvious. In late 1974, Cunningham signed a lease for (and later bought with a $75,000 Kresge Foundation grant) a former office building two blocks west of Madonna. Dario Bonucchi, the architect who was then Focus: HOPE's board chair, oversaw the renovation of the building at 1355 Oakman Boulevard. Cunningham, who had decided to bring on two black men as assistant directors, Robert Brazelton and Gil Maddox, wanted the building ready for use quickly. He assigned three former seminarians—Klapp, Bidleman and Lemenu—to put a fresh coat of paint on the inside concrete walls and ceiling.

A special paint was donated by a machine shop owner down the block. "This was the paint they used inside of plants and it's got a heavy latex base to it. Once it's on the walls, it is there forever. It's very expensive paint," Armstead said. Whether they didn't have the proper equipment or training on its application, the crew hated that paint. "This stuff was horrible," Bidleman said. "You put it on with a roller and it spun off like cotton candy." It was hot, sticky work that left them panting, sweaty and covered by sticky thick paint drips.

When they took a break and walked back to the rectory, Cunningham took pity and told them to have a beer from a cooler in the garage that was left over from a Madonna parish picnic. "Our attitudes were getting worse as the week went on," Bidleman said. "To drown our sorrows, we went down to the garage" for more beer.

"It was such a horrible job that we would break for lunch a little bit earlier every day and go on and have a beer every day for a week," Klapp said. Then, Cunningham "had somebody over for lunch and he went out to the cooler and there wasn't a beer left. He went storming into the Resource Center and I came in dressed up from painting with (paint) all over my face and he said, 'All the beer? You drank all the beer?' And he just turned around and stormed out again. I felt awful."

U.S. Agricultural Secretary Earl Butz had chosen the 1974 Christmas season to announce plans to scale back the federal food stamp program and to freeze the amount of food being sent to Detroit in the CSFP. Cunningham and Josaitis flew to Washington several times that winter to lobby against Butz.

Cunningham called upon friends and volunteers to write President Ford and demand that Butz be stopped. Detroit Mayor Coleman A. Young wrote the president, blaming Butz for lackluster food stamp and food distribution programs. "Unfeeling debates and blundering" at the USDA had limited the food programs to a fraction of the actual need, Young said. The letter-writing campaign was working. One USDA official told Cunningham: "We don't count your letters any more. We weigh them."

On March 17, Gov. Milliken and other Midwestern state governors had dinner with President Ford at the University of Notre Dame in South Bend. Suddenly, the problem with Butz was solved. On March 18, Milliken announced that the USDA was doubling the amount of CSFP food—more than $2.5 million worth—to be shipped annually to Focus: HOPE for distribution to the poor. At the time, Focus: HOPE was budgeted to distribute monthly food allotments to 17,000 people, but had managed to feed 20,563 people in February alone. "I was pleased with the President's response," Milliken told the *Free Press*. Josaitis credited Michigan's Republican Senator Bob Griffin who, "when no one would touch us two years ago ... was in there helping us fight for more food." Cunningham called it "a moral victory."

The increase, however, meant Focus: HOPE needed a new facility. It wasn't easy because federal rules required nonprofit organizations using federal money for facilities to have only one-year leases. "There's no way on earth that you're going to get a building of any value in the city of Detroit in a fairly good neighborhood, on a railroad siding to receive the food, without rats scurrying all over on a one-year lease, at a price that you can afford to pay," Cunningham said.

A new problem: Will Kraus, the owner of the building Focus: HOPE now leased as its only food distribution center, had decided to sell the building back to the Ex-Cell-O Corporation. Ex-Cell-O needed to expand tooling production to fulfill its multi-million dollar contract with the Soviet Union to build a truck factory. Kraus decided to sell and told Focus: HOPE to get out.

Cunningham refused, but he didn't have a miracle up his sleeve—yet. Kraus went to court. A few days later, Wayne County Sheriff William Lucas called Cunningham to say he had a court order to evict Focus: HOPE from Kraus's building. According to Armstead, Cunningham asked for "a little more time." The sheriff gave him two days. Cunningham still did not resolve the problem. Lucas told the priest he had to follow the law and act. "When we got down to the wire, Father said, 'Look, if you want to evict us you'll have Channels 2, 4 and 7 out here watching you throw these mothers and babies out in the streets.' Everybody began to get a little nervous at this point," Armstead said. "At the last minute, we got the Louise Tuller Miller Trust at the National Bank of Detroit to purchase the building for us," Armstead said. "Ex-Cell-O backed off and the Trust leased the building to us, eventually donating the building to us for $1."

In late May, Shaw College in Detroit invited Cunningham to participate in an unusual fundraiser at Olympia Stadium: To be among a select group who would lace up boxing gloves and participate in exhibition matches with Muhammad Ali, then the world champion.

The night before the bout, Cunningham, Eleanor and Don Josaitis, Bonucci, Armstead and some other Focus: HOPE folks had dinner at the Normandie Bar & Grill across the street from the Fisher Building. Eleanor was worried about Cunningham's safety, and not just in the ring. He was a white man, a Catholic priest no less, who would be surrounded by Ali's corps of black Muslim bodyguards wearing dark shades, leather jackets and black berets. No one doubted that some of them would be armed. "People thought that they [black Muslims] were very angry and hated white people," Armstead said. Josaitis, he said, kept pleading with Cunningham: "Bill, Bill, why are you doing this?"

"Eleanor was really afraid. And Dario was needling Bill: 'Bill, he's going to kick your ass!'" Cunningham seemed nonplussed and responded, "Eleanor, it's going to be all right."

At Olympia before the bouts, Cunningham, Armstead and his "trainer," folk musician Ron Coden, made their way to Ali's dressing room. It was crowded with stern-faced bodyguards, Shaw college staff, and some of the people chosen to box the champ. Cunningham "goes up to Ali who's got a little girl on his lap, 6 years old, and he doesn't look up, just talking to the little girl," Coden said. "Cunningham waits and waits; Ali doesn't even acknowledge him because he's focused on this girl." Finally, the girl was ushered away and Cunningham got to talk with the champ. "Ali, how is this going to work?" Cunningham asked, according to Armstead. "You know how it's going to work. Just try to hit me," Ali said. "Bill's face dropped; he thought it was going to be a scripted thing. You could see he was getting a bit nervous," Armstead said.

Cunningham changed into the boxing trunks and white silk robe with the Focus: HOPE logo made by a group of Madonna women, everything black and white and shiny. He matched the outfit with his bib-like black rabat and white plastic Roman collar over a white T-shirt, and waited his turn in the ring.

Ali had agreed to spar with several opponents on June 6, including three professionals. Ali said one boxer, Johnny Hudson, "can take it and the nigger hits hard." Another bout with professional boxer Ron Gentry ended, and Ali pretended that Gentry, a white man, had made a racial slur.[24] Ali had to be "held back" from brawling with Gentry by his handlers. Gentry returned the favor by mocking Ali's prancing. Then Ali exaggerated his prances even more as the crowd, numbering only in the hundreds, laughed.

---

24   *Ali played similar pranks on many people, including the author of this book during an interview in 1997.*

When it was his turn, Cunningham entered the ring, handed Coden the robe and sat on the stool in the corner. The bell rang and the priest walked out. Ali raised a gloved fist and stopped him in his tracks, saying he would not fight anyone wearing a priest's collar. "What he didn't want was some religious thing," Armstead said. "I snatched the collar off Bill and threw the thing over in the corner.

"The first round and Bill's dancing around, showing off some of his stuff, bobbing and weaving, a punch here and there," Armstead said. The priest, who had learned the rudiments of boxing in high school, was a natural athlete and he'd been jogging more frequently in preparation for the match. But he was 45 and not as strong or as fast as he once was. "Ali just did a right hook, just a slow blow" that caught Cunningham off guard. "Bill's hair went that way, his mouthpiece went this way, and snot started coming out of his nose," Armstead said. "It caught his attention. He gets his mouthpiece back in, they mess around some more." In the second round, "Ali said, 'Throw the right! Throw the right!'" Coden said. "He threw it. Ali goes down. But it was so cute, Cunningham almost tripped over him." As the priest stumbled across the ring, the crowd broke into applause.

At Madonna Church, Cunningham was thinking of remodeling. Having won his battle with the archdiocese on the Madonna parish debt, he decided the sanctuary was too dark and they needed to spend some money to lighten the place up. Dario Bonucchi, an architect and designer, thought the south wall of the Madonna church sanctuary would be a great place for a large stained-glass window. Cunningham loved the idea but did not want depictions of Jesus, Mary or the Saints. His vision was of a large candle in the center representing Christ and smaller candles encircling it.

Cunningham contacted the most renowned stained-glass artist in the Detroit area—Margaret Bouchez Cavanaugh, of Warren. She came to Madonna and sat in the church while the priest explained his vision. "He always talked about being candle people," Sister Cecilia said. "He envisioned this window with this big candle representing us. [Cavanaugh] was back in a couple of days with this design that caught the colors that are in the side windows. She just had this gorgeous 15-foot window design."

In the spring of 1975, work began. Workers stood by as Cunningham climbed scaffolding in the alley behind the church to take the first whack at the wall with a sledgehammer. A frame was installed, then Cavanaugh brought dozens of pieces of stained glass to Madonna and leaned them against the back wall. Cecilia was surprised to see Cavanaugh going around with a hammer and chisel, breaking and chipping away at the pieces of glass to make the smaller pieces she needed. "I thought she was going to ruin the window," Cecilia said, "but she said, 'No, that's what's going to make it beautiful.' She chipped at it to make it sparkle, so it reflected the sun. She was right."

An unsigned article written in 2006 and published on the Madonna parish website described Cunningham's concept: "He was inspired with the vision of a large stained-glass window for the south wall of the church designed in such a fashion that light would fill the worship area on Sundays and other times of worship. ... Christ is the great center candle. The smaller lights that surround are the people of God. Together we bring warmth and light to the world. As the candle is consumed by the flame, so are we in our love and service for others. Within and beyond these walls and windows we live the dying and rising of Jesus Christ. We rejoice with those whose vision and artistry have given us this beautiful expression of faith."

Top: Father Cunningham (fourth from right) and other American clergy meet with German Catholic, Lutheran and government officials in 1975.

Bottom: The Focus: HOPE leadership team in the mid-1970s from left: Eleanor Josaitis, Gilbert Maddox, Robert Brazelton and Father Cunningham. Maddox and Brazelton were brought on to increase racial diversity at the top of Focus: HOPE.

Credit: Top photo courtesy of Bishop Roger Morin, bottom photo courtesy of Focus: HOPE

11

C.P. Time

WITH ARTICLES ABOUT Focus: HOPE appearing in *The New York Times* and *The Washington Post*, as well as his frequent lobbying trips to Washington, Father Bill Cunningham became something of a national figure in 1975. That relative fame led to the West German government inviting him to an all-expenses paid trip to advise them on how religious institutions can better provide social services. "We invited Father Cunningham because he has been active in the social field," said Volker Anding, the West German Vice Consul in Detroit.

Cunningham was among eight clergymen from across the United States, including a priest operating a feeding program for the hungry in New Orleans, Father Roger Morin. While waiting for their flight in Chicago, Cunningham and Morin found they had much in common. Morin knew a bit of Cunningham's program in Detroit. Cunningham, too, had heard about Morin's work turning a summer education-recreation program for inner-city kids into neighborhood community centers that operated year round. The centers also distributed government food commodities to soup kitchens, food pantries and the needy. Unlike

Cunningham, who made sure to keep Focus: HOPE independent of the Archdiocese of Detroit, Morin had been assigned to run the church-sponsored programs by New Orleans' Archbishop Philip Hannan.

In Germany, the group made several visits to churches and hospitals called *crackenhauses*. Cunningham often steered the discussion toward other issues, including the Holocaust. "Bill could never resist the hard questions," Morin said. "After we saw the Catholic and Lutheran churches, he kept wanting to know where the closest synagogue was. An awful lot of conversations were with leading Catholics and Protestants who had been older, been there during World War II, almost with tears in their eyes. Either they had failed [to stop the Holocaust] or they didn't know what was going on. I think finally we got to see the remains of what had been a synagogue in West Berlin."

When the tour ended, a German official asked if there was anything else the Americans wanted to do or see. Cunningham didn't hesitate, asking to meet a celebrated Catholic prelate at that time, Cardinal Alfred Bengsch from the eastern sector that was under Communist rule. Bengsch, known as the "Cinderella prelate," had authority over Catholics on both sides of the Berlin Wall. But East German authorities refused him permission to leave the Communist country for more than a few hours at a time and then only on certain days each month. If he was late returning to East Berlin, border guards would refuse to let him back in, hence the Cinderella moniker. When Cunningham was asked why he wanted to see Bengsch, he responded "because he's really a cosmopolitan cardinal; he has been suffering for nearly a decade."

Because of the political division between East and West Germany, it was a delicate matter. But the next morning, the Americans were called early and told to appear in the lobby immediately. Cunningham said they "whisked me into a Mercedes limousine, no word where we were going." They were taken to the chancery, where Cunningham surmised that "something was afoot, monsignors began to flutter in and out in their, uh, marvelous elegance. … I knew something great was about to happen and in came Cardinal Bengsch." Cunningham was introduced and the cardinal said, "I understand you have been asking to see me."

"We had a very pleasant and interesting meeting," Morin said. Bengsch "was sort of a gruff German gentleman. Big cigar-smoking fellow. And I think it was Cunningham's question… he wanted to know the cardinal's opinion on what was at that time a Christian-Marxist dialogue." A priest interpreted Cunningham's question as Bengsch chomped a cigar. The cardinal's reaction was "that was a whole lot of bull crap. … There was no such thing as a Christian-Marxist dialogue because there wasn't any foundation for a dialogue."

Cunningham also asked Bengsch if he thought an American could be elected pope. "To have an American pope with the ideals that you cherish, for the freedoms you've expressed, with the wealth that you possess, to lead this Church would be a disaster," Bengsch said. "Well, that set me back on my heels again," Cunningham said.

Cunningham's third question had to do with a movie, *The Shoes of the Fisherman*, in which a priest imprisoned in a Siberian prison eventually is elected pope and then uses the Vatican treasures to care for the poor. Bengsch hadn't seen it, so Cunningham summarized the plot: "It was such a moving thing for me, to see this pope from behind the Iron Curtain, giving up the riches of the Vatican to feed the poor. … And the pope then, after taking his tiara off and offering it to the crowds in St. Peter's Square, and then did the beautiful thing that I would've wished the popes could have done over the ages: 'I invite, I invite'—such a nice word, sounded almost like Jesus. 'I invite the nations of the world to join me in this, to give up what they had to feed the poor.'

"So, I said to Cardinal Bengsch, 'You won't let me have a pope from the U.S., what would you think about a pope from behind the Iron Curtain?'" Cunningham asked. The cardinal responded: "You remember my answer about the American pope? That would be doubly foolish—to have a pope come from behind the Iron Curtain would be to ask for the imposition of authority on the Western World that you have never understood because all we know is what I've told you: Unless there is inexorable discipline and authority, the people will not be free. To come with that culture, to come with that understanding of the world, would be anathema to the people of the west. Pray, that you have another Italian pope." (Three years later, a Polish cardinal, Karol Josef Wojtyla, was elected and became Pope John Paul II.)

While Cunningham was in Germany, his 87-year-old father suffered a mild stroke. When Cunningham returned, "he went right over and stayed right there with his dad," Sister Cecilia said. "Every Sunday he would go and get his dad and bring him over to church for Mass and his dad would stay for breakfast, then Father would go and spend the rest of that day with his dad."

When Focus: HOPE's new headquarters building at 1355 Oakman Boulevard opened in 1975, there were offices for two new assistant directors, both African-American men of some distinction: Robert F. Brazelton had been appointed by former Mayor Roman Gribbs to the Mayor's Committee for Human Resources Development, and Gilbert A. Maddox, Ph.D., a former professor at the University of Michigan and one of the earliest blacks on Detroit television, hosting three shows: *Blacks and Unknown Bards* (1959), *CPT* (1968; a title that obviously played on the "Colored People's Time" stereotype), that aired on Detroit Public Television and *Profiles in Black* on NBC-affiliated WWJ-TV, Channel 4 (1969-74).

Maddox, who had grown up in Detroit's Brewster Projects, had been a member of the Focus: HOPE board of directors since 1970. His concern was poor communication between whites and blacks in the country and particularly in Detroit. Cunningham, Maddox said, "was a courageous Roman Catholic priest who was a beacon of liberal thought. And he was speaking out very forcefully on how the white community had essentially failed to address the problems of urban America. At the time, you had black leadership speaking out forcefully, but very few whites were addressing the issue of racism."

Brazelton was amazed that Focus: HOPE was recruiting him. At their invitation, he met Charlie Grenville and Eleanor Josaitis for lunch at a Howard Johnson's restaurant on Woodward in Highland Park. "Eleanor suggested that I come work with them, kind of offhandedly," Brazelton said. "It wasn't as if it was a job offer. It was like, 'Bob, you'd make a good part of this team, you know.'"

Both men started work the same day, June 24, 1975, taking desks on the first floor. "On the first floor was this open area so that everyone was facing in to each other. I think Father Cunningham rather liked the idea of this collective synergy, if you will, between various persons and various programs," said Maddox who became Focus: HOPE's assistant director of communications, media and education projects. Brazelton, who had problems with alcohol and marijuana that he thought were secret, was named assistant director of Personnel Management and New Program Development. He was in charge of administration—in name only, though, because Associate Director Josaitis always was there to run things and make major decisions under Cunningham's authority.

Maddox helped put the final touches on a report that Cunningham was producing about metropolitan Detroit school desegregation. Schools in Detroit still were mostly segregated. Middle-class suburban schools were nearly always all white. The Detroit School Board was "an agency under the control and supervision of the state ... consciously drew attendance zones along lines which maximized the segregation of the races in the schools, exacerbating the effects of extensive residential segregation," the Focus: HOPE report said. "Schools were constructed in locations and in sizes which ensured that they would open with predominantly one-race student bodies."

The Michigan Legislature also had passed Act 48, a law signed by Governor Milliken that blocked a voluntary high school desegregation plan by the Detroit Board of Education. In response to the U.S. Supreme Court directives to integrate public schools in two *Brown v. the Board of Education* (in Kansas) decisions handed down in 1954 and 1955, the Michigan Board of Education initiated a small busing program between students from Ferndale—just across Eight Mile Road at Woodward from Detroit—and Detroit.

A federal case brought by the NAACP in Detroit, *Bradley et al v. Milliken at al* represented a significant shift nationally from desegregating schools in the south to the north. The lawsuit alleged that the state had failed to provide a quality education for black children in Detroit. U.S. District Court Judge Stephen Roth held that a variety of causes, including acts of commission and omission by suburban governments and the state legislature, had the effect of concentrating black citizens in Detroit's inner city. Whether it was their intent or not, governments at the federal, state and local levels, combined with "private organizations such as loaning institutions and real estate associations and brokerage firms," had established racial segregation in the Detroit area by virtue of restricting where blacks could live and, thereby, limiting access to quality schools by black children.

To remedy this discriminatory conduct, Roth ordered that 53 of the city's 85 outlying suburban school districts bus thousands of white students from the suburbs into the inner city to attend school with blacks, while busing thousands of black students to schools in suburbia. Roth's plan would have created one metropolitan school district with 780,000 students, of which 310,000 would be put on buses every day to achieve the goals of desegregating the metro area.

Roth's court orders were denounced by state legislators and suburban residents. Michigan's appeal made its way to the United States Supreme Court, which overturned much of Roth's decision on February 27, 1974, marking the first time in 20 years that the high court had not supported school desegregation. In his dissent, Justice Thurgood Marshall, the first African-American to serve on the high court, wrote: "We deal here with the right of all our children, whatever their race, to an equal start in life and to an equal opportunity to reach their full potential as citizens. Those children who have been denied that right in the past deserve better than to see fences thrown up to deny them that right in the future. ... For unless our children begin to learn together, there is little hope that our people will ever learn to live together."

Focus: HOPE's report on education released in the simmering summer of 1975 garnered little attention in local news media because of some major news events. Those included a riot on July 28 on Livernois Avenue near Fenkell after a white bar owner shot a black teenager he thought was tampering with a car parked outside. One person, a Polish immigrant on his way home from work, was killed, and the mayhem added to an environment of fear that fueled the migration of white Detroiters to the suburbs. A bigger story that made national news was the July 30 kidnapping of former Teamsters Union President Jimmy Hoffa outside a restaurant on Telegraph Road in suburban Bloomfield Township. The crime never was solved despite decades of investigating by the FBI, who believed Hoffa was killed by the Mafia.

Cunningham was fearless when it came to confronting white people living far from the problems of inner-city Detroit. "His spiel was talking about people's moral and religious responsibility to wipe out hunger in this country," Thom Armstead said. "This country is a land of plenty. Shame on us." Everyone was too distant from the lives of the poor to understand. Why is it that we cannot ensure that every baby in the U.S. has enough nourishing food to eat? If you put a hungry baby on Earl Butz's desk at the USDA, he would feed that child, Cunningham would say. "Institutionally, we insulate ourselves from these things," Armstead said.

Cunningham "wasn't asking people for money, but he told them they had a moral obligation. In many cases people were a little upset, but you could see them nodding their heads," Armstead said. "But in many meetings people were hostile. I remember a lot of visits and Bill would say, 'Thommy, we have to have my dog start our car when we leave.' Those folks, he would lambaste them. He would make them feel real ashamed. He certainly could sense the crowd, read the crowd and he knew how to work a crowd. He knew what they needed. If they needed to be hit on the head with a 2-by-4, he would hit them square between the eyes. Generally, folks would come up after and say, 'Thanks, I needed that.'"

Focus: HOPE held another march on November 2, 1975, with four groups starting from different points, including Birmingham in the north, and Grosse Pointe in the east, converging at the State Fairgrounds at Eight Mile and Woodward. Folk musician Ron Coden often teased Cunningham about holding his walks in the fall when the weather was unpredictable. "The weather for some reason always turned out fine. He'd come in with a big smile on his face. I'd say, 'All right; you did it again.'"

Just nine days after the walk, the housekeeper caring for "Pop" Cunningham called the Madonna rectory to say she needed help for the old man and didn't know what to do. Father Cunningham was out of town so Bidleman and Lemenu rushed over to the home on Boston Boulevard to find the old man dazed and afraid. They called 911, and then helped him into the ambulance. "He looked back at the house like this was the last time he was going to see it," Lemenu said. This time, the stroke was far more serious, and he lingered at a hospital and two care facilities. "At that point, Grandpa just slipped away," said Father Cunningham's niece Betty Edwards. "He had been fighting, the doctor said, to exist, but the stroke was so complete there would never have been a Grandpa again. He was severely mentally impaired, probably on machines over a week, maybe 10 days. ... Bill was like giving him permission to quit fighting. It was such an emotional time. The kids and I were in tears." Will Cunningham died on December 15.

"My father is very important to me," Father Cunningham explained to a reporter in 1972. "I have a lot of respect, love for him—as a friend, as a human being—I've completely forgotten about him as a father. I just think this old man is something unusual—long white hair, big choppers, mod suits, 85. He'll climb on the motorcycle and we'll take trips. ... He's great on the back of the bike. We went up to Cadillac this year and it was colder than the devil and I'd say, 'Are you tired?' 'No, you tired?' 'A little bit.' 'We'd better stop then.' He's this kind of person. He's gorgeous. He did not want me to be a priest."

"Bill, his beliefs were that his father was in a better place," said Coden who attended the funeral at Madonna. "There was the sadness, yet a celebration." After the service, the ladies of the parish put on a luncheon in the church basement. Peter Deegan, Cunningham's cousin on his father's side, went downstairs to find an interesting mix of people. Deegan and Cunningham were chatting despite interruptions from folks paying their respects. "One African-American lad, I would guess would've been in his mid- to late-30s, came in, well dressed with a Superfly hat on," Deegan said. "He was very articulate, talking with Father." Cunningham introduced Deegan, who was then an assistant prosecutor in St. Clair County, to the man in the drug-dealer getup. "When he left, Father said, 'You know, Pete, that is one of the sharpest guys in our area here and you wouldn't let him into your law school.' I stopped and looked at Father and said, 'Yes, but you wouldn't let him into your seminary, either.' He said, 'Touché!'"

Without neglecting his pastor's duties, Cunningham kept an almost nightly schedule of speeches before various groups across metropolitan Detroit. In March 1976, his talk at St. Raymond parish before a testy group of more than 100 erupted in angry shouting led by Donald Lobsinger of the fringe group Breakthrough. Lobsinger and six other protesters shouted at Cunningham and prevented discussion. "Have you talked to businessmen in East Warren and other areas harassed by criminals or visited high schools like Denby?" Lobsinger demanded to know. "You're giving these people an 'Alice-in-Wonderland' view of the city."

Following Cunningham's "forthright presentation on the importance of integrated and stable neighborhoods, where all could live together in harmony," St. Raymond's priests asked for comments from the congregation. One parishioner's comment was written on an offertory envelope: "This offering was mailed to Billy Graham. I just could not sit and listen to more of your love the damned nigger talk." Another was carefully typed on a card. It was entitled "A message to the Negroes of America" and demanded that blacks pay $500 billion to white people "in payment for your education, and for the damage you have done to us and to our nation." The typed and unsigned note said, "Now, I know what a Black Irishman is." The third was a handwritten note to Cunningham and St. Raymond's pastor, Father Larry Ventline: "Dear Bill and Larry. Congratulations on 'Dialogue on Neighborhood Sunday.' I wish I could have been there to watch the Holy Spirit at work. Honest, Reflective, Courageous, Forthright Direction. Genuine leadership on display. You make a great team."

Despite the work of Cunningham and others to ease the fears of whites, thousands were pulling out of Detroit as soon as they could sell their homes. On July 17, 1976, the *Free Press* ran a front-page story that said, "The number of homes for sale in many of Detroit's finest neighborhoods has risen sharply in the past year, particularly on the northeast side, and is probably at an all time high." Rising crime frightened white and black alike. Detroit's two daily newspapers published one horrific murder story after another. Most television newscasts led off with a bloody tragedy. When the police weren't quelling potential riots and investigating shockingly vicious violent crimes, they were battling each other over Mayor Coleman Young's affirmative action policy of promoting black officers over white ones.

As crime rose, Cunningham urged people to address challenges with optimism and hope. "Crisis evokes courage, forges endurance, excites invention, rouses apathy, lances cynicism, sharpens vision, and ennobles every human passion," he wrote in November 1976. "If Detroiters will survive, all Detroiters, black and white, city and suburb, it will be because we came together, struggled to solve our problems, met together our fears, together rose to stop the lawlessness of street crime and social crime."

Turning his attention to Detroit's neighborhoods, Cunningham had Focus: HOPE volunteers organize citizen block clubs as a counter to local homeowner associations that were seen as anti-black. The new block clubs "all have names with initials, all have self-appointed officers, all hold their local meetings in churches, and all seem to have miraculously started shortly after a visit to Detroit by Fr. Cunningham of Focus Hope," said a front page article in the *Harper Woods Herald* on April 14, 1977.

In a follow-up article in the *Herald*, Cunningham responded: "We want to wipe away the panic-selling that destroys our neighborhoods and creates blighted communities ... When people starting families or those looking for a nice place to live try to find a house, they will see in our pamphlets what schools, parks and organizations our Detroit neighborhoods have. Hopefully, they will buy a home on the northeast side, and with these big three and four bedroom houses we have, they will choose Detroit."

Cunningham could not slow down, despite always being late. Bidleman chuckled whenever Cunningham said he had 20 minutes to get somewhere. "Everything was 20 minutes, whether it was Port Huron or the east side." Having a motorcycle helped him maneuver around traffic deftly and speed without too much risk of getting a ticket. But when the weather caused him to drive his Volkswagen, the priest had to slow down a bit.

On one lobbying trip to Washington, Cunningham, Charlie Grenville and Eleanor Josaitis were late getting out of Focus: HOPE headquarters. Cunningham had to stop at the bank, making them even later. As the minutes ticked by, Josaitis told Grenville to get him or they'd miss their flight. According to Josaitis, "Charlie says, 'Eleanor, the man is 48 years old. Now, you're going to have to let him grow up if he's ever going to know that he is totally and absolutely responsible for getting us to that airport in time.'

"Twelve minutes to the airport, 128 miles an hour down the expressway we go," Eleanor said. "Bill, in all his magnificent splendor, jumps out of the car, runs in with the tickets. I jump out with the briefcase, run through the Geiger counter [she meant the metal detector]. Charlie takes the car and parks two miles away at the lot. I'm standing at the Geiger counter. Bill is God knows where. Charlie comes huffing and puffing down the ramp and we run together to the plane, only to see 'Captain Cunningham' standing with his hand on the door and his other hand on the pilot, saying, 'I'll be with you in a minute, folks.'"

Cunningham had his charming Irish smile on, but Grenville was not amused. "I remember laughing my ass off and how livid Grenville was," Bidleman said. "Charlie wouldn't talk to [Bill] the rest of the trip, he was so pissed off. It was very illustrative of Bill's style."

That flight to Washington was one of many that saved the Commodity Supplemental Food Program (CSFP). After the efforts of Michigan Senator Don Riegle (who was elected to the Senate in November 1976 after Hart retired due to cancer) and South Dakota Senator George McGovern, legislation was passed in September 1977 that guaranteed the continued existence of the CSFP. The bill also established a clearer funding mechanism at the USDA to pay for administering surplus food distribution programs.

Getting the law passed and signed by President Jimmy Carter was a significant accomplishment. But, as the saying goes, the devil is in the details—in this case in the writing of regulations that would put the law into effect. USDA bureaucrats wrote tentative guidelines that Focus: HOPE found unworkable. "The guidelines were cumbersome, and involved regulations we have never been subject to before," Josaitis said. "We knew it would take four times as much energy to change the guidelines once they were adopted as to stay with them until they were acceptable." During the delay, Focus: HOPE nearly ran out of money to cover payroll for its employees working in the food program. U.S. Senator Don Riegle arranged a $50,000 advance to Focus: HOPE from the USDA's Commodity Services Administration office in Chicago.

Congressman Bob Traxler, D-Bay City, a rookie who was appointed to the House Appropriations Subcommittee on Agriculture, and his aide Roger Szemraj played key roles in getting the USDA to fund and expand the feeding programs. In an interview years later, Traxler said that he "was totally enamored with what they were doing. …It struck me as one of the finest projects I had ever been asked to be of help to."

Mary Ann Gideon, the Presbyterian anti-hunger activist, began working for Focus: HOPE as a volunteer public relations specialist that year. It didn't take her long to realize that Cunningham would listen to her advice, but then do it (or say it) his own way. Once, the priest was being interviewed by J.P. McCarthy on WJR-AM and Cunningham told the radio host that "he didn't like Billy Graham"—one of McCarthy's favorite religious personalities. "J.P. was just crazy about Billy Graham. ... [Cunningham] didn't like that fundamental religious type," Gideon said. "I tried my best and suggested later that he call McCarthy and apologize or fix it up." She got him to call J.P. after the show, but the priest only "made it worse."

Cunningham had been handling his own media requests, but his propensity for being late frustrated some in the media. Reporters "didn't want to go through me; they'd call him direct if they could," Gideon said. "That was a big mistake if you were booking him to be on a show. I went with him to make sure he got there."

Gideon said she once told Cunningham that he was running on "C.P. Time," which the priest took to mean "Colored People's Time." "That's racist!" Cunningham told Gideon. She responded: "No, it means Catholic Priest Time." They both laughed.

Young Focus: HOPE supporters in front and key adult volunteers in the rear posing on the lawn of a neighbor across the street from the Josaitis home in Detroit's Sherwood Forest community. Father Cunningham is wearing a white shirt on the left.

Credit: *The Michigan Catholic*

12

Trust

IN A CABIN at Walden Woods near Hartland, Father Cunningham stood in the back of the great room crowded with weeping teenaged boys and girls—white, black, brown and yellow. He, too, was in tears as Eleanor Josaitis described her passion for civil rights in the context of her own life, her own outrage at injustice, and her own guilt over the sorry state of Detroit.

Standing before teens who had been through an emotional wringer wrestling with their prejudices for the past two days, Josaitis looked each kid in the eye. She talked about the turning point of her life: seeing peaceful blacks beaten by police in Selma, Alabama, on television in 1965. She told about Father Cunningham responding to Dr. Martin Luther King Jr.'s call to march with him in Selma, and Cunningham's visions of hope for Detroit. She talked about moving into the city in 1969, infuriating members of her family who thought she was crazy and endangering her five children.

Each of them was responsible for bringing peace to their schools, she said, their neighborhoods and their homes, even if their parents or classmates were suspicious and angry. "You are going to have to learn to trust one another," Josaitis said, grabbing the hands of one white kid and one black kid, bringing them together, forcing a clasp. "This is my goal." By the time she was done, the teens were a joyfully tearful group hugging each other, professing how much they loved and respected their new friends.

Running the organization on razor-thin budgets in the 1970s, Cunningham never stopped pushing to expand Focus: HOPE, particularly into the city's high schools that were on the cusp of a racial crisis.

In February 1974, when the U.S. Supreme Court overturned federal Judge Stephen Roth's orders on cross-district busing of students between Detroit and its suburbs, the high court left intact Roth's orders to desegregate schools in the city itself by busing students. Detroit Public Schools planned to begin busing black kids into predominantly white schools in the district that fall. Roth's order had the unintended consequence of increasing white flight from the city. Cunningham was critical of the Supreme Court ruling, but he knew complaining was pointless. He believed Focus: HOPE should find ways to prevent racial tensions in the six public high schools involved in the busing plan.

Focus: HOPE had no funding for any new project, of course. But during several freewheeling staff meetings, it was decided that two staffers—former seminarian Carl Bidleman, who was white, and Monica Emerson, a young black woman—would form a biracial team to attend student assemblies and present the facts about racial injustice and the impact of segregation on the entire region. "We thought that in addition to the message, the visual itself, a black female and a white male, working hand-in-hand together toward a common goal, helped them get along together and really embrace each other," Emerson said. Focus: HOPE provided the service free of charge to any school that asked.

Charlie Grenville, Focus: HOPE's resident intellectual and a lapsed Catholic priest, was enthusiastic about an effective program in the schools and shaped Cunningham's thinking on how it could be done. Grenville found a source of federal funding that could let them get involved in the racial integration of schools in a sustained way.

The Emergency School Aid Act (ESAA) of 1972 offered grants to nonprofit entities to reduce the effects of minority isolation in majority white schools. Grenville took the lead in developing a detailed proposal with input from Cunningham, Josaitis, Gil Maddox, Bidleman, Emerson, Ken Kudek and others. The result was a comprehensive plan to identify 50 youth leaders in each of the six Detroit high schools affected by the desegregation order: Redford, Ford and Cody on the west side, and Denby, Finney and Osborn on the east side.

The project was called Training for Trust and, according to the proposal, it "has two major objectives: To eliminate racial tension, polarization and hostility in six Detroit public schools and to prevent the re-segregation of those schools and their communities. ... The balanced racial composition of those schools provides the opportunity for quality, integrated education available nowhere else in the metropolitan area."

Focus: HOPE asked the feds for $553,000—virtually the entire amount allocated to Michigan under the ESAA. The proposal required approval by the state and city boards of education, school administrators and a representative panel of teachers, parents and students prior to submission in February 1976. Cunningham and Josaitis visited dozens, asking for their support. As usual, Cunningham wasn't willing to wait for anyone's go-ahead. Cobbling together small grants from DPS, the General Motors Foundation and the Ford Motor Company Fund, Focus: HOPE hired John Staniloui (pronounced STAN-eh-loy), the former principal at St. Brigid Catholic Elementary School in Detroit, and began training student leaders and teachers that spring.

According to a report by Grenville, a panel of independent reviewers ranked Focus: HOPE's plan first among proposals submitted from Michigan. Nonetheless, the U.S. Office of Education approved a grant of only $94,000, less than one-fifth of the request. Despite the setback, Cunningham was confident that more funding could be found and the project began with training sessions for smaller numbers of students and teachers that spring and summer.

With the support of DPS superintendent Arthur Jefferson, the six high schools were designated as Trust project sites. In each school, 50 kids identified by peers as leaders academically, socially, athletically or otherwise—including gang leaders— were invited to a weekend away from home. Cunningham was a longtime believer that well-structured retreats can changes lives, and he sunk thousands of dollars into providing them in a safe remote setting. For many teens, it was their first experience with the great outdoors or even going beyond city limits.

Over a series of weekends in August and September in 1976, each of the six initial Trust groups was taken to a remote location, like Waldenwoods in Hartland. The goal of the retreat was to train kids not well-acquainted with each other to understand, communicate and peacefully interact with youths of another culture or ethnicity. Those leaders in turn would return to their schools and, with the assistance of Focus: HOPE staff, be ambassadors of hope, nonviolent conflict resolution and community service.

"The essential plan was to attempt to identify in every school the positive leadership and the negative leadership," Maddox said. "Then we brought these leaders together in retreats and training activities to get them to relate to each other in a positive fashion, and then to begin to relate to the school and the student population in terms of activities which encourage integration of students racially."

Cunningham usually kicked off the retreats with words similar to these quotes reported by Bidleman in a later newsletter: "The fundamental problem of America is that, black and white, we don't trust one another. There is a lot of stuff that we don't know about one another. We hope to get that out on the table right away." The kids were then led through facilitated group discussion to build teamwork and respect. Students were assigned to share a room with someone from the opposite race, the first time many of them had experienced integrated living. "Nobody got any sleep," one student told Bidleman. "But that was the best part. You really get to know people when you share a room with them."

Small group discussions initially focused on helping the kids relate to each other in a respectful way so that everyone had a chance to be heard. "By assuring equal, positive value for every person, the process also tends to enhance self-concept, to build trust and to allow for honest exploration of fundamental values, differences and concerns," a 1978 Focus: HOPE report said.

Mary Kay Stark, then a Trust coordinator at Osborn High School, said retreats often included a "string ceremony," in which a ball of yarn is used as a tangible symbol of unity. Each person, one by one, takes the ball and thanks someone in the group for something they had done or said and then passes the ball to that person still holding the loose end of the yarn. By the time everyone has had a chance, the entire group was holding on to the same string, intertwined and connected.

Cunningham opened the retreats, but it was Eleanor's emotionally honest talk at the end that many remembered. "When you listened to Bill's and Eleanor's two speeches you'd be wiped out," Stark said. Jerry Lemenu said Eleanor's speech—even though "sometimes it was over the top"—brought everyone, including Cunningham, to tears. "My experience is you bring kids on this kind of thing, you tell them they're leaders, give them a safe place to talk and then demonstrate how you can be revealing and pour your heart out," Lemenu said. "They really are desperate for a place to feel safe, reveal and tell their secrets. Someone like Eleanor does that."

Horace Sheffield III, then a young Trust coordinator at Finney, said Eleanor would "have these kids crying, literally in the palm of her hands." He said he would never "forget the first time I saw her do this—I thought, my God, this woman! I need to have her in church on Sunday morning," Sheffield said. "Even in that setting on occasion there were a couple of kids who literally had emotional breakdowns. They were unable to stop crying, feeling guilty about some previous acts, wondering how they were going to go back home to a house full of hatred and bigotry."

Thom Armstead said he once saw three teenage black boys after Eleanor's talk. "They were walking and one said to the other, he said, 'Man, if that bitch don't make a motherfucker cry there's something wrong with him.'"

Typically, when a retreat ended, kids gathered in the parking lot before boarding buses back to Detroit. Cunningham had the final word inside each bus: "Six high schools that are the hottest site of court-ordered desegregation are going to determine how this city goes, and may well determine how this nation goes. As a group of young leaders, you are going to impact beyond your school to the whole community—your family, neighbors, real estate companies, the government, the police department. You may have impact way beyond the limits of the city of Detroit, as this affects the nation."

Cunningham left it to Maddox to figure out how to continue the Trust program in the schools through the entire school year. Maddox found a structured method of fostering better youth communications called Participation Training created by Dorothy Minion of Indiana University. Minion was brought in to train Focus: HOPE staff and to participate in the initial retreats. "The beauty of it was, you had 16 [youths] in a circle and you take two of them out as observers who report what they saw," Staniloui said. "It was awesome, fantastic."

They began in September 1976 at two high schools—Redford on the west side and Denby on the east side. Bidleman was sent to Denby and Staniloui handled Redford. Staff was hired for the other four Detroit schools over the next six months as funding came in. Bidleman and Staniloui spent several days talking with students and staff at each school to identify student leaders. "You had to know how to pick leaders," Staniloui said. "I talked to every single junior and senior in the high school—the kids were the ones running the show. You had to get the right kid." Leaders of gangs were intentionally selected to help bring troublemakers into the process.

Redford High School drum majorette Anne Kelly was standing outside the school on Detroit's far northwest side, just twirling her baton and hanging out with her friends when a young, rangy, long-haired white man approached. It was Staniloui. "He walked up and struck up a conversation with some of my friends and me. I remember the oddness of that. … He was asking poignant questions about the school and how we were getting along with one another."

Kelly learned that Staniloui was from Focus: HOPE and he was there to help white and black teens integrate into a better, more socially engaged student body. She had actually seen Cunningham and heard a lot about him from her mother Marian, a Cunningham fan. "My parents were very Catholic and always raised in the Catholic Church and she described this amazing priest … this amazing man who lead this march in the city and had a whole food program."

With court-ordered busing that year, Redford's student body was a little more than half black. The limited busing to achieve racial integration in Detroit was going far smoother than in Boston where court-ordered school desegregation was met with weeks of violence that left several people dead. "At least Detroit was actually integrated," Kelly said. "For us, 1967 was only nine years previous. Most of us were very much conscious of the possibility of violence right there, all the time. Plus we had heard what had happened in Boston. We saw fights. We knew kids getting beat up. We knew of guns and knives and threats. … There was violence and fear, and a lot of us at Redford were determined to have peaceful integration."

Kelly attended the Trust program retreat. On the first school day after the Redford group's retreat, Kelly and the other chosen students gathered outside before class and chanted "Focus: HOPE! Focus: HOPE!" A female student made a speech at the school flag pole asking why black students always used one door into the school and white students another. When the school bell rang, the students walked in together chanting "Focus: HOPE."

When the kids at Denby returned, they "formed an impromptu circle in the parking lot … joined hands and sang, 'We Shall Overcome,'" a Focus: HOPE newsletter article said. "The next day they spoke about the conference in their regular classes and made a presentation to the Denby Mothers Club.

They organized the first homecoming parade in recent memory on nearby streets, with a large well-integrated turnout of students, teachers and administrators, and carried a 'Let's Get Together' banner and Focus: HOPE placards." A few days later, the Denby kids joined the Focus: HOPE Walk along East Eight Mile Road, and they later put their stamp on the 1977 school yearbook by choosing "We Have a Dream" as its theme.

Sheffield said it was a huge undertaking just to get the parents' permission for their kids to attend a Trust retreat. "When they came back home, the white families were over here and the black families were over there and the kids got off the bus together," Sheffield said. "They left as foes and they came back as friends. Literally, when they got off the bus these kids were hugging each other, crying again, talking about they were so glad they had an opportunity to have their eyes open. It was just amazing. … We had more problems when we got back with the adults than we did with the students."

As part of the effort, DPS and Focus: HOPE organized a series of "mini-conferences" that year, beginning in November with a meeting of about 300 academics and community leaders at Mercy College to study "The Impact of Mass Media on Urban Life." The keynote speaker was Benjamin Hooks, then head of the Federal Communications Commission, who lamented the portrayal of blacks on television. "The average white viewer comes to know black[s] and Hispanics principally through commercial TV," he said. "And what they know is someone who's always in trouble. And it's about time that someone other than hustlers and prostitutes were held up to our black youth as heroes."

As busy as Focus: HOPE volunteers and staff had been since Focus: HOPE was founded in 1968, things were about to get even busier. Cunningham summed up the situation in his "Muddling Thru" column published in the August 1977 *Focus: HOPE News*: "Perhaps Focus: HOPE is attempting too much with the feeding program, media and T.V. projects, equal employment litigations, desegregated schools, neighborhood stabilization. Perhaps this article will ask too much of you. On the other hand, all of this may be long overdue. No sadder thought or more sour taste than a dream never dared, or a courage never tested. When Focus: HOPE was born nine years ago out of the fire and ashes of 1967, it was born from the confusion of blacks and whites asking: 'What can I do?' Focus: HOPE's answer was: 'Whatever we do, let's do it together.'"

Maddox and Staniloui pushed to hire two coordinators for each school, teams that they hoped would be balanced by race and gender. JoAnn Watson, who had attended Madonna parish school in the 8th grade and was inspired to academic success by the nuns, was then a young vice president of the NAACP's Michigan chapter, and a University of Michigan journalism graduate. Maddox, who had been one of her U-M professors, recruited her to work at Focus: HOPE. She already knew about Cunningham and liked the idea of working in schools to foster better race relations among the students. "I was enamored of him," Watson said. "He lived what he preached. I loved that about him."

Watson was teamed with a young white woman, Valerie Snook, for the Trust program at Redford. "The kids loved it," Watson said. "Some teachers, they smiled on the outside, but I picked up a little resentment. Not so much with the subject matter, but it was the influence of Father Cunningham to access us to the classroom. We were not typically certified teachers, even though we all had degrees. But it was their hallowed ground."

Staniloui said the Trust project exposed ineffective leadership at some of the schools. Denby, according to Staniloui, had a weak principal and Cunningham worked behind the scenes, probably with Superintendent Jefferson, to have the man replaced. Under the new leadership, Focus: HOPE was given complete access to the school and students earned school credit for participating in Training for Trust. "These kids met every day for an hour," Staniloui said. "That's' how we stopped the riots at Denby. They had rioted seven straight years, and this year there was not a riot."

At Cody, "the principal would hide in the office; the gangs were running the school big time," Staniloui said. Cunningham frequently clued Jefferson in about what was going on in DPS, and he got Cody's principal replaced by Henry Baum, a Jew and Holocaust survivor. Baum brought a new concept to DPS—using computerized data to manage 2,000 high school students. Baum also trusted Focus: HOPE. "We were given a list of problems by principals every day and we were allowed to pull any kid out of class for whatever reason," Staniloui said.

Sheffield said that at Finney the principal "did not like me with a passion and he disrespected me because I had more control over the students than he did. He would holler and scream at the students, threaten them all the time." That principal was black, Sheffield said, but the black students "disliked him more than the whites." The principal, Sheffield said, "was set against Father Cunningham; he didn't like the program, and he would say, 'I don't give a damn what Arthur Jefferson said I got to do.'"

When Cunningham came to Finney to meet with students, he got an earful about the principal. "The kids were able to give him far more detail on how recalcitrant he was," Sheffield said. That principal, too, was replaced.

Participation Training, which required students to communicate about issues through writing assignments, was good for the retreats. But when it came to the every day work at the schools, Staniloui believed Positive Peer Culture, a new group behavior modification dynamic, would be more effective. PPC—which Staniloui re-named Positive Peer Influence (PPI) so the organization did not have to pay a royalty fee—worked better day-to-day in the schools.

The PPC model was designed to make the group responsible for correcting an individual's behavior. Complete confidentiality was necessary, even though kids disclosed behavior that should have been reported. "We talked a lot of kids into leaving their guns at home; it was a common thing for us. In two of these groups, two kids admitted killing somebody," Staniloui said. "It was such a high level of group process. You could talk about anything in the group. Who's dealing drugs—that was a big thing. Which teacher was screwing some kid. Who was going to beat up so-and-so."

Word about the Trust project soon got around. Administrators at suburban and parochial schools asked Focus: HOPE to include them. In June 1977, Southfield Public Schools hired two Focus: HOPE Trust coordinators for Southfield High School and Southfield-Lathrup High School beginning in September. The cities of Southfield and Lathrup Village had sizable Jewish populations and were just beginning to see an influx of other ethnic groups, including middle-class blacks and Chaldeans, Catholics from Iraq.

"When black kids started coming into Southfield High School, maybe a half dozen kids, it generated almost immediately a hysteria and a crisis," said Bernie Sucher, then a student at the school. "There was physical violence and threats of worse. Incredible angst, and hatred and fear." Sucher, then editor-in-chief of the student newspaper, was among the first group of leaders attending a Trust retreat. "I didn't want to be there," Sucher said. "I was a typical journalist; I had a job to do there, but I didn't want to participate in this. I was reporting on other people solving the problem or dealing with the issue."

Cunningham, however, singled Sucher out of the group and "convinced me I needed to be part of the Southfield High leadership of Focus: HOPE." Sucher wrote a definitive account of a Trust retreat for *The Southfield Jay*, the school newspaper. "The primary working factor involved in the 'Training for Trust' program is the discussion group. At the retreat, three such groups were formed, each consisting of students and faculty, each racially and culturally balanced," Sucher wrote. "Helping on the training were Focus: HOPE people, usually one or two to each group. These staff members helped guide discussions through the outline of the established training scheme. Groups were free to discuss any topic of common interest. Issues discussed included drugs, school policies, Detroit, busing, race relations, school violence, Principal [Daniel] Hogan and Coleman Young.

"Group discussions were made by consensus. In other words, all had to be in agreement. An important factor in the discussion was the emphasis placed on involving all present. Reluctant or shy individuals were encouraged to speak; everyone assumed special roles (leader, observer, recorder) at least once. To encourage direct speaking, eye contact and the use of names were constantly suggested.

"With this relatively simple process, Focus: HOPE helped transform a collection of skeptical and sometimes hostile individuals into a group which, after two and a half days of training were mixing freely and openly amongst each other," Sucher wrote.

Sizable portions of the Southfield-Lathrup High School student body were either Jews or Chaldeans, with a few Hindus and ethnic whites thrown in the mix. "This was a school that had gone through some pretty dramatic changes in student population," said Lewis Rudolph, the Focus: HOPE coordinator at the school. "It wasn't a black/white thing. There was Jew Hall, Camel Hall, Jock Hall, Burnout Hall. Chaldeans were treated as Arabs. There were these territories, a whole ecology where they hung out between classes.

"When I picked my students to go to the retreat at Waldenwoods I had, of course, the president of the student body, the football captain, the cheerleader. But the group also had the burnouts, the kids who didn't go to class, who just hung out and smoked weed. My goal was to work with one half of one percent of the school community and to create some sort of program that could spread to the entire school," Rudolph said.

Cunningham brought a diversity of speakers to that retreat, including Tom Fox, an African-American reporter for television station WJBK Channel 2 in Southfield. Two respected leaders in the Chaldean community, Michael George and Afram Rayis, appeared with an owner of Chatham supermarkets, Harold Weisberg, a Jew. George was the owner of Melody Farms, a dairy wholesaler, and was informally known as the "godfather" of the Chaldean community for having helped many immigrants from Iraq open grocery and convenience stores. "We went out to this retreat and each of us spoke about the relationship we had between the four of us," George said. "We talked about business and social relationships. We talked about the importance of getting along, our backgrounds. It made a world of difference, even though it was only a two-day seminar."

During the retreat, the students discussed the Camp David Accords, a historic peace agreement reached in September between Egyptian President Anwar El Sadat and Israeli Prime Minister Menachim Begin. The accord came after 12 days of secret talks convened by President Jimmy Carter and inspired the kids on retreat to write a "Framework for Unity" pledge. Returning to school, they spent a few more weeks honing a message, crafting the words in four languages and engaging the school's art class to inscribe it in English, Hebrew, Arabic and Hindi on a scroll several feet in length. More than 1,000 students, faculty members and staff of the high school signed it: **"We, the undersigned, do hereby pledge our solemn oath to avoid allowing our differences of nationality, religion, or race to divide us, but rather to strive to understand and appreciate our diverse heritage while working to unify our school and our community."**

At an assembly at Southfield-Lathrup on December 13, Bill Brodhead, who had moved from the state legislature to Congress, accepted the scroll and promised to give it to President Carter so it could be shared with Sadat and Begin. "I went directly from that meeting with Father Cunningham and the students, flew to Washington and, instead of going home from the airport, I went to the White House," Brodhead said. "I walked this thing in and I figured they would have it signed then and there and give it back to me." As it turned out, Carter had pressing matters and he didn't see the students' scroll until shortly before Christmas. The president seemed impressed, writing in his own hand a thank-you note to the students: "I am hopeful that actions such as yours will contribute to a lasting peace and understanding in this region."

Despite being a skeptical young journalist, Sucher was blown away by Cunningham. "I had literally never met a human being like Father Cunningham," Sucher said. "I wasn't prepared. At an intellectual level, I remember it being such a shock that there were people that were like this out there. The guy just was the most powerful, committed person that I had met at that point in my life."

One of Sucher's teachers, Ken Siver, said he found Cunningham to be "unbelievably charismatic, a wonderful and captivating speaker. ... He had a very calming effect on people and he was funny besides. There was a certain amount of self-deprecating humor. The term I would use is disarming. I think some people were afraid that you're going to bring this guy in here and he's going to tell us how to behavior what to believe or that we got to like our neighbor. And he wasn't that at all. ... He inspired. He really inspired people."

Cunningham used his "Muddling Thru" column in late 1977 to ask Detroiters to hang tough and work through their problems together, as black and white citizens of the same city: "Detroit is the center of the nation's crisis. Therefore the hope of America's future focuses on us. ... In the schools students are together, physically, under one roof, mathematically measured, equally black and white. But they view one another suspiciously, testing turf, establishing within the de-segregated building separate exits, separate activities, separate sports, separate sides of the classroom. Herein lies the beauty, the challenge, the hope of the city and perhaps of this nation—for in Detroit, east side and west side, crisis has reached its height. Out of this sow's ear is the making of a silk purse."

A breeze blows Father Cunningham's leonine mane during a
Walk for Justice.

Credit: John Collier

13

Lion

A PRIVATE EYE was snooping around, trying to find some dirt on Father Bill Cunningham on behalf of his client—the Automobile Club of Michigan. Auto Club executives couldn't quite believe that the priest hadn't yet given up on his quixotic quest to make them pay for abandoning Detroit. They were frustrated and growing desperate, asking friends and business associates to not support Focus: HOPE financially.

In court, the Auto Club filed a motion for a judge to order an independent audit of Focus: HOPE's finances. If Focus: HOPE lost, the Auto Club would demand that Cunningham's nonprofit organization pay the company's considerable legal fees. Could Cunningham pay up if he lost?

Despite the priest's relative fame in Detroit, there was no shortage of people who disliked him and his organization of do-gooders. In the nervous white neighborhoods of Detroit, Cunningham was riling up many residents with speeches in church halls and schools. He challenged whites to allow a peaceful integration of their neighborhoods as a sign that Detroiters had the moral character to welcome black families moving in, rather than letting greedy real estate agents trick them into panic selling. Some of the priest's harshest critics came from home-owner associations fighting tooth-and-nail to keep blacks out. When you can't beat them, Cunningham reasoned, out-organize them. He sent Focus: HOPE staff to create mixed-race block clubs in the same neighborhoods.

Cunningham also waged a public shaming campaign against the city of Birmingham, the posh Oakland County suburb that abuts Bloomfield Hills, one of the wealthiest zip codes in the country. On April 3, 1978, Birmingham voters soundly defeated a proposed real estate development that would have used federal funds to build housing for low-income people, including blacks. Cunningham saw the vote as hypocritical and racially motivated. "What really troubles me is a kind of moral rupture—the tearing away from, the blind denial of, something which made the vote in Birmingham possible: the freedom that people to choose to deny a part of their freedom to others," he said.

He was harshly critical of the Michigan Legislature and the State Board of Education for doing nothing to address the huge disparities in outcomes between white and black kids. "Presently there is an uneven and unequal school system," he told *The Michigan Catholic* in 1975. "If we are preparing children mentally and physically to be part of our society they're going to be frustrated when they enter school—it's inadequate. We want the state to give the children their full constitutional right to a quality education. This responsibility doesn't lie with the local school boards or municipalities."

Adding an element of danger to his life, a right-wing nut-case, Donald Lobsinger, would occasionally pop up at a public meeting, threatening and heckling him, demanding to know if Cunningham was a card-carrying communist. "Finally, Cunningham tried the ploy of humbly admitting that, yes, he was a card-carrying member," Carl Bidleman said. "Lobsinger freaked out."

Reflecting on the first decade of Focus: HOPE in his "Muddling Thru" column in March 1978, Cunningham wrote: "Ten years later, still learning, still growing, still surprised at the tenacity of ignorance and bias, Focus: HOPE is celebrating with a few over-the-shoulder glances. Perhaps the best thing about Focus: HOPE—whatever the achievements and mis-starts of the past ten years—is that we haven't forgotten why we started. Focus: HOPE began with the conviction that racism is this nation's greatest moral obstacle to survival. … And perhaps most critical to Focus: HOPE's beginning was a certain light-hearted arrogance: Getting it done means doing it yourself—and if that doesn't work, we have only ourselves to blame. A kind of kitchen philosophy and Gospel blend. Oh, and one other thing, when it doesn't work, stay up all night until it does. That's called muddling thru."

What was actually muddled was communication between the Trust project staff in the schools and their colleagues at Focus: HOPE's headquarters. The Trust job was tough and exhausting with late hours, problematic and needy kids, angry or apathetic parents, resentful teachers, turf-protective administrators, and limited help from the home office on Oakman Boulevard. "Many times, it felt sort of isolated," Bidleman said. "That was part of the problem." Some coordinators couldn't handle the rigor. Others had transportation problems. Some of the black coordinators became disillusioned with Focus: HOPE and quit. They said they felt they were being used as black faces fronting for an organization that, when all was said and done, still seemed to be run by white people.

One of the black Trust coordinators, Daisy Brown, was disciplined for being chronically late. She had a schedule full of evening meetings and weekend events to attend on behalf of Focus: HOPE. And, she didn't think she always had to be at work at 8:30 a.m. Brown was the leader among several dissidents who demanded a meeting with Cunningham to discuss what they saw as racism and injustice within Focus: HOPE itself.

In a two-page memo to him dated May 3, 1978, they denounced the "subjective supervisory performance evaluations to delay or deny salary opportunities to employees" and "the application of arbitrary, disparate standards in regard to hiring, assignment, and other terms and conditions of employment."

The memo concluded: "We find it ironic that while Focus: HOPE is working to halt the racist practices of a corporate giant (AAA), Focus: HOPE is itself guilty of perpetuating the same unfair employment practices with respect to Black employees. That Focus: HOPE programs, in application, are diametrically opposed to the organizationally expressed philosophy demonstrates lack of genuine commitment to the ideals of racial harmony."

The group may not have known that funding for the Trust project was dicey. Cunningham expected approval of Focus: HOPE's most recent request for $305,249 from the federal Office of Education—he'd already expanded the program to several parochial schools without an assured source of funding. But on June 30 the Department of Health, Education and Welfare (HEW) announced that three Michigan organizations would be awarded a total of $507,670 in grants under the Emergency School Aid Act: Latin Americans for Social and Economic Development, Ren Outreach and the Metropolitan Detroit Youth Foundation. Focus: HOPE got zilch, a potentially fatal blow to the Trust project.

Cunningham, of course, would not take no for an answer. He and Eleanor Josaitis worked their friends on Capitol Hill and developed a campaign that included letters of support from Detroit Superintendent of Schools Arthur Jefferson and Mayor Coleman A. Young. The mayor wrote a letter to HEW Secretary Joseph A. Califano saying the Trust program was "critical in resolving two major concerns of my administration—the necessity of interracial understanding and collaboration in the rebuilding of Detroit, and our commitment to improve the quality of public education. ... People at all levels of the Detroit school system insist that the continuation of this project is crucial, and I would agree."

Cunningham told the *Free Press* that he kept the Trust project going by pooling money from other Focus: HOPE programs and cutting wages in half while also looking for other grants. HEW wouldn't budge. Maddox said the program was "the victim of bureaucratic change and insensitivity to the realities of the harsh climate of a city like Detroit." By August, though, Michigan's Congressional delegation worked with HEW and found $220,000 that was then allocated to Focus: HOPE. But the disruption and uncertainty resulted in several payless weeks for Trust staff.

Other Focus: HOPE programs were growing substantially. With federal grants totaling nearly $6 million to operate the Prescription Food Program, Focus: HOPE suddenly was one of the largest charities in Detroit. Its 1978 annual report lists the names of 77 employees on the back cover. But the growth had its downside. Its workforce was no longer just a committed group of former volunteers who shared Cunningham's vision and passion and who would follow the priest anywhere and rarely ask about getting a raise in pay. The huge government grants meant hiring dozens of people to do the work required under those grants. Many new employees perceived Focus: HOPE simply as an employer, not a call to service. They expected to be paid decently and treated fairly under clearly defined rules.

On May 8, a meeting of the full staff was called to air grievances. An internal summary of the meeting listed the issues raised:

- "Discriminatory treatment of black staff. One hundred percent turnover among black members of education staff. Subjective and inconsistent management practices which can discriminate against black employees. Office cliques which form along racial lines. Neglect of black perspective. Should be able to discuss issues such as making the anniversary of Martin Luther King's death [sic] a holiday.

- "General Management Practices. Ideology and Goals. Staff members need to operate out of a similar frame of reference, i.e., all should know what institutional racism is. Need to discuss overall goals of the organization. Need to agree on objectives, or we won't be able to measure whether or not they've been met.

- "Some felt there was not enough of an opportunity to discuss what direction the [Trust] program is going in. Focus: HOPE activities don't always get at the real problem, i.e., teacher appreciation day doesn't touch the problem of dirty bathrooms. Program doesn't acknowledge that most of the schools have a black majority, and tries to make black students conform to white cultural norms."

Josaitis assessed the meeting in a handwritten note to Cunningham: "My feelings are that the black staff mainly in the resource building plus some members of the white staff are feeling so very insecure that they are unable to function either as a group or individually. They are searching for direction and understanding. It is also my feeling that the ones doing the loudest yelling are producing the least."

Cunningham and Josaitis met with Brown and other troubled employees on May 26, 1978, a meeting that satisfied neither side. Brown wrote a second memo that amounted to an indictment of Cunningham and Focus: HOPE. It cited "fraternization, apparently along racial lines, [that] inhibits job efficiency" and an "indefensibly high rate of turnover among black employees." Focus: HOPE didn't even have a written personnel policy or employee manual, Brown pointed out.

Brown's memo actually was a fairly accurate description of problems in an organization that was not functioning under the ordinary rules of business or nonprofit management. Typically, issues were thrashed out in freewheeling fashion at staff meetings where everyone had the chance to say something that they would then have to defend. Arguments were loud and passionate. But it was always Cunningham who made the final decisions and Josaitis who enforced them.

Issues of employee compensation often were decided subjectively—a man with a wife and children to support was routinely paid more than a single woman performing the same work because that's what Cunningham decided. Mary Kay Stark, a Trust coordinator at Osborn, once heard another coordinator ask Cunningham if the staff would receive a raise. "He goes,

'Well, Mary Kay doesn't need a raise, and neither do I.'" That was an exaggeration; Stark certainly could use a raise but she was too intimidated by the priest to contradict him. Stark said Cunningham "thought we were all getting out of hand."

More ominously, a few colleagues distrusted the priest. Some employees thought he was raking in the money. After all, he owned a flashy Harley-Davidson motorcycle, smoked cigars, enjoyed good scotch, and wore fine clothes, although they mostly were black suits, and if you looked closely you could tell they were well worn. Cunningham had many wealthy friends. Some employees presumed that Cunningham had inherited his dad's mansion on Boston Boulevard and a large bank account. (Actually, Father Cunningham's share of the estate was worth about $200,000.) What the disenchanted employees may not have known was that Cunningham worked as executive director of Focus: HOPE for no pay and often dipped into his own pocket to make up shortfalls in payroll.

Brown ended her memo by asking: "If we—intelligent, civil rights workers with a 10-year (or more) history of involvement in the struggle—cannot work toward a solution of our own racial problems, what business do we have crusading in the larger society under a banner of civil rights?"

While Brown took the lead in the dispute, Josaitis believed the main instigator of the racial disharmony afflicting staff in 1977 and 1978 was a former Black Panther named John LeRoy Williams. A Cincinnati native who had served in the U.S. Marine Corps in Vietnam, Williams was an intelligent, eloquent and charming man who found an outlet for his distrust of whites and the capitalist economic system—the Black Panther Party. In 1968, he said in an interview some 30 years later, the Panthers sent him to do community organizing in Detroit. But Williams said he was disappointed by the lack of fervor in Detroit where, in his view, Black Panthers were more interested in doing drugs and having sex than in revolutionary politics. To Williams, the black militant scene in Detroit was a media-hyped fraud. "Black people were more afraid of other black people than they were afraid of the quote unquote white majority," Williams told friends.

A friend suggested going to Focus: HOPE, which was hiring coordinators for the Trust project. During the interview process, Cunningham and John Staniloiu asked Williams a lot of questions about his racial attitudes. "What do these folks know about racism?" Williams said he thought to himself. Keeping his natural tendency toward sarcasm in check during the interview, Williams talked about the need for blacks to gain economic power in order to control their destinies.

Staniloiu said Williams had presented himself as "very charming, very bright, an intellectual." But, "he hid his other side. Focus: HOPE and myself were not that good on checking people's backgrounds. We probably should have put his Social Security number through the FBI and CIA to give us more of the real truth." The next day, Staniloui called Williams to say he was hired. He started working at Osborn High School with Mary Kay Stark. By then, the school's student body was less than 20 percent white. "It was a tough, hard job, and a hard sell (to the school staff)," she said. Williams often displayed behavior that came off as "militant and angry," Stark said.

In March 1977, Williams called in sick after getting stabbed in the abdomen. According to a police report of the incident, he said he was trying to break up a fight between two other people, whom he could not identify, when he was stabbed. When the police arrived, Williams was the only person left at the scene. "He was laid up and we had to replace him," Staniloiu said. "Those school jobs were 100 hours a week. We had to have someone in there immediately and he couldn't go back to work for an extended period."

After he returned to work in the late summer of 1977, Williams came to Focus: HOPE for a Project Trust meeting and announced that he had changed his name to Azizi Adisa Masai, a name he chose to emphasize his African heritage. The name means, "your friend, a warrior of the Masai nation, who makes his point known," Masai said. He said he wished to become a true Masai warrior. To be Masai, he must kill a lion and he was looking for a lion to slay.

Staniloiu saw Masai as "seething with anger" and believed that he was casing Focus: HOPE for some sort of stunt. "I told Bill we need to get rid of him, but we didn't know how," Staniloiu said. "We knew he'd take us to court, pull some shit, holler racism."

At the Trust retreat in October 1977 for Osborn student leaders, the guest speakers included Wilfred Little, the older brother of Malcolm X, an ex-convict who later joined the Nation of Islam and became an outspoken black militant. He became a martyr in 1965 when he was assassinated. Wilfred Little, however, was no radical. "Will Little was as unlike Malcolm as anyone," said Gil Maddox. "A quiet, soft-spoken person who was dedicated to the idea of change and wanted to see change take place, and who did not necessarily believe that Malcolm, his brother, had taken the correct route." As a young man, Little had worked as a machinist and knew the trade could serve as a path out of poverty for many black men and women. Little later became an executive at Michigan Bell Telephone Co.

Little's conversations with Trust kids always were soft-spoken, elegant and understated. He said people should work together and love one another. He touched their hearts and opened their minds.

When Little finished a talk, kids grabbed what they could—napkins, even—to get his autograph. Then it was Josaitis's turn to give her emotional talk. Her story about moving into the city and the sorry mess that Detroit's black children were in rankled Masai. He hated her stump speech about what racism had done to black people: Black children going hungry, black men not working, black kids growing up into killers because there was no hope.

What right did this white woman have to preach about the ills affecting black people? "*Kiss my black ass,*" Masai thought. "Damn! We might be allergic to milk, did she ever think of that? If we need baby formula, Karo syrup mixes up real well with some water." On his second retreat with Osborn students, Masai cut Josaitis off and ushered the kids to another activity.

Later, Josatis fired Masai for making a sexist remark. A few days after his firing, Masai walked back into Focus: HOPE carrying his infant son, also named Azizi, and asked Cunningham humbly for his job back. The priest relented and Masai's dismissal was reversed. Deemed unsuited for Project Trust, Masai was assigned to help Ken Kudek in the Auto Club lawsuits organizing thousands of documents and scheduling depositions of witnesses and plaintiffs. Despite getting a job back, Masai continued to pester Focus: HOPE. Masai protested the policy of mandating employees to work on the Rev. Martin Luther King Jr. birthday-holiday, by coming to work wearing a slave's coveralls and a white kerchief tied around his head. He walked around the office stooped low with a sign hanging around his neck that said, "Is Slavery Dead?"

Despite his suspicion of whites, Masai said he enjoyed the intellectual challenge of matching wits with Cunningham. He loved the philosophical arguments he shared with the priest, sometimes over scotch. Masai was fond of accusing Focus: HOPE's white staff of being inherently incapable of understanding the deep effects of racism on people of color. The whole organization, Masai thought, was just shy of being a bunch of poverty pimps.

One night, Masai, Kudek and Gary Faria, who was then in law school, got roaring drunk in Kudek's apartment. Faria's home in Detroit had been broken into several times but he refused to get a gun for protection. Masai claimed a measure of expertise in the matter of guns and suggested that Faria should just go out and shoot one "like a man." Masai even offered to show Faria how to fire it. About an hour and several rum-and-cokes later, however, Masai came to his senses: "Wait a minute! What the hell am I doing teaching a honky to shoot?"

Father Cunningham surveys the mess left by a 1978 fire.

Credit: Pat Beck/*Detroit Free Press*

14

Person of Interest

FATHER CUNNINGHAM HAD not been sleeping long when fire truck sirens snapped him awake. He pulled his leather motorcycle jacket over his black T-shirt. Then, fear in his eyes and his chest heaving, he ran 200 yards west down Oakman Boulevard, each step bringing him closer to the realization that Focus: HOPE's headquarters was engulfed in hot smoke.

He stopped abruptly, standing in shock at the sight of smoke billowing through a broken second-floor window. He saw firefighters pry open the building's roll-up security steel doors and drag hoses inside to douse the flames and save the structure. After the fire was knocked down, an assistant fire chief told Cunningham that the inside was a mess, but the building was salvageable. A delay of another 15 minutes in reporting the fire might have meant a total loss of the building. Garfield Jones, a security guard at the Ex-Cell-O plant across the street, had seen smoke coming from the roof of the Focus: HOPE building and called 911 at 3:12 a.m. Cunningham sought Jones out and bear-hugged him, thanking him over and over.

Then, the priest hurried back to the Madonna rectory and called Eleanor Josaitis. "The pain in Bill's voice" lingered in her mind, she said. She brewed some coffee and filled thermoses while waiting for Tony Campbell to pick her up. They got to Focus: HOPE around 5 a.m. Focus: HOPE's headquarters and its contents were a soggy, sooty mess. Josaitis found Cunningham and embraced him. "Let's pray," he said.

At daybreak, investigators were sifting through debris, fishing in ashes for evidence, taking pictures and making observations for several hours. The two lead detectives were Marv Monroe, a veteran Detroit Fire Department arson investigator, and Lloyd Eagle from the Police Department's armed robbery unit. They had recently become partners on a joint task force fighting a growing number of arsons in the city. In many cases the suspect turned out to be whoever would benefit from the insurance policy. Selling commercial and residential real estate in Detroit had become more difficult and some owners found it easier to have their building burned, collect the insurance and walk away.

Monroe scanned the charred scene with his trained eye and described evidence to Eagle who took notes and learned. Monroe explained that the undersides of shelving that held reams of paper had burned before the tops, indicating that the fire had risen from the floor. Monroe also observed six distinct locations where flames ignited. He guessed that the initial fires had burned for about three hours before the security guard called 911. "Christ, this thing is arson," Monroe told Eagle. "You tell me its arson, I'll get the guy," Eagle responded.

When they were finished, they let the crew from Focus: HOPE inside—Cunningham, Josaitis, Campbell, Thom Armstead, Charlie Grenville, Dave Klapp, and others who had arrived for work only to find a disaster. While the rest looked for things to salvage, Josaitis grabbed a broom and started sweeping the mess out. Campbell, the organization's finance director, had been working late the night before preparing for an audit, and he'd left Focus: HOPE's general ledger book open on his desk. People from the Arthur Anderson accounting firm were expected at Focus: HOPE that morning, October 16, 1978. The audit would not begin that day.

The detectives took Focus: HOPE staff members aside for some questions before approaching Cunningham, who was thinking that the fire had been caused by faulty wiring in the hastily refurbished building. They met him in a secluded area and decided to lay out what they knew so far in their investigation. As Monroe spoke, Eagle watched the priest for reactions. He told Cunningham that it looked like someone had deliberately set the building on fire. Monroe said there was no sign of a break-in, so whoever did it must have had a key.

Who would have a motive to try to burn the place down? Having spoken to several staff members, Monroe already knew that in the past four years, Focus: HOPE had received millions in federal grants, as well as hundreds of thousands of dollars from foundations and private donors. That's a lot of money to be accounted for, he told Cunningham. Someone at any struggling nonprofit organization might have a reason to destroy records, especially when facing an audit.

"What are you trying to say?" Cunningham asked, according to Monroe, who said years later that he had a good memory of the interview. "We just found out you were supposed to be audited this morning," Monroe told him. "Your books were out on the desk."

"What does that mean?" Cunningham looked sharply at Monroe. "That means you have the right to remain silent, anything you say can be used against you in a court of law," Monroe said. When he started to tick off the rest of the standard Miranda warnings, Cunningham interrupted. "You don't think I did it?" "Wait until I finish with your rights," Monroe told him.

As Monroe continued with the required warnings, Eagle watched the priest closely. Both detectives saw Cunningham grow angrier as he realized the implications of what had happened to Focus: HOPE. Monroe said Cunningham looked like he "wanted to punch me in the nose." He forcefully denied knowing anything about the arson. Monroe said he'd probably have to take a lie detector test.

Then Monroe asked if there was anyone on the Focus: HOPE staff who might have a reason to do it? Cunningham said he didn't think so, then turned away from the detectives, made a quick decision, and strode into the smoky and waterlogged conference room where Josaitis was organizing the cleanup. Everyone hushed as Cunningham approached. His eyes blazing, Cunningham told his staff that someone had tried to burn down Focus: HOPE. His voice was pained, but he spoke in a confident tone. Monroe, who had followed the priest into the room, said Cunningham "was a hot ticket; there were a lot of people gasping." Sensing the staff's shock and despair, Cunningham used his anger to rally them. "We're going to rebuild this damn place," he said.

He then introduced the two detectives and said they were going to find out who was responsible. "Everybody's going to take a lie detector test," the priest declared. Eagle, a tall, thickly built American Indian with a no-nonsense demeanor, put a heavy hand on Cunningham's shoulder. "Wait a minute," Eagle said. "We'll decide who's going to take a polygraph."

As Cunningham mulled over who hated Focus: HOPE enough to burn it down, he kept coming up with only one answer: The Automobile Club of Michigan. The two federal class action lawsuits accusing the Auto Club of discriminating against its employees on the basis of race and sex were nearing a climax after years of litigation. By late 1978 Focus: HOPE had won a series of pre-trial motions, and appeared to have the upper hand. Was it a coincidence that the Resource Center fire broke out almost exactly a year after the Auto Club had been fined $52,000 by a federal judge for misconduct in its dealing with Focus: HOPE? The Auto Club was appealing and still hadn't paid the fine.

Cunningham was convinced that the Auto Club had hired someone to set the fire. "Thommy," he told Armstead, "I know it was those sons of guns."

At one point, there was a tentative offer from the Auto Club for a nominal amount of money in return for a pledge to hire more black people. But Cunningham refused to settle unless the insurer admitted its guilt in a public way and took affirmative action to help those impacted by its racist and sexist policies. Cunningham was skeptical of the company's sincerity. If the way its lawyers behaved was any indication, Cunningham believed, the Auto Club was determined to win the case and put Focus: HOPE out of business whatever the cost.

Monroe and Eagle discussed Cunningham's conspiracy theory. "You can't go off on tangents," Monroe instructed Eagle. "You write them down, but you go with the obvious. If you don't, you get buried in speculation and you can actually destroy your own case if you don't pursue the obvious avenues."

With arsons at businesses, an investigator has to consider whether the owner was in financial distress. Another possibility could be a disgruntled employee, someone with a personal motive to hurt the organization. It didn't take the detectives long to identify a serious rift at Focus: HOPE that had been simmering for more than a year.

Problems at Project Trust mounted, including funding shortfalls and restive coordinators working at nearly a dozen disparate schools. Several Trust coordinators either quit, were fired or transferred to another department because of budget issues.

In July 1978, Masai sent a memo to Kudek: "I am demanding to be formally laid off from Focus: HOPE due to the fact that adequate funds have not and currently are not available for past services rendered. I expect the effective date to be 7/7/78; the last full day worked."

A layoff would allow Masai to collect unemployment checks, and Kudek refused. Masai threatened to file a complaint with the Michigan Office of Equal Employment Opportunity (EEOC) charging arbitrary and subjective disciplinary actions. He claimed he would expose the "misfeasance and malfeasance of the Executive Director [Cunningham] and the Associate Director [Josaitis] of Focus: HOPE with no pending disciplinary actions for deliberate program overspending."

If Masai's allegations became public, it could seriously damage Focus: HOPE's carefully nurtured public image and threaten fundraising. The EEOC complaint was settled relatively quickly.

Masai and Focus: HOPE signed an agreement on October 10, 1978—less than a week before the arson fire—in which Masai agreed not to sue under the 1964 Civil Rights Act. Focus: HOPE agreed to adopt within 90 days a written personnel policy governing grounds for discipline, a grievance procedure, a job performance evaluation process, a standard vacation policy and "statement of goals for Affirmative Action at all levels of the organization."

Although Masai got no money and no admission by Focus: HOPE that he had been mistreated, he counted the dispute as a victory. Masai's claim for unemployment benefits still was pending before the Michigan Employment Security Commission.

Whoever torched the Focus: HOPE Resource Center must have had a key, the arson detectives kept reminding Cunningham. Yes, Masai had left under difficult circumstances in July, Cunningham told them. But Focus: HOPE had changed all the locks after he left. Curiously, Cunningham said, he had found a key broken in one of the new door locks in August. New keys had been distributed to just 13 Focus: HOPE employees and the detectives carefully questioned each. None would admit that he or she had given anyone a key to Focus: HOPE.

In typical arson investigations involving businesses, police protocol called for a polygraph test for the top management team or owners. Many confessions are taken from suspects frightened by the thought that they might not be able to hide their guilt from the machine. And when people passed their lie detector tests, detectives use that fact as leverage with the prime suspect, suggesting that he or she should take one, too. If the suspect refuses, you've probably found the culprit.

Monroe respected polygraph examiner Chet Romatowski of the Michigan State Police. The tall, professorial-looking Romatowski was the son of immigrant Polish Catholics, a man steeped in respect for the Church.

From reading the newspapers, Romatowski knew about Focus: HOPE feeding the poor in Detroit and of Father Cunningham's reputation as a high-profile, motorcycle-riding, long-haired priest; a liberal who preached about racism and white guilt. But Romatowski was not in awe of Catholic priests, having administered polygraph tests to a handful of priests over the past several years. In the case of the "Oakland County child killer" who kidnapped and murdered at least four children, Romatowski gave a lie detector test to a priest from Farmington suspected of having a fondness for altar boys. When he sat for the test with Romatowski, the priest broke down and confessed that he had molested several children. But the priest denied he had ever killed anyone and the lines on Romatowski's graphs showed the pedophile priest was telling the truth.

When Cunningham arrived for his lie detector test, he shook hands with Romatowski who purposely called him Bill, instead of Father. The examiner tried to impress the priest with the invincibility of the polygraph. Subjects have to believe in the test in order for it to work. "I could fool you and you could fool other people," Romatowski said. "There's one person that you cannot fool and that's yourself. You know whether you're telling a very significant falsehood."

In a typical polygraph test of the time, pnuemograph tubes were stretched across the top and bottom of the subject's chest to monitor subtle changes in breathing, heart rate, temperature and perspiration. The examiner got normal readings through a series of "easy" questions to set a base level, such as "Do you live in Michigan?" "Nobody can beat the test," Romatowski said. "But they try."

"Well, I don't lie," Cunningham said.

"That's fine. But if you set this fire, I'm here to find out," Romatowski said.

Romatowski read Cunningham his Miranda rights warnings one more time. "You have the right to remain silent. Do you understand that?"

"That means I don't have to say anything," Cunningham said.

"Good."

After many more questions, Romatowski finally got to what it was all about.

"Do you know who set the fire?"

"No, wouldn't be here if I did."

Truth.

Finished with the questions and certain that Cunningham had nothing to do with the arson, Romatowski thanked the priest. "Well, Father, in my opinion you're telling the truth." It was the first time Romatowski called him "Father."

Cunningham was impressed with Romatowski. The priest was invited to speak before various law enforcement groups and promoted polygraph tests. He even helped Romatowski lobby Lansing against legislation that would restrict their use in employment situations.

Tony Campbell and Gil Maddox were next on the polygraph parade. Campbell's test came the day after Cunningham's, and Maddox's was taken on Nov. 2. Each took half a day to complete the test and both passed.

With Cunningham and other managers cleared, the insurance company finally agreed to pay Focus: HOPE's claim. The company's initial settlement offer of about $30,000 was paltry and wouldn't begin to repair the damage, Cunningham said. He fought loud battles over the telephone and in person until he browbeat the insurance company into forking over $150,000, which enabled Focus: HOPE to refurbish the entire structure, including building a mezzanine above the main second-floor area.

During the drawn-out investigation, Monroe and Eagle often stopped by the Focus: HOPE Resource Center after work to talk with Cunningham and Josaitis over a scotch. One day, Josaitis mentioned that her sister Margaret Kruger was a psychic. Josaitis said her sister could come to the Resource Center and give her impressions to the detectives. Monroe's experience with psychics had been positive and he convinced the skeptical Eagle to at least talk to the woman. Their unit commander was against it, but Monroe and Eagle arranged to do it on their own time. Cunningham went ballistic when he heard about it. "You're not holding a goddamn séance in my building!" he yelled. "Why don't you join us, Father?" Monroe asked. "I'll lose my parish! I'll lose everything!" Cunningham relented but he refused to be present when Kruger walked through the place.

It was after dark when Kruger met the detectives. As they approached the Resource Center, she grew nervous and upset. The lights were off and the detectives used their flashlights as they fumbled with the keys that Cunningham had lent them. Both detectives were taken with Kruger's beauty and, well, her sexiness. "She can't be psychic," Eagle whispered to Monroe. "If she knew what I was thinking right now, she'd slap my face." They started walking back to where the print shop had been and the fire had been set. Suddenly, Kruger started shaking uncontrollably. She gasped for breath and the detectives had to help her out of the building. They went for a cup of coffee at a diner on Woodward Avenue and Kruger spoke expansively as Monroe jotted on a napkin, notes that he later typed up for the file.

"It's a black man," Kruger told them. She described a man in his mid- to late-20s, tall and thin. She said the man was wearing a "very colorful rag around his head. He's got a long stick. It looks like there's a rag on the stick and the rag's on fire. He's walking around in a big room, touching it down all over the room. There's anger. I can feel the anger. That's all I can tell you."

Monroe and Eagle looked at each other, amazed at how close she came to describing what they believed happened as shown by the evidence. Monroe later told Cunningham about Kruger's psychic impressions and asked if he knew a black male of that age and build, someone who was very angry. Cunningham said that Focus: HOPE had fired a guy who matched the description.

The detectives went looking for Masai. They found him working at a low-wattage radio station run by one of Detroit's best-known black separatists, the Rev. Albert Cleage, a founder of the Christian Shrine of the Black Madonna. Masai's office was decorated in African style: zebra skins on the walls, carved wooden lions, romantic prints of an African warrior's life. He wore a *dashiki* and a cap replete with the colors associated with black power in Africa: red, green and black. As the detectives introduced themselves, Masai immediately became defensive. Monroe asked questions that sounded to Masai more like accusations. He told them to "go see Eleanor Josaitis and Bill Cunningham about that fire."

Monroe told Masai that Cunningham and others already had passed a lie detector test and asked if he would voluntarily take one, too. When Masai said, sure he would, Monroe was surprised. They made arrangements for the next morning, December 12. Masai said in an interview years later that he "figured the police have to investigate everybody." But he didn't like being "pictured as this crazy radical just because I attended church at the Shrine of the Black Madonna."

Just as they had done with Cunningham, Monroe and Eagle picked Masai up early in an unmarked police car. On the way out to Northville, Masai kept up a nonstop patter about educating, empowering and organizing black people for the struggle against the whites in power. At the post, Romatowski went through the usual orientation procedure with Masai who kept interrupting. "I didn't do it," Masai told Romatowski. In over 40 years of experience, Romatowski had gotten nearly 1,000 people to confess to crimes through the process of preparing for or taking a lie detector test. But not this time. Masai had copped an attitude of noncooperation.

"Do you live in Michigan?" Romatowski asked in one of the baseline questions.

"No, Canada," Masai said. "Use that to set your gauges."

Masai's sarcastic responses were throwing off any ability to test the veracity of his statements. After more than a half-hour, Romatowski called a halt to it, concluding that Masai "was deliberately attempting to distort the polygrams to prevent a definite analysis to be made," according to his police report. "However, there are sufficient emotional responses to show deception," he wrote in the report. "Therefore, it is this examiner's continued opinion that Azizi Adisa Masai is not being truthful to the pertinent test questions."

Later, Monroe asked Romatowski for his impression of Masai. "This guy is more like a soldier than a criminal," Romatowski said. "If he did it, it wasn't for profit. He could have done it for a cause. This is a guy who's on a mission."

A failed polygraph exam is virtually never allowed as evidence in a criminal trial. The detectives could not get any of the 13 people known to have keys to Focus: HOPE to admit lending out a key, although they suspected one of them had. Without being able to put a key to the Focus: HOPE Resource Center in the arsonist's hand, the detectives basically had no case to present to the Wayne County Prosecutor's Office. They were stumped.

But Masai wasn't done with Focus: HOPE. In June 1979, he saw a newspaper article on the Auto Club sex discrimination lawsuit going to trial and called the reporter, Martha Hindes of *The Detroit News*. Masai gave her a story that ran on the front page on July 8, headlined: "Rights unit hit by bias complaint." Hindes reported that even as Focus: HOPE was fighting the Auto Club on allegations of race and sex discrimination the organization "was itself charged a year ago with discrimination against blacks on its payroll. ... The whole episode escaped the attention of the media, which had given supportive coverage of Focus: HOPE's 11-year crusade for racial brotherhood. Now the complaint of discrimination inside Focus: HOPE has been revealed, by Masai."

Hindes had called Cunningham for a response and the priest reacted angrily. "If he's really interested in civil rights, why would he bring up something like this now, when the Auto Club is at trial?" Cunningham asked. Hindes' follow-up report suggested that Cunningham's image as a rebellious, motorcycle-riding cleric with long hair was an act designed to attract media attention. She wrote that "some" called Cunningham "Father Chutzpah" and that his following was mainly "affluent white liberals—the type who refused to move from Detroit after the riot when everyone else was running, and who made sure they mentioned this wherever they went."

Cunningham's anger at the *News* was deep—he always preferred the liberal paper, the *Detroit Free Press*, where his friend Neal Shine was an editor. "I think Eleanor and Bill were really, really hurt by the article," Thom Armstead said. Cunningham called for a meeting with Bill Giles, the cantankerous executive editor of the *News*. The priest marched into Giles' office and demanded a retraction. Giles countered that the accusation had been made in an official manner and was fair game for news coverage. Besides, wasn't it true that many blacks had recently quit their jobs at Focus: HOPE? Giles asked.

Cunningham admitted that, yes, black employees had been leaving his organization but only because they were being offered more money than Focus: HOPE could pay them. He said Hindes' article was unfair and had a negative tone. Why didn't the *News* look into Masai's background and see what's really going on here?

Giles told Cunningham that he stood by his reporter and that no one, not even Father Cunningham, was going to tell him how to run a newspaper. That's when things became heated. Giles, Armstead said, called security to his office to escort them out, making Cunningham even madder. "Wow, Bill lit into his ass! Goddamn!" Armstead said. "Eleanor was so apologetic. They ran [Cunningham] out of there and Eleanor was apologizing all the way out the door. And, Bill was so damn mad that she was apologizing. He ripped her—'What the hell are you apologizing for?'"

Cunningham had coffee with Shine a few days later, according to a "Muddling Thru" column the priest wrote. Shine said he'd warned Cunningham. "I told you eight years ago when you took the AAA to court over the move to Dearborn that you were playing hardball. ... You've got to expect this kind of stuff," Shine told the priest. Cunningham said Giles' defense of the stories was hypocritical, given that several female employees had recently filed a lawsuit against the newspaper for alleged sex discrimination. He noted that *The Detroit News* had moved its printing operations from downtown Detroit to Sterling Heights—a suburb often called "Sterling White." And, in late 1979, the *News* was embarrassed by the leaking of a memo from one of its editors, Mike McCormick, which told reporters to find stories targeted at readers who are 28 to 40 years old, making at least $18,000 a year and who live in the suburbs. Such stories "should be obvious; they don't have a damn thing to do with Detroit and its internal problems," McCormick's memo said.

Focus: HOPE's top leaders held several meetings to discuss what to do. Armstead and Ken Kudek began work on an employee handbook, and Cunningham wrote another piece for a "Focus: HOPE Special Report" newsletter in which he defended the organization's record on relations with black employees. "FOR THE RECORD: At the time of my writing there are 54 black employees full time at Focus: HOPE and 24 white employees," Cunningham wrote. "Focus: HOPE Administration at the time of the charges consisted of one white male, two black males and one white female. The annual average salary of the two black administrators was $23,500. The one white female administrator received $18,000. The white director received no salary and no expenses." The white director, obviously, was Cunningham himself.

In September 1979, Masai got bad news from the Michigan Employment Security Commission. The MESC found that he was trying to scam the unemployment system and that he had lied when he applied for unemployment. He had found a job within two months at New Detroit at a higher rate of pay. Masai was assessed a penalty of a six-week disqualification period for lying about his job status, and he was forced to refund the $472 in unemployment checks to the state.

Masai later worked as an administrative aide to Detroit City Council President Erma Henderson and in the Washington office of Congressman John Conyers. By 1998, Masai was counseling unemployed people at the Detroit Jobs Commission, referring many clients to Focus: HOPE's Fast Track and Machinist Training Institute.

"I still call him one of my mentors," Masai said of Cunningham. "If I hadn't worked with Bill Cunningham and hadn't gone through the things he took me through, the training on how to cope with shit, I'd never had worked for City Council. I'd never had worked in Congress. A lot of that came from Bill. He taught me how to stand up to them."

Gary Faria, who completed law school, left Focus: HOPE and became a corporate attorney, ran into Masai at the Pretzel Bowl bar in Highland Park a few years after the fire. "He immediately started going into this monologue about the fire," Faria said. "He was complaining how people hassled him about the fire."

"They all thought I did it," Masai told Faria.

In an interview, Masai said he is proud of what he did at Focus: HOPE and to Focus: HOPE. "We went toe-to-toe and they lost so much money during the EEOC case," Masai said. "When it hit the newspapers, they really lost money." Masai believed he accomplished his mission to become a true African warrior.

"Focus: HOPE, I always say, was the lion I slew."

Father Cunningham and architect Dario Bonucci in 1977 at the State
Fairground amphitheater at the end of the Focus: HOPE annual Walk.

Credit: Focus: HOPE

15

Still Here

THE CROWD ATTENDING a Focus: HOPE Christmas
folk-music spectacular at the Raven Gallery in Southfield was
momentarily stunned into silence when, during a barnburner of
a speech, Father Bill Cunningham dropped the F-bomb. Then,
they erupted in laughter and applause.

"I was floored," said folk singer Charlie Latimer. "Everybody is stunned, just stunned. But it was OK because it was Bill."
With the crowd still applauding, Cunningham walked off the
stage and took a staircase upstairs to "chill" a bit in the green
room, Latimer said. "He walks in the dressing room and I'm
standing there, and I said, 'Nice set, Bill!' It was all I could think
to say." Cunningham laughed hard. The audience may have
been stunned, Latimer said, "but they sure did cheer him on,
believe me."

It was a momentary slip for a man careful of his reputation as
a Catholic priest; albeit one quite comfortable using "goddamn"
and "bullshit." But he certainly showed how fired-up he could
get when his sense of justice was outraged. Not surprisingly, on
this particular occasion, his ire was directed at the Automobile

Club of Michigan. He still believed the insurance company was behind the arson at Focus: HOPE's Resource Center, although no evidence of that was ever found.

Temporarily ensconced in the Madonna rectory after the fire, Cunningham, Eleanor Josaitis and Dario Bonucchi were taking calls from people wondering if Focus: HOPE was still functioning. Bonucchi, the architect and folk music impresario who was Focus: HOPE's most active volunteer, took to answering the question: "We're still here!" Others picked it up and the phrase became a rallying cry for Focus: HOPE—a sign that they weren't going to let a cowardly arsonist slow them down.

Most of the staff was relocated to the Focus: HOPE warehouse on East Davison, but Cunningham and Josaitis wanted to make a statement by using their desks at the Resource Center, even as refurbishing was underway. They were soon busy with another crisis that came on December 13. The U.S. Department of Agriculture issued a recall of 6,000 cases of spoiled infant formula that had been distributed by Focus: HOPE. Seven infants in Detroit and dozens nationwide developed severe diarrhea after ingesting the formula.

Josaitis organized a rapid response, mobilizing dozens of staff and volunteers to contact thousands of families that had received the tainted formula. She and Cunningham got help from several local businesses, including the Ex-Cell-O Corporation, which loaned Focus: HOPE 20 office telephone lines in its building across the street for volunteers to use. Michigan Bell installed an extra 30 temporary phone lines at the Focus: HOPE's Food Prescription Program building to be manned by volunteers. Xerox donated copy machines to help with the extraordinary effort. "Our theory is that it takes a long time to build any kind of trust in the community and we are going to be more concerned than we have to be with this," Josaitis told a reporter.

For several weeks that winter, Bonucchi had been ill. He spoke of stomach upset, and began gobbling Tums antacid tablets by the handful. On Saturday March 3, 1979, he managed to take in Phil Marcus Esser's new production, *Vanities*, at Vittorio's in Livonia, and then caught a set performed by another friend, Ron Coden, at the Railroad Crossing on East Eight Mile Road in Detroit. Bonucchi spent Sunday afternoon at Eleanor and Don Josaitis' home. Typically, Dario didn't complain about his health, but that afternoon he told Eleanor that his chest felt heavy. Bonucchi returned to his home—a three-room carriage house apartment in Grosse Pointe—but soon telephoned Josaitis to say he wasn't feeling well. She asked if she should come over. "Yeah," he said. The phone went quiet, but he had not hung up. She and her husband Don rushed over and found Bonucchi slumped on his desk, the phone off the hook. He was dead of a massive heart attack, four days before his 46th birthday.

"Dario couldn't sing and he couldn't play the guitar but he brought more music to Detroit than anyone else," Coden told the *Free Press* for an obituary. "We know of no one who has given more of himself with such energy to the cause of justice in this city," Cunningham said. At his funeral at Madonna church that Thursday—Bonucchi's birthday—Cunningham noted that the architect had designed the layout of Focus: HOPE's Resource Center when the building was purchased in 1975 and had been working on plans to refurbish it after the fire. Cunningham pointed to the church's new stained-glass window depicting a large candle and compared Bonucchi to "a candle who brought light into people's lives, showed us the way and whose spirit had kindled a hundred good projects."

"I think the loss of Dario really broke his heart," Latimer said of Cunningham. Wanting to memorialize Bonucchi in a lasting way, Josaitis decided to adjust the date of the founding of Focus: HOPE—from March 6, 1968, when Cunningham and Father Fraser gathered a large group of priests and lay activists at Sacred Heart Seminary to March 8, 1968, Dario's birthday.

Bonucchi had been working on organizing Focus: HOPE's biggest music festival to date at the Music Hall performance center in downtown Detroit. Esser and others stepped up to finish preparations for the show scheduled for April 23 and given the title *We're Still Here* by Dario's folkie friends. Besides Latimer, Coden and Esser, performers included Ortheia Barnes, Barbara

Bredius, Mary Ann Pacquette, Pamela Smith, Josh White Jr., Pete Hendricks, Dean Rutledge, Scott McCue and the St. James Missionary Baptist Church choir. Eleanor Josaitis took the mic and told the audience that she was certain that by the following weekend, "Dario would have a folk festival organized in heaven."

"There was such a love for Dario. Some people you just really embrace right away," Ortheia Barnes said. "Dario had that kind of character and warmth about him. So we were endeared to him and yet very hurt [when he died], yet encouraged that we knew Dario would want us to continue this legacy and not let it go. What had been created by him must live on—we're still here."

Josh White called Bonucchi "an honest, sincere person with a goal to help someone else. You feel that. You felt that from him. You felt it from Cunningham. There was no ulterior motive, nothing in back of what they're doing except for those who don't have it as good."

In May 1979, the long-awaited trial for one of two class action lawsuits brought against the Automobile Club of Michigan by Focus: HOPE was about to begin. Evidence uncovered by Ken Kudek and Gary Faria, combined with the work of diligent lawyers Jane Burgess and Marilyn Mosier proved a pattern of discrimination at the insurance company not only against blacks, but also against women. Sex discrimination was added to the allegations against the Auto Club by Focus: HOPE-assisted attorneys.

In 1975, U.S. District Court Judge Charles Joiner ruled that the six African-American women plaintiffs could represent a class of black employees or a class of women employees, but not both in the same case. A separate class action lawsuit alleging sex discrimination against 7,000 women was then filed against the Auto Club. That case was assigned to U.S. District Court Judge John Feikens, with both sides agreeing to forgo a jury. The race discrimination case before Joiner was delayed several times by the Auto Club's appeals of the judge's rulings, including one unsuccessful appeal to the U.S. Supreme Court.

Testimony for the trial in the sex discrimination case began on May 15. One of the first witnesses at trial was plaintiff Carolyn Madden Hall, who said she was hired by the Auto Club as a clerk in 1965 at salary of $59 a week. For 10 years, Hall said, she tried to get a position as a computer operator without success. After she filed a civil rights complaint, she was given what she called a "dead end" computer librarian job. She left the insurance company in 1976 and eventually got a job developing computer systems with Northern Telecom Systems, Inc. in Southfield. Another plaintiff lost her job because of the Auto Club's policy on maternity leave—there wasn't any. Like other women working at the Auto Club, she had to quit and then re-apply. She was rehired later at a wage level two grades below what she'd had before pregnancy.

In 1978, 65.5 percent of the Auto Club's employees were women, but many of the women complained that they were systematically denied a chance to get better-paying professional, technical and sales jobs, as well as supervisory positions, in the company. When women were placed in professional areas they still were paid significantly less than men doing the same job, according to an analysis of payroll records by Mark Killingsworth, a professor of labor economics at Rutgers University.

When the trial opened, there was extraordinary tension in the courtroom, according to Helen Fogel, a *Free Press* reporter. Fogel wrote that in cross-examining Hall, Auto Club lawyer Joseph A. Sullivan wryly suggested that the lawsuit was just a "tactical device" in the long-running and very public battle between Focus: HOPE and the Auto Club. "I suggest to you that you are completely wrong," Hall responded angrily, according to Fogel. "This is for me. This is for the injustices I suffer." Fogel ended her May 29 report with a quote from an anonymous "seasoned courtroom observer:" "The tension in this case is just terrible. They are all so angry, so angry. You can feel it every time they speak."

One should clarify the distinction between Joseph A. Sullivan, a former Wayne County Circuit Court judge and one of the Auto Club's attorneys, and another lawyer with a similar name,

Joseph B. Sullivan, who became Focus: HOPE's Board Chair after the death of Dario Bonucchi. The two Joe Sullivans, who attended the University of Detroit at the same time, are related only by marriage. Joe B. Sullivan married Joe A. Sullivan's sister Mary who, obviously, didn't have to change her last name. Mary and Joe B. Sullivan were far more liberal than Joseph A. Sullivan. They lived in the Sherwood Forest neighborhood across the street from the Josaitises, and were fervid supporters of Cunningham and Focus: HOPE. Joseph A. Sullivan, on the other hand, was a fierce competitor who believed that Cunningham was full of baloney and Kudek had acted unethically and possibly illegally while investigating the company.

Killingsworth, who also had testified the previous year in a more celebrated sex discrimination case against *The New York Times*, said there was a "substantial" difference in pay between female and male employees of the Auto Club—a difference of between 30 and 55 percent, or about $12,000 a year on average. "One should not draw any hasty conclusions from the testimony given thus far," Joseph A. Sullivan cautioned *Free Press* reporter Tim Kiska in August. "We fully expect that conclusion to be refuted by our experts in the field."

In an 87-page opinion released on February 15, 1980, Judge Feikens found the Auto Club guilty of discrimination against its female clerical workers in two forms—"impact" and "treatment." Answering the notion that Focus: HOPE was not a party in the case and had no business standing up for women not in its employ, Feikens said: "In the open society in which American ideas and ideals best flourish, there must always be room for advocates, private attorneys general who seek to implement these rules of law."

The evening of the big win Josaitis called Mary Sullivan offering to mitigate any hard feelings between her and her brother, Joseph A. Sullivan. "He's never forgiven Cunningham," Mary Sullivan said in 1998 of her brother. "He's bitter about it to this very day. When Joe loses a lawsuit, he never forgives the other side." Her husband added that his brother-in-law "never forgets and never forgives."

But the case was far from over, as the Auto Club appealed and dragged its feet on following Feikens' orders. For the next 16 months, attorneys representing the women—primarily Jane Burgess and Marilyn Mosier—successfully fought the appeal, and then negotiated a settlement with the company, culminating in a press conference on July 30, 1981. The Auto Club agreed to immediately deposit $3.5 million into an account jointly controlled by the company and Focus: HOPE and from which the 7,000 women—past and present employees, and job applicants—could be paid compensation for the discrimination they had endured.

"This is the finest affirmative action program for women in the United States," Cunningham boasted at the news conference. "This commitment of the Automobile Club will make them a model for other corporations in Detroit and across the nation. ... There are rumors around the country that civil rights is dead. But this is an indication of how wrong those rumors are." The settlement—in which the Auto Club did not admit wrongdoing or discriminatory practices—called for a court-monitored affirmative action program in which women would receive two-thirds of all professional, technical and unit managerial openings; 35 to 60 percent of all managerial openings, 42 to 48 percent for all commissioned sales openings, and 20 to 25 percent of all top management openings.

Sadly, Burgess was unable to attend the press conference. She'd been diagnosed with a brain tumor in early 1980 and suffered a stroke. Mosier, too, was diagnosed with cancer in February 1981, but continued working on the case. Despite both women suffering ultimately fatal illnesses, they fought hard—and they won. To attend the news conference, Mosier left a hospital bed where she was undergoing chemotherapy. "They've given six years of their career and sacrificed their health to fight for justice," Cunningham said, "his voice full of emotion," according to *The Michigan Catholic* article by Thomas Ewald. "It's moving for everybody here to see Marilyn come from her hospital bed to finish this up. These two attorneys expended themselves tremendously." Cunningham also praised Kudek, saying "Ken's years of research and his sacrifice helped to win justice and equity for women and blacks at AAA."

Two of the named plaintiffs in the suit still were employed at the Auto Club, including Arquita Thomas, who told *The Detroit News* that she'd been with the company for 10 years— virtually the entire time of the litigation. "I always knew we'd win," Thomas said. "Now if AAA would just follow the judge's orders, working conditions would be improved." The settlement included $500,000 to be shared by the named plaintiffs and witnesses who testified, and $250,000 for eligible female employees whose employment was terminated for pregnancy.

The issue of costs was still unsettled, with the Auto Club strongly opposed to Focus: HOPE's claim that it was owed more than $1 million. Feikens was well aware that the case had been litigated for eight years and that the relationship between the parties and their legal teams was fraught with hard feelings. Focus: HOPE "had won against the Auto Club and then they wanted to recover costs and fees, so they hired me," said Gerald Rosen, then with Miller-Canfield, and later a federal judge.

The fight over costs continued into the fall. Cunningham insisted that his time spent on the case also be included in those costs and fees—even though the priest volunteered his time at Focus: HOPE and Rosen advised against asking to be compensated. "Cunningham felt very strongly that even though he was not paid that he should get an hourly rate for the amount of time he put into the litigation," Rosen said. "I kept trying to tell him there was no precedent for that. He wanted the money, but he was much more concerned about establishing a precedent." Rosen said he put Cunningham on the witness stand during the hearing for costs but during his testimony the priest uncharacteristically had a moment where he couldn't answer a question. "At one point, he just kind of clammed up. He lost his train of thought. He had a deer-in-the-headlights look," Rosen said. "That's a horrible feeling for a lawyer, to have a witness go dark on you like that."

When Feikens' office said the judge's opinion and order on costs was ready, Rosen hurried to the courthouse to get a copy and skipped to the last page. "I was floored by the number," Rosen said. "At the time, in terms of cost and fees under Title VII, it was the largest in history. ... Basically, we got everything we asked for except for Cunningham"—no costs awarded for his time. "I called him up. I was ecstatic and very happy about it." Cunningham seemed miffed: "What about me? Did he give me anything?" When Rosen told him no, Cunningham said: "God-damn it! Tell Feikens he owes me one." Rosen said he passed that on to the judge. "That always became a standing joke with Feikens who became a close friend and a mentor." Feikens liked Cunningham, Rosen said. "He thought he was a lovable-rogue type guy."

The new, more conciliatory approach to Focus: HOPE began when the Auto Club's board appointed Jack Avignone as president in July 1981. Avignone apparently decided to cut the insurer's losses and settle the cases with Focus: HOPE, ending a public relations nightmare for the company. At a news conference in December 1981, Cunningham made a surprise announcement—the Auto Club and Focus: HOPE also had agreed to a preliminary settlement in the race discrimination case before Judge Charles W. Joiner. That month, the Auto Club contributed an additional $4 million to another joint account to dispense to thousands of African-Americans who were discriminated against. The company had already built and occupied its new headquarters in Dearborn, but in a unique twist about $1.5 million was set aside as a "mortgage subsidy fund" for minority employees of the Auto Club to purchase homes in Dearborn and surrounding areas at lower interest rates, and to provide a low-interest loan program for employees to buy cars to drive to work.

The year 1980 contained significant milestones for Cunningham—his 50th birthday and his 25th anniversary as a Catholic priest. Harry Cook, the *Free Press* religion writer, interviewed Cunningham for a question-and-answer column for a regular front-page feature called "Q." Cook focused on Cunningham's paid job, as a Catholic priest:

Cook: "What was your vision of the priesthood 25 years ago and is that vision valid for you today?"

Cunningham: "My vision? Well, it was of a Disneyland idealism, a great drama of stepping into some awesome space of goodness to do great things. It was a combination of 12th century knighthood and a reform of the Benedictine order. Indeed, my vision has changed substantially."

"Cook: How so?"

"Cunningham: Priesthood now seems to me a matter of dealing with the problems of individuals and communities as a whole. It seems clear to me that the great, abiding problem of this country, or at least this city, is race. And I mean by that we have created a vast group of urban poor who are unemployable, who have been ruled out of the productive, consumption system. And of course, the most marvelous hypocrisy of our time is that the Church has gone hand in hand with that oppression. Why is the Church black in one place and white in another, all the same time we are praying 'that we may all be one'? Why?"

"Cook: Does the church look different to you now than in 1955?"

"Cunningham: I love the Church, but, you know, sometimes it reminds me of one of those Italian traffic policemen in Rome. They seem so preoccupied with their symphonic gestures and whistle blowing and impeccable grooming. They stand up there and wave their arms, and nobody pays a damned bit of attention to them. They just drive."

"Cook: How about the changes in the Catholic Church since the ascendancy of John Paul II? Have the reforms of the Second Vatican Council been left behind?"

"Cunningham: Well, it certainly seems like a fortress mentality that the Holy Father is featuring for us. He's strengthening definition. He is retrieving the Church from any kind of sense of adventure. The Church ought to be a place of adventure. But he's receiving a lot of support from people whom the adventurous Church developed by John XXIII threatens and makes insecure and even angry. I think these people welcome the move back behind the wall. I think the whole business of curtailing ecumenism and closing off the possibility of freedom of conscience in moral matters stems from the man himself. His whole priesthood was spent behind the Iron Curtain where, if Christianity did let its authority sag and offer freedom of conscience, the state rather than the church would form that conscience."

"Cook: Is the Vatican's recent ban on priests being involved in politics—in particular Father Robert Drinan's being barred from running for re-election to Congress—a part of that?"

"Cunningham: Sure. And it's not an unhealthy thing for us to deal with this pope. For one thing, I think he's right about Drinan and priests in politics. We don't belong in elective politics because we need to be clearly a moral light, idealistic and uncompromising. And isn't the very nature of politics making things work by compromise? What bothers me about the Drinan affair is the authoritarian way he was dealt with, by the very methods that violate the ideal of freedom which is the soul of the Church."

"Cook: But you're involved in politics."

"Cunningham: Ah, yes, but in the sense of being active *with* politicians, getting their attention, educating them as to the needs of people and working with them to get what people need."

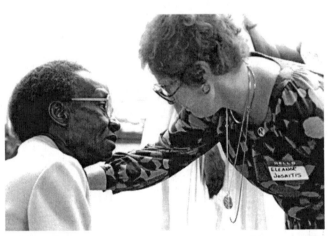

Eleanor Josaitis hears Annie Harris's story of hunger and poverty with nowhere to turn.

Credit: Focus: HOPE

16

Bad Cop

IT WAS STANDING room only at the Detroit City Council meeting in the spring of 1980 when Father Cunningham came to present a slide show about Focus: HOPE's newest idea: getting the federal government to approve expanding the Commodity Supplemental Food Program (Focus: HOPE called it the Food Prescription Program) to needy senior citizens. But the crowd, including all major news media outlets in town, was not there just to see Cunningham. Mostly they were protestors, angry about a new auto assembly plant that General Motors wanted to build in parts of Detroit and Hamtramck—cutting out a chunk of the heart of Polish culture.[25]

Cunningham and Thom Armstead arrived at the 13th floor auditorium of the City-County Building with seating for more than 200 carrying a slide projector and handouts. Cunningham

---

25   *After years of legal battles and a 29-day sit-down strike, residents lost the eminent domain argument in 1981. Some 1,300 homes, 140 business, six churches and one hospital then were demolished and 4,200 people relocated so that GM could build the Poletown plant.*

was fired up, Armstead said, and prepared to blow everyone away. Alas, he was about to lose face.

"Marianne Mahaffey gave us 15 minutes to make the presentation to the world about our senior food program," Armstead said. But, "the slide projector got stuck. We spent about 5-10 minutes trying to get it going. Finally, they said, 'OK, Father, go get the equipment fixed and you can make the presentation another time.'" Cunningham was silently steaming when WXYZ-TV Channel 7's long-time irascible political reporter Jim Harrington walked up. "Ahhhh, Father Cunningham," Harrington said. "Is Focus: HOPE out of focus today?"

"Bill was so pissed off," Armstead said. "He gave Jim Harrington a look to kill. He didn't say a word to anybody. He just told me to grab the equipment. He drove all the way back to Focus: HOPE, pissed off all the way. And he went into the video room and chewed Carl out." That would be Carl Bidleman. No one had tested the equipment before hand but it really wasn't Bidleman's fault that it failed. "But, damn! He chewed Carl's ass out," Armstead said. "Goddamn! I think that was the worse ass-chewing I'd ever seen." Bidleman, he said, took it stoically, "twisting his mustache about a dozen times" as the priest—his beloved mentor—raged.

But it was just a bump in the road. Eleanor Josaitis had gotten a call in 1978 from an elderly woman asking about getting food from Focus: HOPE. The woman, Mary Washington, "said, 'I understand you give away food,'" Josaitis said. "I just start running my big mouth about this fabulous program for pregnant women, nursing mothers and young children. When I finished bragging, that's when she screamed into the phone at me: 'I'm 72 years old and you want me to get pregnant before you help me?'" The call changed the way Josaitis thought about what Focus: HOPE was doing with the food commodities supplied by the U.S. Department of Agriculture. "She had me flat on the ground. She called me everything but a child of God."

At first, Cunningham was against it. But Josaitis wouldn't stop talking about starving seniors and finally wore the priest down, Armstead said. How hard could expanding the program to the elderly be? All they had to do was get Congress, the USDA and maybe even the President of the United States to agree to the idea— challenges that never gave Cunningham pause. Complicating their plans were a bad economy, a weakened President Jimmy Carter, and a surging, conservative, anti-big government wave of mostly white voters eager to blame the national economic malaise on high taxes and liberal policies. Cunningham knew he'd have to convince conservative Republicans.

"Bill told me once that it was much easier to get federal support from Richard Nixon than it was from Jimmy Carter," said John Ziraldo who worked in Focus: HOPE's Trust project from 1980-83. "He believed that Republicans did not have answers to social problems. They didn't have a clue and were willing to listen to Bill and Eleanor. Carter's people thought they knew what the answers were. Democrats think they can solve these problems" and, hence, had little interest in Cunningham's far-fetched ideas.

The call from Mary Washington came three years before the federal class action lawsuits against the Automobile Club of Michigan were won. To any rational mind, Focus: HOPE was in no position to take on a new cause in 1978—the nonprofit had zero reserve funds and the legal bills for the two federal lawsuits were mounting. But getting food to the destitute elderly of Detroit was important to Josaitis and Cunningham—they'd just have to figure out how to do it.

In September 1979, Focus: HOPE got $60,000 in grants from the Detroit Free Press Charities and the Ford Foundation to purchase video equipment, including cameras, microphones and editing consoles. Initially, the idea was to produce simple videos to help clients of the Food Prescription Program learn how to be creative when preparing meals using the food commodities but a new video department would soon be documenting all Focus: HOPE activities and public relations material.

Cunningham assigned Gilbert Maddox, who was then heading up Focus: HOPE's Education Department, to take responsibility for videos. Maddox was a former television talk show host and behind-the-scenes producer, but he wasn't an engineer familiar with the new Beta technology. Shooting the video, recording voice-overs and other sound, then editing it all together was a process that appeared to work. But, for some reason there were technical glitches that distorted what came out on screen. "Every time they'd go to play show-and-tell the [equipment] would not work correctly," Bidleman said. "Nobody knew how to figure it out."

Another misstep caused by their technical inexperience came during a news conference about the food program where Cunningham planned to show off new videos to help people learn about healthy living. "It was going to be a new process by which willing young people would get educated about nutrition, health and general information about the community, and it would be shown continuously while people shopped," Armstead said. But the video equipment again failed. And, Channel 7's Harrington was there to needle Cunningham. "Jim Harrington was there for the premiere of the food center video and he made a wisecrack," Armstead said. "He told Bill he was not impressed. ... The film was horrible. It was all distorted, not very well produced, and we had all these press people here reviewing this new concept. ... Gil was talking about a time-based corrector—he may not even know what it was."

Maddox suddenly resigned. "I thought Eleanor and Bill were a little naïve about the pervasiveness, the deviousness of this thing called racism," Maddox said. "I think they erroneously thought that if you bring information to people that they will see the error of their ways and they would change. ... Let's just say we had philosophical differences."

"And then Cunningham came to me," Bidleman said, "and asked, 'Do you want to take over the video department?' I said, 'Shit, yeah! Let me figure it out.' This would've all been taking place literally at the time that Dario Bonucchi died." Bidleman had no experience with video whatsoever, but took on the task with his usual aplomb. If Cunningham thought he could do it, who was Bidleman to doubt? "I basically scrambled real quick and got some engineering help to figure out how this stuff worked. I just started learning and doing." The problem with the videos was relatively easy to fix. "They were editing wrong. When it was played back the tape was all stretched and skewed." Bidleman conquered the glitches and began producing videos to be shown while people "shopped" at the food center.

Campaigning for the Republican presidential nomination at the University of Michigan-Dearborn in April, George H.W. Bush said there was a clear difference between him and his chief rival, Ronald Reagan, on social issues. "He wants the cities and states to take full responsibility for welfare payments. What he doesn't tell us is where the money would come from if state and local jurisdictions were forced to accept this responsibility," Bush told students. "In my opinion, such a proposal would bankrupt not only Michigan, Detroit, and other states, but virtually every state and major city in the nation." With polls showing Michigan in play, Bush campaigned hard and wide in the state, including a visit to Focus: HOPE and meeting Father Cunningham a week before the May primary.

In the primaries, Bush won Michigan and five other states, but withdrew after Reagan piled up an insurmountable lead, eventually carrying 44 states. Reagan won the nomination during the Republican convention in downtown Detroit in July 1979. The only drama was over his choice for vice president. Some Republicans wanted Reagan to tap former President Gerald Ford of Michigan. But Reagan chose Bush to be his running mate, a move designed to shore up support in Texas, the Midwest and the Northeast where Bush had run strong.

During the 1980 presidential campaign, Reagan mobilized what was called the Moral Majority, religious conservatives who wished to abolish abortion, strengthen the military and shrink the federal government. With the religious right's backing and the poor economy buffeting Jimmy Carter, Reagan won in a landslide that helped Republicans take control of the U.S. Senate for the first time in 28 years. Reagan's election ushered in a period of conservative dominance known as the "Reagan Revolution." "It is likely that, all by himself, Father Cunningham outnumbers the Moral Majority," wrote the *Free Press'* liberal columnist Jim Fitzgerald in January 1981, shortly before Reagan was inaugurated. "At the close of a speech given at a fundraiser, Father Cunningham talked about the old people who too often become lost. He didn't call them lambs. He called them important, and valuable, and he urged that they not be forgotten by younger people. ... Father Cunningham's voice choked as he talked, and his eyes teared. It was an emotional moment ..."

Less than a month after taking office, Reagan announced that his administration would eliminate future federal Title VII CETA funding for thousands of state and local government employees. In Detroit, that meant the loss of $28 million in federal money—funding for 1,500 jobs, including 420 police officers, 150 sanitation workers, 120 firefighters and 120 recreation department workers. Mayor Coleman Young's administrative assistant William Beckham Jr., said the city would find ways to keep the employees on the payroll, despite a $135 million deficit in the fiscal year ending that June. The Focus: HOPE team—Cunningham, Josaitis, Armstead and Charlie Grenville—recognized the new dynamic in Washington. Besides controlling the Senate, Republicans also had gained 35 seats in the House although Democrats kept their majority there. In general, Democrats were decidedly more sympathetic toward Focus: HOPE's humanitarian objectives, but Cunningham had been savvy to cultivate friends among Republicans like Vice President Bush.

Cunningham began drawing more attention from national news outlets. On April 15, 1981, *The New York Times* published an article by William Serrin (who had covered the 1967 riots for the *Free Press*) about Focus: HOPE's Food Prescription Program that was "highly praised in Detroit and by food activists across the country" because of its "creativity." Serrin described Cunningham as "an imaginative, shrewd Catholic priest." In the article, Eleanor Josaitis said Reagan's proposed budget cuts to programs serving underprivileged people as "the kind of things that are so disheartening."

Despite the political climate, Cunningham and Josaitis strategized on how to expand the CSFP to seniors. They needed a partner with credibility, experience and resources to provide compelling data. The Detroit-Wayne County Area Agency on

Aging stepped up in July 1979 and commissioned Focus: HOPE to conduct a survey, research relevant data and create a video to educate policy makers and the general public.

With the $18,400 grant, Bidleman hired Dave Gregorich, a video arts instructor at Macomb County Community College, as co-director and co-producer, and Dennis Seegars as a technical assistant. Using leads provided by the Area Agency on Aging, the crew visited elderly folks in Detroit and the enclave of Highland Park, recording seniors who subsisted on meals of oatmeal cookies and tea, yet insisting that they didn't need help. The crew taped a 74-year-old woman, Annie Harris, who was eking out her existence on an income of just $1,600 a year, barely surviving on a diet of eggs, lunch meat and bread. She'd become so hungry and depressed that she had considered suicide, an option she said she rejected because she was a Christian. While Bidleman and the video crew were at her house, Annie fainted. She was rushed to a hospital suffering from heart trouble and chronic malnutrition, all in view of a Focus: HOPE camera.

"Broken Promise" was the video's title. "It grabbed the emotion, and that's what we were trying to do, grab the emotion," Josaitis said. She contacted all the legislative aides of every member of Congress Focus: HOPE had ever met, and organized a screening of "Broken Promise" in a meeting room on Capitol Hill in Washington. "On the day that I showed it to the staffers, it was extremely moving to them," she said. "They asked a lot of questions, but they were bound and determined to do something."

A couple of weeks later, in early April 1981, the documentary was shown to the nutrition sub-committee of the House of Representatives Agriculture Committee chaired by Fred Richmond, D-New York. "Fred Richmond was so taken with the videotape showing what was going on with senior citizens that he ordered the videotape shown on the House closed-circuit network so all members of Congress could see what the needs of senior citizens were," said Roger Szemraj, then an aide to Michigan Congressman Robert Traxler. "That was really the first use of video technology in congressional testimony to get a program going."

Jeanne Findlater, general manager of WXYZ-TV, an ABC affiliate, saw the video and, despite its lack of polish, immediately wanted to air it. It was featured on Channel 7's "Kelly at Night" show on April 25, 1981 with host John Kelly. The show was expanded to a full hour for the occasion and featured a studio audience for an on-air discussion with Cunningham after the showing. The video, "rough edges and all, packs a powerful wallop," gushed *Free Press* television critic Mike Duffy. *The Detroit News* critic Ben Brown also noted the rough production style. "But the more powerful message is delivered by the seniors themselves," Brown wrote. "We see them in dank apartments and hotel rooms, in broken-down houses; the story they tell is one of deadly depression and anger." In the film Nellie Cuellar, an elderly Detroiter and member of the National Black Caucus on Aging, said: "When they no longer need you … they do you like they do racehorses … Only they don't shoot you. They starve you inch by inch."

Coordinating lobbying trips to Washington, Cunningham, Josaitis and Father Roger Morin of New Orleans created messages tailored for certain politicians. Josaitis and the two priests developed closer relationships with congressional staff, most importantly Szemraj on Traxler's staff, and J. Bennett Johnson who worked for Representative Lindy Boggs of Louisiana. Morin said it was something like the "good cop-bad cop," routine. Morin would play the good guy, and Cunningham would bring the fire. "There was a passion rooted in justice," Morin said of Cunningham. "Bill was always on. I think he played his part to the nth degree. He got their attention, the intensity of his voice and the glare in his eye." Eleanor "had an impassioned approach, a moderate approach, and she was able to balance off Father Bill."

Szemraj said Cunningham and Josaitis were formidable lobbyists. "It was always a very, very powerful team," Szemraj said. "And people were always respectful about meeting with a priest. And in some respects I think you got a little bit of the good cop-bad cop routine. Eleanor was the good cop throughout. And then Bill was there to push the hard stuff, whatever it was that had to be pushed. And, frankly, I don't think he was beyond taking advantage of his collar, to make people feel guilty because he believed he was fighting for a higher cause. I know that one of his favorite phrases throughout all the years was the fact that it was immoral that we did not do more to take care of people who needed assistance."

Congressional aides were reluctant to speak openly, but Morin said key staffers would tip them off about relevant hearings or provide intelligence about what arguments might work with a given congressman. Eleanor kept a notebook with notes on each policymaker they visited. "Eleanor carried this enormous briefcase, bigger than I'd ever seen any man or woman carry," Morin said. "She had all kinds of stuff in there. We were all carrying something, but when it came to the actual physical load I think Eleanor was carrying more than anybody else."

When lobbying, Morin spoke on behalf of the Archdiocese of New Orleans. Cunningham and Josaitis made it clear that they represented just Focus: HOPE, not the Archdiocese of Detroit. "There were all kinds of affiliated groups that were interested in terms of child nutrition issues and ways to get as much good, high-quality food to children as possible," Morin said. "They were aware of the negative outcomes of a lack of proper nutrition. Through the years, we were blessed; we met many, many people willing to help." At the end of the day, the group would meet for drinks and strategizing. "We did enjoy sitting down at the end of the day either licking our wounds or celebrating our victories for the day," said Morin.

By fortunate happenstance, Congresswoman Boggs was assigned the office next door to Traxler's and both served on the Appropriations Committee headed by legendary Congressman Jamie Lloyd Whitten of Mississippi, who would become the longest-serving member of the U.S. House of Representatives in history—until Michigan Congressman John L. Dingell passed that record in 2009. Whitten began his career in Congress in 1941 and, a southern Democrat, was a segregationist who voted against five civil rights acts in the 1950s and 1960s. But his racist leanings mellowed over time. He later apologized for his record and voted for the Civil Rights Act of 1991. Boggs and Traxler persuaded Whitten to expand the CSFP to the elderly poor. "We always had a routine with Ben Johnson and Father Morin coming to visit Lindy and Bill Cunningham and Eleanor Josaitis visiting us," said Szemraj. "And then the four of them would hook up together and go visit everyone else."

Whitten had a reputation for not supporting federal subsidies for farmers. But, Traxler and Boggs persuaded him to expand the food program through that year's Farm Bill in a subsection on "contingent appropriations," meaning that funding would be provided once the legislative authorization to create the program is achieved, Szemraj said. "The long and short of it was, we got the program approved in the Farm Bill in the House. Bob and Lindy went to Jamie Whitten and said, 'Jamie, we got this program in the Farm Bill and we want to make sure there's money to run this program as soon as it gets underway.'

"The funny thing was, Jesse Helms, then chairman of the Senate Agriculture Committee—Republicans had taken over that year—was arguing against the program, saying it's just another program, and we don't need to start up another program" Szemraj said. No transcript of the Senate hearing could be found, but according to Szemraj, Republican Senator Thad Cochran of Mississippi said: "Mr. Chairman, I don't know what all the fuss is about, but we just funded that program in the appropriations bill." "When Cochran said that, Jesse Helms dropped his opposition," Szemraj said. "That was how we got the legislation in to start the senior program."

The House approved the final legislation the week before Christmas 1981 by the closest of votes, 205-203, approving pilot projects for programs in Detroit and New Orleans. Cunningham told *The Michigan Catholic*'s Thomas Ewald that Josaitis deserved the credit. She had accomplished the near impossible through "superlative effort" the priest said. "They also voted to increase funding for the [infant] feeding program. We have a lot to be thankful for." Ewald called Josaitis "the sparkplug behind getting this program for Detroit," and wrote that Focus: HOPE's reputation for success in feeding 36,000 mothers and small children was key to getting the federal approval.

"The next step is to meet with the Agriculture Department to write up the guidelines for the program," Josaitis told Ewald. "Then the specifications have to be sent to manufacturers who will bid on filling the orders. There's also the possibility that the department might prolong getting this program going but we hope not. ... There's a new awareness of the needs of the elderly and this program will enable us to feed some hungry senior citizens, especially those who call each month begging for food."[26]

But the USDA failed to act. Cunningham, Josaitis, Grenville and Armstead went to Washington frequently to speak to members of Congress, their staffs and various officials, trying to push the USDA to get the program going. An irritated and impatient Cunningham spoke before several congressional committees, including before the Senate Special Committee on Aging on February 25, 1982: "This morning we are players in an utterly predictable scene," Cunningham began. "Our elderly poor will be described and counted. Good people will plead the cruelty of new program cuts. Then some more good people from the Department of Agriculture will say what they are supposed to say, or they will be fired. Everybody knows that. The agents of the Department carry an awful burden—not to reveal here what each knows, or should know, about hunger in America, not to say what each feels in his heart and conscience or should feel, but to defend ideological course.

"Their department—established to assure adequate and equitable production and distribution of food—is again held hostage by the Office of Management and Budget, to be used in an ideological and political standoff at the expense of its constitutional mandate. They will be loyal to this Administration, an otherwise

---

26   *In the final bill, though, a mistake was made. Only Detroit and Des Moines, Iowa, were named as sites for the pilot program. New Orleans had been left out as an earmark in the legislation. The two priests and Eleanor worked their behind-the-scenes magic and New Orleans was included later when the Agriculture Department wrote the rules.*

necessary quality in government service, at the expense of a higher moral requirement to relate facts to the well-being of the commonwealth, the service of the American people and the protection of their rights."

The Congressional Record does not describe the emotion in Cunningham's voice or the tears that welled in his eyes, but his passion came through loud and clear: "Hunger in Detroit is desperation. It is old people in restaurants ordering a cup of tea at an un-cleared table and furtively eating leftover scraps of French fries and sandwiches. ... It's 75-year-old Annie Harris, full of pride and dignity, confessing that after her last trip to the hospital for starvation, she would have killed herself if she did not believe in Jesus. Hunger in Detroit is constant worry. It's worrying whether the partial loaf of bread, the remains of jam, and the last box of macaroni and cheese will take you through three days until the Social Security check arrives. ...

"Hunger in Detroit is loneliness. It's not having anything to offer company, if there were company. Hunger in Detroit is illness, another trip to the hospital because an egg in the morning, tea and toast at noon and hot dogs at night are not enough. Hunger in Detroit is guilt. It is old people who won't tell you their children's names because they don't want to be a burden. It is the guilt of sons and daughters who have to abandon their parents because, in today's economy, they can hardly feed their own children. And hunger in Detroit is anger. ... The anger of old people is quiet despair, knowledge that the refusal of food is a final rejection, that one's fate is a lingering and lonely and fearful and disregarded wait for death."

While Cunningham's soaring speeches could move policymakers to tears, that alone would have gone nowhere without his team, principally Josaitis and Charlie Grenville. The studious and cerebral Grenville was essential to Focus: HOPE's success yet never fully recognized for his work. "Charlie was a genuinely brilliant man," said Ziraldo. "The folks at the USDA were very enamored with the results that Focus: HOPE got. When a couple of [USDA's] senior executives came to town, they took Charlie out to dinner. They said, 'we want to do this in other

cities but there's not a Focus: HOPE in other cities.'" They asked
Grenville if he could design a commodities food distribution
program for a city without a Focus: HOPE. Grenville "took out
a cocktail napkin and sketched it out for them. That's how the
USDA's WIC program came from. WIC comes after the Food
Prescription Program and scales it up. It was designed to do the
exact same thing."

In July 1982, the USDA finally agreed on rules that would
govern two pilot programs within the CSFP to distribute
food to indigent elderly people. With $480,000 in federal
funds for administrative costs available for immediate distribution, the USDA chose Focus: HOPE in Detroit as a pilot
project. Focus: HOPE was required to obtain $62,869 in match-
ing funds, excluding volunteer time and effort, to receive its
$240,000 in federal funds as well as increased shipments of food
commodities.

The funding allowed Focus: HOPE to distribute packages
of commodities that included dried milk, dehydrated potatoes,
farina, egg mix, evaporated milk, canned meat or poultry, vegetables, fruits and fruit juices, peanut butter, dry beans and cheese,
to 1,561 seniors who lived in Wayne, Oakland and Macomb
Counties every month. That's less than one percent of the eligible indigent poor elderly in the tri-county area. The funding
supported the program only for the 14-month period of August
1, 1982, to September 30, 1983. But Cunningham wanted to
show that the program would surpass expectations so that Congress would not only continue the funding, but increase it.

In an updated request to the USDA, Focus: HOPE asked for
more shipments of food commodities to allow the organization
to feed 50,000. "I think we'll get it, we just need the additional
money to operate the program," Cunningham told *The Michigan Catholic*'s Ewald. Cunningham said turning people away has
been tough on Focus: HOPE staff, and that he's had to con-
sole them spiritually in the face of such need. "The workers see
a seemingly healthy kid and his mother come in for food, but
some old folks on canes come in for food and we have to say 'no.'
They're crying at the check-out line, the workers are so upset.

But we have to preserve the integrity of the pilot program if we ever hope to do for the older folks what we're doing now for the youngsters and mothers."

Top: Machinist Training Institute (MTI) students.

Bottom: Thom Armstead, who headed up several Focus: HOPE projects, including the food program and the MTI.

Credit: Focus: HOPE

17

Industrialist

FOCUS: HOPE'S SENIOR staff was accustomed to Father Cunningham coming up with bold, innovative and expensive ideas—without explaining where the money could be found. But, this time the priest had pierced the stratosphere on his way to outer space. He wanted to buy the Ex-Cell-O factory across the street for $300,000.

In late 1980, Thom Armstead heard a rumor that Ex-Cell-O was preparing to sell its facilities on Oakman Boulevard. Armstead said he talked to the plant manager about the company donating some of its parking lot to Focus: HOPE. The manager said they might be able to work something out, adding that his boss had been talking about wanting to meet Cunningham. Coincidentally, Armstead got a call from Ken Davis, the owner of a machine shop housed in the Ex-Cell-O complex. "He said he [had] called Ex-Cell-O and he and five other businessmen were interested in buying the property and converting it into an industrial mall," Armstead said. "A number of light industrial businesses in there could support one another and take over the facility." But when Davis called Ex-Cell-O, he was told that

Focus: HOPE already owned the building, even though, Armstead said, "we hadn't even made an offer at that point."

Davis and the group of other business owners, including Braun Engineering, had been talking about buying the Ex-Cell-O buildings to bring their businesses together to lower costs and increase productivity. They figured they could share both their specialized machinery and the skilled machinists who knew how to operate them. Braun liked the idea of a "synergy" of industrial companies in an "Industry Mall." Plans were for Braun to create components, such as car manifolds, that could then be machined to precise yet variable specifications by the other companies in Industry Mall. The companies could all save money in transportation, engineering and warehousing. It was an idea Cunningham would come to embrace.

A meeting was set. "These five guys come over, and Ken Davis pulls an article out of his wallet from *The Wall Street Journal*, talking about this program down in St. Louis that's training screw machine operators very successfully," Armstead said. "All the graduates are getting hired!" Immediately, Armstead said, Cunningham "really got geeked." This was perfect—Focus: HOPE could train disadvantaged people for skilled jobs in the machining industry, creating job opportunities and supporting economic activity in Detroit.

The *Journal* article published in April 1980 said that federal CETA funds had been used in 1979 to start an automatic screw machine operator-training program in St. Louis. The 36-week apprenticeship program taught low-income people how to operate "multi-spindle automatic screw machines." The article provided a good explanation of what metalworking screw machines, sometimes called lathes or turning centers, do—making parts for everything from watches to semi-trucks. Screw machines make the mass production of industrial goods possible, and made Detroit the "Arsenal of Democracy" during World War II.

Focus: HOPE could scrape together $5,000 for a down payment, but no one—especially Cunningham—knew how they would raise the rest of the $300,000. "His dad being in the real estate business, he knew that he had to grab as much real estate as he could grab up in the area," Armstead said. As they walked to the Focus: HOPE Resource Center, Armstead said he told Cunningham that the staff was "going to commit both of us to a mental institution."

With the staff gathered around the conference table, Cunningham explained Ex-Cell-O's proposal.

"Nobody was for it," Armstead said. Gary Faria, who was working with Ken Kudek on the AAA lawsuit, said everyone but Eleanor "just told him he was nuts. We were beside ourselves. We were short on money and having difficulty keeping other stuff going, and he was gung-ho to go down this road."

Cunningham had often pondered how to create a more thriving business environment for minorities on that stretch of Oakman Boulevard. He had watched when the factory shift changed at 3 p.m. with workers rushing to get home, and regretted the lost potential. One time, Cunningham shook his head and said: "Thommy, look at those guys racing out of here to go home to Livonia and get in front of the boob tube. All that talent could be here training our guys. ... He almost had a tear in his eye."

Armstead said Ex-Cell-O's offer was something "we hadn't expected. ... We weren't looking for a 300,000-square-foot facility." Heating costs alone would be more than double than the 40,000-square-foot food center. But Ex-Cell-O kept sweetening the deal, offering to close off parts of the buildings to reduce utility costs and help Focus: HOPE find clients to rent space on the factory floor. Cunningham, Armstead said, "was salivating," about the prospect.

By 1980, a generation of skilled machinists had begun to retire or die off. The average age of skilled machinists in the United States was 55 and rising. The unglamorous trade was difficult and dirty. The work was tedious, boring and somewhat dangerous.

Most machining companies had trouble keeping skilled tradesman on the payroll because they knew they could always find a job somewhere else. When company owners and factory managers considered whether and when to upgrade equipment like screw machines, the decision often boiled down to whether someone qualified could be found to run them. They knew that if they trained someone to operate the newer machine, a competitor would likely come along and poach that employee. Some companies found it cheaper to hire skilled machinists from another company even at a premium, while others resorted to shipping specialized work to other areas of the country or even overseas.

Some saw the dwindling numbers of experienced machinists as a direct threat to American industrial know-how, and even the nation's way of life. A 1981 article in *TIME* described the loss of the nation's machining edge in a global economy, with the United States dropping from 21 percent of production of machine tools worldwide in 1964 to just 7 percent in 1980.

After being inaugurated in January 1981, President Ronald Reagan announced the largest peacetime buildup of the United States military in history, proposing to spend a trillion dollars to modernize the Army, Navy, Air Force and Marines, despite rising federal deficits and a rush to cut taxes. With Reagan's ascendency, Detroit lost much of its federal support, tens of millions of dollars. But where some saw crisis, Cunningham saw opportunity in Reagan's planned military buildup—which would put him at odds with local pacifists, including a well-known Detroit bishop.

Cunningham, Josaitis and Armstead toured the St. Louis CETA program that trained low-income people, preparing them for entry-levels job in machine shops for as much as $10 an hour, high enough above minimum wage for a man or woman to support a family.

Cunningham asked Kudek and Faria to research the issue further. They interviewed officials with the Department of Labor and combed the Congressional Record and the Federal Registry. "They came back with reams of information on what the Labor Department was saying," Josaitis said. The team identified 1,322 shops that had openings for machinists in the metropolitan Detroit. Cunningham believed those jobs should be filled by people of color who had been denied careers in skilled trades for generations. The priest saw an opportunity for Focus: HOPE to evolve from an organization that metaphorically gives someone a fish to eat to one that teaches people how to fish, as Cunningham frequently said. The Ex-Cell-O complex across the boulevard would be a perfect location for Focus: HOPE to train Detroiters for good paying jobs as machinists.

To sum up, the audacious Cunningham proposed to simultaneously buy an industrial complex for $300,000 that Focus: HOPE didn't have, equip it with dozens of expensive pieces of heavy machines they'd get from God-knows-where, and start an industrial training program out of whole cloth, all while developing a handful of start-up businesses to provide jobs for student machinists.

Oh, and he wanted the whole thing up and running in six months. The effort would involve complicated negotiations with dozens of small and large businesses, as well as several federal, state and local government officials. They would have to find funding from foundations, corporate sponsors and banks. Cunningham never wanted to waste time, but he instinctively knew that a window of opportunity had opened and he'd have to act boldly and quickly to pull this off before it closed.

As a favor to Cunningham, the Ford Motor Company evaluated the condition of the Ex-Cell-O complex. In nearly continuous use since the late 1920s, the complex was not in great shape. For example, 12,700 of the 50,240 square feet of floor in the B building needed repair. One fix was to pour four inches of concrete over the entire floor at ground level, but the cost was about $250,000. On the positive side, the boilers and steam pipes were in decent shape. "There are certain trade-offs involved in the choice between replacement or repair of physical property," a Ford report said. "Replacement usually results in longer-term trouble-free usage, but requires greater initial capital expenditures. Repair minimizes initial expenditure, but in most cases results in higher expenditures long-term for maintenance." There never was any question about which approach Cunningham wanted—he would replace and refurbish. He wanted to polish what he considered industrial gems along that stretch of Oakman Boulevard.

Kudek went to work on Gilbert Hudson of the Hudson Webber Foundation, which in 1981 authorized a one-year grant of $100,000 for what Cunningham called the Machinist Training Institute (MTI). The Foundation's award letter made a subtle suggestion that it would not consider a second-year request for the same project. Hudson, Kudek claimed, said that the foundation's board of directors was leery of the concept. According to Kudek, Hudson said, "the road you've chosen to follow is full of snake pits." Over the next few years, Hudson Webber donated another $200,000 for the MTI.

Getting companies to lease space in Industry Mall was essential for Cunningham's plan to work. "Suddenly, we had this enormous amount of expense coming on the books as we acquired this property," Kudek said. "With the acquisition of the Ex-Cell-O property, just the gas bill alone was a horrendous increase in expense. What we needed was one or more key leases."

They also needed a faculty. Cunningham wanted retired machinists to teach neophytes with limited job experience how to operate the precision equipment, but also engineers who could help with drafting, design and specifications. The priest told his staff not to worry, that Focus: HOPE always managed to find key people when it needed them. Small business owners like Ken Davis, Earl Allard and others agreed to help sustain the complex by operating their for-profit businesses in Industry Mall while supporting the Focus: HOPE's training center with technical support and apprenticeships to graduates of the training program.

Armstead told Cunningham about how computer numerical control (CNC) and computer-assisted design (CAD) machines would soon become ubiquitous. Owners of small metal working shops around Detroit would need workers trained on computer-assisted machining. "I told him I think there also would be a market for people who work in small shops where the owners just got a little CNC machine and they need someone to operate it. They could send their people to us" for training, Armstead said.

After the priest talked about his plans during his homily at Madonna one Sunday, parishioner Edna Jackson approached Cunningham and commented: "You know, you're not a business-man and you don't know anything about engineering. You don't know how to run an engineering school or how to get people to become engineers." She looked him in the eye. "If you make that work, I'll eat my hat," Jackson said. "OK, you're going to have to eat your hat," Cunningham answered.

Cunningham hired Jackson for the food program, but he soon switched her job to recruiting engineers for the MTI faculty. "He said, 'I don't want all white people and I don't want all black people,'" Jackson said. "It was always his idea that minorities and women never had an opportunity to enter the world of engineering, and he wanted desperately to make that happen." She tried various sources in and outside of union circles, but couldn't find any black engineers. "I said to Cunningham, I said, 'there are no retired black engineers;' and he said, 'yes there are.' I said, 'I beg to differ.' He said, 'There are some and you will find them.' I said, 'If you say so.'"

Jackson sent recruitment letters to newspapers and one ran in *The Michigan Chronicle*, the city's black weekly newspaper. A black machinist named Ira Hatcher heard about MTI and "came in to look around," Armstead said. He and two buddies had taught at the Ford Trade School machinist apprenticeship program for high school students and the three of them volunteered to come in and help. "One guy was a descendant of Thomas Jefferson's black mistress," a slave, Armstead said. Then, someone at the U.S. Army's Tank Automotive Command (TACOM) brought up the name of Claude Harvard, a black machinist-engineer-inventor at Ford Motor Company who had introduced Henry Ford to George Washington Carver in 1935. Harvard had designed and invented many automated machines that helped Ford out-perform the competition in Detroit's cutthroat car-making business. In 1981, Harvard came to Focus: HOPE, liked what he saw and signed up.

That summer, retired Rear Admiral Lee Landes of the Naval Reserves got a call inviting him to a dinner party in Warren. He wasn't sure why, but he was well-connected at the Pentagon and at the Ford Motor Company where he also had worked. The party was at the home of a retired Army Colonel who had been working for TACOM building tanks. It was a set-up for Cunningham to meet Landes. Conversation eventually "got down to something called the Machinist Training Institute," said Landes. "I asked what is a priest doing in a machinist program?" Landes said. "What they needed was jobs [for poor people]; what they had was the food program." Cunningham told him about America's aging workforce of skilled machinists, and how that threatened national security. There was an urgent and critical need, and Cunningham said he aimed to address it by training blacks and other disadvantaged people as machinists. Landes said he asked Cunningham when he was going to start the program. The end of August, Cunningham responded—just weeks away.

Landes asked how many students the MTI could handle.

"We can probably teach a class of about 50," Cunningham said. "You have 50?" Landes asked. "I have 2,500 applicants," the priest said. "How are you going to get down to 50?" Landes asked. "Now you know why you were invited to dinner."

Cunningham persuaded Landes to let Focus: HOPE use the Navy's aptitude test for recruits. He agreed under two conditions: One, that the tests be administered by Naval Petty Officers in uniform ("Done," Cunningham said immediately) and, two, the Navy was to be granted access to those applicants not chosen for the Focus: HOPE program. "For the next maybe six years, we got about 11 interviews a month for the service" because of Focus: HOPE, said Landes, who had been an aide to Robert McNamara when he was president of Ford in the early 1960s. Landes was invaluable in helping Focus: HOPE build connections to the Defense Department.

Cunningham met with the first class of students in November. The priest "gave everybody a pep speech, talked about the purpose of the program, how much he wanted us to succeed," said John Wilford, a member of that first class. "Everybody was very appreciative of him helping us. His motto was: 'If you want to pay me back, do good.' That was his motto." Most members of the first class were young black men like Wilford, but he was the only one with a criminal record. Overcoming that, Wilford became a "star" at the MTI.

"It's not an easy trade; if it was an easy trade everybody would be doing it," Wilford said. Cunningham set high standards and demanded that MTI graduates have a strong work ethic because they had to perform well if the trade school was to be sustained. The future of the program was on their shoulders.

The fact that Focus: HOPE had no money to buy the buildings or the equipment needed for a complicated training program never seemed to give Cunningham pause. Confident in his vision of hope for the city, Cunningham went anywhere and everywhere for money, including foundations, corporate offices and boardrooms.

Someone at TACOM told Armstead about a small-time machine shop owner named Abraham Minowitz who was known for seeking out smaller TACOM jobs—called "one-sies" and "two-sies"—that most shop owners couldn't be bothered with. TACOM regularly sent out requests for parts machined in relatively small quantities without a complicated bidding process. Minowitz "had mastered the whole art of one-sies and two-sies," Armstead said. The folks at TACOM said there were plenty of these types of jobs available, if Focus: HOPE wanted in.

Cunningham's ace up his sleeve was U.S. Sen. Carl Levin, D-Michigan, who sat on the Senate Committee on Armed Services. Levin opened many doors at the Pentagon for Cunningham and Josaitis. He forwarded them a copy of a December 1980 report from the House Armed Services Committee, in which the nation's dwindling machine tooling capacity was discussed in the context of national defense: "Although the industry uses a wide variety of sophisticated and expensive machine tools, its real asset is the highly refined skills of its innovative toolmakers, mold makers and machinists. That skilled worker is eroding at an alarming rate."

Framing the argument for funding a machinist-training project in terms of national defense might just work, Cunningham thought. Charlie Grenville and Gary Faria began to research grant opportunities among a myriad of federal authorizations, including for the Departments of Defense, Labor and Education. There was no precedent for grant-making at Defense. Certainly the Pentagon had entered into countless contracts with manufacturers for matériel and other goods or services to the military. But it had never just given money to a nonprofit organization because its mission coincided with the military's.

In a 1981 "Statement of Need" document to help Cunningham sell his idea to the feds, Faria summarized points made in the House report on the dwindling number of skilled machinists: "Many tooling and machinery firms complain of being forced to turn down defense-related work while machines sit idle because of the lack of skilled workers. Many tooling and machining firms are aggressively recruiting overseas for skilled help. They are filling American jobs with foreigners while national unemployment continues to rise—a truly sad commentary."

Levin told Cunningham something that few people knew about: For decades, the military had been stockpiling thousands of pieces of heavy machine-tooling equipment. The machines were packed in grease and warehoused in limestone caves and in de-humidified warehouses around the country. The government was keeping the tool-making machinery so that in the event of war industrial machines could quickly be unpacked and put into production of war matériel.

Focus: HOPE's formal application to borrow the equipment was sent on June 17, 1981, to Colonel Francis J. Sciples, commander of the Defense Plant Equipment Center in Memphis. The cover letter from Cunningham said: "We anticipate making a major contribution to the rapid growth of our machinist industry, and our capability to do what we did during World War II, as America's Arsenal." Cunningham's "wish list" included 15 screw machines, five turret lathes, 10 engine lathes, six grinding machines, 14 milling machines, three drill presses, two boring machines, and a shaper. Sciples gave tentative approval.

Even as initial classes began, MTI students and Focus: HOPE volunteers got busy cleaning and re-painting B Building, as well as putting up walls to make classrooms. But they had none of the precision industrial equipment needed to provide any kind of meaningful training. "There was a little snafu at first," Armstead said. "We didn't have the [CETA] funding for the training and when we went after the machines they said, 'Well, you got to have the funding; you get the funding, we'll give you the machines.'" The CETA funds were needed to pay for the training, a "Catch 22."

The Detroit officials overseeing disbursement of CETA funds told Focus: HOPE that it would look bad if they gave federal money to a job-training program that wasn't even set up yet. "They liked Focus: HOPE and they liked what we were doing but they didn't want to stick their necks out like that," Armstead said. Then someone remembered that the then-closed Wilbur Wright Vocational School in Detroit used to train kids in the rudiments of tool-and-die making. A few phone calls and a meeting later, the Detroit Public Schools agreed to provide about 20 machines—lathes, mill grinders, drill presses, borers and shavers—for MTI. The Detroit Office of Manpower then approved a $550,000 CETA contract to train up to 60 precision machinists.

Faria wrote a nine-page document about MTI specifically for Vice President George H.W. Bush and sent it with a cover letter from Cunningham dated September 22, 1981. "If this nation is to be secure, economically and otherwise, it simply must decrease its dependence on other countries for the tools of production," the document said. Bush, who had been introduced to Cunningham by Governor William Milliken, was sold. His support was critical, with military officers repeatedly mentioning the vice president while meeting with Focus: HOPE.

In July, Secretary of the Army John Marsh visited Focus: HOPE while in Detroit. Impressed with what he saw, Marsh assigned two Lt. Colonels to liaison with Focus: HOPE, and to participate in meetings Cunningham would be holding over the next several months in Washington.

While thanking the Army for the promised loan of 46 pieces of precision machinery, Cunningham added another request for a $2 million grant from Defense for training. At an Oct. 1 meeting at the Pentagon, Cunningham was told that Secretary Marsh strongly supported the project and that $2 million a year did not even "amount to a whisper around here, but [the] problem is how to give it to you. ... If people knew that the Vice-President is interested, they find ways to do things they don't think they can do," according to a memo written for Cunningham by Congressional aide Pete Teeley.

Cunningham and his team, often including Landes, also lobbied Labor Secretary Raymond J. Donovan. The Labor Department granted Focus: HOPE permission to "perform manufacturing contracts in the training context, which will in turn generate revenue to support the program." In effect, the machinists in training would be working on actual parts under contracts with TACOM and local machine shops and manufacturing plants—real world, hands-on experience that also would generate revenue for Focus: HOPE.

Focus: HOPE raised considerable private funds for the MTI from several organizations: the C.S. Mott Foundation ($200,000), the McGregor Fund ($50,000), Ford Motor Company Fund ($25,000), Michigan Bell Telephone Company ($15,000), American Natural Resources Company ($5,000), Burroughs Corporation ($5,000), J.L. Hudson Company ($5,000), and Detroit Edison ($10,000).

"They were just doing groundbreaking work," explained William S. White, the long-time Mott Foundation president. "They were trying to do something positive for Detroit, and always it was at its core more of a civil rights organization but turned into one of the most effective community development organizations around."

Senators Levin and Don Riegle wrote to Defense Secretary Caspar Weinberger in November, thanking him for the loan of the machinery to Focus: HOPE but asking for a $2 million training grant. Weinberger wrote back that while he agreed with Focus: HOPE's mission to help prepare for possible war, the Pentagon did not have funds to train private sector employees. "I support Focus: HOPE's efforts to create a program to train skilled technicians; as you know, we are committed to helping alleviate the critical skills shortage," Weinberger replied in December. "However, beyond loaning equipment to be used for training purposes, the Department is very limited in the assistance it can provide."

Nothing was easy about creating the MTI. "Enormous levels of physical energy stretched throughout the developmental stage—painting, constructing classrooms; preparing floors and walls; obtaining classroom and office furniture, holding open houses for the community and business leaders; locating machinery and arranging for delivery; cross-country trucking; machine rebuilding, painting, electrical and mechanical hook-up; hiring staff; selecting curriculum; recruiting volunteers, and testing applicants," wrote Carol Jachim, then the editor of Focus: HOPE publications.

Out of more than 4,000 applicants, just 55 were chosen by Focus: HOPE to begin training at the MTI. Among the 55 trainees, seven were women. Classes started at 7:30 a.m. with 30 minutes of calisthenics and ended at 4 p.m. The eight-month training program proved that many disadvantaged people had a strong work ethic. Most were recruited by local machine shops, earning decent wages. "Companies were trying to get students before they completed their course work," Armstead said. "We had a very good reputation in the community for providing employees who were well-trained."

The vice president was invited to the MTI ribbon-cutting ceremony in December 1981, but could not make it. However, Cunningham and Josaitis were invited to sit with the vice president and Barbara Bush in the owner's box during Super Bowl XXIII on January 24, 1982, at the Pontiac Silverdome. The San Francisco 49ers won their first Super Bowl that year, defeating the Cincinnati Bengals 26-21. But before the end of the game, Josaitis excused herself to leave and, as a courtesy, two Secret

Service agents offered to escort her to her car in the VIP lot. Despite their protection, Josaitis slipped and broke her pelvis.[27]

During the game, Cunningham urged Bush to visit Focus: HOPE as soon as he could fit it into his schedule. Bush admired the organization's mission of helping the poor help themselves. People who had lost hope suddenly were becoming educated and picking themselves up by their proverbial bootstraps. They could now get higher-paying jobs that would get them off of welfare. In June, Cunningham announced that Bush had helped secure a $200,000 grant from the Labor Department to expand the MTI. Hundreds of thousands of more federal dollars also would be appropriated in the coming months.

Everything seemed to be going well. But then another bureaucratic glitch developed: While the Pentagon could loan machines to an institution for training purposes, they could not be used to make products that would be sold for a profit. Yet, for the MTI business model to work, students must make parts under contracts with the military and corporations. Focus: HOPE intended to make a profit and churn them back into the training program.

Rear Admiral Landes held the opinion that the military made regulations and the military can damn well change regulations. The logical point of contact, Landes advised, was Vice Admiral

---

27   *A well-known quirk at the Silverdome was its inflatable roof that was kept erect by powerful fans that pushed the dome up and air out of the arena, causing a disorienting rush of air for people entering or leaving the building. Negotiating the exit with a hand on the arm of each Secret Service agent, Eleanor fought the rush of air, lost her footing on the icy carpet and fell. "I guess that draft just sucked her down," Don Josaitis said. She insisted that she be taken to Henry Ford Hospital, 30 miles away in Detroit, and the two agents drove her there. She had broken her pelvis. Don said that a couple of years later, he and Eleanor were with Cunningham at a pub for a fundraiser when a man came up and asked how she was doing. He was one of the agents who had taken her to the hospital that day. Eleanor asked how he could remember that so well, according to Don, and the agent said, "I couldn't forget someone as nice as you."*

Eugene Grinstead of the Defense Logistics Agency, a former Navy combat scuba diver during World War II.

Cunningham had planned a visit to Capitol Hill for February 1982 and Grinstead agreed to a 30-minute meeting at the DLA in Virginia. Landes was to fly to Washington and meet Cunningham at the Pentagon. From there, they'd be driven to Fairfax to meet with Grinstead. Cunningham already was in Washington to lobby for the food program. But, a severe snowstorm hit Washington and Landes' flight was cancelled. Most of Washington was shut down, but Cunningham took the Metro to the Pentagon and was driven to the meeting with Grinstead. Since other appointments had been cancelled due to the weather, Grinstead, a Catholic with several kids, and Cunningham worked for hours with military lawyers and other officers to iron out the problem with regulations. They came up "with a loophole in the regulations that allowed us to start making products," Armstead said.

In August 1982, 44 men and three women were honored at a MTI graduation ceremony. Mayor Coleman Young and 400 other people participated in the festivities. "We're just delighted with the quality of the students and their ambition to be the best," Cunningham told *The Michigan Catholic*'s Tom Ewald. "After only one year of training, their knowledge and capabilities are equivalent to those who have been in the trade for two or three years. ... Our candidates are not only adept at reading blue prints and doing quality machine work, but they're able to do computer work and load a numerical control machine— there's not too many machinists who know how to deal with computers."

Word finally came that the vice president could visit Focus: HOPE on October 5, 1982—less than a week before the next Walk for Justice. Cunningham's team, already working hard to organize the walk, kicked into high gear. Some 65 dignitaries, including the head of every major company in the area, General Decker of TACOM; *Free Press* executive editor, David Lawrence Jr.; and several elected officials were invited. The visit was scheduled minute by minute from the time the vice president's plane touched down at Metro Airport at 3:05 p.m. to his arrival at Focus: HOPE at 3:30 to his departure by motorcade for downtown at 4:57 p.m.

Cunningham, Josaitis, Armstead and Kudek greeted Bush and introduced him to the VIPs one by one. Bush then toured the MTI, visiting with students at various stations. Cunningham introduced John Wilford to Bush as the MTI's "work horse" because he always was on time, studied hard and stayed late— and had turned his life around. "The thing that makes me feel good is this here: he knew he was dealing with an ex-convict," Wilford said. "All the important people I met, they all shook hands with me. They all treated me nice."

At precisely 4 p.m., Bush began his public remarks:

"This is a marvelous combination, cooperative effort between government—and mainly private sector—and I would salute Mayor Young and the business community of the Detroit area and I wouldn't want to leave out the untold volunteer efforts that make this program possible." Bush went on to announce two more grants for Focus: HOPE—$450,000 from Labor for job training, and $730,000 from Health and Human Services "for rehabilitation, maintenance, and other needs to maintain this complex." Bush pulled an envelope out of his suit jacket pocket and held it up. It was an actual government check to Focus: HOPE for $1.18 million.

"We look on Focus: HOPE as exactly that—a hopeful thing," Bush said. "We think it can serve as a model, a shining example for the creation of similar programs throughout the country. The program is efficient. It produces the necessary job results which are skilled trade jobs that are not only needed by the unemployed, but jobs that industry wants to fill but is having difficulty filling today. So it is filling an economic need."

On Sunday, October 10, 1982, the day of that year's Walk for Justice, the *Free Press* published a column by Neal Shine who wrote that he no longer doubted Cunningham: "I now tend to list all Focus: HOPE projects as probable successes. When Father Cunningham pointed to the empty Ex-Cell-O Corp. plant across from his Church of the Madonna a year ago and told me he was going to use the old factory to start a program to train young people as machinists, I simply asked him when he expected to graduate his first class. He said in August. Last August, the first 44 people were graduated from the program."

In less than a year, using charm, charisma, his moral authority as a Catholic priest and his unshakeable faith that others could be persuaded to join his cause, Father Cunningham had accomplished what had seemed impossible. He had gotten a Republican administration generally hostile to liberal do-gooders to support a program that would help underprivileged minorities get jobs to lift them out of poverty, in a northern city with a majority black, primarily Democratic population—Detroit.

"It was phenomenal," Armstead said.

David Ciesnicki, the white bearded fellow, and two Machinist Training Institute students listen as historic inventor Claude Harvard explains drafting.

Credit: Focus: HOPE

18

Victim

IN A STAFF meeting about Focus: HOPE's upcoming Walk for Justice, Gary Faria commented that the annual walks might not be worth the tremendous amount of staff time. Donations from participants never came close to covering expenses. Wasn't it time to do something different? Weren't the walks passé? Faria asked innocently. With furious anger, Cunningham jumped up. His eyes bulged as he leaned toward Faria. What kind of idiot would come up with that cockamamie idea? His rant went on for several unrelenting moments.

It was Edna Jackson's first day at Focus: HOPE, and she stiffened, not knowing what was going on. "It scared me half to death," she said. "And then Bill quieted down, and Eleanor took Gary into [a different] room and closed the door. When he came out, you could tell the poor man had been crying like a baby."

The tenor of Focus: HOPE meetings took some getting used to. Surprising to some was the mild profanity that came from the priest and, to a lesser extent, Eleanor—liberal use of the words "goddamn" and "bullshit." In early 1981, John Ziraldo, a new coordinator for Project Trust, attended his first staff meeting and was dumbfounded at what seemed to be a lack of decorum. "Bill was arguing with someone on the staff. Within moments they were cussing each other out—Bill to this staff person, this person back at him," Ziraldo said. "Life went on. Nobody got fired. People were passionate in the way they represented their views. ... They would argue all day long, that was their style. ... The whole thing was this kind of brilliant dysfunction in some way, because it worked. You cannot argue with the results."

Despite his occasionally fiery temper, senior staff would follow Cunningham anywhere. No one could light up a crowd like the unconventional priest both on spiritual and practical levels. He and Eleanor were totally committed to Focus: HOPE and they expected absolute loyalty and 110-percent effort. You had to work late and on weekends if need be. While Eleanor usually was more diplomatic, Cunningham was blunt when people didn't measure up, sometimes hurting feelings. He challenged assumptions, criticized lack of follow-through and insisted that they improve. He told them that they could and would do better, but he seemed unconcerned about the effect his harsh criticism could have on colleagues.

The office set-up at the refurbished Focus: HOPE's Resource Center headquarters was a wide-open room with Cunningham and Josaitis sitting at adjacent desks at one end within sight and sound of other staffers working nearby and in a mezzanine above. Everyone heard everything. If Bill and Eleanor needed privacy, they retreated to a conference room or took a drive to Belle Isle to talk without distractions.

Ziraldo said Cunningham had "this smart, insightful thinking, a cut-to-the-marrow kind of approach to solving problems. He was a highly emotionally manipulative person at the same time. He was this terrible blend of the two." The priest's eloquence in cutting colleagues to the quick left many shaken, upset and angry. "The thing was, Focus: HOPE used to chew them up and spit them out," Ziraldo said. "There was only so much of that kind of drama that people were willing to put up with, so people moved on. I'm one of them. I just wanted to go somewhere

where life was a little less turbulent. ... I do admire the folks who could stick around for the long term."

One staffer who wasn't afraid to stand up to Cunningham was Sarah Whipple, a no-nonsense former U.S. Navy WAVE officer during World War II and a former Glenmary sister who became the priest's secretary in the early 1980s. Whipple "would get after him if he wasn't doing things on time, taking care of the newsletter or something sounded not right," said Patsy McMahon, another ex-Glenmary sister and Focus: HOPE employee. Cunningham thought Whipple was stiff, so he nee-dled her whenever he could—most of which she took with resigned humor.

"Bill always had Sarah doing stuff over and over again—just one little thing, do it over again," said Thom Armstead. "This particular day, at the end of the day, she came and brought a bunch of letters for his signature. ... So Sarah came over and dropped them on his desk and said, 'Father, I've got to go home now.'" As she walked away, Cunningham made a crack about having to now fix Whipple's mistakes himself. A few moments passed, then Whipple "came all the way back in, walked up to his desk, leaned over and said, 'Fuck you, Cunningham!' He almost fell off his chair. He thought it was so funny."

Preparing for a visit by dignitaries or the news media was always high priority. Jerry Lemenu, the resident artist who drew countless cartoons and graphics for Focus: HOPE publications, was assigned by Cunningham to get the new food distribution center on Detroit's southwest side ready for a grand open-ing. "All of a sudden, I'm interior decorator," Lemenu said. He worked all day and into the night making the place present-able for celebratory opening. "I was putting up curtains I had picked out the night before the opening. I thought things were pretty much done except for a hole in the wall for a new door." Lemenu planned to use part of the curtain to hide it.

"Cunningham had been staying away—a new strategy of 'hands off,'" Lemenu said. "Here it is 9 o'clock. I'm doing what I can, hanging up these curtains. He finally shows up, sees this hole in the wall. I was the only person there. He reamed me, just blew up. I don't remember his exact words, but it felt really personal. 'How could this be left here? It's just incompetent!' His eloquence—as much as I admired it in some occasions, I hated it in others. I was just stunned. I basically stood there in stunned silence. When he left, I just started throwing things, and I just walked out. The next day, I was steamed about it. I didn't go to the opening, a big to-do with Coleman Young.

"The following day, I went straight to Bill's desk and said, 'you owe me an apology! What you said was personal. It wasn't my responsibility. It was way too personal. I didn't deserve that.' He knew that that was real important to me, and he knew that it took some courage on my part to do that, to confront him. So, he apologized. He didn't say one word to defend what he said. That was sort of a turning point in our relationship."

Lemenu, one of the former seminarians who gravitated to Cunningham's cause, said that there were "three stages of knowing" Father Cunningham: "The first stage, you are just totally enthralled. He was just a charismatic figure and you want to be around him. The second stage, if you are around him, you become disillusioned. There were a lot of things very human about him that aren't very wonderful. ... If you persevere, then you'll come back around and see all the wonderful things he is. Combined with his humanity, it makes him all that more admirable."[28]

On October 4, 1981, about 3,000 people joined Cunningham and the rest of the Focus: HOPE crew for the annual Walk for Justice. The goal that year was to raise $100,000 for the Machinist Training Institute, which would open the following month. The route began at the State Fair grounds at Eight Mile Road down Woodward Avenue to Hart Plaza at the Detroit River. Cunningham told *Free Press* reporter Andrea Ford why holding

---

28   *In the March 1981 Inside Hope newsletter for employees, Cunningham went out of his way to praise the work done by Lemenu and others to get the Southwest Food Center ready for the opening: "My personal congratulations to everyone who was involved in the opening of the Southwest Food Center. I was extremely proud of the appearance of the Center and all the preparations for the opening."*

the march was important: "A lot of people in our town are facing a lot of insecurity and a lot of pain," he said. "There's a tremendous amount of pressure on these people, and the walk takes on special meaning for them."

That same day Cunningham's friend retired Navy Admiral Landes lost his son George, who was killed by a drunken driver. Looking for a way to turn his tragedy into something positive, Landes met Candace Lightner, the California-based founder of Mothers Against Drunk Driving (MADD), when she came to Detroit to appear on a talk show that December. Landes decided to organize the same advocacy program here.

The new Michigan Chapter of MADD scheduled its first candlelight vigil for February 17, 1982, in front of the Spirit of Detroit statue at the foot of Woodward Avenue. Cunningham provided glass-enclosed votive candles from Madonna and he, Thom Armstead, and Eleanor and Don Josaitis attended— all of them moderate, but regular, drinkers. "It was about five degrees that night; wind blowing, a lot of snow in the air, and my wife was sick as a dog," Landes said. "We brought her there in a wheelchair wrapped in a sleeping bag." It was a somber and sobering beginning for a chapter that would grow into a statewide advocacy organization with thousands of members.

A few weeks later, Landes saw Cunningham having dinner at Opus One, an upscale restaurant downtown. "He was having some drinks," Landes said. Something must have bothered Cunningham about the encounter, Landes said, because, "the next time I saw him he said, 'Let me ask you something. Do you think I drink too much?' I said, 'What do you think?' He said, 'I don't know how much too much is.' I said two drinks an hour of beer or wine or cocktails is too much." "OK, I'll cut back," Cunningham said. "Whether he did or not, I don't know," Landes said.

Between fighting for every dollar of available federal support for the MTI and advocating for an expansion of the Food Prescription Program to seniors, Cunningham and Josaitis were travelling to Washington at least once a month. Often Armstead, Grenville or Bidleman would go along. The schedule of meetings was grueling, designed to waste not a minute. "We'd come in the night before, have dinner with a couple of folks, cocktails back to the hotel and then meet with another group after then, maybe 8-9 o'clock," Armstead said. "The next morning, they'd work two, three breakfasts with [members of Congress and their staff] before they went to work. They'd try to set up lunches, try to catch people when you could. We'd get back on the last flight out at 9:30. Be at work the next day, no problem."

Armstead said that to save money, they would stay together. "All four of us in the same suite. Eleanor would get the bed. We'd get the couch or the floor. One time, Carl [Bidleman] and I and Eleanor and Bill were in just like a sitting room with one bed and patio doors." Didn't matter the weather, Cunningham insisted on opening the window or door. "It'd drive me nuts! He had to have fresh air at night! The only thing that allowed fresh air in was the patio door. I used to freeze my ass off sleeping in the open air."

The full-court press on Washington by Cunningham and Focus: HOPE worked remarkably well. Credit Cunningham's intelligence, passion and charisma, as well as Josaitis' politesse as she prodded congressional aides to overcome bureaucratic inertia. The follow-up notes and phone calls, flowers and boxes of Sanders chocolates she sent to delighted staffers were all part of Josaitis' considerable arsenal of charm. "It was phenomenal how quickly we were able to get through the road blocks" for the MTI, said Armstead.

The afternoon of August 15, 1982, was calm, sunny, about 80 degrees and pleasant on Belle Isle where the Madonna parish was holding its annual picnic. Cunningham and parishioner John Covin were visiting tables, when a man came up behind Cunningham and swung a steel bar at his head. "I didn't realize, but he sneaked up behind us and he hit him. He was going to his head, but he throwed his arm up," Covin said. "I pulled Father away." The man, a member of the parish, had been drinking and he'd used a steel stake from a game of horseshoes to attack his pastor. Two or three blows fell on Cunningham's left arm and back, dropping him to his knees. The attacker was stopped before more damage was done. Covin said he tried to pummel the man, but people intervened and the drunk stumbled off. Cunningham had arm fractures in two places. Armstead said the priest later told him what the guy's beef was: "He said he was in church and Father had sprinkled holy water on his girlfriend, but not on him. … Man, if he hadn't blocked it, that horseshoe stake would've gone straight to his head," Armstead said.

The priest preferred that no one call the police and he refused to file charges. He explained that in his "Cunningham's Comments" in the next parish bulletin: "I regard the man who struck me as very dangerous, but also as a member of our parish family, and therefore it is most important to me that we handle this as a family matter. I sincerely hope everyone understands. I am not angry and I am proud of that. I hold absolutely no grudge. I do have a very painful arm, but it reminds me that all of us hurt one another—and I also am guilty of that. Let us pray for one another."

On November 12, 1982, a debate about President Reagan's cuts to domestic programs for the poor while increasing defense spending by billions was held at a meeting of the Greater Detroit Chamber of Commerce, later known as the Detroit Regional Chamber of Commerce. Cunningham was on a panel that was to discuss "morality, jobs and defense spending." Roy Levy Williams, president of the Detroit Urban League, told the crowd that, "the U.S. ought to be biting the bullet, rather than building the bullet." Williams said that for every $1 billion spent on defense about 67,000 new jobs are created. But for every $1 billion spent on education, 187,000 jobs are created and if spent on construction about 100,000 new jobs would be created.

Cunningham, who was seeking millions of dollars in equipment and in contracts from the Defense Department to operate the MTI, also spoke. But he didn't buy into Reagan's "trickle-down economics." Spending on defense is fine, he said, but "the people in Detroit need something to defend. … Of course we need an adequate defense, but when 52,000 people in Wayne County are living on less than $1,600 a year, you have to look at the priorities. People first need a country where they can work and live in dignity." When people questioned Cunningham's embrace of the Pentagon, his "dark, Irish temper flared" during the discussion, *The Detroit News* reported. "While the Rev. William Cunningham of Focus: HOPE didn't surprise anyone by condemning nuclear weapons, his defense of defense did," the *News* said.

"Morality cannot abide people who refuse to get their hands dirty with the building of a just society," Cunningham told the crowd. "There is no question that those of us who will not engage as a society in an active defense of situations and ideals we call a civilization, are as guilty as those who devise atomic weapons. ... It used to be that our priority was to 'bring us your poor, your huddled masses.' America was a place of eminent promise and productivity. One of the best places to live was Detroit, where you could own your own home and be somebody. Now *that* was something to defend."

Among the dozens of people Focus: HOPE hired to staff the MTI was a burly blond-haired pacifist with a bushy beard, an all-city football player from the Jesuit-run University of Detroit High School from which he was graduated in 1975 before attending the University of Michigan. David Ciesnicki, who began volunteering at Focus: HOPE while still a high school student, was a pacifist to the core, a young man who kept a well-thumbed copy of Mahatma Ghandi's book, *For Pacifists*, on his desk at the MTI, along with piles of notes about people he knew needed help. "Being a firm believer in the idea of racial unity is the first step we must take so we can begin to alleviate the suffering and misery of millions in this country," Ciesnicki wrote in a July 1979 letter to Grenville asking for a job. "I view this opportunity as a godsend for it will allow me to work in a socially progressive manner in a community that I love dearly."

Ciesnicki, had fallen in love with another U-M student, a young black woman named Denise. They married despite opposition from members of both families, who couldn't abide interracial relationships. When the Project Trust program ended due to funding shortfalls, Ciesnicki was moved to the MTI. He befriended everybody and encouraged students to work hard and do their best.

John Wilford, who was then a 34-year-old ex-con and heroin addict trying to get his life turned around by getting trained at MTI, said his life was saved by Ciesnicki who encouraged him again and again to stick it out. "I didn't think I could," Wilford said. "Dave told me I would. There were no maybes about it. I would. But I would have to do something, too. I would have to have good attendance at the shop, good grades. He gave me the confidence I needed. He kept pushing me to do better. And once I did better, to do better than that."

Wilford said Ciesnicki invited him for dinner and when he arrived he was surprised because Ciesnicki had never mentioned being married to a black woman. "He said, 'John, this is my wife, Denise,' and I could tell how he was looking at my face for a reaction. I think I passed the smell test." Wilford often found himself at Ciesnicki's house watching football and talking over a beer.

Despite family difficulties, the love between David and Denise was evident to everyone, and their toddler son, David, was cute as a button. They lived a life of compassion, love and justice-seeking and were admired by many colleagues at Focus: HOPE. On Thanksgiving Day 1982, Ciesnicki carved off a leg of the family turkey, wrapped it and other food from their table in aluminum foil, and then drove the food package to an elderly woman who had called Focus: HOPE, saying she hadn't eaten in several days. "He would get 'thank you' letters from students he had helped ... and that was his feedback," Denise Ciesnicki later told *The Detroit News*. "That was the way he knew he was doing something right. It was sweet to get those letters and they always seemed to come at just the right times, just when he began wondering if he made any difference."

Wilford helped the Ciesnickis move to a better home in Detroit near the intersection of Grand River and the Southfield Freeway in the middle-class community of Rosedale Park. In the early morning hours of December 5, 1982, the three were asleep when a man forced his way through the back door, went upstairs, encountered David in the hallway and stabbed the young father at least 18 times, killing him. The killer did not harm the child, but then abducted Denise. She was repeatedly sexually assaulted. When she finally escaped and found her way to police, the man had disappeared. A police detective called the killer "one vicious son of a bitch."

David Ciesnicki was just 25, and a memorial service at Cunningham's Church of the Madonna was both sad and uplifting. "He was open, he was trusting, he was trusted," eulogized Armstead. "He was an architect of sorts—a builder of bridges between all people, young and old, black and white. He believed, he encouraged, he listened." Ortheia Barnes led the crowd in singing "Amazing Grace," leaving many in tears. Cunningham, who said he almost didn't hire Ciesnicki as being too young, said, "For a man his age, he had an incredible passion for justice and civil rights." Josaitis said that Ciesnicki "was a talented young white man, married to a beautiful black woman, and he did everything humanly possible to improve relations between the two races."[29]

Crime in Detroit continued to rise, contributing to increased white flight from the city and widening swaths of blighted neighborhoods. Enrollments at Sacred Heart Seminary in Detroit, where Father Cunningham had both studied and taught, continued to decline steeply in the early 1980s. Also alarming to many Catholics was the veritable exodus of ordained priests discouraged by many Church policies, particularly its celibacy mandate and the hierarchy's teachings on divorce, sexuality and birth control.

William F. Kienzle, the former editor of *The Michigan Catholic* newspaper turned author of church-themed crime novels, told *Free Press* religion writer Harry Cook that he had stopped waiting

---

29   *In January 1990, Fred Moore, a Detroit police identification specialist using a new $22 million state fingerprint computer system broke the Ciesnicki murder case open. A fingerprint left at the crime scene years earlier, was finally identified as belonging to Eris Montgomery, then a 27-year-old ex-con. Montgomery was arrested, tried and—after less than an hour of deliberation—convicted by a jury of first-degree murder and first-degree criminal sexual conduct, breaking and entering and armed robbery. He was sentenced to life in prison without possibility of parole.*

for the archdiocese's sluggish bureaucratic process of marriage annulments and applications to remarry. "I quit [the priesthood] over the threat of suspension for marrying people out of accord with canon law," Kienzle told Cook.

One of Cook's main points was the challenge of fewer Catholic priests willing to serve in the inner city where they were dealing with impoverished parishioners who needed help on many fronts. Of course, Cook called on Cunningham to comment as a priest who was somehow managing to minister to a parish while running a growing nonprofit organization. Could there be a conflict between his duties as a priest and as the leader of Focus: HOPE? "It's the Gospel in action, a very natural outgrowth of what the church is here to do," Cunningham said. "I don't see any conflict whatsoever."

Much of the poverty and despair in Detroit was caused by a sharp decline in car manufacturing. During the 1980s, dramatic changes in global economics hastened the loss of manufacturing jobs in Detroit and Michigan. Foreign carmakers began beating Detroit's Big Three—General Motors, Ford and Chrysler—on price, quality and miles-per-gallon. Oil producers in countries like Iraq, Libya and Iran that were run by dictators raised prices. The impact in Michigan was profound. Thousands of good jobs were lost, pushing the poverty rate higher. On December 16, 1982, with the state's official unemployment rate at 17.2 percent, Republican Governor William Milliken declared a "human emergency" and asked the Legislature for emergency help for heat and food for the poor.

Focus: HOPE turned to the federal government to help Detroit's suffering people. It took several months and support from Michigan Congressmen William Broomfield, a Republican, and Democrats Bob Traxler and Bob Carr, as well as help from Michigan's two Democratic Senators, Carl Levin and Donald Riegle, for Focus: HOPE to expand its network of food distribution centers. The Reagan Administration had to be pressed hard to provide enough food commodities to feed up to 15,000 poor women, children and elderly people in Oakland County alone.

While the number of people living in poverty could be measured by the Census Bureau, some measures of human suffering were not precisely known, particularly when it came to hunger. Presidential advisor Edwin Meese made that point inadvertently in December 1983 when he told reporters in Washington that some people go to soup kitchens "because the food is free and that's easier than paying for it." Meese added that he had seen no "authoritative evidence" that there were hungry children in the United States.

Cunningham told the *Free Press* that Meese's remarks were "insensitive, callous, so grotesque. ... He's spitting in the eye of the poor. Has he stood in those [soup] lines, been to places like the Capuchin kitchen?" Organizations like Focus: HOPE had for years fought to get programs like WIC (Women, Infants and Children) to feed poor and hungry children, Cunningham said. "We've had to practically bludgeon Washington to get this help."

On February 28, 1985, Cunningham was participating in a "round-table debate on religion and politics" at the Episcopal Church's Barth Hall in Detroit. Other debaters included Michigan Governor James Blanchard, former Governor and current state Supreme Court Justice G. Mennen Williams, Rabbi Stanley Rosenbaum of B'nai Moshe, Rev. Dr. Frederick Sampson of Tabernacle Baptist Church, Sister Rachel West of the Groundwork for a Just World organization, and state Rep. Lynn Jondahl, a Democrat from East Lansing who also was a minister with the United Church of Christ. Apparently, Father Cunningham stole the show, at least according to *Detroit News* religion writer Kate DeSmet whose subsequent column was headlined "Fr. Cunningham hits 'em where they live."

The discussion centered on finding political answers to help the poor and the hungry in the context of religion. Cunningham "approached the subject with nary a cautious bone in his body," DeSmet wrote. President Reagan, Cunningham said, "does sometimes become pope and forgets his role by calling on the Church to do their thing, and then gets upset with Church leaders who call on him to do his thing." Cunningham talked about the movie, *Shoes of the Fisherman* with Anthony Quinn playing a fictional humble pope who challenged religious leaders to give up the trappings of wealth. "This new pope tells a crowd in St. Peter's Square that the Church's first action will be to sell all the things of the papacy" and use the proceeds to help the poor, Cunningham said. "Churches must divest themselves—sell it; get rid of it to feed the hungry of the world. ... If we have it and won't give it to them, then we are responsible for every one of those in the epidemic of hunger. We are as responsible as if we walked into their homes and took their food away. What we need are a lot of bishops, sisters and priests standing naked in a snow bank having given everything away. You develop that kind of morality by leadership."

DeSmet wrote: "A good guess is that his message would be the same even if it were delivered to a roomful of bishops. There's something to be said about this priest's public chutzpah factor. Like, we could use a couple of buses full of it."

Faculty and staff of the Machinist Training Institute with Claude Harvard—the inventor and mechanical genius who introduced George Washington Carver to Henry Ford in 1935—front and center. On the left is MTI dean Suzanne Young and on the far right is Thom Armstead.

Credit: Focus: HOPE

19

Harvard

ANY THRILL FATHER Cunningham felt when the vice president of the United States personally handed him a check for $1.18 million was soon dissipated by the hard reality that there were serious strings attached to it. Focus: HOPE was now obligated to quickly find 175 qualified applicants to the Machinist Training Institute, train them in basic machine tool operations and place them in actual jobs—within one year.

Cunningham, Thom Armstead and a handful of tool-and-die shop owners were making it up as they went along. And they'd seen success. Of the initial 55 students at MTI, 44 had completed the nine-month program. But now Focus: HOPE would have to quickly recruit and train four times as many low-income people for entry-level manufacturing jobs in just 32 weeks. The only option was to reduce the quality of the training, so that graduates could work some factory jobs. But they would not be skilled machinists.

"If you give people basic skills like blueprint reading, how to read a micrometer and the basic operations of a piece of equipment, that's all the industry really wanted," Armstead said. "If you got to hire someone off the street, you might as well hire somebody who could read a blueprint and a micrometer."

Neither Cunningham nor Eleanor Josaitis expressed any worry about making it all work. But in order to reach that 175 enrollment they were forced to admit youths who had not mastered 10th grade level math. Both later acknowledged that mistake, and another: becoming contractually obligated to place all graduates in jobs within one year. If Focus: HOPE didn't perform, it might have to return money to the federal government and probably lose future opportunities for funding. "We blew it," Josaitis told the author. "People were coming in, they wanted to come in, but they couldn't pass the math test. We just said, OK we'll lower the standards to get the next cohort. It wasn't a washout, but we made a serious mistake. We learned a lesson because they weren't prepared."

This was not just a problem for Focus: HOPE, but for employers across the state. Increasing numbers of kids, especially those from families living in poverty, were dropping out of school before graduating. Many graduates soon learned they did not have the math and reading skills required for higher wage jobs. "I'd say one out of 10 had algebra," said Frank Bugg who worked at Focus: HOPE for nearly a decade. "When I went to discuss this with Father Cunningham, he said clearly we need to be able to get kids' math skills up to the level they needed fast in order to get into the MTI, or the MTI would die."

They began offering after-hour tutorials at no charge. Remedial math and reading classes at the MTI were multiplied. More kids were getting it, but many still were failing. Cunningham wanted them to try the latest idea in education: teacher-guided computer education programs that allowed students to learn at their own pace. Cunningham wanted underprivileged Detroit kids to be ready for the high-tech future he saw coming. The idea didn't work. Most of these kids still needed a real teacher who cared about their success and inspired them to learn.

The students who passed math and reading went to the shop floor. After safety procedures were explained, experts— both white and black retired machinists—provided hands-on instruction in the use of boring mills, shapers, lathes and other machinery. MTI students weren't just practicing; they were making real parts under contracts with TACOM, General Motors, Ford and other manufacturers. Cunningham's plan was to have enough production contracts for the MTI to cover costs.

With a gargantuan effort, most of the federal requirements were met, and Focus: HOPE succeeded well enough for continued government funding. Cunningham pushed MTI managers, especially new dean Suzanne Young, to get the education program accredited so students would be eligible for federal financial aid, including Pell Grants, Stafford Loans and Veterans Education Benefits. Three years later, the Council for Non-Collegiate Continuing Education accredited the MTI, thanks to Young, an ex-nun and former principal of St. Mary's of Redford High School.

Among the cadre of engineers and machinists who comprised the faculty of the MTI, two stood out as "stars" of the program—Claude Harvard and Wilfred Little. Harvard, a native of Georgia who moved with his family to Detroit at age 10 in 1922, had high aptitude for mathematics and a curiosity for machines and radios. At age 15, he was among a handful of black kids allowed to enroll in the Henry Ford Trade School. Harvard faced the same challenges as previous black students, who were expelled because they were provoked into a fight by white boys. Harvard, however, kept his cool in the face of racist behavior.

Working as the first black in Ford Motor Company's design and experimental department, Harvard created the company's first piece of automated precision machinery. His piston pin inspection machine evaluated the metallurgical strength, the precision of the pins to 1/10,000 of an inch, as well as their smoothness while sorting them, automatically rejecting defective pieces. Henry Ford himself chose to send Harvard to display the innovation at the 1934 World's Fair in Chicago. The following year, Harvard presented a speech on behalf of Mr. Ford at the Tuskegee Institute in Alabama, and a year later introduced Mr. Ford to George Washington Carver when Carver visited Detroit. Among other inventions, Harvard also created Ford's first in-car cigarette lighter by finding a metal alloy that would "pop-out" when it glowed red hot. Former Focus: HOPE colleague Tom Ferguson said the invention came about because both Harvard and Edsel Ford were smokers.

Wilfred Little, the older brother of Malcolm X, had been volunteering for Focus: HOPE in its Project Trust training program for high school students for several years. When the MTI opened in 1981, the Michigan Bell Telephone Company loaned Little, the manager of the company's urban affairs department, to Focus: HOPE and continued paying his salary for several years. Little had endured many heartbreaks, including the apparent murder of his father in East Lansing in the mid-1930s, the institutionalization of his mother in a mental hospital in 1938 and the scattering of his siblings to relatives and foster homes. As a 14-year-old boy in Lansing, Little enjoyed a printing class offered in school. But the white teacher told him that, "colored kids can't be printers." Little got into the class, however, by telling the teacher that his family was moving to Africa and he wanted to have a skill in order to find work there. The teacher allowed him to stay. Little used a similar tactic with the white teacher in shop class, eventually working during the summer with that teacher on machining jobs. "He taught me how to make jigs and fixtures, and he taught me a lot of things I didn't know were special until I got out into the field later," Little told amateur biographer Paul Lee. That teacher helped Little land a job at Reo Motors in Lansing with such an effusive recommendation that the company had to hire him as a skilled machinist despite his black skin.

Like Harvard, Little was a gifted student who had to overcome the racism endemic in Detroit's gritty industrial milieu. In 1943, he joined Elijah Muhammad's Nation of Islam and served as a minister at several Michigan NOI mosques. Wilfred and his brother Reginald Little introduced their younger brother Malcolm to the NOI when Malcolm got out of prison. Malcolm, too, joined the NOI, but in 1964 became an outspoken critic and embraced Sunni Islam. He was assassinated in New York in 1965 by NOI agents.

"Integration is part of [Focus: HOPE's] philosophy," Little told *The Christian Science Monitor* in 1988. "After all, our students are going to have to work in an integrated world. We give blacks and whites exposure to each other. They learn to work together to communicate. Some of them have never had any close contact with a person of the other race before. They find they enjoy it."

Armstead said employers from several machine shops around Detroit began showing up for a tour of Focus: HOPE. On the shop floor, they checked out good students surreptitiously and offered them jobs. "Those guys were trying to pull people out of the school before the training was over," he said. "Your math had to be good, blueprint reading had to be good. The instruction from the teachers, Claude Harvard, Will Little and others, was excellent, and we had some very good folks on the [shop] floor. Those kids could read blueprints. The employers loved their skills. There were a variety of machines they got a chance to operate. They weren't just one-trick ponies. They could operate boring mills and all specialty machines."

So, why were the city's public schools producing so many young Detroiters without an adequate education, a high school diploma or a path to a job or career? Why were so many children in the city undernourished? On April 18, 1983, Father Cunningham was invited to be the keynote speaker at a Michigan State University conference entitled "The Crisis of Michigan Cities: Unemployment and Hunger." His speech before an audience of graduate students, teachers, professors and advocates for the poor put the blame on poorly trained teachers:

"What we do at Focus: HOPE has to do with the radical concept of what it means to be a teacher. What that means to me is to do well in certain areas and to assemble young people, enthusiasts and idealists about you and say to them, in a sense of the Scripture—and I don't mean this blasphemously—'Come, follow me.' I have never been comfortable with a teacher who did not point to self in the classroom and say, 'Write as well as I write, invent as well as I invent, critique as well as I critique, work in the political system as well as I do.' The phenomenon of teachers that I've known as well as faculty members with whom I've developed bonds of friendship over the years, generally are those who are less good at writing, less good at politics and less good at science. I know that threatens the academic world, but we have a price to pay for your being less good sometimes at what you do."

Despite Cunningham's oratory about what Focus: HOPE had accomplished with the MTI, nothing was ever hunky-dory. For one, the tutorial program still wasn't working well. In 1986, Cunningham asked Ferguson, a former *Free Press* reporter and editor, to study the program and report back to him. The result after four months was a thoughtful and perceptive 11-page report:

"First, it's worth recognizing that 90 percent of the Machinist Training Institute's failings have been pre-destined," Ferguson wrote. "The school, for better or worse, was created by matching apples and oranges. The apples are students who predominantly are long-term unemployed, black and/or female, whose work habits have deteriorated (or never existed), many of whom have had problems with the law or with the euphemism du jour, 'substances,' and virtually all of whom are impeded in their progress by other pieces of 'baggage,' as we are wont to describe various side effects of poverty. The oranges are machine shops with the most stringent attendance rules of any business I know, 58-hour weeks, and a workforce that is not only white but, to indulge in stereotype, historically racist and entirely male. If you set out to construct a more impossible training/placement task you would fail. ... Anything remotely approaching 90 percent success with such students is 100 percent impossible."

Ferguson noted that MTI had placed more than 90 percent of its graduates in manufacturing jobs. "Relative to other job training programs for those in poverty, our record is tremendous." But "only a small percentage ... will become, and remain, machinists. ... This is what is meant by 'pre-destined' failings. They have very little to do with how the school is run or how teachers teach. They just come, sadly, with the turf."

Ferguson said some MTI staff resented Cunningham's repeated statements about becoming the "Harvard of machinist schools." Staff at MTI wanted to help people get out of poverty, period, Ferguson said. Most of the applicants to MTI weren't interested—and probably didn't have the aptitude for—careers as skilled machinists. They just wanted a job. That conflict led to many students dropping out and for many graduates to quit the trade after getting a machinist job.

Ferguson offered a "radical idea" for Cunningham to consider: Create something called a Focus: HOPE Academy where everyone who qualifies could get a month of intense remedial instruction in math and reading, as well as training in resume-writing, interviewing, attire, even professional niceties like shaking hands correctly, avoiding profanities and looking others in the eye. Ferguson called it "a kind of boot camp for people desiring to lead productive lives."

Cunningham liked the idea. He tasked Armstead, Young, Charlie Grenville, and a young Jesuit-educated do-gooder named Kevin Gordon to create a short-term academy to help youths who had graduated but still did not have the math and reading skills needed for the MTI or for any sort of other career.

In typical Cunningham fashion, Fast Track was launched before there was money to pay for it. But the concept was attractive to potential funders and donors. In June 1988, the Kellogg Foundation approved a three-year $786,000 grant for Fast Track. IBM agreed to donate 64 desktop model 286 computers, then among the most modern personal computers, 60 workstations, two file servers and the latest math-reading learning software.

Grenville, who had been disappointed that Cunningham had pulled the plug on Project Trust, designed a two-part Fast Track program. The first part was six weeks of intensive remedial instruction in mathematics and reading, resume-writing and workplace etiquette. The other was more personal: regularly meeting with kids still in Detroit's high schools to encourage them to study and enjoy math and science. Grenville hoped to stimulate their imaginations through exposure to high-tech manufacturing, including robotics. "Very high tech and space age,"

Gordon said. Grenville "didn't think that this little six-week Fast Track by itself was going to work."

Cunningham looked at Fast Track as an essential step, but only a step toward his idea for Focus: HOPE's biggest enterprise yet: a cutting-edge manufacturing and engineering college—the Center for Advanced Technologies. He expected the best MTI students to continue their education at the CAT where they could earn associates and bachelor's degrees. Initially Cunningham insisted that all kids entering Fast Track would have high school degrees. But Focus: HOPE soon learned that wasn't feasible and that "the G.E.D. kids were actually testing higher than the kids with high school diplomas," Gordon said. "The first couple of [Fast Track] classes were a disaster."

Outwardly, Cunningham painted a rosy picture for the press. "We found the challenge of the machinist industry, particularly the mathematics, to be very demanding," Cunningham told *The Michigan Catholic* in March 1989. "Our Center for Advanced Technology will need capable young people and this is one way to ensure that they'll be there. We know we need good candidates, but we also know that not everyone will be a machinist. Those that can't or don't want to be will be prepared for a good future."

Josaitis made a surprise visit to Fast Track in April 1989, and was discouraged. "There were nine students in the class, two arrived late, one absent," she wrote in a note to Cunningham. The Fast Track manager was fired due to poor record keeping, and they put Gordon in charge. Gordon could get the paperwork straightened out, but they still needed someone who could improve student performance in the classroom.

At about the same time, Cunningham asked Lt. General William S. Flynn, the top commander at TACOM, if he knew someone who could instill military-style discipline in the Fast Track program. Flynn mentioned a key assistant, Sergeant Major Thomas Murphy, who had recently retired from the U.S. Army. Flynn asked Murphy to call the priest. "He said, Father Cunningham is looking for somebody down there to, the way he put it, to kick ass and take names," Murphy said. "Sergeant

Majors, that is mainly their job. They make sure that the soldiers work, and do their job, what they're supposed to when they're supposed to. That's what a Sergeant Major's job is."

Gordon called Murphy a "character, a little guy from Ireland, face like a bulldog." Murphy and Cunningham hit it off like two Irish drinking buddies, although Murphy, who emigrated from Ireland at age 17 and joined the U.S. Army at age 19, didn't drink. "I really liked him," Murphy said of the priest. "You know, no holds barred. He talked to Murphy like Murphy talked to him. … I was impressed with the fact that he had a training program to get these people into a career field."

Cunningham gave Murphy the authority to run things the way he saw fit. "I set it up myself," Murphy said. "OK, business starts at 8:00 in the morning—three minutes late and you're required to come to school on Saturday morning. That started right away, getting them punctual, being there on time. If they had a doctor's appointment, don't tell me after the fact. I want to know before the students had to log in every morning."

For the first class Murphy handled, he passed out a written set of rules that had been approved by Cunningham. "If you're not going to abide by this, you might as well leave now because I'll kick your ass out," Murphy told them. One tardy was one point; an unexcused absence was two points. "If they got to six points then they didn't graduate. They could go home. As far as I was concerned they weren't serious about it." Murphy said. Murphy was an incredible workhorse and arrived at work every day by 4 a.m., driving in from New Baltimore, about 40 miles away.

One of the first things that got scrapped under Gordon and Murphy was the idea that the kids could learn by simply working through a program on the computer. "First of all, the majority of the students coming in there were computer illiterate," Murphy said. "They got classes, actual classes, teacher to student. … Unless you're actually there seeing them doing it all the time, they do what the hell they want to do." Between them, Gordon and Murphy turned the program around and got positive results. "We would have these high school kids come in. If they tested at 8th grade reading and math, we found we were usually pretty good at getting them up to 9th and 10th grade in six weeks. But the reading scores didn't come up the way the math did."

"For a priest," Murphy said of Cunningham, "he was very down to earth. He didn't have himself up on a pedestal. He didn't mind getting his hands dirty. We pulled it off, but I think he gave guidance. He had people, smart people, in the fields that would get this stuff done."

Over scotch in 1985, Cunningham and his friends Neal Shine, managing editor of the *Free Press*, and Don Haney, a black television personality, concocted yet another innovative program: the Focus: HOPE Journalism Olympics. The idea was to bring dozens of teens from a wide swath of Metro Detroit to Focus: HOPE where they would spend the morning learning about the civil rights organization, then have lunch with mentors, who were professional journalists. The teens were then set loose to explore the Focus: HOPE campus and interview whoever would let them: staff members, Fast Track or MTI students, volunteers or food recipients. The students were to find a story, interview sources, come back to a Focus: HOPE classroom and type their stories up, 300 to 500 words maximum, by the 4:30 p.m. deadline. The results would then be judged by a panel of journalists and the winners, to be announced in a few weeks, would share $2,000 in scholarship money, mostly provided by WXYZ-TV (Channel 7) anchor, Bill Bonds, another Cunningham friend.

All told, 52 students from 30 high schools competed in the Journalism Olympics, mentored by 29 professional journalists from print and electronic media. Ann Walker, then Focus: HOPE's special projects coordinator, told *The Detroit News* that the Olympics were successful at bridging the city-suburban gap, but that she was "really disappointed" that only two Detroit public high school students participated.

High school students comprised probably the largest group of walkers at the annual Focus: HOPE Walk for Justice in 1985. That year, Cunningham changed the route to focus on the communities around the Catholic Church of the Madonna and the areas that in 1967 saw the worst of the riots. He wanted to emphasize life in neighborhoods where people were struggling to get by even as city leaders were lavishing money on down-town developments. "We have deterioration, and that has to be attended to," Cunningham said. "But by starting and ending the walk at Focus: HOPE we are showing what we have done and what we have to do here. ... I think they'll get an education in a few hours, have some fun and make a contribution to an organi-zation that is trying to make a difference in the future."

Vice President George H.W. Bush and Michigan Governor William
Milliken listen to Father Cunningham discuss his ideas for a greater Detroit
through Focus: HOPE's innovative job training programs in 1982.

Credit: Focus: HOPE

20

Miracle Worker

FATHER BILL CUNNINGHAM and Gerald Rosen, a friend from former Senator Bob Griffin's office, carefully made their way into the abandoned factory where the priest proclaimed he would create a world-class center for high-tech engineering. Rosen, then working for the Miller, Canfield law firm in Detroit, was skeptical. "There were holes in the ceiling, water coming in all over the place," he said.

Cunningham was enthusiastically explaining how he would build a futuristic learning environment for underprivileged youths. "And, it's going to have a Star Trek theme with a bridge!" Rosen quoted the priest. "I kept thinking this guy just lost it. I finally said, 'Bill, where are you going to get the money for all that?' He looked at me and said, 'God will provide.'"

Focus: HOPE had just purchased that factory and two other empty industrial buildings another two blocks west on Oakman Boulevard for $700,000—money it had borrowed. It was more money than Cunningham wanted to spend, but he was up against a deadline for a $6 million HUD grant that Charlie Grenville had found that would let them pay for remodeling.

The cut-off date was looming and Cunningham knew he couldn't get a grant to refurbish buildings Focus: HOPE didn't own. But the sellers—a group of real estate speculators—wouldn't budge on the price, so he grudgingly signed purchase agreements and borrowed the money.

"Once we got the keys, we found all kinds of stuff in there," Thom Armstead said. "The roof was leaking, paint was falling off the ceiling. It was a mess." David Lanius, a process engineer at Detroit Diesel advising Focus: HOPE, assessed the place: "What a disaster!"

"The Ford engine plant, you open the door and you were in mud and goop knee-deep," Lanius said. "That was a really sorry looking mess. The windows were out, the roof was open, the floor was in muck and dung, birds, critters of any kind. Critters had come in and died in there and were all over the place."[30]

When the deal was done, Cunningham shook off any negative energy and declared that in two weeks they'd celebrate with a big party announcing what would become the Center for

---

30   *David Lanius and his wife Sarah (known as Sally) was invited by Bill Sullivan at Focus: HOPE to come to the Catholic Church of the Madonna to hear its charismatic pastor who, strangely, was involved in the auto industry. "We went to his church," said Lanius, a Lutheran. "We listened to him pray. We listened to him give sermons. We listened to him do all of those kinds of things. In addition to that, he knew then that I was an engineer." Cunningham's Focus: HOPE, Sally Lanius said, "was lots of prayer, logic and sweat." Lanius had spent four years in Brazil leading a team that created an entire plant to make diesel engines and was uniquely qualified to help the priest build an industrial operation. At Cunningham's request, Lanius took a tour of Industry Mall. "There was no equipment that was useful in a very fast action," Lanius said. He was alarmed because the MTI's old equipment was unsafe. He was appalled that steel pieces being milled or drilled were not held as securely in place as they needed to be. There were "17-year-old kids standing here looking at it with their mouth open waiting for something to happen." He told Cunningham and Armstead that the process was inefficient and laden with risk. The priest scoffed, saying that nothing had happened so far. "I said, OK, that's fine. Be happy that it hasn't because somebody could get hurt badly," Lanius said.*

Advanced Technologies. Oh, and they'd hold the party inside the oily, grimy, vermin-infested engine plant that was to become the CAT. Focus: HOPE staff and volunteers got to work. "We swept all the water out, cleaned the floors and put up a lot of Visqueen on the walls," Armstead said. "A stage was set up, we set up a bar. Coleman Young came out. We had all the industry folks out. ... It was horrible, but it's funny. ... People were standing around and they would be having cocktails, waiters were serving a great open bar, a nice little orchestra playing, and just days before rats were running around, the roof was leaking and there was grease all over the floor," Armstead said.

The party was Cunningham's first opportunity to sell the CAT to potential donors, including many powerful Detroiters. He knocked them out with his exuberance. He described his vision that he said would transform Detroit's aging manufacturing infrastructure by providing disadvantaged people the linguistic, mathematical and hands-on technical knowledge that it takes to operate the precision robotic manufacturing equipment of the future. And, he said, the U.S. Department of Defense would help make it all happen.

Aubrey Lee, then a National Bank of Detroit regional director, was at the party. Cunningham said he needed a $1.5 million line of credit from the bank. Lee, the first African-American to rise to vice president of a major bank in Detroit, said NBD "had a lot of faith in Focus: HOPE. We had faith in them because they produced. They produced and they were great supporters of Detroit. In my opinion, Father Cunningham was not only a great priest, but he was a businessman with a collar. ... It sounded unbelievable, what he wanted to do. But as someone who had worked very closely with Father Cunningham and Eleanor and who knew their history, I thought he would be able to do it."

Focus: HOPE got its first computer numerical control (CNC) and computer-assisted design (CAD) machines in January 1983. Programming and operating such machines was just one of the skills Machinists Training Institute graduates would have, Cunningham said. With the math and technical knowledge, they could be craftsmen, machine repairmen, tool-and-die machinists, hydraulics repairmen, and electronics technicians. The CAT would go light years further, training candidates for degrees in engineering. Cunningham had met dozens of machine shop and tool-and-die operators who had gotten rich by being very good at creating machines that manufacture parts for the automobile industry. His goal was to help low-income people get the skills they needed to not just work for an hourly wage, but to become engineers and owners of industrial operations.

Lud Koci, another executive at Detroit Diesel who met the priest in 1985, said Cunningham was right about the employment crisis and his ideas made sense, as grandiose as they seemed. He believed Cunningham "to the extent I believe any Irish priest. He was typically full of blarney. You had to listen to what he told you and then think it through: Gee, that's where he aims to get at. But it's going to be a long time betwixt the cup and the lip."

Even as Cunningham, Josaitis and the Focus: HOPE team planned this new, unique and creative project, they had to once again fight powerful figures in Washington working to de-fund the food distribution program at Focus: HOPE. Josaitis and Cunningham continued relentless lobbying on Capitol Hill and at the Pentagon for the food program, MTI and, now the CAT. The pair—sometimes accompanied by Armstead or Grenville—worked meetings with key policymakers in the Senate and the House and their staffs. By March 1986, Cunningham had testified 11 times before congressional committees, and Grenville three times. The official Focus: HOPE count does not include dozens of other trips to Washington at which Cunningham and Josaitis held small-group meetings, presented videos, discussed data and gave heartbreaking descriptions of the bleak conditions faced by the poor in Detroit.

Focus: HOPE's Food for Seniors program provided nutritional foods specially designed to augment the diets of senior citizens who take multiple prescription drugs and who are least likely to have access to protein, fresh fruit and vegetables. Federal funding had been allowing Focus: HOPE to serve 7,700 seniors every month, but there were more than 16,000 eligible elderly people on a waiting list—seniors who had called Focus: HOPE asking for help. On their trips to Washington, Josaitis lugged an oversize briefcase with a stack of green-tinted paper that was five or six inches thick. It was a list of names of impoverished seniors waiting for food. It made an impressive thud when dropped onto a conference room table or a bureaucrat's desk. Help us expand the program to those other needy seniors, they pleaded and pleaded again to staffers and policymakers on the Hill. Success was a matter of getting to the right people with the right message, suggesting solutions, making connections and always remembering to say thank you in written follow-up notes.

In the spring of 1986, after years of lobbying by Cunningham, Josaitis and Father Roger Morin of New Orleans, Congress finally approved an expansion of the Food for Seniors program nationwide, appropriating $3.5 million that agencies or organizations could request to administer the programs. The legislation specifically set aside $700,000 for Focus: HOPE.[31]

To Cunningham and Josaitis, getting the legislation passed should have made it a done deal. But the U.S. Department of Agriculture and the federal Office of Management and Budget (OMB) were dragging out the regulation-writing process for the program. The regulations should not have been that difficult to write. General eligibility standards already existed in the program: Persons aged at least 60 with singles having incomes of $569 a month or less ($6,828 annually), and couples having incomes of no more than $764 a month or $9,168 a year. An estimated 100,000 seniors in the tri-county area were eligible for the program. And even though the Food Prescription Program had been closely scrutinized, often visited and always praised by federal bureaucrats and policymakers, some officials in the Reagan Administration did not want to release the money. Not only

---

31   *The $700,000 that finally came from the federal government was needed to help Focus: HOPE keep the Food Prescription Program alive—it was not and could not be used to re-pay the $700,000 borrowed to purchase the three industrial buildings.*

was the expansion in jeopardy, but the entire program was in danger because it was running out of money to operate.

By late June 1986, the prospect of shutting down Focus: HOPE's signature program was under serious consideration. The Reagan Administration apparently had decided to let the handful of programs that distributed government-purchased food commodities—like Focus: HOPE's—to end. "The OMB wants to kill this program, and they want to do it by denying us the funds to store and distribute the food we have," Cunningham told the *Detroit Free Press*. "When an old person who has been receiving food on our program dies, OMB wants to snatch back the food from the next old person waiting in line."

Josaitis went to work, speaking to several people on the staff of U.S. Senator Bob Dole, R-Kansas, who was the chairman of the Senate subcommittee on nutrition. Many commodities to be distributed, of course, were produced by farmers in his home state. "Dole had a big interest in this," said Rosen. "I knew Dole's staff and I helped organize their coming and testifying through that contact."

With Dole and other Republican Congressional support, the USDA and OMB folded and released $700,000 to Focus: HOPE to increase distribution to 16,000 senior citizens. Cunningham told the *Free Press* that including all seniors on the waiting list was unexpected, but certainly welcome. "It's always a surprise when something happens on this scale," the priest said. "We were hoping to get some of the elderly poor off the waiting list—to have them say we'll take care of all 16,000 on our waiting list is probably the most dramatic news we've had around here in 15 years. An unusual amount of credit has to be given to Sen. Dole for his unswerving commitment to taking care of hungry people in this country."

Josaitis was "walking in the clouds; she's fought for this moment for five years," Cunningham told *The Michigan Catholic*. He said that as many as 4,000 of the elderly on the waiting list had died while the government dragged its feet: "Just about every parish in the tri-county area has seniors who are hungry and have a right to this food. This is not a handout. This is food designed especially for their diet needs."

While the CAT was still in development, Cunningham and Josaitis never forgot about Mary Sullivan's offer to start a proper day care center at Focus: HOPE. "Eleanor and I had always talked about a Center for Children," Sullivan said. "I said at the time that when you get some space I'll start a little day care center; maybe one of those little storefronts" on Oakman Boulevard.

As part of the three-building deal in 1984, Focus: HOPE bought an empty supermarket that once had been a Massey-Ferguson warehouse at the corner of Oakman Boulevard and Linwood Avenue. "I went out and looked at it and it was a pit, an absolute pit," Sullivan said. "It had been a supermarket and it was just in shambles. Ford had used it as a place to stick their pallets; huge, huge pallets, all rusty, stacked up 6 feet high, with rats running around. I said, 'If there ever is a day care center on these grounds, it'll be a miracle.'"

Still, Sullivan felt a spiritual connection to Cunningham and believed in his vision. "I really felt that God wanted a day care center there and that He chose me specially to put a day care center there because I think nobody in their right mind would try to do it. I was afraid that if I didn't do it, nobody would do it."

Cunningham put Sullivan in charge of the whole project: site cleanup, renovation, architect work, the contractor, as well as designing the Montessori-like program that she would eventually run. "I said to him, 'You know I've never done this before.' He said, 'You know, my dad always told me if you want a job done well give it to somebody who isn't quite sure of themselves. They'd do a better job because they work harder at it.'"

Articles of incorporation for the Focus: HOPE Center for Children were drafted on November 16, 1984: "The purposes of the corporation are to root out racism, poverty and injustice, to provide for the relief of the poor, the depressed or the underprivileged, to lessen neighborhood tensions, to eliminate prejudice and discrimination, to rectify the effects of prejudice and discrimination and to combat community deterioration by developing and operating programs for the education and care of children, including, without limitation, one or more licensed child care centers, admission to which will not be denied because of race, color, creed, sex and national origin."

Grenville's team added grant-writing for the Center for Children to their growing list of Focus: HOPE projects that needed funding. Grenville's experience, knowledge about federal opportunities, and uncanny ability to distill Cunningham's over-the-top rhetoric into a clearly written work plan, were essential. Grenville "particularly took that project (Center for Children) to heart," Sullivan said. "He wanted to have that money for that project because he had felt that as a child he himself had been so neglected. And we would talk about what children need and the dignity and the respect you have to have for children so they grow up to respect themselves. Charlie would say, 'I wish I had been to a school like that and treated like that.'"

Words on the page weren't quite enough for one improbably large grant request that Focus: HOPE made to the U.S. Department of Health and Human Services (HHS): $1.3 million for the Center for Children. Grenville, who had taken two months off in 1986 after surgery to remove cancerous tumors in his esophagus (likely a byproduct of his smoking and drinking habits), was under extraordinary pressure to find the ever-increasing amounts of money required to fulfill Cunningham's vision. "To pull that whole thing together was stressful, to pull all those matching grants together, it was so difficult," said Kevin Gordon, who came to work for Focus: HOPE's Development Department in 1988. Proposals written by Grenville and his team also were sent to several local foundations, principally the Troy-based Kresge Foundation, then known for funding brick-and-mortar projects. Kresge soon approved a $500,000 challenge grant, meaning that it would grant Focus: HOPE a half-million dollars if an equal amount was raised from other sources.

HHS turned Focus: HOPE down flat. But Cunningham refused to accept that as their final answer. As it happened, HHS Secretary Margaret Heckler, an appointee of President Reagan, was scheduled to attend a conference at Cobo Hall in Detroit in October 1985, one of her last public appearances outside of Washington before becoming the U.S. Ambassador to Ireland in December. Sen. Carl Levin, who knew about Focus: HOPE's grant proposal, also was scheduled to attend the conference luncheon and had been told he would sit next to Heckler. Levin offered Cunningham his seat and the priest found himself with a captive audience of one. "He sat next to Heckler and charmed her over the luncheon," Armstead said. The priest undoubtedly spoke passionately about the underprivileged and how brain science showed how important the pre-school years were. He would have talked about the greatest obstacle for low-income parents looking for work was a lack of day care. He undoubtedly added large measures of his Irish Catholic humor and charm. "A lot of Irish bullshit," Armstead said with a laugh.

Kresge's deadline for Focus: HOPE to achieve the match was November 15, 1985. That day, just hours before the offer would expire, an aide to Heckler called Cunningham to say that HHS was granting $851,000 for the Center for Children. "Like a miracle, the call from Jerrold Speers came late on November 15, the very day the Kresge Foundation had established as the deadline for meeting its challenge grant," Cunningham wrote in a thank-you letter to Heckler. Cunningham also expressed thanks to several Republican officials, including Michigan Congressman Carl Pursell, Labor Secretary William Brock and Vice President George H.W. Bush.

The vision of an early childhood learning center was extraordinary, but the details in re-purposing a site that was possibly contaminated with chemicals into a learning place for toddlers provided plenty of headaches for Sullivan and the architectural firm, Robert Sassak Architect, Limited. The idea was to try to save as much of the building as possible, but "there was so little that we could actually use from the old building," Sullivan said. 'The only thing we ended up using was the foundation; everything else had to be new. And then we had a lot of problems with oil drums buried on the grounds. There was oil in them and we couldn't build on the property unless they were empty. There was a lot of expense in finding out whether those oil drums were full of oil."

Cunningham generated most of the headaches by adding upgrades that drove costs skyward. In a January 21, 1986, letter to Sullivan, Sassak said that his first proposal to Focus: HOPE dated September 12, 1984, was for a building estimated to cost less than $500,000. By November 1, 1984, after several meetings with Cunningham, cost estimates rose to $850,000 and then $1.1 million. Focus: HOPE's payment of the firm's $86,000 fee for designing the building and managing the construction bidding process—generally 8.8 percent of the total project's cost—had been spent long ago. Sassak included a list of 38 areas that were changed or added on by Cunningham during that first year, including: "Prolonged Contract Negotiations," "Landscape Development," "Play Area Development," "Steel Fencing Development," "Project Security Systems," "Double Sprinkler System at ceiling and above," "Kitchen Equipment Plan Revisions," and "Overall Upgrading of Approach to Project per ongoing directives from Fr. Cunningham."

By Labor Day 1985, the cost estimate had risen to $1.65 million. "Since then, at Fr. Cunningham's direction, the project continues to be inhanced [sic] and expanded," Sassak wrote, including expensive small-size toilets that toddlers and preschool children could use. "Obviously, the project we began is not the project we are finishing," Sassak wrote. "Taken individually, the changes have not been prohibitive. Taken collectively, the changes have redefined the nature of the project and restructured the scope of the work in ways neither you or I could have foreseen until you determined your exact program requirements, item by item, as we worked our way through this phase of the project. … We have not received compensation for services since our October 1 [1985] invoice, and yet we continue to work to complete the project while expanding the scope of the work."

Sullivan, too, was frustrated by the ever-changing nature of Cunningham's vision for the day care center. Her needs were simple: a decent and clean place to teach and nurture young children. Cunningham wanted a large helping of that, plus a certain wow factor for visitors. "We had a lot of disagreements," Sullivan said. "He was very interested in the building and making it a beautiful, beautiful structure for the children. My concern was the interior, of having the things inside that the children were going to need, the equipment. I was afraid we were going to run out of money before we got to the inside. He wanted a special tile on the roof and things like that that I didn't feel were as important. I used to say that I'm going to be out on the street with a babushka. We're going to have a beautiful building and I'm going to be out on the street begging for a little folding money like the gypsies in Ireland."

Have faith, Cunningham advised. In June 1986, ground was broken for the Focus: HOPE Center for Children. It took more than a year to complete the modern, spacious and beautiful building. The final cost was $2.7 million and it came from various sources, primarily HHS, Kresge, the Skillman Foundation, the McGregor Fund and the Gannett Foundation—all grants that Grenville and his team worked hard to capture. "Imagine, the development officer and the price keeps going up and up, and Charlie's got to keep up," said Gordon. "He would just fume in private."

Focus: HOPE needed money, but there were lines Father Cunningham would not cross. That December he got media attention when he turned down cash raised by a group of nude dancers at Jason's, a bar in Windsor, Ontario, across the river from Detroit. The topless-bottomless dancers had held a "Christmas Charity for Children" party to raise about $17,000. In a single day, they had sold pictures of themselves, garters and T-shirts and danced nude at customers' tables to earn $5 tips for charity. The dancers had included Focus: HOPE among the charities it planned to donate to. "We're going to refuse it," Cunningham told the *Free Press*. "The purpose of Focus: HOPE is civil rights and … we view [nude bars] as part of the problem… We feel that the misuse of women that is Jason's commodity is contrary to the principles of Focus: HOPE."

An opportunity to provide miraculous assistance to Focus: HOPE's MTI graduates came in 1986. Lud Kodi's wife, Trudy, had only met Cunningham a few times and didn't really know him well. But while planning a 50th birthday party for her husband, Trudy called the priest for help deciding what to ask invitees to do in lieu of gifts. Her husband really didn't want or need anything. The priest told her that many MTI graduates could get a better start in their careers if they owned the tools of their trade: basic things like micrometers, gauges, T-squares, prime squares, levels and heavy duty tool boxes. Those tools are expensive, but if a skilled tradesman doesn't have them they have to work with somebody who does and can never be truly independent. "She threw this big party and we told people instead of bringing me gifts, to bring tools for the MTI," Lud Koci said.

"We invited Father to come; he was just so thrilled," Trudy said. A beaming and grateful Cunningham asked Lud Koci to speak at the next MTI graduation where he could present each graduate with one of the gifts. None of the machinists could have hoped to own such tools that weren't already battered from years of use. "Father would never accept anything other than new for his people—never," Koci said. "One year, a guy brought him a whole bunch of toys for Christmas for kids that his own kids were done with. They looked like new, but Father called him and told him to come pick up his garbage. 'Would your kids like getting someone else's used toys?' was how he put it."

However, Cunningham "did take a used truck from us at Detroit Diesel that was in pretty good shape," Koci said. "We took a lot of pictures with Roger [Penske] and myself and him. Then Roger looked around for someone to drive the truck to Focus: HOPE, and Father said, 'I'm here!' He said, 'I drove a truck for years!'" Skeptical, Koci said he cautioned the priest that, "This was a full-size, Class A truck; you can't just drive it away."

"Sure, I can! Just watch me," Cunningham said. To Koci's and Penske's amazement, the priest got in the cab and drove it around the parking lot once just to show them. Then, he drove it to Focus: HOPE. "There wasn't much he couldn't do," Trudy Koci said.

Cunningham, of course, got a first-class building for the $2.7 million spent building the Center for Children. The high-quality early childhood education program would initially be offered only to the children of MTI students, employees of Focus: HOPE's for-profit industrial operations, or regular staff members. "The Center for Children was the carrot, as he called it, to bring people into the machinist training program," said Sullivan who had also supervised the design of various rooms where different age groups of kids could play, learn, eat, nap and exercise. "I wanted a kind of homey atmosphere," Sullivan said.

All reviews of the Center for Children were positive with reporters hyping another triumph for Cunningham and Josaitis. As usual, Cunningham waxed eloquently when speaking about the children Focus: HOPE expected to serve in the spectacular new building. "This center is dedicated to inspiring children with the wonder and joy of an inscrutable future, rather than the fear and hate of an unknown darkness," he said. "We can't provide road maps or star paths. All we can provide is a child whose heart and mind are filled with hope for the future—lifelong hope, founded on the energies of love."

One feature of the Center for Children was a closed-circuit television system that allowed Focus: HOPE employees and MTI students to check on how their children were doing during the day without leaving their workstations. Cunningham had wanted a wow factor, and he got it—a childcare center that was safe, clean and nurturing, an architectural jewel in the heart of a struggling Detroit neighborhood. "We want to convey a message that the children of Detroit are important," said Angus McMillan who ran the center with Sullivan. "They are the future."

"One of the values we try to instill in workers in the mall industries is that they are only helping themselves but that because they are being productive, their children can have a chance at a better life, too," Cunningham told Pete Waldmeir for a column published in *The Detroit News* in March 1988. "So if, say, a young mother who has an infant and is working at her first job with us knows that her child is in the same class with the kids of people who have achieved something in life, she'll work hard to stay employed with us—if for no other reason than to give her child that added chance. ... Does that make sense? I guess we'll find out, won't we?"

Father Cunningham prepares to sign papers creating Cycle-Tec. Others from left are Michael Lewis, an attorney, John Rye, head of Lamb Technicon, and F. James McDonald, president of General Motors.

Credit: Focus: HOPE

21

Profiteer

JOHN CARDINAL DEARDEN may never have realized that a boon he granted to Father Bill Cunningham in 1980 would lead the nonprofit Focus: HOPE to expand beyond a machinist training program and into for-profit industrial manufacturing that would generate millions of dollars for Focus: HOPE.

"Bill called Dearden and asked if he knew Jim McDonald," Thom Armstead recalled. McDonald, the president of General Motors, was a member of the "Cardinal's Club" of business leaders. "The cardinal said he'd give him a call. The next thing I know, McDonald's secretary was calling and setting up a meeting for Cunningham and me with Jim McDonald." Cunningham needed McDonald's help finding jobs for a dozen MTI graduates who had not been hired.

They parked outside the General Motors Building on West Grand Boulevard and rode the elevator to the 14th floor to meet McDonald. A large group of GM purchasing directors had to wait for McDonald to finish up with Cunningham. Then, "he introduced us to all his purchasing agents. We went and made our pitch to this group and McDonald said, 'we want to help out.'" McDonald gave each director a specific number of MTI graduates to hire. For the next few weeks, human resources people from several GM plants came to Focus: HOPE to interview MTI graduates. But the industry was in a slump. There was a hiring freeze, and the company was laying off employees. None were hired.

McDonald didn't give up, Armstead said. "He sent out the head of labor relations for GM and the top representative for the UAW to Focus: HOPE. … Everybody thought it was a great idea." But when the UAW representative reported back to union vice president Stephen Yokich, the notion of GM hiring new people when union members were losing their jobs was nixed. The only play available was to make Focus: HOPE a GM contractor. "He called Cunningham one day and said, 'Father, if we give you these contracts can you hire them?' Of course, Bill said, 'yeah!' And we started a little company, F&H Manufacturing, and we hired those 12 folks to work in F&H. And then McDonald continued to help us out."

As production plans ramped up, Industry Mall and the MTI needed more machine tools—lathes, grinders, mills, shapers, and especially more complex machinery like dynamometers. "He was begging, borrowing machine tools where ever he went," McDonald said of the priest. "We certainly had some machines in storage in various plants that we could make available to him." McDonald also opened doors for Cunningham to meet people in important positions in the industry. One of them was John Rye, the head of the Lamb Technicon, a major producer of parts and tooling machines for the automotive industry. A master mechanic and engineer, Rye had worked for GM for several years. But in 1952 he quit GM and bought a tool-and-die shop from his uncle Joseph Lamb near Stroh's brewery.

Rye specialized in engineering better machines to make parts like spark plugs. Mechanizing as much of the engineering process as possible meant more precise and consistent metal shaping—a better product for a lower price. Eventually, Rye took what would become Lamb Technicon into the business of making machines that make other machines, allowing for higher productivity, quality and profit. John Rye held more than 2,000 patents, mostly in the automated system-building manufacturing process, his son Jonathon Rye said. Under his father, Lamb Technicon became a pioneer in robotic manufacturing. His creativity, work ethic and talent made him a millionaire.

John Rye met Cunningham at Focus: HOPE in 1981, and soon Rye, McDonald and Cunningham were tossing around ideas about how Focus: HOPE could insert itself into the hyper-competitive automobile business.

"At that lunch, they came up this idea to create a factory to rebuild transmissions at Focus: HOPE," Jonathan Rye said. John Rye would invest a chunk of his company's resources into the enterprise. McDonald promised to produce a contract to rebuild defective transmissions through a company called Cycle Tec, a subsidiary of Lamb Technicon. Cycle Tec would hire MTI students to break down GM transmissions, examine fluids and parts for anomalies, replace worn parts, and then rebuild the transmissions perfectly enough to be sold.

Although top Lamb Technicon managers were not thrilled about the idea, Jonathan never doubted his father's business acumen or questioned his charitable nature. So he carried out his dad's directives to get Cycle Tec going. "My dad did it just to be a good Christian," he said. Armstead thought that while John Rye was generous to Focus: HOPE, there was a certain amount of self-interest at play, too. "Politically, (Rye) knew that the president of General Motors was supporting Father Cunningham in our project and this could possibly mean some additional business for him," Armstead said.

With the GM contract in place, Cycle Tec took over about 130,000 square feet of space in Building B of Industry Mall. "They brought equipment, conveyor lines, a dynamometer that takes components like transmissions and tests fluid pressures, timings, spring tensions and other properties to make sure the machinery is functioning properly," Armstead said. Operations began in early 1982 and in that year Cycle Tec hired 107 new employees, many of them MTI students who could work on the transmission rebuilding line while still studying to become machinists. Although Cycle Tec wasn't doing actual machining, it served as real hands-on work in an industrial production setting. Rye put Lamb's engineers, marketers and finance people at Cunningham's service.

"It goes into a real industrial operation, as opposed to a little mom-and-pop transmission shop," said Ken Kudek, who in 1985 would become general manager of Cycle Tec. "They're collaborating. But it's not like Cunningham's creating the business model for Cycle Tec; that's happening between McDonald and Rye. Let's call it a win-win-win. Rye gets a place at an advantageous rate for the rent, Focus: HOPE is relieved of this large economic burden and makes a little money off of the rent, and it supplies support for MTI."

The transmission GM selected for Cycle Tec was the "350" that had been used in most cars and light trucks for several years. "Instead of having these transmissions go to the AAM-COs and others, GM decided it would capture the market by re-manufacturing them and giving them the Mr. Good Wrench certification," Armstead said.

The damaged 350s came in by the truckload and Cycle Tec workers would bring them to a disassembly area "where it's all broken down to parts with certain parts discarded immediately," Kudek said. "The engagement of the clutch is fiber against metal, and you get rid of the fiber, drain the oil, the torque convertor gets put into a bin and can't be reused without being re-manufactured. The good parts, the reusable parts, you wash and you feed them into the part system where they're inspected for wear and those kinds of things. Then to various departments doing things like rebuilding the valve body or the clutch and all sorts of other parts. O-rings, like washers, are replaced 100 percent. And you rebuild the transmission according to the type of vehicle or vehicles it's going to go onto." The re-manufactured transmissions would sell for $600. Seemed ideal on paper, but the problem was that virtually every car mechanic in America knew how to fix a 350 for about $200, although the "fixes" often were temporary.

By the end of 1982, Cycle Tec workers had disassembled, cleaned and rebuilt thousands of 350 transmissions shipped to Focus: HOPE from dealers all around the country. The quality of the work was excellent, but the re-manufactured transmissions were not moving from storage racks. Shipments from GM slowed to a trickle and Cycle Tec laid off most employees—making John Rye rethink the viability of the whole idea and putting Cunningham in the uncomfortable position of watching people he was trying to help become unemployed.

Cunningham wrote a letter to McDonald on February 11, 1983, asking for help: "After a spectacular beginning, exceeding production schedules and quality standards—meeting and surpassing all of GM's requirements, the company has now been forced to lay off due to poor sales." Writing with an understanding gleaned from the countless conversations he was having with engineers, production managers and line workers, Cunningham offered some ideas on how to get the re-manufactured 350s gathering dust at Focus: HOPE sold and keep Cycle Tec operating. He suggested extending warranties on the like-new transmissions from 90 days to one year and cutting the price to $250 or $275, well below cost. "Perhaps the transmission could be a loss-leader until the pipeline is cleared. In any case, the promotion should increase consumer return to dealers from the present 5 percent to better than 50 percent of the transmission aftermarket overnight. The full cost would come to about $350, providing a high quality, fully warrantied product that would rock the Royals and the AAMCOs. And from my side, the excellent performance of our workforce would be appropriately recognized with steady employment."

The priest ended his letter by saying, "Thank you for permitting a cleric to tramp through your marketing place." McDonald wrote back that some of Cunningham's suggestions already were under study. In truth, nothing would solve Cycle Tec's immediate problems. "John Rye at Cycle Tec ends up with all these 350 cores, all of these parts sitting in the pipeline and all of these re-manufactured transmissions for which there is really no market," Kudek said. "But, they've got a work force and all the attendant costs."

"They didn't have an easy time of it," Jonathan Rye said. "The auto business has always been cutthroat, always. And it became apparent that the Japanese were coming on strong. It was a very tough business in the 1980s."

Fortunately for Focus: HOPE, GM decided to change its primary transmission from the hydraulic 350 to an electronic one called a 700 R4 for a new line of cars, including front-wheel drive models that GM was bringing along to compete with the Japanese. "When GM decided to go all front-wheel drive, that's when the industry exploded," Jonathan Rye said. "It was huge for the machine tool industry. From that technology, we went into other areas of factory automation and then we got into complicated parts production ourselves."

The original idea of Cycle Tec being owned one day by its minority employees was put on hold until a business model that worked could be put into place. But it was obvious that Lamb Technicon couldn't continue losing money just to support Cycle Tec. "John Rye decided that he'd sunk enough into it," Kudek said. "But he is willing to sell the business, with McDonald's encouragement, to Focus: HOPE. And then, Focus: HOPE will introduce this new re-manufactured product."

Jonathan Rye said that by 1984 he and his father had put about $2 million into Cycle Tec and decided to more or less donate the business to Focus: HOPE with the understanding that eventually it would be turned into a minority-owned business that could earn the owners profits. Jonathan Rye handled details of the transfer of Cycle Tec to Focus: HOPE, coming to Cunningham with a "fire sale" price of $350,000. Kudek urged Cunningham to push for a lower price, say, $150,000. Rye agreed to the lower figure. "It's all set up for 150," Kudek said. Then a GM insider advised Cunningham to ask John Rye to simply donate the business for one dollar. A day or two later, "Cunningham, McDonald and John Rye get together at McDonald's office and they sign the papers," Kudek said.[32]

---

32   *On September 17, 1986, John Rye was convicted by a federal court jury on four counts of income-tax fraud for failing to report $1.3 million in income from 1979 to 1982. Father Cunningham testified on his behalf, emphasizing Rye's work with Focus: HOPE and personal integrity. Cunningham also appeared at Rye's sentencing in January 1987. A remorseful*

"Part of the deal was GM was to send in two guys to run the company [Cycle Tec]. One was an old GM management type who had been in the transmission business." Some aspects of that arrangement worked better than others. "Within less than a year, they put us in a position of facing a union election."

The priest asked David Lanius, a Detroit Diesel engineer experienced in designing manufacturing plants, to organize a production facility "that would allow us to build parts for people for profit." Lanius devised a small contract with Detroit Diesel for Focus: HOPE to produce a variety of pulleys and then retired to work for Cunningham, setting up the manufacturing system to fulfill the contract. "It was not a huge amount, about 1,000 pulleys," Lanius said. "We didn't give them the equipment, but they had enough good equipment to provide that kind of activity."

Cycle Tec and F&H Manufacturing, wholly owned subsidiaries of the nonprofit Focus: HOPE, produced parts under contracts with the U.S. Army Tank-automotive and Armaments Command (TACOM) in Warren and with Detroit Diesel, GM and Ford. Ford alone came up with eight contracts for Focus: HOPE's Industry Mall, primarily due to the support of company president Harold Arthur (Red) Poling.

One day, Armstead and a volunteer-advisor were looking over a blueprint with specifications for a Ford transmission casting that Focus: HOPE was about to begin machining. "This guy,

---

Rye got three years in prison (all but five months suspended), five months at the Community Corrections Center on Cass Avenue, and 1,250 hours of community service for each year of probation. He also was ordered to pay $115,000 in fines. Rye's attorney, Robert Schwartz, told the judge at sentencing that Rye had already paid $1.7 million in back taxes and fines, and had given $625,000 to charity, and had sold a $1.5 million business to Focus: HOPE for one dollar. "I am a child of God. I err," Rye said tearfully. Much of Rye's community service was performed at Focus: HOPE where Eleanor Josaitis regularly reported to the federal probation department that Rye had been diligently helping develop business for Industry Mall, as well as consulting on the development of Cunningham's next big project, the Center for Advanced Technologies.

one of the GM or Ford advisors, looked at the blueprint and saw this upside down triangle. 'Do you know that's a delta item?' the guy said. I said, 'what's a delta item?' A delta item is one of those safety items like the brakes or steering, one of those things that if you screw up it's a big deal. You can get sued big time for failure of a delta item." Armstead said he went to Cunningham immediately to warn that they were at high risk. If a delta part failed and someone got killed or seriously hurt, they could be sued. "They could have all of Focus: HOPE, the Food Center, everything."

Cunningham's short-term answer was to stop referring to F&H as a department of Focus: HOPE and to create a measure of legal separation. To provide some distance from Focus: HOPE, F&H Manufacturing was incorporated on May 2, 1984, with a three-person Board of Directors: Cunningham, president; Kudek, secretary; and Tony Campbell, treasurer. F&H "is a medium to high volume machining and assembly company with heavy emphasis on metal removal," a Focus: HOPE document explained. "Process capabilities are milling, drilling, boring, tapping, turning and grinding. F&H's primary market is the automotive and related industry, off-highway vehicles and aircraft industries."

Although the new company's trustees were all white men, at some future date F&H "will be a minority owned and operated company with substantial employee ownership." At the first corporate meeting, the board voted to allow Cunningham to issue 500 shares of the corporation's common stock at $1 per share to Focus: HOPE for cash, a whopping $500 to operate the company. Eventually, F&H was shut down in favor of Focus: HOPE's nurturing of for-profit companies it did not "own" such as Oakman Industries and Acu-Tec.

In an April 1984 *Michigan Chronicle* article, reporter Danton Wilson profiled a black man named Kevin Moore, married with four children, who was a new owner of a machining business thanks to Focus: HOPE. Moore said that three years earlier he was unemployed with fading hope when he heard about the Machinist Training Institute. "Father William Cunningham was on television talking about it," Moore said. "As soon as I heard it, I jumped on the phone. Fortunately, I was one of the people picked to join that first class."

After completing his training as a skilled machinist, Moore and a few others got help from Focus: HOPE in setting up their own business, Oakman Industries. Besides providing space in Industry Mall, Focus: HOPE also helped with bookkeeping and contracting services. And MTI instructors would always be available with advice and know-how as the need arose. Moore began hiring a few MTI students. "Right now, we have several contracts with the auto companies and the Defense Department," Moore told Wilson. "And we're making headlight parts for Buick and other General Motors cars. We have a mass-production set-up. We produce a high volume of parts. ... Soon we will become self-sufficient. The Focus: HOPE program gives you an opportunity to really be independent, to stand on your own two feet as it were."

About half a dozen businesses were developed inside Industry Mall from 1982 to 1986. They used precision machining equipment on loan from the Department of Defense and space underwritten by foundation and corporate grants to Focus: HOPE. Even with significant help some of the businesses failed. But many of the owners and employees were successful enough to leave Industry Mall and open up their own machine shops.

Thanks to GM's McDonald, Focus: HOPE got a valuable piece of used equipment, a dynamometer that had been getting rusty in a company storage yard in Detroit. The dynamometer, which was about 8 feet tall, 18 to 20 feet long, 7 feet wide and weighed more than a ton, is used to test engines, transmissions and other assembled components to see how they function while in operation. A dynamometer is a complicated and expensive testing device. Getting a working model was essential to Focus: HOPE's industrial operations.

"That control box itself had to be lifted with a hi-lo," Armstead said. Back when that dynamometer was functioning, it was configured to test the 350 transmission. GM was giving Focus: HOPE the machine for free, but no one could get it to work.

"For days we tried to get that thing going," Armstead said. All they had to show for their efforts was a pool of hydraulic fluid under the dynamometer. "That thing was leaking all over the floor like an ice rink," Armstead said. "It was a nightmare. We had to buy shoes for those guys because the transmission fluid wore through the damn stitching on the safety shoes."

John Milam, a GM engineer on loan to Focus: HOPE, knew "two farmers" who were adept at fixing complicated machinery. The two men—Jim Dunmeyer, who was in farm irrigation, and his friend Murray Hall—were persuaded to come to Focus: HOPE and get the dynamometer working and re-configured to test the newer 700 R4 transmissions. For more than a month, the two men carefully disassembled the dynamometer, keeping track of what went where. "They had wire strung out of that machine all the way to the back of the plant," Armstead said. "They tore everything loose and just rewired everything. That thing was beautiful, a mechanical work of art."

One of the companies started by Focus: HOPE, Acu-Tec, was owned and operated by its four employees: John Wilford, Joe Mason, Graylon Edwards and Joe Morris. "It was a business sponsored by Father Cunningham," Wilford said. "Our machines were placed in certain areas—Bridgeports, lathes and grinders. There were jobs that was given to us by the auto industry, that Father Cunningham had convinced them to. We made parts for headlights on GM cars. We made a lot of injection molding parts, a few gauges, plastic melts [forms]."

Armstead said that he frequently had to encourage or cajole the employee-owners of Acu-Tec and Oakman Industries to keep up with production schedules while also focusing on quality. "They got behind in their schedule," Armstead said. "It was important to keep up with the schedule, to keep production and quality up, so this thing could be successful." Repeatedly, Armstead would remind them that they were the owners and were responsible for fulfilling terms of all contracts: "Business owners don't get paid time and a half. You guys are going to have to decide how to expand your schedule, come in on Saturday or Sunday. But you got to get your schedule caught up." Wilford and Edwards grasped that concept and put in extra hours, getting in early before the others, staying late or working all day on Saturday. Some of them, though, were slackers and Cunningham eventually shut the companies down.

Being a new GM product, the 700 R4 electronic transmissions that were being built in a Hydramatic plant on Nine Mile Road in Warren had glitches that angered customers and frustrated dealers, according to Armstead. "There were more transmissions being shipped back than were going out the door every day," Armstead said. "They had major problems across the country, all these returns. They had cars on the hoist and no transmission" to install. The company was forced to send new transmissions made in Toledo to dealers to replace defective ones, crimping the production of new vehicles. Suddenly, GM needed what Focus: HOPE had to offer—a process and a work force that could get defective transmissions rebuilt and ready to install quickly. "In the first contract, they said, can you do 25 a day?" Armstead said. "Within two, three months, we went from 25 to 200 transmissions a day. We had to make all the engineering changes, reassemble them and get them out the door—200 a day."

The work required hiring and training dozens of people, but the money Focus: HOPE grossed that first year on that one GM contract was phenomenal—nearly $14 million. "We used all GM parts; the only thing we had to purchase was the transmission fluid and the labor costs. It was sweet," Armstead said. "Boy, were we making a profit!"

The money was amazing for a nonprofit that just a few years earlier was close to insolvency—but like a lot of things in the risky auto business, the bottom dropped out the following year. Repairs were made under GM specifications, but those specs kept changing. By Armstead's count GM made nearly 100 engineering changes to the 700 R4 over the first couple of years as new problems emerged. "A transmission is a very intricate piece of machinery," Armstead said. "There are over 1,100 parts inside a transmission. The tolerances are so close on that piece of machinery that any outside debris or something as small as a human hair can cause a failure."

Cycle Tec had to continuously respond to the engineering fixes by retraining workers and changing production lines. Not surprisingly, the transmissions Cycle Tec remanufactured began to fail in large numbers. "At one point, we had 11,000 transmissions shipped back to us, ones we'd already worked on," Armstead said. "We had such a high incidence of failure in the remanufactured transmissions that they shipped them all back. Jim McDonald was getting all kinds of heat. Eventually, they had to shut down the Toledo transmission assembly plant for a weekend, and retool the line to get those transmissions done."

McDonald was under pressure from the GM board when he called the head of Hydramatic, Tom Zimmer, and asked him to help Cunningham. According to Zimmer, McDonald told him: "There is a place called Focus: HOPE and the guy who runs it is Father Bill Cunningham. There isn't a day goes by that I don't get a call from that guy. He's driving me nuts and I got better things to do. You take him on and keep him away from me. Find out what's he's bitching about and what we can do to help him."

Zimmer said he drove from his office at the old Willow Run bomber plant in Ypsilanti to Focus: HOPE at about 6:30 one night. "There was nobody there, except there was a light on in an office and the door was open," Zimmer said. "I stuck my head in and there [Cunningham] was." After some pleasantries about their backgrounds, "we got down to it," said Zimmer. "I am offering my services to you because of Jim McDonald," Zimmer said he told the priest. "As we got into it, then he began to pontificate. He could just wallow in himself with great relish." After about 10 minutes, Zimmer cut him off: "If you think I'm here to hear you pontificate about things, I've got better things to do. If you want to talk business, I'm ready, but if you want to blow smoke at me, I'm going home."

For Zimmer, after hearing the priest out and considering the situation, it all came down to a simple truth: Cunningham and the people at Focus: HOPE had no idea what they were doing with Cycle Tec.

Technically, Focus: HOPE's contract was with GM's Service & Parts Operations (SPO) and not with Hydramatic, but Zimmer and his Hydramatic colleagues provided invaluable hands-on and behind-the-scenes assistance. The re-engineering work on the transmissions was complex, yet had to be done quickly, resulting in high failure rates. "Through the grapevine, we had heard that they [GMSPO managers] were trying to deep-six us," Armstead said.

At the time, GM management was under intense pressure from Wall Street to reduce costs, improve quality and increase profits. Managers at Hydramatic were trying to squeeze every dollar of profit while ramping up production of better performing transmissions. "Some of [Zimmer's] people were not happy with some of the things that happened quality-wise and wanted to cut us off," Armstead said. "So Father and I had a meeting with Tom Zimmer, and we were walking down the parking lot to Cycle Tec. He said, 'Father, what do you want to be—a business or a charity?' Bill told him, 'I want to be a business.'"

Focus: HOPE had to meet the same quality standards as any other GM supplier, and Zimmer "was a tough task master," Armstead said. Under the terms of their contract, Cycle Tec was to pay GM for every transmission that was returned to Focus: HOPE for a do-over. "We had to tear each of them down and give them a report on each transmission, a quality control root analysis. We lost our ability to produce more until we were able to get all 11,000 transmissions torn down." It took several months with costs swallowed by Focus: HOPE. "We had to disassemble everything, re-assemble it, put in all the engineering changes, and test so many a day," Armstead said. "Of the 11,000 that we sent back, many were good but because of the failure rate in random samplings, they rejected the whole thing."

Cunningham "was not happy," Armstead said. "We had to assemble the staff, we had to pay the salaries to the staff assigned to this job over six months. And then they let us go back into production, but we could only produce one transmission a day. Then it was five, and then they ramped us up to 25." Cunningham exacerbated the problem by simultaneously pushing the plan to turn over ownership of Cycle Tec to its minority employees despite the production problems.

"We started giving these bonuses at the end of every quarter," Armstead said. The bonuses were a strong incentive to rebuild more transmissions—but often resulted in shoddy work. "Everybody wanted more and more, faster and faster, but the quality was gone," Armstead said. Cunningham replaced Kudek with Armstead who began to stabilize Cycle Tec. "Things were starting to come back and we started to get back into the black again," Armstead said. "And then there was a movement to unionize Cycle Tec."

Armstead said he tried to emphasize that "sweat equity"—rather than production bonuses—would pay off for employee-owners in the long run. "There were some who thought it was a grand idea, but who couldn't see the big picture and were unwilling to wait five years for the company to be turned over to them." If employees voted to unionize, they hoped to become members of UAW Local 40 where it was unclear if the local supported the idea. "There was a reluctance to mess with Focus: HOPE, but we assumed it was because one or more employees asked" to unionize, Armstead said. Cunningham's "instruction to me was: 'Why do we need a third party to negotiate for employees who are going to be owners?' He was busting his ass. They never could understand the contract. He was not anti-union. But, the biggest mistake was paying bonuses much too soon. A few months later, we said your bonuses aren't going to get renewed but you'll be putting sweat equity into the company. They didn't want to do that."

Finally, Cycle Tec employees voted to join the UAW, and contract bargaining began. By that point, Armstead said, Cunningham "was against the whole damn union. But he let me handle it, if you know what I mean." Recognizing a potential public relations problem, Cunningham's resistance to unionization was concealed as much as possible. The priest tried to stay above the wrangling, even as he directed Armstead to keep pushing back.

Cunningham was frustrated, but once again GM management came through. "They asked us if we would be interested in a new project, and that project was identifying and shipping transmissions 'just in time' to the four companies that were doing the re-manufacturing," Armstead said. Cycle Tec would be closed and a new entity called Tec Express would be set up to quickly evaluate faulty transmissions from across the country and then ship them to factories with the capacity to re-manufacture them.

It was a good deal for GM and for Focus: HOPE. "GM could save millions of dollars if they had a central facility to sort out and send those parts to where they needed to be re-manufactured," Armstead said. "All transmissions would come to Cycle Tec and we were to redistribute them based upon the production schedule for that particular plant."

They took over an old building on Fenkell Avenue. "We set up some conveyor belts and had a couple of engineers design some overhead hoists that could pick up the cases with the transmissions, set them over the line, identify them, stack them up and put them on the trucks. It was 'just in time' and it saved time and money. We would get the trucks in, five to six trucks a day, unload them, identify the transmissions and then ship them out the door to plants in Oklahoma and North Carolina, but none in Michigan."

Cycle Tec no longer existed. Several employees lost their jobs as Focus: HOPE created a new business model for a for-profit subsidiary. "There were a lot fewer employees, but they were very efficient. And we did OK; again, nothing but labor costs— no parts, no costs at all outside of that," Armstead said. "And the union problem went away."

Michigan Senator Carl Levin, Father Cunningham and General Colin Powell, former chair of the Joint Chiefs of Staff, during a 1993 visit to Focus: HOPE.

Credit: Focus: HOPE

22

Pacifist

"IT WON'T WORK!" Father Cunningham nearly shouted as he slammed the palm of his hand onto a Washington, D.C. conference table, startling the top federal official from the Commerce Department sitting across from him. It was late afternoon, March 5, 1987.

Cunningham was asking Commerce for $6.5 million to support development of Focus: HOPE's Center for Advanced Technologies. The official, assistant secretary for productivity, Bruce Merrifield, had suggested that the priest look to the private sector to create such a thing.

No, Cunningham told him forcefully, that's already been tried at the University of Michigan. U-M's research and development of a flexible machining training center "ran aground ... because of the dearth of skilled workers to operate and maintain the equipment." When the high-tech machinery inevitably broke down, the facility was paralyzed, he said. The nation needs the CAT to train the operators who know how to use and fix the new equipment, Cunningham said. Without it, the United States could "lose its manufacturing industries."

There simply were not enough skilled people to repair computerized machinery, and the shortage had delayed integration of more high-tech manufacturing, resulting in a drag on the nation's economy, said Cunningham. The CAT was the answer to the problem, he said.

Merrifield considered the priest's arguments, then said he was convinced. He agreed that this was a major issue "to which he had no solution," according to notes of the meeting. "He was willing, however, to use his persuasive powers whenever and wherever necessary to help this proposal to move forward."

Cunningham was going boldly where no one had gone before—creating an unprecedented funding partnership between four federal departments: Labor, Education, Defense and Commerce. The CAT would be a true collaboration between several government agencies, universities, science, industry and the non-profit Focus: HOPE.

Cunningham's extraordinary vision would be expensive, and the federal government's role was critical. Focus: HOPE's ace development officer, Charlie Grenville, found potential sources for funding in the budgets of all four departments. Grenville's projections included $55 million in new machines and equipment (Defense), $1 million for machine foundations (Defense), $5.5 million for building refurbishing (Commerce), $500,000 for installation and start-up (source not identified), $1.5 million for production, quality, certification and training (Labor) and $11.3 million in other start-up costs (not identified). Education would be asked to provide millions for the training program.

Cunningham, usually accompanied by Eleanor Josaitis and CAT project director David Lanius, went to Washington once or twice a month where aides for Michigan Senators and members of Congress, steered them toward meetings with key officials at the Pentagon and the Reagan Administration. Cunningham and Lanius brought a slide show, which was helpful. But the priest's performances in those meetings was spectacular—"electrifying," one aide called them.

Cunningham told the feds that the CAT would be "self supporting after start-up" with production contract income bringing in $38 million a year. But to get going, Focus: HOPE needed tens of millions of federal dollars to refurbish old factories and install the latest computerized machinery. The CAT, he said, required cutting edge production machines. And it all had to be brand new—not just brand new, but not even invented yet. That's why the largest amount requested, $55 million for equipment, was critical for the success of the entire project.

"As you can see, the DOD is being asked to provide the lion's share of the start-up costs ($56.5 million)," wrote Mike Cummins, an aide to Senator Carl Levin, about a meeting with the four federal departments. "When questioned about this, Fr. Cunningham tore into the DOD policy of stockpiling ineffective and un-useful military hardware, and demanded instead that monies be channeled into developing a competitive manufacturing force so that our future military hardware can be purchased at home, instead of placing the U.S. at risk by being dependent upon substantial outsourcing. …

"In response to [Cunningham's] electrifying foray on the DOD, John Mittino of the DOD went to the podium and explained that although he likes what he sees at Focus: HOPE, the DOD is moving towards being strictly a purchaser of finished goods, and the development and competitiveness of the suppliers is left to industry. [Cunningham said] it was obvious that Mr. Mittino does not understand the tie-in between industrial competitiveness and military security. Industry will be forced into one of two scenarios: either outsource more of the production (putting the U.S. at risk), or import highly skilled manufacturing labor (which industry is seriously looking at, but which hurts our domestic workforce)."

The frequent trips to Washington were necessary, but exhausting. To make the complex task of selling the CAT easier, Cunningham and Josaitis decided to repeat their successful 1983 collaboration with the Ford Motor Company to bring the feds to Detroit to see for themselves. Ford had let them use its corporate jet to fly a dozen federal officials to and from Detroit to see Focus: HOPE's food program. This time, they would need a bigger plane. With a grant from the Ford Motor Company Fund,

Focus: HOPE chartered an airliner to bring federal officials to Detroit for the day.

Early on the morning of November 11, 1986, Cunningham and Josaitis were at Washington National Airport to greet invitees from Defense, Commerce, Education and Agriculture, as well as the National Science Foundation. They made good use of the one-hour flight to the Motor City, selling Focus: HOPE and the CAT.

It was the most important visit to Focus: HOPE since 1982 when Vice President George Bush came to deliver a government check. Josaitis was in charge of making sure everything was perfect for the few hours federal policy makers were on the campus. Focus: HOPE "colleagues"[33] were expected to be waiting at their stations when the dignitaries arrived. The group arrived by bus at Focus: HOPE at 10:30 a.m., then heard from Machinist Training Institute Dean, Suzanne Young, and Associate Director, Ken Kudek. They toured Industry Mall, met machinists in training and those working for the for-profit start-up companies like Cycle Tec Remanufacturing and High Quality Manufacturing. They re-boarded the bus to drive past the old Ford Engine plant down the street where the CAT and the Center for Children would be built. Then, back to the Resource Center for a special lunch.

"Eleanor wanted to make sure that they ate commodity foods," said Edna Jackson who then headed up the Food Prescription Program. That meant creating dishes using canned beans, peas and corn, rice, and canned chicken, turkey and beef—the same commodities provided by the federal government to be distributed to eligible poor people. Josaitis wanted to prove that the food was not only nutritious but also delicious when prepared correctly.

They turned to a Madonna Church parishioner Jackie Crowder, then the nutritionist for Macomb Public Schools. Crowder, helped by her son Dennis, who was a professional chef, agreed to prepare the important meal. The visitors "were

---

33   *Eleanor Josaitis insisted everyone working with Focus: HOPE was a colleague, a step above just an employee or volunteer.*

all shocked," Jackson said. "One, because they had never had anyone do that to them before—feed them government surplus commodity food. Second, they could not believe that this was happening in the city of Detroit, something so cool in the city. And thirdly, nobody had ever invited them anywhere to see what was happening with federal dollars." The Defense Department's Mittino still had a fond memory of that lunch 27 years later. "They served a lunch which I never did forget because the lunch was composed of government-provided food of different sorts," Mittino said. "The lunch was delicious."

After the satisfying meal, the government people listened to presentations from several corporate leaders, including Stephen E. Ewing, President and CEO of the Michigan Consolidated Gas Company, who sang the praises of Cunningham and Focus: HOPE: "As a member of Detroit's business community, I can tell you the motivation, dedication and productivity exhibited here is the envy of many a corporate executive."

The MichCon Foundation, along with the Ford and General Motors corporate foundations, already contributed to the development of the CAT, Ewing said. "If past accomplishments are a window through which you can see future possibilities, Focus: HOPE will achieve the goals they have discussed with you today." Another executive, William Bournias, who was president of Lamb Technicon's Machine Tool Group, told the feds that the U.S. could lose the global industrial competition because there weren't enough trained Americans to operate and maintain high-tech machines. "The economic impact is that we in the western world spend twice the capital equipment to produce the same volume," Bournias said. "What's the key difference? It's not technology. It's highly trained, well-managed, motivated people."

Cummins outlined for Levin what had happened during the trip, which, he said, "was very professionally done by Fr. Cunningham and crew." A reception at the Resource Center ended the visit. "During the cocktail hour at the end of the day I spoke with many of the participants, and it became clear that we are Focus: HOPE's greatest hope in getting the necessary support from the DOD," Cummins wrote—the "we" being Levin's office. "I did get a chance to chat and exchange friendly compliments with Mr. Mittino. He complained about the politicians getting their noses into every little nit-picky DOD budget item, and I politely listened. I stated that the Senator was very concerned about DOD financial support to Focus: HOPE. He did relent that the Senator had suggested some very good programs for the DOD recently."

Cunningham couldn't wait for the slow wheels of the federal bureaucracy to get going. "Fr. Cunningham wants to get this start-up in gear within six months," Cummins wrote. "The initial monies needed are the $5.5 million from the Department of Commerce for the building refurbishment. I would expect [Senator Don] Riegle's office to take responsibility for seeing it gets provided, although it sounded like Commerce wanted guarantees from the other Government agencies along with industry that they will follow up with their share of the commitment."

At a meeting in Washington on November 25, Cunningham, Josaitis, Cummins, Lanius and Brian O'Malley of Michigan Congressman Dennis Hertel's staff, met with several federal officials. Fred Haynes, a Commerce Department official who had been on the trip, "opened the meeting and, 'speaking for the Department of Commerce,' pledged five and one-half million dollars for the renovation of the building presently owned by Focus: HOPE, attendant upon a commitment from the Department of Defense. Haynes stated his belief that Focus: HOPE is perfectly suited for and capable of carrying out this project."

Haynes "suggested that DOD offer Focus: HOPE an exclusive contract in advanced composites manufacturing, in the range of $60 million to $90 million annually. Haynes suggested that composite technology is 10 years away from large-scale application by industry and that the time to train is now. He emphasized that technology developed in the U.S. is increasingly slipping offshore, and that the composites can be a major turning point for U.S. competitive edge in manufacturing in the next 15 years.

"Richard Donnelly [another DOD official] expressed some unease concerning the ability of a nonprofit organization to compete successfully in this arena. Cycle Tec Remanufacturing, Inc. was cited as evidence of Focus: HOPE's ability to manage a large-scale profit-making industrial enterprise. ... At this point, Mittino suggested we inspect machinery in DOD holdings heretofore inaccessible to Focus: HOPE. Lanius explained that equipment necessary for the CAT project is not yet in existence. New machinery is an absolute necessity. Retrofitting equipment was insufficient due to the need for optimal flexibility for training and prototypical purposes. Training on dated equipment would be self-defeating for the CAT.

"The central argument boils down to the difference between, on the one hand, stockpiling industrial and defense equipment and, on the other, training a world-competitive workforce in durable goods manufacturing. ... DOD reps raised the question of why private industry does not invest in this type of human resource development. Cunningham answered that while industry trains for its own restricted purposes, general technological and broad-based cross training must come from the educational institutions in consort with industry and government. The CAT would be a model of such technological education and training. The meeting ended with a sincere commitment on all sides to look for areas of support."

Grenville led the task of putting the concept into writing, a document well over 100 pages. Focus: HOPE's "Unsolicited Proposal to the U.S. Departments of Defense, Commerce, Labor and Education" was sent to all four departments in Washington on May 22, 1987. The cover sheet for a "Center for Advanced Technologies, A National Cooperative Demonstration Project," had the signatures of Cunningham as executive director and project manager. Lanius, Grenville, Josaitis and five other staffers also signed in a show of pride. By then, the price tag for the CAT had grown to $78.3 million. There were many more lobbying trips to be made.

A series of important meetings began on June 12, with Cunningham, Josaitis, Lanius and others meeting with top deputies in the four federal departments. Cunningham presented a one-pager that described the progress to date: "In two years, Focus: HOPE has brought the Center for Advanced Technologies from concept to the verge of realization. Right now, we need some help to overcome a critical impasse with the Department of Commerce. … The Defense Department has approved a $15 million expenditure to supply the first phase of advanced manufacturing equipment, and will provide another $27 million in subsequent phases. The other key partner at this stage is the Economic Development Administration (EDA) an agency of the Commerce Department, which has been asked to provide a $3,750,000 grant to prepare the facility. That is one-half the cost estimated for Focus: HOPE by Albert Kahn Associates.

"The problem is that Commerce assistant secretary [Orson] Swindle, who heads EDA, is now insisting that the agency won't spend any more than it has on other large projects in recent years, about $1.5 million. Unless Commerce provides the full amount, the Defense Department will not go forward with its commitment on machinery. … Secretary [Robert] Mosbacher's signature on this document, and his direction to assistant secretary Swindle to fund EDA's full $3.75 million share of the facility preparation budget, will unlock the whole process. We need your help to draw his attention to the importance of doing this before June 30 when Congress needs to have the signed Memorandum of Understanding (MOU) in hand."

The Focus: HOPE contingent flew home to Detroit later that Friday for the weekend. But they caught a return flight Sunday after Cunningham's Masses at Madonna to be ready for more meetings. The schedule for Monday, June 15, was crammed: a 10 a.m. meeting with two officials from Education, lunch with someone at the Pentagon, a 2:30 meeting with advisors at Bush's office, and a 4:30 meeting with Michigan Congressman John Dingell. They ended the day with a 6 p.m. dinner at The Dubliner Restaurant with six staff members working for Senators Levin and Riegle, and staffers for Congressmen William Ford, Carl Pursell and Bob Traxler. The following day brought 10 more meetings on Capitol Hill, followed by a single large meeting scheduled from noon to 2 p.m. At that meeting, assistant secretaries for the four Departments were present, as was a domestic policy advisor to Bush and Senators Levin and Riegle.

A record of the meeting prepared by Levin's staff said that the Senator and his brother, Congressman Sander Levin, made opening remarks citing Focus: HOPE's remarkable record of success. Then Jim Koontz, director of the National Center for Manufacturing Sciences (NCMS), pointed out the need for innovative approaches to advanced technology training, and pledged that NCMS would work with Focus: HOPE because it represents "a positive U.S. response to intense global competition." Joann Nueroth, director of operations for the Michigan Strategic Fund, told the group that foreign competition and changes in technology were forcing the country to quicken the pace of the development of high-tech manufacturing. Grenville spoke next about using the CAT as a cooperative demonstration project, stressing the lack of high-tech skills in the nation's labor force, and how the proposed MOU between the federal departments would work.

Merrifield, from Commerce, "strongly recommended the federal agencies move forward and approve the proposal, and suggested that Focus: HOPE begin mobilizing their plans as soon as possible."

Levin laid out a three-step process with deadlines for everyone in the room: "The first step is for Focus: HOPE to give clear dollar projections of the private sector's total commitment in the project to the federal agencies by July 2. The second step is for each of the federal agencies to provide Senator Levin and Senator Riegle's office[s] with any additional legislative authorization language it deems necessary to proceed by July 2. The final step is for the Department of Defense to form and lead an inter-agency task force that will develop and deliver a signed Memorandum of Understanding to Senators Levin and Riegle by September 1, 1987."

The MOU was needed to convince Congress to establish a $145 million fund for a Defense Manufacturing Initiative. Carl Levin then organized a letter of support for the money's inclusion in the final bill before the Senate Appropriations Committee that was signed by 19 senators, including Republicans Bob Dole, Orrin Hatch, Christopher Bond and Rudy Boschwitz. The money was included in the final defense appropriations bill.

In October, the EDA announced it was committing $3.75 million to Focus: HOPE for renovation of the former Ford Motor Company engine plant to house the CAT. Corporations and foundations matched that amount. Then Navy Captain Ralph Mitchell at the Pentagon declared that Focus: HOPE was a candidate for a $15 million grant to establish a national high-tech training center.

But back in Detroit, Cunningham's wooing of the Pentagon was causing friends and allies to wonder what the hell a priest working to help the poor was doing getting in bed with the military.

"I'm appalled," the Rev. David Kidd of Central Methodist Church told the *Free Press*. "It's not swords into plowshares at all. … They've really sold out. I'm sure it's a terribly difficult decision when $15 million is at stake, but this is not a time to make compromises." Another anti-war activist in Detroit, Carol Park, noted that Focus: HOPE's symbol of a black hand and white hand reaching for each other was a "profound contradiction" to a civil rights organization becoming a defense contractor. The Pentagon's money was "designed to produce weapons that would destroy people," Park said. "It's a profound ethical dilemma, and I don't envy Bill Cunningham having to wrestle with it." Cunningham said he "didn't wrestle at all. … It would be one thing if my motive were to put people in the position of grinding out more sophisticated weapons, but my motive is to give people the finest technical know-how so they'll be in the mainstream of the economy."

Bishop Thomas Gumbleton, a longtime supporter of Focus: HOPE and Cunningham's friend, strongly objected to the deal. "The Pentagon isn't going to give money out carelessly," the bishop told *The Michigan Catholic*'s Tom Ewald. "They expect a return on their money. Even if all the trainees don't participate in research and development programs for the Pentagon, some will. And by that very fact, you're participating in the total activity of the Pentagon."

Gumbleton—then national president of Pax Christi, a Catholic peace organization—said that Focus: HOPE's arrangement with the Pentagon "means building weapons for the arms race." Remember, Gumbleton said, Pope Paul VI called the building of weapons of mass destruction while the needs of the poor were unaddressed "abominable." Further, Dr. Martin Luther King Jr.,—one of Cunningham's heroes—had pleaded with the government to stop the arms race, calling it a "spiritual evil." "It's very difficult to be against something providing skills to inner-city youth," Gumbleton told the *Free Press*. "I'm not saying my judgment is the only judgment or that I know any better than anyone else. But it's a Pentagon program. I would not take the money."

Cunningham publicly responded in May 1989 when he answered questions from *The Detroit News* about his plans for the CAT. "Why go to the Department of Defense for millions to train people to work in the defense industry?" the reporter asked. "It's called beating swords into plowshares," Cunningham answered. "I'm pulling it out of a budget that would normally be used to build weapons for defense or killing. It gives the Defense Department a couple of bangs for the buck. It enhances their capability and at the same time produces a trained work force. ... A country's strength is in its capacity, not in its storage of 30mm bullets. ... I think the Defense Department understands more than anybody else what the deficits are in our schools, in mathematics, in science. I know it's an uneasy relationship, and I'm not unaware of the criticism. But the bottom line is jobs and the bottom line is who will pay to try.

"War is absolute insanity. I live in a country that still thinks its strength is in its military, instead of in the resources of its young people. What we're asking the Department of Defense to do is to buy into—as a defense measure—the developing of those resources. It's not like building an atom bomb. It's like building a better scientist. If that scientist has turned to make a bomb, that's his perversion."

Cunningham said he had gotten no "flak" from the Catholic Church for seeking money from the Pentagon. "That's the most appealing thing about this to me. If I have $100 million of defense money sitting out there, are you saying to me the best thing to do with that is to buy guns? Or the best thing to do is give it to Focus: HOPE so they can buy machine tools? That's what it amounts to. ... It's important to have a department of Defense. It's important for me to be a pacifist, but it's wrong if I demand that society follow my pacifist feelings or that I demand that people become pacifists."

"I've known Bill Cunningham for a long time," *Detroit News* columnist Pete Waldmeir wrote. "He's a realist, one of a small number of liberal clergymen who understand that the realities of working to help the poor sometimes requires compromise and cooperation with folks you wouldn't necessarily want to make a retreat with. ... Father Cunningham isn't some kid, some novice cleric-turned-entrepreneur who has conned or flimflammed his way to the position of power he occupies today in the Civil Rights movement. ... From the shaggy looks of him, I've often wondered if he can afford a haircut. He busts his fanny, day after day, so that people can have jobs, collect a paycheck, see that their kids have food, clothes and schooling. So they can walk proud."

The liberal *Free Press* also came to the priest's defense with an editorial supporting him while admitting that Cunningham and Focus: HOPE now found themselves "handmaidens of the Defense Department." "What he is doing is grabbing every spare dollar he can lay his hands on to retrain people who have dropped out of school or gotten a wretched education and turn them into effective workers," the editorial said. "Father Cunningham's approach may be—in fact is—often unorthodox. ... That doesn't make it wrong, misguided or a sell-out."

Whether in public or during meetings at Focus: HOPE, Cunningham gave no hint that the negative reactions from allies from the peace movement bothered him. In response to a comment that the Pentagon's money was somehow tainted,

Cunningham quipped: "They say the money's tainted. They're right, It 'taint enough."

Money—not all of it taxpayers'—was rolling in. In September 1989, the National Bank of Detroit (NBD) made its largest charitable gift ever—$500,000 over six years—to Focus: HOPE for the CAT, also making it the largest corporate gift to the civil rights organization up to that point. "For years, NBD has believed that education is the key to Detroit's future, and for that matter, the competitive future of the country," NBD chairman and president, Charles T. (Chip) Fisher III, said. "After looking closely at the Center, we think it will make the most dramatic and positive impact in the area."

One significant funder of Focus: HOPE William S. White of the C.S. Mott Foundation in Flint said he worried that Cunningham was overreaching with the CAT. "We felt that that was too far in advance and that we were afraid that it could overburden the organization," White said in an interview. "And so we were nervous about it. We supported it but we felt it just could be too big of a dream, and too much at one time."

Focus: HOPE's 14th annual Walk for Justice in 1989 was launched for the first time outside the organization's Resource Center on Oakman Boulevard for an eight-mile stroll around the neighborhood. The controversy over the organization's dealings with the Pentagon may have affected attendance. The *Free Press* reported about 3,400 people participated in the October 6 walk, fewer than previous years when more than 4,000 people attended.[34] Marchers knew about the controversy over the Pentagon, with one couple holding a sign: "Trillions for Weapons and Waste! The Pentagon Produces Poverty!"

Cunningham, who knew that the $15 million was just the beginning of his plans to tap into Defense Department's resources, said no weapons were being produced in the CAT program and that the training would lead young people into a variety of careers, yes, including with the military. "What those young people do with their capability is up to their own

---

34   *Cunningham's guestimates of 10,000 at most of those marches were wildly optimistic.*

conscience," Cunningham told the *Free Press*. "But to say we should deny them those skills because the money comes from the Department of Defense is irresponsible."[35]

---

35   *Technically, Focus: HOPE was not producing weapons for the Pentagon, but the Pentagon contracts did involve making parts for weapons. An article in the Free Press on November 6, 1993, said a $50 million Defense Department grant to Focus: HOPE to develop a new type of piston made of aluminum and reinforced graphite that was lighter and harder than existing pistons allowed the Pentagon to study "whether carbon-reinforced aluminum will allow low-cost methods to make the warhead of a missile." And, the Defense Week newsletter published in Washington, D.C. on October 4, 1993, said: "Some Focus: HOPE products are already being used in Pentagon weapons. The Center manufactures pulleys for Detroit Diesel, which are used in engines for the Bradley Fighting Vehicle, M109 howitzers, M113 armored personnel carriers and ammunition haulers among others."*

Lobo, a Bouvier des Flanders, was Cunningham's favorite dog.

Credit: John Collier

23

St. Francis

SYMBOLS BEING IMPORTANT to Father Cunningham, he
challenged his Madonna congregation to become "candle people," Christ's light for the world. The Focus: HOPE logo of two
hands, one black and one white, metaphorically reaching toward
each other, yet not touching, was his symbol of hope for Detroit.
The Roman collar he wore as a Catholic priest was a sign of his
commitment to Jesus's directive to work and sacrifice on behalf
of the disadvantaged and the poor. But one symbol that might
have been Cunningham's—the honorific title of "monsignor"—
was one he could not accept.

No titles of monsignor had been awarded in Detroit since the
late 1960s after the Second Vatican Council that had encouraged a simpler, more humble, servant Church. The title of
"monsignor" was purely honorific (monsignors do not out-rank
priests) and seemed no longer necessary or appropriate to most
bishops as they implemented the reforms of Vatican II. Cardinal
Edmund Szoka, who had been Archbishop of Detroit since 1981,
decided to renew the tradition. In 1990, Szoka learned he would
be promoted to President of the Prefecture of Economic Affairs

in Vatican City State. Szoka petitioned Pope John Paul II asking his Polish friend to bestow the "monsignor" honor on more than two dozen diocesan priests, including Father Bill Cunningham. Some weeks later, word came from the Vatican that the Pope had approved Szoka's request.

In late March or early April 1990, Cunningham and 28 other priests were called to a meeting in the new office building attached to Blessed Sacrament Cathedral where Szoka said that all of them would be recognized for their valuable service to the Church. Also in the group was the first African-American priest in Detroit to be so honored, Father James Robinson, pastor of Blessed Sacrament Cathedral, and several of Cunningham's friends and classmates, including Ed Baldwin, Tom Finnigan, Gerry Flanigan and Anthony Tocco.

Cunningham said nothing then, but later met privately with Szoka to say he could not accept the honor, according to Ned McGrath who later became spokesman for the archdiocese. Cunningham cited a pledge he had made to himself while in the seminary high school and after joining the Third Order of St. Francis—to not accept ecclesiastical promotion in the Church. The Vatican was informed, but no one else in Detroit—except the Cardinal's secretary Father John Zenz—knew about it until the priests met a few weeks later at a prayer service ceremony to make it official. Several noted Cunningham's absence. When the announcement was made on May 16 that 28 priests would be recognized as monsignors, reporters soon learned that the most famous Catholic priest in Detroit at the time, Bill Cunningham, had turned down the honor and that became the main angle for their stories.

"Let me say very quickly that I deeply appreciated the thoughtfulness of the cardinal and told him I sincerely join in the celebration of the priests whom he has honored," Cunningham told *The Detroit News*. "They are fine guys, good priests, and I'm really glad he's honored them. ... But I promised myself when I was much younger that I would not accept any titles. It's a very personal thing—that promise made at 14—and I wanted to keep it, so I deferred the honor. ... Since I was a kid, my hero has been Francis of Assisi. … I admired the simplicity of his life and his commitment, and accepting a higher title would not be in keeping with that. Francis of Assisi would not even accept becoming a priest."

Like St. Francis, Cunningham loved animals. But he adored dogs since his boyhood at St. Mary's of Redford parish where he often could be seen walking a tall Irish Setter named Horace. "I had a Boston Terrier and he accused me of having a 'puppy' and asked when I was going to get a real dog," said classmate Doug Donner. Cunningham, who had been playing violin and guitar, broke the little finger of his left hand when it got twisted in his large dog's leash once, ending his playing of stringed instruments.

As an adult, Cunningham's lifelong love for dogs was evident in the sermons he would preach and even in the book reviews he later wrote for *The Michigan Catholic*. A 1965 review he wrote about a book featuring a grumpy old lady whose heart is changed by a pet mouse begins with a discussion of a boy and his dog. "Ever watch a small boy cross-legged on the floor, his dog stretched out before him, head cradled over the boy's ankles, brown eyes wide, upturned? … Now they look and love. Francis of Assisi was known for his love of animals. He called them his brothers—even the rats that clicked over the floor at night, beady red eyes searching the cracks for crumbs. Philosopher Martin Buber believed that men who loved animals had a higher degree of spirituality, more gentleness than other men."

Crime around the Madonna complex was frustrating for Father Cunningham. Thieves targeted cars parked by people attending Mass on Sunday or for a community dinner meeting. "We lost a car right smack in front of his house one Sunday morning," said Mary Sullivan. "We stopped over, went to Mass there, decided to have coffee. … Our car was gone."

An insomniac, Cunningham was known to walk the neighborhood around Madonna late at night with Lobo and another Bouvier, a female named Dynasty. Jan and Marion Cunningham, who lived in the Madonna neighborhood, were coming home around midnight and were surprised to see Cunningham on a dark street with one of the dogs. They stopped their car to make sure he'd be all right. "He said, 'Nobody's going to bother me,'" said Marion Cunningham, an African-American who is no relation to the priest.

"He loved his Bouviers," said Sharon Agnew, his longtime administrative assistant at Focus: HOPE. "One particular time, his big Bouvier got out, and they found him. Where? Laying on my porch. I don't know whether he picked up my scent, but I came out my front door and this Bouvier is laying on my porch. ... I knew whose dog it was. I called Father and he laughed, 'Oh, my goodness, smart dog!'"

Cunningham didn't always take Lobo when he jogged. Once, according to Leddy, the priest was jogging down Oakman at 3 a.m. and "here comes a black man the other way." Lobo, who was watching from the rectory's second floor balcony, "didn't think the guy was innocent," Leddy said. Lobo leapt from the upper porch and rushed at the perceived threat to his master. Lobo knocked the man to the pavement and pinned him, baring his teeth but not biting, as he was trained. Cunningham came up and held Lobo while the man hurried off, uninjured.

Despite the dogs, the crime problem around Madonna festered for many years. "They were breaking in cars up there at the church, stealing the stereo equipment and the air bags out of the cars," said Nathaniel Leotus (Lee) Williams. "He had some dogs that someone gave him that wasn't no good for guard work." Williams, whose mother belonged to Madonna Church, was hired in 1990 to be a "senior host" at Focus: HOPE. Cunningham learned that Lee Williams owned a 17-acre farm in Tuscola County and raised dogs that he trained for security work. Williams said he told Cunningham what was wrong with his security dogs: "They were too friendly. They raised them up at the Children's Center and they loved children. ... We had to go through them and weed them out and train them."

Cunningham fired the man in charge of the dogs and convinced Williams to take over the canine corps. But instead of being an employee of Focus: HOPE, Cunningham convinced Williams that he should own his own business and be a private contractor. "I know he played hard ball with everybody he came in contact with," Williams said. "He would get you. In business, he was notorious. … I found that odd when we talked about my raises. I'd have to come in, sit like I was at a summit meeting and negotiate. If I wasn't careful, I'd get the short end of the stick. If I wasn't sharp and stayed focused, I'd get screwed. He gave you contracts and stuff. You'd better live up to them, too."

Cunningham personally had just two Bouviers—the formidable Lobo, and Dynasty that Williams said had come from the line of night security dogs at the old Hudson's Department Store downtown. "Dynasty had a mild temperament, but protective. Lobo was a good watch dog, but only Father could really handle him." Then, Lobo bit his master. "He was trying to separate the dogs, one of them was in heat," said Greg Petty, a deacon at Madonna. "Lobo nicked him on the knee. He was shaken. He put peroxide on it. I offered to take him to the hospital, but he said, 'No, Greg, it will be OK.'"

Williams also got bitten by his Rottweiler that he had tied up for a minute outside a party store. When he came out, the dog was acting crazy. Williams believed someone had maliciously given the dog a piece of crack cocaine to eat. "When I came out, when I went to walk him, the cocaine took effect and he went into a reaction," Williams said. The dog turned on him, mauling its master viciously. "The guy at the store had to come out and shoot him." Because it was a serious dog attack, a necropsy was conducted and Williams said they found traces of cocaine.

The dog had torn up an arm and his ankle had to be rebuilt with titanium. "I had over 1,000 stitches, all up and down my arm." Williams spent months in a wheelchair and didn't think he'd ever walk again. Then, Cunningham called and told him to come back to work. Cunningham and Josaitis insisted that Williams walk up to the second floor at the Resource Center every week to meet with them. "Miss Josaitis told me to come up there. Was I going to believe what those doctors said?" Williams said. "By me going up to his office every week, it built my leg up and after me walking up all those steps I found out I didn't need no wheelchair."

Williams said he worked from about 4 a.m. until 6:00 at night, seven days a week. One Friday, he took the day off for his daughter's wedding. He left the Focus: HOPE/Madonna canine corps in the care of a new man whom Cunningham had hired based on Williams' recommendation. Somehow Lobo got out and ran into Oakman Boulevard. "A truck coming hit him and killed him," Williams said. Someone called Cunningham and he was there in a flash. Sobbing, he picked Lobo up and carried the body down the street to the Shrine of St. Peregrine. Someone fetched a shovel and Cunningham dug the grave himself, praying, crying and making the sign of the cross over the corpse.

"Father, he was messed up for weeks. He loved his dogs and that really hurt him," Williams said. "I was supposed to get a raise, but I didn't get one. He told me I didn't get no raise cause that dog got hit. And I wasn't even working. That wasn't fair. ... He blamed me for what happened." The man who had let Lobo out was fired immediately.

Eleanor Josaitis and Bill Cunningham on "the bridge" of
the Center for Advanced Technologies designed to
resemble the fictional Starship Enterprise.

Credit: Focus: HOPE

24

Trekkie

LATE-NIGHT REPEATS OF the old "Star Trek" television series may not have been the inspiration for Father Cunningham's visionary Center for Advanced Technologies. But judging by how much he talked about Gene Roddenberry's concept of the crew of the starship Enterprise led by a charismatic Captain Kirk, it very well could have.

"If America is to compete in the global economy, it must go boldly where no one has gone before"—if Cunningham said it once, he said it a thousand times in speaking to government officials, military brass, captains of industry, the clerical community, news reporters and the foundation community.

Architects from the Smith, Hinchman & Grylls (SHG)[36] firm were excited by Cunningham's concept and began planning the transformation of the rusty old Ford engine factory designed by Albert Kahn in 1929 into a modern high-tech facility that would evoke the feeling of entering something akin to the fictional starship Enterprise.

---

36   *The firm later was known simply as the SmithGroup.*

Doors would "whoosh" open electronically, activated by computer-recognition of a palm print. Sink faucets would turn on and toilets would flush automatically with motion detectors—a feature that was rare until later in the 1990s. Glass-enclosed escalators would whisk people between floors with a clear view of internal mechanisms. It would be among the first to have lighting that automatically turns on when someone walked into a room, then turn off when vacant. Three large generators were to be installed so natural gas could be turned into electricity for the entire Focus: HOPE campus.

But the pièce de résistance would be a "bridge" evoking the fictional starship Enterprise where visitors could oversee the shop floor and view real-time closeups on two giant TV screens that would be interactive. The idea was to allow school children to converse with a machining student or engineer at the far end of the shop floor through both audio and video—a concept later enhanced by software innovations such as Skype. Captain Kirk and Mr. Spock would probably feel comfortable at the CAT, but Cunningham intended to spark kids' imaginations and get them interested in engineering, mathematics and science.

Choosing the distinctive color for the CAT's floor covering was an unexpected challenge. The material would be imported from Germany, a mixture of epoxy and rubber that was durable, stain- and chemical-resistant, nonskid and with a certain bounciness to minimize fatigue for people working on their feet all day. Typically, U.S. factory floors were made in grime-hiding brown, gray or black. But when SHG designer William Jay Hartman researched flooring he saw that builders of many European factories had chosen brighter colors. And he liked it.

"The Europeans have a much more daring understanding of color than we do in North America," Hartman told *Detroit Monthly* magazine in 1994. Hartman brought a sample book of European colors, including pink, bright yellow, loud purple, electric blue and a startling bright green. "So the three of us sat down and this meeting took about three hours. All we were trying to do was pick a floor color," Hartman said. Josaitis wanted pink as a message to the "old-boy network" that controlled the auto business in Detroit. Cunningham was thinking yellow, a metaphor for opportunity and streets paved in gold. Hartman thought purple might be best. Finally, Josaitis brought in three or four others on the CAT executive committee. "Father said everybody pick a sample," said Tim Sullivan. "Everybody grabbed a different color. The only one that was left was this green one. That's what Father chose, this Granny Smith apple green."

How Cunningham became enthralled with "Star Trek" isn't clear, although he would certainly agree with an article written in 1969 by Father Andrew Greeley, a Catholic priest, sociologist, journalist and popular novelist based at the University of Chicago. Writing about "Star Trek," Greeley said that Captain Kirk and the Enterprise "symbolize the Church on pilgrimage" with each episode a sort of morality play. Greeley praised "the qualities of confidence and hope and integrity displayed by the Enterprise crew." Despite futuristic weaponry, "the Enterprise finds its strength … in the friendship and loyalty of the crew to one another. Kirk is the respected and loved leader, but he is also the dedicated friend of his crew. His decisions are brave and forthright, but never made without consultation. And when the chips are down, the triumph of the Enterprise comes not from sophisticated gimmicks but from the force of such unconquerable human emotions as friendship, trust, courage and love."

Obviously, Cunningham was the "Captain Kirk" of Focus: HOPE. "I didn't really appreciate Mr. Roddenberry's extraordinary faith and strong moral value systems until after he died" in 1991, Cunningham said during a speech at Sacred Heart Seminary in 1995. "He was certainly a holy man. The concept of going boldly where no one has gone before is not new to 'Star Trek.' It was exactly the path that Jesus Christ laid for us, and laid for us more specifically by his chief disciple, St. Paul. That concept is reiterated as the Church developed institutionally over the centuries."[37]

---

37   *Nichelle Nichols, who played Lieutenant Uhura on the show, often told about meeting Dr. Martin Luther King Jr., who said he was a huge fan of hers and "Star Trek." King told Nichols that "images on television permeate the culture, either for the good or the bad, and this is for the highest*

With government funding committed, an ambitious reconstruction schedule was set up for the CAT. All plans would have to be approved by the feds. The federal Economic Development Administration would dole out millions in grants if Focus: HOPE adhered to a strict timeline for reconstruction. By April 30, 1990, architectural/engineering plans would be completed and approved by the EDA. By May 30, bid advertising would be finished. By June 30, the construction contract would be awarded, and reconstruction would be completed 16 months after that, by October 1, 1991.

The R.A. DeMattia company of Plymouth, Michigan, was selected to manage the project. "The actual construction of the CAT building has been broken down into two stages," Focus: HOPE grant writer Laura Blyth (later Poplawski) wrote in a 1990 memo to Charlie Grenville. "The first stage will cost $7.5 million. ... The shell of the building is to be completed during the first stage. This includes the roof, windows, grounds, etc. The building will appear finished, with second stage work to be completed inside.

"The following will be completed in the first stage: three power towers (out of nine total), three classrooms, four unisex bathrooms, three conference rooms, an open air office space, four labs (electrical, material, measuring, tool crib), 22 machining cells, a loading dock receiving department, and lighting through the occupied area. A medical office (first-aid station) with two examining rooms. The first, second and third floor will be stripped and readied for second stage work. The major demolition project is the replacing of the roof. ... The first stage will be completed by January 1992 ... the whole construction will be finished by 1995 or 1996."

---

good." In a 21st-century PBS-produced "Pioneers of Television" documentary series, Nichols said she had been thinking of quitting "Star Trek" due to the hate mail she had received. But King talked her out of it. She quoted him: "You cannot abdicate to your position. You are changing the minds of people across the world. For the first time, we see ourselves, what can be, what we are fighting for, what we are marching for."

One of the biggest challenges was cleaning up the site. Underground oil storage tanks had to be drained, inspected and usually dug out. Old electrical transformers were leaking dangerous chemicals, PCBs, and all the lead paint in the buildings had to be sandblasted away using regulated environmental safeguards.

As for the new high-tech machine tool equipment, Cunningham and advisors Vern Lovse, a retired GM truck plant manager, and Ray Billingsley, an industrial control engineer, visited companies designing machines that would fit their needs, including Cincinnati Milacron in Cincinnati and K.T. Swazzy in Cleveland. "The final purchase of machinery depends on the securing of CAT production bids, namely the Detroit Diesel contracts. ... Focus: HOPE has submitted various bids to Detroit Diesel for production of pulleys and flywheels [basic service, low-production engine components], a total of 320 parts. We are expecting word on the pulleys from Detroit Diesel within a week. Flywheels will be a later decision," Blyth reported.

"The equipment was all American-made machine tools, that was how he sold the CAT," Sullivan said. "That was important to Father. His spiel was always, 'I want to prove that American machine builders are just as good as the Japanese, and they can compete and produce products just as well, even better.'"

With manufacturing processes becoming more and more precise, the CAT would need the latest innovations in machinery. "For example, a balancer—something similar to when you get new tires balanced. A pulley, because it is round, has to be balanced too, because it's coming from a steel casting," Sullivan said. One balancer cost nearly $400,000 in the 1990s and Focus: HOPE would need as many as it could get.

Sullivan said Cunningham brought his "salesmanship" to bear on negotiations for the specialized computer numerical control (CNC) equipment. "To negotiate contracts with Cincinnati Milacron, he'd say, 'I need four, but I'm going to buy three of them and you're going to donate the other one.' And they'd do it," Sullivan said. What Cincinnati Milacron got out of the deal was a tax write-off and a place to send customers to see a new flexible manufacturing process in action. With flexible manufacturing, the process of producing goods can readily adapt to unexpected changes in product design.

"The future of Michigan's economy depends upon diversity in durable goods production and the capability to make rapid changes in flexible machining and manufacturing processes," Cunningham said in a 1987 speech before industry leaders. "To achieve this, thousands of new workers must be prepared to enter the labor force with high levels of academic and technical skills. We do not have a moment to waste."

While Cunningham worked with the architects and the contractor refurbishing the CAT he struggled with a critical component—a curriculum and a faculty. He had trouble with the academic egos from five culturally distinct universities. Curriculum was the only area of development that Cunningham was unable to highlight in updates to the U.S. Departments of Education and Labor about Focus: HOPE's progress.

Call it karma, providence, or God's plan, but Cunningham got lucky (again) in 1991 when he met Leo Hanifin, then the dean of the Rensselaer Polytechnic Institute of New York. Hanifin, a University of Detroit graduate, had written "a paper on the concept of a teaching factory, having people learn in an actual production facility, somewhat akin to a teaching hospital. That concept was intriguing to me." Fortunately for Cunningham, Hanifin was moving to Detroit to become dean of University of Detroit Mercy's (UDM) College of Engineering.[38]

Deans of engineering schools at Wayne State University, Lawrence Technological University and the University of Michigan had tentatively agreed to collaboratively educate students at the CAT, who would then receive degrees from those institutions. But UDM had not been asked to participate. Hanifin—who had earned his engineering doctorate from UDM—asked Cunningham why UDM was not part of the CAT collaborative. It was, after all, a Catholic institution with an excellent engineering program. Cunningham didn't have an answer, but Hanifin soon got the UDM engineering college involved.

---

38   *The University of Detroit merged with Mercy College in* 1990.

Hanifin set up a "war room" in UDM's engineering building, where about 25 members of what became the Greenfield Coalition team labored to create a manufacturing education model that would transcend the differing cultures and systems of each institution. They were trying to "create a learning process that would link what students are learning [in the classroom] with what they're doing in the plant," Hanifin said. "So, if you're going to learn about metrology, measuring parts, you would get assigned to the quality control unit and learn how to program coordinate-measuring machines."

The coalition partners worked to develop a curriculum that would impress the National Science Foundation. Charlie Grenville would craft a proposal. Cunningham and Josaitis already were building relationships at the NSF, but they needed a proper curriculum, and academic inertia was holding things up.

With Hanifin taking the lead, the deans of engineering at Lawrence Technical University and Wayne State University and lower-level academics from the University of Michigan, Lehigh University from Bethlehem, Pennsylvania, and Central State University in Ohio began figuring out a new curriculum not confined by the traditions of typical engineering colleges.

Their mission to transform how engineers and technicians are educated required a "fresh approach." The objective was to "develop a proactive engineer who seeks and applies deep knowledge to grasp technological opportunities which provide an advantage for manufacturing enterprises," according to a position paper written in 1994 by Hanifin and Paul J. Eagle, an associate professor at the University of Detroit Mercy's College of Engineering and Science.

While Cunningham was no engineer, he knew what he wanted to see as an end result—a six-year process by which disadvantaged young people could go through the Fast Track program to improve math and reading skills, learn the fundamentals of machine work at the Machinist Training Institute, enter the CAT for advanced training in high-tech operations, and finally emerge with associate and bachelor's degrees in engineering.

Of course, Cunningham thought he knew how the process should work. But, he would come late to meetings and then argue with the academics about what they'd been discussing for the past two hours. "Bill didn't like words like 'classroom,' of course. He wanted them to learn by doing," Hanifin said. Cunningham also "didn't want [students] to go into a classroom, sit down and be lectured to about any subject." Hanifin said Cunningham's idea was to "convert the sage on the stage to the guide on the side." The priest also didn't want them to use the word "students;" the young people would be "candidates" for degrees. Eventually, the academics began using code words to avoid annoying Cunningham. "We created a new language where a banana was a classroom and an apple a course," Hanifin said. "As a joke, when he'd come in the room, we'd start talking about apples and bananas. ... We wanted to grant them credits. The coin of the realm was credits and grades and when you stack up enough of them you get a degree. He wanted the degree, but he wanted far less structure and more computer-based learning."

Cunningham declared that candidates would learn on computer modules at their own pace—a concept called "active learning." But, Hanifin said, most of the students were disadvantaged and didn't know where to begin. They had been "out of the academic mainstream for most of their lives and they needed some significant handholding." How to educate them "didn't fit with academic structure."

An answer to the prayers of Cunningham and Josaitis suddenly appeared in the form of Lloyd Reuss, a General Motors executive and a protégé of company president Jim McDonald. Reuss became GM's president in 1990, although he was demoted and then fired due to declining market share, quality issues and losses in the billions.

But Reuss found another calling at Focus: HOPE, where he took on the task of getting the academics from the six universities to hammer out details for the CATs curriculum. And he helpfully connected Focus: HOPE with manufacturing executives he knew.

"I grew up in the transmission business," Reuss said in a 2013 interview. "When I went down there as a volunteer, Father—I'm sure he never said this quite deliberately—knew that people like myself that I recruited and retirees I recruited were never part of the financial equation" of Focus: HOPE. In other words, the value of their volunteer work could not be found on any Focus: HOPE balance sheet.

Cunningham and Josaitis said Reuss was essential to their plan to train "renaissance engineers" who would first learn how to make things, and then anticipate and design things that need to be made. Reuss was the "keeper of the tension" between academia and industry, Josaitis said. "We were blending the academic world, the chief of the hierarchy in the colleges of engineering, together with the executive concept of the manufacturing world," Cunningham told *Detroit Monthly* magazine in 1994. "And as we pulled these two together, wrenchingly, we got great negative response from the academic community: 'How dare you call somebody a dean? You don't have any right to call anybody a dean.' And then, of course on the manufacturing side there was just a kind of wistful response, saying, 'Well, it could work but it never has.' Because the manufacturing community by and large benignly tolerates the academic community, sees them off in foo-foo land."

In May 1993, Focus: HOPE announced that Reuss was now Executive Dean of the Center for Advanced Technologies. In contrast to his $1.2 million salary package at GM, Reuss's compensation from Focus: HOPE would be—zero. (He had a GM pension worth an estimated $350,000 a year.)

The coalition eventually decided on a "continuum of experiences from a technology course to an engineering course," the 1994 paper said. "An engineering course emphasizes analysis and design and, to a lesser extent, experiences with specific technologies. On the other hand, a technology course emphasizes the development of skill and experience with specific technologies with less emphasis being placed on analysis."

Credits could be earned from each of the universities, but the track for candidates called for an associate degree in manufacturing technology to be awarded by Lawrence Tech after two years, with qualified candidates moving on to a four-year bachelor's degree in manufacturing engineering technology from Wayne State after four years, or a bachelor's degree in manufacturing engineering from UDM after about four and a half years. Development projects for the first year were designed to draw on the strengths of each university. Central State would handle technical graphics and design; Lawrence Tech materials science, Lehigh manufacturing systems; UDM machining processes; U-M statistical methods, and Wayne State computer applications.

Meanwhile, the rest of Industry Mall was showing its age. The hasty refurbishing of the old Ex-Cell-O plant that was done in 1981 badly needed updating. The whole plant's air exchange filter system was 50 years old and needed to be brought up to OSHA codes for the health and safety of people in the buildings. A third of the shop floor was unusable, there was not enough classroom space, the entrance and lobby needed work, and restrooms needed to be handicap-accessible. They also needed better equipment to meet industry standards and a metrology lab. The old grinding equipment retrieved from storage in government caves was insufficient. Their CAD-CAM (computer-assisted-drawing and computer-assisted manufacturing) machines were only two-dimensional, not the three-dimensional machines that were now industry standards.

Grenville and his staff went to work on identifying a source of funds to refurbish the MTI, and found it at the Office of Community Services, an agency of the U.S. Department of Health and Human Services. Hundreds of thousands of dollars for the MTI came to Focus: HOPE in October 1990 and September 1991. The metrology lab that was added in February 1991 featured more than 40 new devices, including assortments of micrometers, gages, calipers, sine plates (hardened precision blocks that hold metal in place during drilling or grinding), other blocks and clamps, comparators (to compare pairs of electrical voltages or currents), and indicators.

The OCS grants also allowed Focus: HOPE to buy a Parker-Majestic Surface Grinder to increase MTI grinding capacity, and the Defense Industrial Plant Equipment Center provided an "Angle-Slide guide cell," another expensive piece of equipment. Focus: HOPE also was able to expand the CAD/CAM laboratory with 17 of the latest model 486 personal computers with 16-inch screens, supplementing the old 286s with 14-inch screens.

On New Year's Day 1991, *The New York Times* published a front page article about Cunningham's vision: "Detroit Priest Preaches Hope Through Job Training." "The center [CAT] represents Father Cunningham's secular theology of economic salvation through hard work and high technology," reporter William Schmidt (another former *Free Press* reporter) wrote. "Inside a gutted Ford engine factory, he has enlisted a cadre of retired automotive engineers and professors from Michigan engineering colleges in the hope of turning his brightest young recruits into skilled industrial technicians, fluent in high math, the intricacies of computer-aided design and manufacturing, and even the rudiments of Japanese and German."

As the 50-year-old Ford plant was transformed into a futuristic computer-integrated manufacturing facility with 220,000 square feet of shop floor, a 40,000 square foot three-story office building and its own power-generating natural gas boilers, staff and finances at the organization rose at a phenomenal rate. Between 1991 and 1992 the organization's annual budget grew from $51 million to $82.5 million with 462 employees, making Focus: HOPE the largest nonprofit in metro Detroit, surpassing the United Way for Southeastern Michigan with its $68.8 million budget, according to *Crain's Detroit Business*.

In manufacturing circles, Cunningham had picked up a nickname: "the industrial priest," a moniker apparently coined by Gary Cowger, executive director of advanced manufacturing for GM, according to a July 7, 1992, article in the *Free Press*. Cunningham was quoted saying that the CAT marks "the first time in the world that people of color have been told you have an opportunity to be superior, to be the best engineers in the world."

Free Press Reporter Pat Chargot noted that the priest's desk was adorned with a "block of gleaming, dark steel riddled with fist-size holes." It was relatively light weight, one of 250 experimental engine blocks that Focus: HOPE had produced for a carmaker he would not identify. Technology, Cunningham said, would allow the United States to downsize its military. "If we're successful—and we will be—then we won't have to store or stockpile weapons anymore," he told Chargot. "We'll be able to build from scratch at any time of defense need within minutes. … While we don't want to brand anyone at the Pentagon as a peacenik, we do want you to be aware that there are intelligent, sound-thinking people in defense who say, 'Why should we build a whole lot of planes or guns that will become obsolete and never be used?'"

That November, Focus: HOPE hosted a Society of Manufacturing Engineers forum at the CAT, still under renovation, that was entitled, "The Renaissance Engineer: An Economic Imperative." Cunningham gave the keynote address, calling the CAT "the crown jewel of Focus: HOPE's commitment to access black men and women, along with many others, into the 'Star Trekian' excitement of 21st-century manufacturing.

"To achieve its ultimate objective, the agile manufacturing facility of the future must be 'online' and instantly accessible to other such facilities across the nation," Cunningham said. "Our industries can no longer afford, and our nation can no longer risk, the practice of warehousing obsolescence. The 'Arsenal of Democracy' served us well 50 years ago. But if we continue to worship its technologies and practices, America could someday be the only cowboy to bring a knife to the gunfight. … The machines and the electronics are here today. We must now begin to build the other half of the equation: the Renaissance Engineer."

General Colin Powell, the former chair of the Joint Chiefs of Staff, addressed the Detroit Economic Club on April 19, 1993, and also stopped by Focus: HOPE at the suggestion of Senator Carl Levin. A month later, Commerce Secretary Ronald Brown came to Detroit to speak at an exporting conference and also took time to see Focus: HOPE. Brown announced that another $3.9 million grant from the Commerce Department would help finish work at the CAT. "That's not a gift. That's because we believe in you," Brown told Cunningham and Josaitis in front of reporters. "We believe in you because of what you have produced."

Brown said the Clinton administration was doing whatever it could to help U.S. business compete globally, even as the president pushed Congress to approve the North American Free Trade Agreement (NAFTA) that would result in increased competition for American manufacturers. "The time for debate, philosophy or trade theology is over," Brown told the Detroit Economic Club a few hours before the Focus: HOPE visit. "We must be unwaveringly pragmatic. We must have a public-private national economic strategy, if we are to compete and win in the global marketplace."

One of the first tasks for Reuss was to help Focus: HOPE get the money to pull it off. The NSF, which funds research and education in the non-medical fields of science and engineering, was the identified source for $15 million. "I worked with [Cunningham] and Lloyd in developing the concept through a number of meetings with other university partners," Hanifin said. Grenville and Focus: HOPE grant-writer Victoria Cole worked with Hanifin to produce the NSF proposal. "We wrote this proposal that would create a learning process that would link what students are learning with what they're doing in the plant. ... I remember working half the night on it. Deadline day. We had to put somebody on an airplane with it to get it to Washington. It was not the era of online grant submission."

The proposal was peer reviewed by NSF consultants across the country. The $15 million would have to be matched from other non-government sources, and Hanifin worked with the academic colleagues to calculate the value of the time professors from the various universities would put into the project, as well as grants from private foundations and the value of donated equipment from corporations. "We had to match dollar for dollar," Hanifin said.

The proposal was selected as a finalist. Hanifin and Cunningham flew together to Washington to make a final presentation to the NSF. Reuss, flying separately, also participated. Cunningham gave his presentation with "just his usual gushing passion, with tears in his eyes," Hanifin said. "And, 'these kids are going to have a different kind of future and they're going to revive the manufacturing base in Michigan and the nation, and we're going to diversify the student body.' All these things were true. This is what we wanted to do. I don't think it was a performance. This was just in his blood. I think he just believed deeply in what he was doing, and the passion and emotion came out."

CAT candidates, Cunningham told them, would work for wages at least 40 hours a week producing items such as pulleys for engines and intake manifolds under contracts with Ford and Detroit Diesel. And the candidates would spend 20 more hours every week on academic studies. "This was a killer team," Hanifin said of the three-man presentation. "I had some cache as the lead. Lloyd had been president of GM and Father Cunningham is bringing his mission of transforming the urban culture, bringing people together. I don't think they could say anything but, 'yes.'" Cunningham wanted the money to come directly to Focus: HOPE, but the NSF said it would have to pass through an accredited institution of higher learning—in this case, UDM as the leader of the Greenfield Coalition.

The announcement came at the end of October 1993. Focus: HOPE's grant was one of the eight engineering education centers projects approved for NSF grants, but the only one with a "teaching factory" at its core. The $15 million multi-year grant was to develop "improved and innovative introductory-level undergraduate courses and curricula in science, engineering and mathematics."

In a news release sent in advance of the CAT's official opening on November 8, Cunningham said: "From the extraordinary vestibule with its three stories of German tile and glass enclosed escalators, the stainless steel clad boardroom and open flexible ambience to the unequaled electronic library, innovative power towers, electronic doors, and sensored lights, there is a Star Trekian, Disneyland excitement."

Reporters had seen the CAT while it was being developed, but the event still excited. Cunningham was even more emotional than usual, his voice choking as he turned to the center's first group of 32 students, most of them black and from Detroit's inner city: "This is the first time they've had that opportunity," he said, "and by God, they're going to make us proud."

One of the two third-floor meeting rooms at the CAT was used on November 13 for a meeting of the Joint Practice Division of the Michigan Society of Professional Engineers, and Cunningham was characteristically eloquent when he addressed the group: "Engineering is perhaps the most ennobling profession a human can have. Your architects and engineers make of this world something that God has envisioned, that none of us can quite see yet."

Cunningham talked about the "new format" of engineering education that was being developed in the heart of Detroit. "We will no longer have electrical engineering, chemical engineering, computer engineering or civil engineering and so on, as separate disciplines. We will no longer have academic departments based upon the latest trend in the university, adding a new course here or there, never changing the departments themselves, and never allowing them to change. That failure to change causes a paralysis of our capabilities in ingenuity as we come into the 21st century."

He spoke, too, in defense of Detroit: "Too many people who don't know this city see it as brutal and explosive rather than muscular and courageous. They mistake our lust for hard work as a lack of intellect. And they confuse our lack of flash and glitter as a loss of spirit. ... This is the city of 141 languages. No other city has such diversification. This is the top of the mountain in terms of human possibilities. And the core of those possibilities is our role as the world's leader in manufacturing. ... Much of this is done not on the basis of intelligence, but on the basis of imagination."

Aunt Callie Fulp took Father Cunningham under her wing when he took over as pastor of the Catholic Church of the Madonna in 1970.

Credit: Josaitis family photo

25

The Women

THE SPRING 1989 raffle drawing at the Catholic Church of the Madonna ended with the pastor coming forward to draw the winner of a new Cadillac DeVille donated by a local car dealer.

Among those clutching their ticket stubs in anticipation was the woman who had sold more raffle tickets than anyone, Callie Fulp, a longtime contributor to Madonna and Focus: HOPE. Fulp was relatively wealthy, a flamboyant dresser and party-giver, as well as a behind-the-scenes fixer in Detroit's black community. For Madonna's raffle, Fulp called in chits from a diverse network of the city's black elite, from business, law enforcement, entertainment and the underworld's pimps, prostitutes and hustlers. Most of them gladly bought the $10 tickets and, as a favor, put Callie Fulp's name on them.

Father Cunningham reached into the tumbler and pulled out the winning ticket. He shocked himself. "Folks, you're not going to believe this," he said. The winner was a Madonna employee, Sister Kathleen Miotke, an Adrian Dominican nun running the parish religious education program. The crowd began murmuring, but Cunningham declared that Sister Kathleen had won fair and square. "When they pulled her name out she said, 'I'm not going to take it,'" Sister Lois Burroughs said. "And everybody jumped on her: 'Oh, yes you are!'"

Kathleen's relatives from Hamtramck had bought a few tickets and had put her name on them. All the nuns, except Kathleen, were overjoyed, but Callie Fulp was fuming. She left in a huff, muttering something about "Buddy Boy," her nickname for the priest that she used when she was mad at him.

The raffle was "terribly embarrassing" to Cunningham, said Tony Campbell, a Madonna choir member and Focus: HOPE's finance officer. There was such a kerfuffle that the priest regretted it. "If I could've palmed that ticket, I would have," he told Campbell. Edna Jackson and her husband ended up buying the Cadillac and with that money Cunningham got a good deal on two compact cars, one each for the two nuns, Sister Kathleen and Sister Cecilia Begin to use on parish business.

When Cunningham became Madonna's pastor in 1970, "Aunt Callie"—as everyone called her—welcomed him with great generosity. She asked what he liked to drink. Later, she sent him a case of Chivas Regal. When it looked like his suit was becoming frayed, she bought him a new one.

Fulp told fascinating stories about her life on a plantation in the South and coming to Detroit where she worked in the Paradise Valley black entertainment district. She began as a waitress at Joe Louis's Chicken Shack restaurant, got married, had a daughter and then was widowed. Callie used charm, extreme hospitality, delicious cooking and relationships to build a small fortune in various business ventures, probably including the numbers racket. She ran a rooming house on Atkinson Avenue called Hotel Callie where gentlemen could hide out from the law or the wife, and be well fed and entertained. Callie was a great cook, specializing in Southern and Louisiana creole cuisine.

A lifelong Catholic, Fulp had supported Madonna's previous pastor, Father Ferdinand De Cneudt, who was a frequent guest at her home. Cunningham, too, attended many of her fancy sit-down dinners with Callie serving food and drink herself. She brought out fine china, crystal and silverware, and nothing but the best liquors and wines. The food and drink were great, but the best thing about Fulp's dinner parties was the storytelling. She insisted that each guest repay her hospitality by telling a story. Since guests could include top police officers, well-healed lawyers, politicians and members of Madonna parish, as well as drug dealers and thieves, the stories were nothing short of amazing.

"She pulled a lot of strings; she had some political clout," Madonna's pastoral associate Greg Petty said. "Callie, she had ties to the underworld and a lot of people would've passed judgment and said, 'we don't want your type.' But not Father. He just lived the Gospel so completely. I think of the parable about who should cast the first stone at the adulteress. So Callie, yes, she fell in love with Billy Boy."

Fulp had plenty of great tales of adventure herself, and her joy was watching other people having a good time.

"She was very colorful; she had a way of expressing herself," Helen Luckey, a Madonna parishioner who was close to Fulp said. "With Father Cunningham, she was a mother figure to him. She taught him about the streets, how to survive and mix with everybody. She was a good woman." She began raising money for Madonna and Cunningham's Focus: HOPE, hitting up her friends in "Superfly" hats and pimpmobiles.

Cunningham always was her honored guest and, frequently, most loquacious storyteller. He compared Fulp to Harry Bailey, the innkeeper in Chaucer's *Canterbury Tales*, who provided food, wine and a restful place for pilgrims on their way to visit the shrine of St. Thomas à Becket at Canterbury Cathedral in England. Innkeeper Bailey, Cunningham told Neal Shine of the *Free Press*, "would feed them, house them and ask only one thing of them, that they tell their story. Like Callie, he never denied them access because of who they were or where they came from—saint or fraud, the toughest felon or the biggest hypocrite. She had a sense of morality, a sense of faith and a sense of God few people ever have."

On Holy Thursday, Fulp would prepare a Passover Seder meal for nearly 20 people—"standing room only," Jackson said.

"She would set a spot up front for Father," and explain that she sat close to Cunningham "because it helps me get a little closer to heaven."

The priest may have unconsciously felt the need for a maternal presence in his life, and Callie Fulp filled that role. "Oh, that lady loved that man, but she loved him like a son and as her spiritual adviser," Jackson said.

Focus: HOPE resident artist Jerry Lemenu had asked Cunningham for years to let him create a portrait, but the priest always refused. Until one day, Cunningham surprised him and asked Lemenu to draw one. "I found out that portrait wound up in Callie Fulp's house and the reason he had it done was if her house ever got raided with his portrait there he hoped the cops would go easy on her," Lemenu said.

"Callie loved the Blessed Mother, loved burning candles and she was so good to everybody, and she just loved Father, just adored him," Sister Cecilia said. "But when she got mad at him, she'd call me and spout off about 'your priest.'" When she was peeved, Fulp would call him Buddy Boy, as in "Buddy Boy, don't get too big for your britches!"

"I think Father thought of her as a mother almost," said Mary Ann Gideon, Focus: HOPE's public relations volunteer for several years. "I remember looking into her eyes one Sunday after Mass. She looked so beautiful."

Cunningham often said he'd like to spend time with Callie Fulp in a cottage in the middle of nowhere and just talk. He wanted to take notes and write a non-fiction book about her life. "They talked about it, three, four, five years," Luckey said. They never did it. Fulp died in 1990, breaking Cunningham's heart. "He could not talk about Callie without crying," Luckey said.

Cunningham brought energy to the moribund parish when he arrived in 1970. But, much of the credit must go to the nuns who lived in the Madonna convent, many of them activists who worked with the poor, the elderly, the drug-addicted or the incarcerated. The nuns from three or four orders added another dynamic dimension to this Catholic community thriving against the odds in Detroit's inner city. "The nuns in the convent, they were going here and there. They were just busy nuns," said parishioner Sadie Guinn, Edna Jackson's sister. "We would go there and have our Bible study sometimes with them." They taught piano to neighborhood children, brought ideas and energy to the parish women's organizations and worked with teenage girls.

Gideon attended Mass at Madonna even though she was a "loyal Presbyterian—I could never be a Papist." She took communion at Madonna, of course. "I always called myself a Cunningham Catholic. I liked what he espoused and believed. ... He was so busy. He was always here at parties and at funerals. So all of our friends, all of my family knew him. How many people? All these people just knowing us, multiply that with all the people at Madonna and Focus: HOPE, all these people had close relationships with him."

Madonna parishioners were nothing if not open-minded about Cunningham's attitude toward some Church rules. Few blinked when Cunningham announced at Mass in the mid-1980s that he was tearing out the confessional booth and would no longer hold regular hours for confessions.[39] According to longtime parishioner Frank Ross, Cunningham told his "candle people" that they were perfectly capable of finding God's forgiveness on their own: "Listen, I am not the man to be the intermediary between you and God. I can help you with your worldly matters, your worldly problems, but I'm not qualified to interface between you and God."

The candle motif was grist for many of Cunningham's sermons. The stained-glass candle window that filled with light each day inspired parishioners to accept their pastor's challenge to take their Christianity out into the streets and take practical steps to help those in need. And they followed him, many to volunteer for programs at Focus: HOPE, others to participate in the parish's many Christian ministry programs. "He had charisma and he just attracted people like a magnet," parishioner Rosemary Abbington said. "He was quite a bit different from other priests I knew."

---

39   *Actually, the confessional booth gained new life as a storage closet.*

Cunningham's typical routine on Sunday morning would be to drink coffee or juice while listening to Sister Cecilia read that day's Old and New Testament readings to him aloud, as well as Father John Castelot's column in *The Michigan Catholic*. "Having a brilliant mind right there, while having coffee and toast, and absorbing the reading and formulating in his mind what he was going to say, and it always came out a masterpiece," Sister Lois said. "That's fairly unusual. Maybe some priests do that but they don't come out with good results like Father Cunningham."

Cecilia said one Sunday morning she was "prattling away" about a recording of Gregorian chant that was getting airtime on local radio stations. "He was standing at the sink with his back to me, never letting on that he ever heard me," she said. "My God, if he didn't bring that out in the sermon! He was hearing everything I was saying. I thought, well, you son of a gun."

At Mass, the Eleanor and Don Josaitis family usually sat on the right side in the first few pews. They were warmly welcome, but Eleanor resisted the urge to get too involved in parish activities. "I remember some of his Sunday sermons," said Janet Josaitis Denk. "He'd bring the Gospel into today, into that neighborhood. And here's this group of black inner-city people who could so relate to this lyrical Irish guy. There were times when he would go and talk about these nuns of his childhood like they were angels. But that was his Irish nature. He could make his story, about his mother, sometimes teary-eyed. Being a little boy growing up in the Catholic Church he wanted them to have the same experience. He could make these people on Linwood experience the same thing he did in his Irish Catholic home 40 years before. That was his gift." Denk said, "Uncle Bill" was "a great argument for the priesthood. He was not bogged down by marriage, by sex, by childrearing, by careers. He was so laser-beamed it made you crazy."

Despite his schedule, Cunningham made himself available to anyone who needed him: parishioner, Focus: HOPE colleague or friend virtually any time, day or night. "I kept hearing about this Father Cunningham like he was, oh my God, the second coming, the Messiah, whatever," said Karen Minard who used to live in the neighborhood around Madonna. "All these people were raving about him. He had black hair and he had this motorcycle. I didn't get it. … My mother wanted me to meet him, and this was out of character."

Minard's mother, a divorced Catholic, had felt judged by other priests. "Here's my mother taking me to the rectory, and my mother didn't go to the rectory. She didn't even go to the church. But she took me to the rectory to meet this man. I remember my words to him. I was cocky: 'So, you're Father Cunningham. What's so special about you?' And he looked at me and he said, 'Absolutely nothing.' He sort of defused me with that. And then I really understood the impact on her."

Another Madonna family close to their pastor was Olive and Fred Burton, Sr., who had known Cunningham and the priest's father since the 1960s when "Pop" Cunningham was living on Boston Boulevard. The priest "was the kind of guy that would always come to somebody's aid," Fred Burton said. "I talked to Father Cunningham many times. All I can see is his eyes, and the way he looked. He had a way of looking at you. It's like God— something you can't explain. Did he say anything? He didn't have to. It was just the way he looked. He understood, that's the way I could say it." Cunningham helped the couple's son, Fred Jr., get corporate help to buy a GM dealership in Ohio.

Fred Sr., was a retired businessman and the longtime volunteer driver for Congressman John Conyers Jr., of Detroit.[40] Burton was an African-American with light skin and salt-and-pepper dark, wavy hair that looked Caucasian. Burton was the same height and build as Cunningham and had similarly handsome facial features—indeed a lot of people thought the two men must have been separated at birth. "I was his black brother," Burton said. "We'd stand there with our arms around us and everyone said we looked alike. Boy, from the back of us you

40   *Rosa Parks, the civil rights icon from Alabama who was living in Detroit, also worked for Congressman Conyers. Fred Burton Sr., became her unofficial driver for the rest of her life. (She died in 2005.) He drove Parks to many events, including those at Focus: HOPE and at Madonna, although she wasn't Catholic.*

couldn't tell us apart. Our shoulders had a little roundness, and the jaws. ... He got a kick out of it, so did everybody at church."

Through all the tragedies and celebrations, Cunningham was there for the parishioners of Madonna. He always rolled up his sleeves and helped when he could in the kitchen or on cleanup duty. "He was an unusual man," said Sadie Guinn. "When we cleaned the church, a general cleaning of the church including the ceiling, he would go out on the street corner for a while and ask men to come and help." The unemployed men were not parishioners, but the ladies of the church always provided a hot lunch for them knowing that they were underfed.

Something about Cunningham allowed parishioners to be themselves. "Most of the priests I had known in the past I felt like there was only certain things I could say around them," said Jan Cunningham, an African-American parishioner who is no relation to the priest. "That might've just been me, not them. But with Father I didn't feel uncomfortable, didn't feel like I had to be guarded." Jan's mother, Marion Cunningham, said the priest loved to play on the fact that they had the same last name. Once, a visitor to Madonna was walking in, the priest introduced himself as Father Cunningham, then said: "And this is Mrs. Cunningham!" "The expression on her face!" Marion said. "He looked at me and said, 'Aren't you Mrs. Cunningham?' I said, yes. He started laughing; he thought it was so funny."

Parishioners were impressed how knowledgeable and passionate their pastor was about racism and its impact on families, communities and metropolitan Detroit. "I remember Father Cunningham standing in the pulpit with tears streaming down his face as he talked about racism and its effect on Americans," Petty said. "His vision of the future, a free and open society based on Christian values. Some of the people in the audience wept as well, so powerful was his presentation. I was just sitting there and watching in awe. ... Over the years, he was such a spiritual leader that our services were always supercharged with this spiritual imagery."

The English teacher in Cunningham would surface during his lengthy homilies. He quoted Shakespeare and Chaucer. "He would make you run to the dictionary," said Sister Ellen Ann Gardner, a Sister of Charity who came to work at Madonna in 1993. "He was proud of his voice, his singing voice, and he always preempted the choir director to lead off with the Gloria or to rev up the choir." If the singing among congregants seemed tepid, Cunningham would proclaim, "full volume!"

Madonna parish was where Cunningham came to "refuel his own batteries," Sister Ellen said. "This was a person who needed two full-time jobs. Cunningham surrounded himself with strong women because they got the stuff done the way he wanted it done."

Cunningham's Masses invariably started 10 or 15 minutes late and lasted way beyond the typical hour. The traditional peace greeting after the "Our Father" and before Communion for most Catholics means a brief handshake or hug with a half-dozen people in the pews nearest them. But at Cunningham's Madonna the sign of peace went on for more than 10 minutes because everyone greeted everyone else in the church.

In just about any setting, Father Cunningham loved to provoke intense, passionate conversations on all manner of hot button issues, like the quality of teachers and racial injustice. His sister Betty, a teetotaler, avoided arguing with him, although her kids and grandkids often found themselves drawn into a debate with Cunningham over any number of topics. Bill and Betty's older sister Rose Marie "would give as good as she got" in arguing with the priest, Betty Edwards said. "A typical brother-sister relationship. She would on occasion try to shock everybody and Bill would take that in stride. She would try to annoy Bill about religion." She'd played the role of a worldly woman "with her voice, with her clothing, not risqué, but definitely far out. She never dressed conservatively."

Rose Marie had long lived in New York City, where she worked as an advertising broker in radio and television and dated a variety of men. She had a long-standing relationship with a Jewish gentleman that she kept hidden from their father because she was afraid of his reaction. Indeed, the elder Cunningham pretty much disowned his eldest child in his later years.

"Rose Marie was a little loony, married a Jewish man and made her old man go crazy," Janet Denk said. (There actually is no record of Rose Marie marrying anyone.) Pop Cunningham was livid that his eldest daughter was living the high life in New York. Her family in Michigan, though, was important to her and every Christmas Rose Marie would fly in to Detroit and stay with her brother in the Madonna rectory. After Masses on Christmas, Bill and Rose Marie would go to the Josaitis' home for lunch and exchange presents. Then they'd drive up to Dryden to be with their sister Betty's family.

Rose Marie "was charming, different, sort of a Loretta Young type person," said Sharon Agnew, Cunningham's administrative assistant. She was referring to the glamorous mid-20th-century movie star known for wearing gowns with deeply scooped necklines. "This one Christmas Eve, Rose Marie came down and she opened up the parish doors. 'Hello, everybody!' She made an entrance, very dramatic. It was cute. We all loved her."

Luckey said that when Rose Marie stayed at the rectory she'd walk around in her underwear. Cunningham always scolded her "not to come down [stairs] unless she was fully dressed." The Archbishop of Detroit, Cardinal Edmund Szoka, was in the rectory once talking with Sister Cecilia while Father Cunningham was busy in the church next door. Suddenly, Rose Marie's voice came from upstairs: "Bill? Is It OK? Can I come down now? I've got my robe on." Luckey said, "Cardinal Szoka shot out of there."

One year after Christmas in either 1990 or 1991, Cunningham asked the Josaitises to fly to New York with him. "We went to New York, Bill, Don and I for New Year's Eve," Eleanor said. "We stayed downtown. Bill went to see her, we did not." Cunningham later pointed out the eye-popping apartment building where his sister lived. "Big, right in Manhattan," Eleanor said. "She was wealthy."[41]

---

41   *Rose Marie Cunningham's apartment was in the Ansonia, 2190 Broadway on the Upper West Side of Manhattan between West 73rd and West 74th. Many athletes and artists had apartments at the Ansonia, including Babe Ruth, Arturo Toscanini, Enrico Caruso and Igor Stravinsky.*

After Christmas in 1992, Rose Marie returned to New York but stopped answering her phone in February, and then she missed calling Bill on his birthday on February 20. Both Bill and his sister Betty Horning called her number repeatedly. Finally on March 1 they called the police. There was no response at the door, and Betty gave police permission to break in. They found her dead in the bathtub of natural causes.

Some may have thought that Cunningham worked so hard at Focus: HOPE that he neglected his parish. "But I think he did a good job with both," said Sister Lois. "If you were to ask me did he neglect his parish, it's a big fat NO. ... The relationship between Father Cunningham and his parish was one of total love and dedication, and with the sisters, likewise."

Cecilia never stopped trying to burst Cunningham's bubble when he needed it. Lois said on one rare occasion, Cunningham arrived at an event before Sister Cecilia because she had gotten lost. When Cecilia got there, she saw Cunningham with a drink in his hand surrounded by several fawning women. All Cecilia heard was the women repeating, "Oh, Father Cunningham! Oh, Father Cunningham!" The next morning, Lois said, Cunningham came into Cecilia's office and she mimicked the women who had doted on the priest: "Oh, Father Cunningham! Oh, Father Cunningham!" "Damn you, Cecilia," Cunningham laughed.

There was an abiding non-sexual love between the handsome, if no longer young, priest and the women of Focus: HOPE and the Catholic Church of Madonna. Women certainly were attracted to him. But he would never jeopardize his celibacy pledge—or give an onlooker a false impression.

Charlie Latimer, one of the folk singers who were friends with Cunningham and performed at both Focus: HOPE and

---

By the 1970s, though, many of the grand apartments had been subdivided into one-bedroom or studio apartments with high ceilings and big bay windows. The building with distinctive French-style round turrets on each corner was well known for a gay bathhouse in the basement, where Bette Midler and Barry Manilow got their start. The bathhouse later became Plato's Retreat, a nightclub where "swingers" could swap sexual partners.

Madonna functions, said the priest "was brutally handsome, he really was. And he was charismatic, polite as he can be, and so much personality, so much passion, so much caring! I mean, women had to drool over this guy and I know they did. He always handled it with the utmost grace. He was human. He had to know he was a good-looking guy. I was around numerous times when they were coming on to him, and he was just as cool as a cucumber, and gracious as all heck," Latimer said. "He was a class act. But, man, you'd better believe it, the ladies would just go gaga over the man."

Cunningham's friend, television news anchor Bill Bonds, was probably drinking with the priest when he asked a question: "You're a very attractive guy, you're handsome, you've got a great body, very attractive guy—I would've killed for his hair, for crying out loud—don't you miss being a father, being a husband, having a wife? Having a family, love?" Bonds said Cunningham responded: "I have my family—these kids down here at Focus: HOPE." Bonds said he commented that it was tough not being sexually active. "It's tough for you, not me," Cunningham said.

Sister Lois attributes some of Cunningham's attraction to his confidence in his masculinity: "Father Cunningham wanted to come across as a 'he-man.' Even the way he walked, with those high-top shoes. I could see him walking down the center aisle on Sundays, almost a trudge. 'Here I am, Paul Bunyan coming down that middle aisle.'"

Cunningham's warmth toward women sometimes resulted in ugly gossip, especially at Madonna where most knew the reputations of married Protestant ministers who were sleeping with mistresses on the side. "There was gossip in our church," said Luckey. "Someone said something that Father might have been going with one of the people that worked at Focus: HOPE." Luckey didn't tell Cunningham but Sister Cecilia heard the gossip in the basement beauty shop of a parishioner while getting her hair done. Cecilia told Cunningham immediately, and "he was irate." The priest showed up unexpectedly at a meeting of the parish women's club, which the rumormonger belonged to. He challenged her to tell him right then what people were saying about him. The woman nervously said she had heard a rumor that Cunningham was having an affair with Eleanor Josaitis. "He was livid, very angry; he was crimson!" Luckey said. "Don't you ever tell a lie like that on me," Cunningham warned that woman, scaring her and everyone else in the room.

Don Josaitis said "there always was talk amongst women: 'How can you stand your wife being with that handsome priest? After all, the guy is human. He's not Jesus Christ.'" Don said that over the years he would hear someone wonder whether his wife had been physically intimate with Cunningham. "I would just say, 'I believe in both people. I don't believe he would ever take advantage of Eleanor, and I don't think Eleanor would ever take advantage of me.'"

Petty said Cunningham would tolerate no loose talk about his morals: "If he was adamant about any point, that was it. He would get angry with women who would announce their romantic intentions. And there were more than just a few. There were letters, there were calls, that kind of thing."

Many of the women in Cunningham's life were relieved in 1989 when Cunningham survived a late night motorcycle accident while on his way to his sister Betty's home in the thumb-area village of Dryden. As usual, Cunningham had been running late and speeding. He didn't see that the recreational vehicle ahead had stopped until nearly too late. Cunningham explained to Campbell that, "the truck didn't have any brake lights when it stopped. He suddenly was going at it too fast and he had no choice but to lay it down." When a police officer showed up, "he saw Bill standing there and he said, 'Where's the body?' [The cop] just assumed that anyone on that motorcycle was dead." Cunningham, however, "was OK; he probably had some minor scrapes and bruises."

The wreck was hauled to Horning's house. "Sister Cecilia said, 'leave it out there; we don't want it back,'" Betty Horning said. She and other women who loved him didn't think it was safe for Bill to run around like a madman on a motorcycle.

"Somebody wanted to give him a [replacement] motorcycle and the nuns talked them out of it," Horning said.[42]

Without the Harley to ride out his frustrations, Cunningham kept his worries at bay by heading down the street to visit small children. The Focus: HOPE Center for Children had opened in September 1987 with three teachers, three assistants and 34 4- and 5-year-olds who were the children of Focus: HOPE's trainees and employees. Going there refreshed his spirit. "He loved it, it was his fix for the day," said Mary Sullivan. "And the children loved him. We always taught them to shake hands with people when they come in and he loved that. They would just gather around him and shake hands."

---

42   *Some years later Horning's son-in-law Pete Rayl took ownership and restored the bike. But Father Cunningham never rode it again.*

Eleanor Josaitis ran a tight ship.

Credit: *Detroit News*

26

Witchcraft

ANN RUZZIN, A longtime friend of Focus: HOPE, was having lunch with Eleanor Josaitis at the Traffic Jam restaurant in the mid-1990s, when Eleanor stopped talking about organizing a Christmas music festival and brought up something that had been bothering her: "Do you think I'm a bitch?"

Ruzzin thought for a moment about all the times she'd seen Eleanor chew out a Focus: HOPE employee, sometimes going way beyond what was called for. "Let's put it this way," Ruzzin said she told her. "You have a strong personality."

"But, am I a bitch?" Eleanor persisted.

"Yes," Ruzzin said, acknowledging that as a boss herself at Kelly Services she'd been called the b-word, too. Then they laughed, and sipped their wine. From then on, whenever Eleanor saw Ruzzin her greeting was: "How is my favorite obnoxious bitch?"

The b-word has a nasty sound, and in Eleanor's case way too harsh and simply wrong. Eleanor Josaitis was proper, polite, helpful, gracious and warm. She seemed to remember everyone's name, and had a good grasp of what their spouses and children were up to. Women struggling against a glass ceiling in the city's corporate hierarchy admired Eleanor Josaitis for her ability to speak her mind and stick to her principles. Over the decades at Cunningham's side, Eleanor became the most beloved professional woman in Detroit.

On the Focus: HOPE campus, it was a slightly different story. The actual word many colleagues used for Eleanor rhymed with the b-word—witch.

The first eye-popping interaction with the tough-as-nails Eleanor for most employees came during orientation. Standing before a group of new hires with fierce determination, Josaitis would begin by reciting the Focus: HOPE mission statement about pledging "intelligent and practical action to overcome racism, poverty and injustice." Then she'd talk about co-founding Focus: HOPE with Father Cunningham in 1968 in order to find practical solutions to the racial problems exposed by the 1967 rioting in Detroit.

Eleanor liked to showcase a sample of the hate mail she'd received. She'd wave a letter up high so everyone could see. She'd then read aloud the racist screed containing several "N-words." Her aim was not to belittle the writer, but to point out that America has a long way to go to before it is a nation that is just—socially, racially and economically. "She kept your attention," said Donna DiSante, who was hired in 1993 to work with Charlie Grenville in the development department. "She had you sitting up straight in your seat, paying attention. It was all: 'No, Ma'am. Yes, Ma'am.'"

Eleanor did not have Father Cunningham's soaring rhetoric or his ability to command a room. But she mimicked his style, confidently speaking to groups large and small, and telling the story of their partnership, forged during a journey to overcome racism. She never attended college, but several universities awarded her honorary degrees, citing her as a role model for women. She inspired people with her passion, grit and determination.

Peggy Shine—the daughter of Bill and Eleanor's longtime friend *Free Press* editor Neal Shine—worked for Focus: HOPE for a few years beginning in 1990. She said Eleanor "was phenomenal; she would make you give up everything to follow her."

Eleanor had complete authority at Focus: HOPE. She saw her duty as making sure the complex was clean, that employees were well groomed, properly dressed and punctual, that colleagues treated each other with respect, and—above all—that Focus: HOPE's good reputation remain intact.

When Eleanor "needed to be hard-hitting, she was," said Mary Kay Stark. "I remember once she gave us a talk about 'dress for success,' how we needed to dress. That may have been just for the women. … She had a lot of compassion, too, yet she was strong. You didn't want to cross either one of them really. You didn't want to make either one of them mad."[43]

Eleanor took her cues on how to manage employees from Cunningham, who did not tolerate sloppiness or laziness. Eleanor, however, took it to an extreme, popping up at odd hours to keep everyone on their toes, complaining when closets or desks were messy, and hollering at colleagues in front of others. "I would see how horrible she could treat people," Peggy Shine said. "My assessment was there were a lot of people who worked there who were young, one of their first jobs, and you had people who were kind of on their way to retirement. My impression

---

43   *Eleanor Josaitis was a stickler for proper dress, her views established in a memo sent to the staff on June 17, 1993, about "Dress Code and Personal Appearance" that was signed by Father Cunningham: "While you are working at Focus: HOPE, you represent Focus: HOPE to the public, to our customers, and to those who serve. You represent the finest and largest civil rights organization in this state, perhaps nation." Banned were jeans, sandals, muscle shirts, sundresses, dungarees, sneakers, tank tops, sleeveless blouses, shorts or skorts, mini-skirts "and/or high splits," halters, jogging suits, sweat suits." Everyone's "hair should be clean, combed and neatly trimmed or arranged. Shaggy unkempt hair is not permissible regardless of length. Plastic caps, rollers and do-rags are not permitted. … If a colleague reports to work improperly dressed or groomed, the supervisor shall instruct the colleague to return home to change clothes or take other appropriate corrective action."*

was she wasn't going to get pushed around; she was more empowered than other people that were there."

Joanna Woods, who started as a teacher at the Machinist Training Institute in January 1986, said that for a time Josaitis "came and lived at the MTI" because she was concerned about high dropout rates. "She was just there giving criticism, making everybody uncomfortable," Woods said. "It was horrible." One staff member, a machinist-instructor, had never been late before but came in a few minutes late while Josaitis was there. She laid into him. "I think I went into total shock," Woods said. "I was like, are you serious? He's never been late. He had been celebrated at MTI. She just reamed him." Josaitis also wanted to sit in the room while students were being tested. Woods said she stood up to Josaitis and told her she'd have to sit by the door so students wouldn't be disturbed during the test. "When I said that, everybody said they thought I was about to be fired," Woods said. "I didn't know, but I knew it was the right thing."

DiSante said Eleanor's harsh criticism of her and others "was cruel; it was awful. Mostly it was Eleanor. But, God forbid, the two of them did it. It was a double whammy. They were tough. And Father Cunningham didn't spare any language." Many times, DiSante thought, they could have handled a particular problem "in a more humane way. ... Eleanor was really the witch. I saw her. She would berate people in front of guests. It was an awful thing. It was really tough."

Edna Jackson was in charge of the Food Center and one day in the middle of an inventory required by federal regulations Eleanor made an unannounced visit. Jackson had not refilled food bins yet because she was busy with the inventory. Eleanor blew up. "Some of the bins were empty or low and she beat me up one end and down the other," Jackson said. "You couldn't get a word in" to explain. "And you were getting beat up because 'you were depriving these people of the food that the government had given them, and they are hungry and I don't care anything about your inventory.' It was a Friday and she had beat me up. And then she left. No chance to respond. I was a blubbering mess. I had to go up to my little cubbyhole and just finish

crying. I didn't want the world to see me carrying on like that."
Jackson called Armstead and said she didn't know what to do
because she thought Eleanor was going to fire her. Armstead
assured her that wouldn't happen and said, "That's just the way
she is."

"Saturday morning, my doorbell rings. I go to the door and
there's a delivery person out there with a whole bunch of flowers.
I looked at the card, where are these from? And it's from Eleanor. Of course, I started crying all over again." Jackson said that
Armstead "helped me understand: She never cared about rules
and regulations if they were going to hurt somebody else. She
just wanted to make sure you treated people right. You make
the Food Center clean and orderly and you let people come
in and get their food and to hell with you and the government
regulations."

The "witch" motif played out for several years. Some colleagues joked about Josaitis "riding her broom" which, according
to then-*Detroit Free Press* reporter Neal Rubin, was "a reference
to her aggressive and sometimes abrasive style." As an ironic
honor for Eleanor, MTI students once used their machining
skills to fashion a stainless steel broom and presented it to her. "It
was basically my idea," Woods said. "It was kind of heavy. She
would bring it out and always make reference to her being the
'broomer.' ... She laughed, oh, she was thrilled with it."

The reputation as a witch that she seemed to relish was
honed over years of inserting herself into virtually every aspect
of Focus: HOPE. One Saturday in 1991, for example, she came
into the Center for Children, where a crew led by Father Cunningham's assistant, Sharon Agnew, had worked for days to
set up for the Christmas folk music festival. "Eleanor is pacing,
walking around that room, looking at all these tables and chairs,
and you knew she was pissed off," said Ann Slawnik, who had
then been working for Focus: HOPE for all of three days. People
were packed in too tightly, Josaitis thought. There should be just
six seated at each table, not eight. She angrily motioned for Dan
Autry, the Focus: HOPE buildings manager, and ordered him to
change the seating to tables of six. Agnew, who normally gave

Josaitis a wide berth, tried to explain why the tables were set up the way they were—many ticket sales were in groups of eight so family and friends could sit together. Agnew knew she was wasting her breath. Eleanor wouldn't budge—six at every table so guests could be comfortable, she commanded. "We got into the biggest argument," Agnew said. "You couldn't win."

When people began arriving, Slawnik said, "the woman at the registration table was completely flummoxed." There was a lot of noisy shuffling as some attendees dragged more chairs up to their six-person tables, leaving other tables short. Slawnik said Josaitis saw the problem she had caused, but it was too late to change.

Perhaps no one endured more criticism from Eleanor than Charlie Grenville, a chain-smoking, hard-drinking lapsed Catholic priest who researched and wrote the grants that made Focus: HOPE possible. Grenville was only rarely quoted in the press and never publicly praised by either Bill or Eleanor for his years of service to Focus: HOPE. An intellectual who was fluent in both French and Dutch, Grenville's forte was taking Cunningham's striking but nebulous ideas, doing extensive research into what might get funded and putting everything into well-written, fact-filled narratives for winning grant proposals. "The three of them had this remarkable set of complementary qualities," said John Ziraldo. "Charlie was really this insightful strategic thinker. Eleanor was the persuader. And Bill was the hammer, the passion behind the whole thing."

The dynamics between the charismatic priest, the feisty and hard-working mother of five and the brilliant loner addicted to tobacco, liquor and clear writing were a wonder to behold. "Between the three of them, there was a contentious relationship. It was very volatile: Three very volatile people," Ziraldo said. Several staffers said they felt Bill and Eleanor sometimes picked on Grenville unnecessarily. For his part, Grenville had learned to keep his head down, quietly take notes in meetings and produce masterpieces of grant writing. He occasionally vented with trusted friends like Ziraldo. "I think Charlie felt a little under-appreciated, but to say that they [Bill and Eleanor] were mean to him, well, they were mean to everybody. ... As much as Charlie might have felt unappreciated, he also felt loved by Bill and Eleanor," Ziraldo said.

Paul O'Neill, who became Eleanor's administrative assistant in 1988, said that the angry arguments between Josaitis, Cunningham and Grenville became an accepted part of any given day. "There was a constant clash between Charlie trying to make his product perfect and thoughtful, and get his plans out ... putting concepts down on something readable by foundations," O'Neill said. "He would be in charge of writing and meanwhile Eleanor and Father Cunningham were still trying to conceptualize what was going to happen." Outwardly, Grenville seemed to bear up under the stress well. "They'd want a proposal to the Kresge Foundation ready by March 1, and they'd call [Grenville] down for meetings that would take up all day and he had to produce a 100- or 200-page proposal," O'Neill said. "And they'd want it perfect. His job was to refine it; meanwhile they were still coming up with concepts. ... It's a lot of pressure."

Usually with a lit cigarette resting in the ashtray on his desk, Grenville churned out thousands of pages of complex, detail-rich yet easy-to-read grant proposals. He sat hunched over a typewriter or keyboard like Schroeder, the piano-playing *Peanuts* character. "The fastest two-fingered typist I ever saw in my life," said Jim Aho, who began working at Focus: HOPE in 1993 alongside Grenville.

"Charlie was one of the most amazing men I ever worked with," said Frank Bugg. "He was in many ways even brighter and more brilliant than Cunningham. Charlie was the mechanism for Father Cunningham who would come up with ideas and dreams for programs and stuff like that. Charlie was able to sit there, visualize what [Cunningham] was saying and put the conceptual stuff on paper."

Unlike Cunningham, who could spin a rapturous, if somewhat fictional narrative about Focus: HOPE's work, Grenville took pains to ensure that every fact in his reports was accurate. "The foundations trusted him and Eleanor. They didn't trust Bill," said Thom Armstead. "A couple of major foundations thought that Bill was giving them a lot of bullshit, too much hyperbole, too much exaggeration of goals. The Walk always had 10,000 people when clearly it was three or four thousand at the most. And he oversold programs. But they really liked Charlie. They knew Charlie was solid. And Charlie, in terms of being a steward to these foundations, if they had any questions or needed any information, he was always on the spot, always on the case."

In 1986, Grenville endured a robbery and beating, and then a cancer diagnosis. Tom Ferguson, a former journalist at the Free Press then working with Grenville, said "Charlie lived on a rough patch of Ferguson street, the only white guy in the neighborhood, next to an abandoned house that had become a dope den." One day, he showed up hours late for work. "His face looked like it had been run over by a tracked vehicle," Ferguson said. "He had stitches and bruises and a badly swollen eye. One arm was in a sling."

Late the night before, someone had knocked on Grenville's door. "Charlie, being a liberal, flung it open as if he were welcoming family for Thanksgiving dinner," Ferguson said. "Instead, it was a delegation from the dope house next door. They invaded, sacked and pillaged." Grenville said, "They even stabbed my water bed!" Grenville was dragged into the street and beaten "within an inch of his life," Ferguson said. While Grenville was talking, Ferguson thought he'd be perfect to play the lead in "The Don Knotts Story"—"a wiry featherweight without the hyper nervous tic that Knotts displayed on "The Steve Allen Show." Grenville said he was glad his attackers hadn't found his TV, which he'd had the foresight to hide inside the oven.

Then, Charlie's bad habits caught up with him. After smoking two dozen cigarettes a day over more than three decades, Grenville was diagnosed with esophageal cancer. He underwent experimental surgery at Sinai Hospital that used part of his large intestine to replace the removed esophageal tissue. He had to give up the drinking and he ate very little, often nothing more than a hard-boiled egg for a meal. But he continued sneaking a smoke or two every day outside behind the Resource Center. "He cut back on cigarettes but was still smoking, which pissed off Cunningham," said Tony Campbell, then finance director. Campbell said Grenville's cancer was the impetus for "making Focus: HOPE a smoke-free workplace."

After the cancer surgery, Grenville's health never really recovered. He caught pneumonia and went on several lengthy medical leaves in the early 1990s, making the job of writing proposals harder when he could work.

While concerned about Grenville's health, Bill and Eleanor continued to rely on him, feeding him information for grant proposals, expanding ideas and sharing hints gleaned from meetings with foundation program officers or congressional staffers. Eleanor would hear a suggestion from someone on, say, Capitol Hill and call Grenville immediately to direct him to insert that idea or wording into a proposal he'd been working on for weeks. The rewriting was nonstop often until seconds before the grant application deadline.

Grenville had decided it was better not to challenge Bill and Eleanor directly in public. "He shied away from the limelight," said Kevin Gordon. "At managers' meetings, he was a very different person: compliant and respectful, but he would often rage" about Bill and Eleanor behind a closed door. Gordon said that Grenville did not resent the news media's refrain about Focus: HOPE being built by Bill and Eleanor all by themselves. "But what really made him angry is they believed their own press, that they didn't appreciate the work, creativity, the energy he put into it," Gordon said. "He was really an intense guy, he really had the stress."

Bill and Eleanor had desks near the center of the large open space, taking up most of the second floor of the Resource Center. People working in the offices on the mezzanine above, like Grenville, heard everything going on down below. You couldn't help but notice when the two of them raised their voices in another "debate." "It was interesting, actually," said Jim Aho, who came to work in Grenville's development office in 1993. "You were so glad you were not a part of it. You were just an observer. The best thing to do was to keep your nose to your computer and pretend you had no clue what was going on, even though you could hear everything."

Tom Murphy, the retired drill sergeant stiffening up students at Fast Track, said he "never had any problems" with Josaitis. "With the chain of command being her as the boss, everything kind of went through Eleanor and right to Father," Murphy said. "She was an ass-kicker and name-taker. … We used to have meetings every Monday morning, Father, Eleanor and all the program managers. If something was screwed up, we got to know what it was."

Gordon found out how tough Josaitis was when he tried to press through a raise that had been promised to one of the math teachers at Fast Track, Monna Wejrowski. "It was a promise, actually written down," Gordon said. Gordon met with Cunningham and got him to sign a form that increased Wejrowski's wage scale. But then Josaitis got up from her desk and in three steps was standing over the priest, having overheard everything. She said: "Bill! Bill! Do you know what the enrollment over at Fast Track is right now?" Lower enrollment rates meant less money coming in. But, Gordon argued, the math teacher is not the recruitment officer and Monna is not responsible for low student counts. Besides, she was promised, Gordon nearly shouted. Bill folded; he would not go against Eleanor on this. "He took the paper and just tore it up," Gordon said. "He would've signed if she wouldn't have come over. And he handed it back to me. That was just the way she could be sometimes."

Gordon said Wejrowski was "incredulous" that her promised pay raise had been nixed by Eleanor. "She was upset, and I couldn't lose her." Gordon pulled out his own checkbook and wrote a check to Wejrowski for the amount of the missing raise, promising to do the same every pay period. Wejrowski was mollified, but Gordon felt he had to tell Cunningham what he'd done. He has a distinct memory of what happened when he did: "I was going to a Jean Luc Ponty concert. [Cunningham] had a briefcase in his hand. He didn't throw it at me, but it went sliding past me. And he was just really letting me have it. 'You opened up this organization to all kinds of liability! How could you betray us? How could you do this?' I was just a kid in my 20s. I was fighting back my tears." A few days later, Gordon got a note from Focus: HOPE's personnel department. Cunningham had approved the raise for Monna after all. A note from the personnel director said Cunningham had directed her to "make sure Eleanor doesn't see this."

Josaitis "was fearless," Gordon said. "She could also be more mean than Cunningham. She could come out of nowhere; you wouldn't know where it was coming from. … You just never knew when a bomb was going to land from her."

Eleanor would pop up unannounced anywhere on the Focus: HOPE campus at any time. While walking down Oakman, she'd snatch litter off the sidewalk and confront a colleague who had walked by without picking it up. She started showing up early at Focus: HOPE before nearly everyone, and then stand at the door waiting for people to come in late. Don Hutchison, Focus: HOPE's star "candidate" student at the Center for Advanced Technologies, said his class had weekly meetings with Eleanor every Wednesday at 6 a.m. "And if you were late, she would lock the door so you couldn't get in," Hutchison said. "One person was late once and [Eleanor] held the door so she couldn't get in. Finally, [the candidate] yanked it open and went into the meeting. The next day, she was removed from our cohort."

Eleanor, Hutchison said, "was very tough, but to her candidates she was very maternal. It wasn't until years later that I heard some horror stories about how terrible she treated some of the other colleagues. I never experienced it personally. I saw how tough she was, but the toughness I saw was warranted."

Although guests and visitors were treated with the utmost deference, Cunningham was known to occasionally let them know he was perturbed with something they said, did or wore. On one occasion, "maybe 10 of them showed up in a van from the Midwest, a nonprofit somewhere, and they had on overalls and jeans and T-shirts," Slawnik said. "As soon as I saw them get out of the van, a little thing went off in my head—this is not going to be good." After their tour and a Focus: HOPE lunch, Slawnik took them to meet Cunningham. Members of the group began asking about Focus: HOPE and how remarkably far the organization had come. The flattery did not impress Cunningham.

"He just laid his arms out so you could see his monogrammed cufflinks on his beautiful French-cuff shirt and he said something like: 'I want you to think about the message you send in the way that you dress as a nonprofit. And I want you to look around at some of our colleagues you've seen today and think about the message you're sending. What we've done from the beginning is to dress as if we were not a nonprofit, as if we weren't unloading dented cans from the back of a pickup truck. I want you to think about that—what you want people to think about you and what to expect of you and them.' They just sat there. He didn't embarrass them, but I think they got the message."

Despite the often unpredictable nature of working at Focus: HOPE, the long hours at nights and on weekends, and the volatile scenes of passionate arguing, many colleagues enjoyed their time there because of its mission and the palpable sense that they were making a difference in the city, indeed in the nation and world. The challenge from Bill and Eleanor was to accomplish great things on behalf of the underprivileged, to solve problems of poverty and racism, to create opportunities for people. And, Focus: HOPE was succeeding!

"When you were at the conference table sitting with Cunningham, you really felt you could change the world," said Gordon. "It was such an exciting time to be there. You just really felt like it was an organization that really and truly had its feet in both worlds. It could make government work for it, just a thrilling thing."

After touring Focus: HOPE President Bill Clinton said, "I have never been in a place as advanced, as upbeat, as hopeful as this place."

Credit: Focus: HOPE

27

Man From Hope

DONALD HUTCHISON, A student at Focus: HOPE's Center for Advanced Technologies, had hidden himself away in an
unused conference room in the complex in early 1994. With his
exhausting schedule of 60-hour weeks—40 hours working in the
CAT's high-tech manufacturing area and 20 hours immersed in
advanced courses in various engineering disciplines—he needed
quiet time to study. "No one ever went there," Hutchison said of
the room where he went to be alone with his books. "There was
just a phone sitting there with dust on it. The whole room had
never been used."

Suddenly, the phone rang. "When I answered the phone they
say, 'Hello, Donald, this is the White House calling. Would you
like to come to Washington to meet with the president?' How
did they know I was here? I never asked. I was so stunned." After
a moment's hesitation, Hutchison simply said, "Sure."

Within a few days, Eleanor Josaitis was driving a group that
included Hutchison, Father Cunningham and another CAT
student to Detroit Metropolitan Airport. It was the first time
Hutchison realized how much authority Josaitis actually had at

Focus: HOPE. "On the way there, I just remember Eleanor saying, 'OK, Bill. You have to see this person and this person and that person, and remember this person helped us with that and that.' I thought, boy, Eleanor is running the place. It was as if she was dictating to him what he should do. Up to that point, I always assumed he was the one running it. When we got to Washington, like clockwork, he did exactly what she told him to do. He went from this person to that person, 'thank you for doing this,' almost verbatim. He remembered everything."

The forum held in a hotel conference room was to focus on developing America's high-tech and highly skilled workforce. Hutchison, Cunningham and the other student were seated on the dais with about 10 other people, including President Bill Clinton. Panelists were asked to briefly introduce themselves to a crowd of about 1,000, but several took advantage of the moment to talk about their particular program in detail. "They talked way too long about their programs," Hutchison said. When his turn came Hutchison gave his name and that he was a student at the CAT in Detroit. Out of respect for everyone's time, he said, "I look forward to telling you more about the program." Cunningham realized that Hutchison wasn't going to talk much about the CAT yet, so "he jumped in" and gave a lengthy spiel about what Focus: HOPE was trying to do.

Cunningham dominated the discussion at the president's jobs summit on February 2, 1994, according to David Everett's report in the *Detroit Free Press*. "Cunningham took as much microphone time as he dared, and then a little more, to brag about the program's successes," Everett wrote. "And Clinton asked one of Cunningham's design engineering students, Donald Hutchison of Detroit, to describe how it helped him."

"The president looked bored, honestly," Hutchison said. "You could tell he had been to a million kinds of events. He kind of sat at the desk with his head in his hand, staring." But, when the forum ended Clinton's demeanor changed and he shook everyone's hand and "was extremely engaged," Hutchison said. "He made you feel as if you were the only person in the room." Cunningham invited Clinton to come to Detroit to see what Focus:

HOPE was doing to help lift people out of poverty through the unique high-tech engineering school under development.

Hutchison was a 1989 graduate of Henry Ford High School in Detroit and his family fully expected him to go college. But he'd attended graduation parties for his friends on their way to college, only to see them return home after washing out. Hutchison did not have a high expectation of success. Then, he went to Focus: HOPE and met Father Cunningham. Focus: HOPE's Fast Track program was the first remedial math program he'd heard about. "I tested fairly high on the entrance exams, but the reason I took Fast Track was I was told if you finish you can get a job at a bank as a bank teller," Hutchison said. "While I was in Fast Track I heard about other programs like the Machinist Training Institute and the Center for Advanced Technologies that was being developed at the time." Still, going to the MTI didn't interest him even though Focus: HOPE managers, especially Fast Track instructor Tom Murphy, were urging him to give it a try.

"Basically, they had to twist my arm to do it," Hutchison said. "I was dead set on becoming a bank teller. They said, 'Why don't you at least take the entrance exam?' I said, OK, I'll take the exam. ... When they told me I had passed and done fairly well, I was surprised. I said maybe there is more to life than just becoming a bank teller."

He enrolled in the eight-month program at MTI, started working with the machines and learning basic blueprint reading, measurements and shop theory. "Suddenly, I had these small successes that started to build my confidence. ... During my time at MTI was when I first met Father Cunningham." The priest was recruiting for the first cohort of "candidates" at the CAT, and he impressed on the MTI students how important this new high-tech engineering education system was to Detroit, to Michigan and to America. "I just remember him being charismatic, very confident," Hutchison said. "He had this presence about him that caused other people to be encouraged, including me. He would talk about the CAT and how grand it was going to be, how spectacular it was going to be. And I bought into that. He made it personal for me, so that I could become this 'renaissance engineer' and accomplish such a goal because of him. ... He made us think that we were going to be better than everyone else, this education and training that we were going to receive was going to be better than any other college in the world. ... Maybe I was naïve, but I believed everything he said."

A few days after the summit in Washington, the Clinton Administration announced that Detroit would host a world jobs conference for the Group of Seven (G7) nations the following month. In 1994, the G7 was an informal group composed of the heads of state, finance ministers or central bank directors from seven countries: France, Germany, Russia, Italy, United Kingdom, Japan, as well as the United States. The G7's mission was to oversee the world's economic system by coordinating policies on international bank lending, trade and global monetary policy. The leaders met once a year at rotating venues.

Everett reported that Clinton chose Detroit for the G7 meeting for a variety of reasons: a "blossoming relationship with the resurgent American automobile industry's top executives, [a] growing alliance with Mayor Dennis Archer [and the] need to repair political damage which organized labor caused by opening new Mexican markets with the North American Free Trade Act." Cunningham's "starring role," as Everett called it, at the previous jobs summit may also have helped seal the deal.

It also didn't hurt that Secretary of Labor Robert B. Reich had been impressed during his visit to Focus: HOPE when he came to Detroit to speak to the Economic Club of Detroit on September 27, 1993. An overflow crowd at Cobo Hall that day heard Reich sing the praises of Michigan's new crop of leaders who were preparing for a high-tech future. "You started doing the thing millions of other Americans will have to do: make the crossing from old work to new work," Reich said in his speech. "I'm not here to flatter you or gloss over the challenges you face. Unemployment in Michigan is still too high and we'd all like to see higher wages. Big manufacturers are still downsizing. And I'm not saying Michigan volunteered to become a laboratory for new work out of patriotism or intellectual curiosity.

Michiganians are adapting to the new global economy because they had to. And they are making it work."

The date set to begin the two-day G7 meeting was Monday March 14, but the question of whether Clinton would visit Focus: HOPE was not immediately clear. If the president came, he would top a growing list of hundreds of public officials, corporate executives, academics, celebrities and do-gooders who came to see Cunningham's miracle in Detroit.

On February 3, the day after the jobs summit in Washington, NASA astronaut Story Musgrave came to Detroit for a visit sponsored by the Detroit Chamber of Commerce. Musgrave had helped repair the orbiting Hubble space telescope the previous year, and he was brought to Detroit to inspire students to study math and science. His sweep through the city came on the same day the shuttle Discovery was launched, the first time a Russian cosmonaut was included on an American crew. At Focus: HOPE, Musgrave told a reporter for *The Michigan Catholic* that, "this place is awesome, as we'd say in the space world. ... The first thing I thought of when I stepped in here was passion. You've got to have passion to do it all. What you're doing here and what we did up there are very closely related. You have to pay attention to every detail!"

No one said anything publicly right away, but many staffers saw the clues and guessed that Clinton was going to visit Focus: HOPE. "It was all very hush-hush because of the Secret Service," said Ann Slawnik, who was in charge of organizing most tours at Focus: HOPE. "Those of us not in the inner circle didn't know until maybe 10 days ahead of time, and then different ones of us were pulled in. I was pulled in because I worked a lot of public relations.

Donna DiSante volunteered to help with communications. "It was really funny because prior to the [G7 summit], we were sitting up there in the peanut gallery looking down and all these men with trench coats and brief cases were walking in," she said. "So, obviously they were Secret Service. ... We could tell. We just said, oh, they're coming."

Everyone got to work at a furious pace once news broke that Clinton would visit Focus: HOPE on Sunday, March 13, the day before he was to give the opening address at the two-day G7 meeting. About 200 foreign officials and more than 500 reporters were expected for the event downtown. It was a perfect opportunity for Focus: HOPE to shine in the national spotlight, since reporters would not have much else to cover on the day before the G7 conference where meetings were behind closed doors. "We had press coming from all over the world, literally," DiSante said. "We were so busy working putting our press packages together; we really worked hard on that to make them look slick."

Air Force One landed that morning at Selfridge Air National Guard base in Macomb County, where "cheering throngs" greeted the president enthusiastically, the *Free Press* reported. The trip to Detroit was something of a respite for the president who was dealing with a much-ballyhooed scandal, a real estate deal in Arkansas called Whitewater that involved the first lady, Hillary Rodham Clinton. Nearly 1,000 people were at Focus: HOPE waiting for him when he arrived at midday. Michigan Governor John Engler, a Republican, and former Governor Jim Blanchard, a Democrat who had been appointed by Clinton to be Ambassador to Canada, stood together in the background and joined Clinton in a receiving line. People on the line were giddy in their excitement. Someone gave the president a T-shirt that said, "Fans of Hillary."

After touring the facility with Cunningham and Josaitis, they came to the raised platform on the CAT's distinctive bright green shop floor. Cunningham had asked Hutchison two days previously if he would introduce Clinton. "I was stunned. I was deathly afraid, because I had never done anything like that before," Hutchison said. "I struggled over what I was going to say all day Saturday and all day Sunday." On Sunday morning, Josaitis and Cunningham listened as Hutchison gave them a preview of his little speech. "They had one minor change, just one word I used that Cunningham himself changed."

Hutchison also was to present Clinton with a plaque inscribed with Focus: HOPE's mission statement. "I remember flubbing the words as I was reading it," Hutchison said. "Almost every dignitary in Michigan was there. The coolest thing was after I gave my introduction, I was able to relax and be able to soak in the moment of being able to stand up on stage with the president. … My parents were really proud, my family was really proud. That was the highlight of my career at Focus: HOPE."

Clinton thanked Hutchison, praised Cunningham and Josaitis and tapped into the theme of hope in the face of huge challenges: "Here we are in an inner-city neighborhood, with building after building and plants that have closed down, which could have become a symbol for the loss of hope."

The president said the deterioration of the manufacturing plants in Detroit and elsewhere dampened people's hopes for a good-paying job and a better future. But, Focus: HOPE was a model for how to counter despair. "Instead of saying 'if,' this is a place that says 'when,'" Clinton said. "This model here could be seen sweeping across America if we had the kind of local leadership that is manifest here by the stunning examples of Father Cunningham and Eleanor Josaitis. I have never been in a place as advanced, as upbeat, as hopeful as this place." Clinton reminded people of his birthplace in Hope, Arkansas, saying, "Now I can say I also believe in a place called Focus: HOPE." The large crowd that included hundreds of Focus: HOPE employees and their families, erupted into wild applause.

All of the hard work was worth it. Clinton's visit to Focus: HOPE received most of the publicity during the G7, outshining a dinner hosted by Vice President Al Gore at the Detroit Institute of Arts in the court dominated by the famous Diego Rivera murals. Cunningham and Focus: HOPE gave reporters a feel-good story line and opportunities for great photos and videos inside a stunning, cutting-edge manufacturing operation that evoked some kind of spaceship.

Clinton's visit could not have gone better for Cunningham, as evidenced by the front-page headline in the *Free Press* the next morning: "Clinton Sees Hope in Detroit; President says Tech

Center is model for U.S." The sub-headline was more detailed: "Surrounded by whirring, buzzing, computerized machinery and hundreds of enthusiastic students, President Bill Clinton rhapsodized Sunday about Detroit's Focus: HOPE, saying its 'stunning examples' could revolutionize manufacturing across the United States."

The *Free Press* report by Bill McGraw and L.A. Johnson said, "the job training and high-tech manufacturing that Clinton saw at Focus: HOPE are part of a vision that will be the meat of the G7 agenda." A piece by *Detroit News'* Washington bureau reporter Richard A. Ryan also was generally positive, quoting Clinton: "I want everyone in America to see you. If we can get rid of all these hang-ups we've got in this country, if we started thinking about what is really important and if we really believe all people are created equal ... then we can revolutionize this whole country. ... And if we can have that in these few square blocks in Detroit, my fellow Americans, can it not happen throughout our country? If we can do this here, we can do it anywhere."

Other media reports had a more skeptical viewpoint on the G7 conference's actual impact on raising employment in Detroit or anywhere else. "It's a good question whether you can duplicate Focus: HOPE elsewhere without also cloning its chief executives, Father William Cunningham and Eleanor Josaitis. But clearly, somebody ought to be trying," the *Free Press* editorialized that week.

The Detroit News' Kim Trent wrote that Cunningham had "spent much of Monday adjusting to his new status as international media star. ... The limelight, however, didn't change the topics Cunningham prefers to talk about, namely Focus: HOPE and his spiritual commitment to it, not his newfound celebrity." Trent asked about his religious faith and the priest responded that, "It's the role of the church to help the people produce and contribute." Cunningham said he thought the media's focus on Detroit had been equally positive. "We've got a lot to be proud of," Cunningham said, referring to the entire metro area.

Detroit News columnist George Cantor said "the high point of the president's stay in Detroit was his emotional visit to Focus: HOPE." But, Cantor wrote, the fact that Focus: HOPE existed was due to the abysmal failures of the public school system in Detroit. Focus: HOPE's "students apparently have come through the public education system without a prayer of finding a good job. They have been prepared for a world that no longer exists... So you must have a Focus: HOPE, in which expectations are matched to reality. But only a fraction of those who need it ever get there. The rest have been destroyed by their education."[44]

In his memoir published a few years later, Reich recalled Clinton's visit to Focus: HOPE to meet Cunningham and the eager students at the Center for Advanced Technologies, although Reich got one fact wrong [Cunningham's eyes were brown, not blue]. The Labor Secretary described a 16-year-old student named "Frank" who, he says, "is jet black and small for his age." Frank explained what he was doing, programming a machine to cut metal "into whatever shape I want if I program it right. ... These machines, they got to be programmed. It's complicated, but I'm getting into it." Cunningham, according to Reich, put his hand on Frank's shoulder and said he's making excellent progress: "He's been with us only three months but can already use statistical process controls. If he continues to do this well, there's a good job waiting for him as a precision machinist." Reich said he asked Frank what he had been doing before

---

44   *Here is a sampling of some of the headlines in 1994 about Focus: HOPE: "Detroit's job-creating gems should shine for G-7" (over a column by University of Michigan professor Noel M. Tichy at the School of Business in The Detroit News), "President Clinton has high praises for Focus: HOPE" (The Michigan Catholic, 3/18/94), "Hard work may bring good jobs" (Cincinnati Enquirer, 3/6/94), "Clinton wants working world" (Arizona Daily Sun, 3/14/94, with a picture of Clinton with Cunningham), "The Faith of Father Cunningham" (Le Monde, 3/12/94), "Spirited training program gives birth to dreams" (Chicago Tribune, 3/20/94), "Area officials pleasantly shocked by Focus: HOPE tour" (Livonia Eccentric, 5/16/94), "No ivy-covered walls for these engineers (Ward's Auto World, March 1994).*

coming to Focus: HOPE. "Nothin'. Hangin' out. Getting in trouble," the teen told Reich.

Reich later asked Cunningham what his secret was. "Secret?" Cunningham responded, Reich wrote. "His blue eyes opened wide. 'How do you do this?'" Cunningham's answer: "These children want to learn. We offer them a clear path to good jobs. You see, most poor kids don't see any relationship between what they do in school and the real world of work outside. In fact, they don't see much of that world at all. We connect the two. This isn't just vocational education. This is education in advanced technology. It's the future. We're giving them real skills linked to real jobs that are in demand. And they know it." Reich wasn't satisfied with the answer, and pressed him on whether this concept could be replicated elsewhere.

"Do we have to clone you to make this work elsewhere?" Reich pressed Cunningham. "Father Cunningham's round pink face turns even pinker. 'Oh, heavens. It's not me, not by a long shot. Of course this can be done around the country. There's a huge need for skilled technicians. And there's a huge number of confused, troubled, poor teenagers desperate to find a future for themselves.' The priest then chuckles to himself. 'Of course, I do have one particular talent. ... I'm very good at knocking people up for money.'"

Reich said he was skeptical. Cunningham told him that the auto companies were a great help. "But," Cunningham told Reich, "I'll let you in on the real secret. *The De-fense De-part-ment.*" (The italics and hyphens are Reich's.) "My ears prick up," Reich wrote. "How the hell did you get DOD money? Pardon my expression."

"By now we're at the car. 'Let's just say there's a senator who's very fond of us, who sits on Defense Appropriations. He's one *hell* of a guy, pardon *my* expression.'" Cunningham was obviously referring to Michigan's senior Senator, Democrat Carl Levin.

Reich continued: "On the way to the Jobs Summit I ponder what I've seen. A lot of America is ready to write off poor inner-city dropouts. But I've just watched a bunch of them master complex algorithms. They're on the way to good jobs and productive membership in society. This isn't magic. It's happening because of a strong-willed, talented man backed by a lot of money." Reich then wrote that at the Jobs Summit he sat next to the British Chancellor of the Exchequer, "a thoughtless disciple of Margaret Thatcher" and a free-market economy. Reich said he felt like "causing an international incident" by telling the "arrogant" Brit what he really thought. "I marvel that this man and Father Cunningham share the same English language and today inhabit the same city," Reich wrote. "They actually live on different planets. I'd rather live on the priest's."

In May, Cunningham and Hutchison were invited back to the East Room of the White House when Clinton signed the School to Work Initiative Act of 1994, part of the president's "lifetime learning" education plan to help the 75 percent of high school students who will not get a college education. The bill provided for $100 million to be distributed by the U.S. Departments of Education and Labor to help states, communities, schools, employers and labor unions begin building a school-to-work network.

"We were late getting to the White House," Hutchison said of the trip. "At the time, [Cunningham] was having problems with his diabetes. … His blood sugar was low, he said. We stopped to get a sandwich, and I think we took a little bit too much time. Or, more accurately we didn't anticipate the traffic. We jumped into a cab and the whole time we were stuck in traffic, looking at our watches. Finally, he said, 'OK, you have to let us out.' And we ran the rest of the way to the White House. … We made it in time but had we not got out to run the few blocks to the White House, we might not have made it."

At the bill signing, Clinton called Cunningham and Hutchison to the dais and said Focus: HOPE was an example of modern job training programs in the country. "Cunningham, he took it all in stride," Hutchison said. "You could tell he was a seasoned veteran when it came to dealing with political figures, even the U.S. president."

Father Roger Morin, Father Cunningham and Sister Agnes Mary Mansour of the Sisters of Mercy who was then the director of the Michigan Department of Social Services. Years of working two stressful jobs, poor sleep habits, lengthy periods without exercise—interrupted by spurts of vigorous work-outs—late-night meals of red meat, excessive alcohol consumption and occasional cigars, eventually caught up with Cunningham.

Credit: Courtesy of Bishop Roger Morin

28

The Needle

WHILE WAITING FOR their lunch orders one day in 1993,
Father Cunningham began downing glass after glass of water
as fast as the waitress could bring them. "He just kept asking for
another glass of water," said Tony Campbell who was with Cunningham and Eleanor Josaitis at a restaurant that day. "He said,
'I'm embarrassed, but I'm sorry; I'm thirsty, I'm thirsty.'"

A few days later, Cunningham's doctor diagnosed type 2 diabetes. It meant drastic lifestyle changes for the priest, whose
biggest challenge was learning to inject himself with insulin. "It
hit him pretty hard; of course, he was pretty upset by it," Eleanor said. "The hardest part for him was he couldn't poke himself.
Knowing Bill's positive attitude, it was just something he was
going to have to deal with."

Cunningham realized that he'd have to start eating better
and cut back on drinking alcohol. He was OK with that, but
really hated the needle. "He used to tell us he struggled with
the needle, how hard it was for him to inject himself," said Greg
Petty, pastoral assistant at Madonna. "I don't know if he was
afraid of needles, but it was a challenge for him. But when he

put his mind to something, he'd do it. He was overweight there for a while, and he said, 'I'm going to lose weight.' And, boom! Weight's gone. He used to enjoy drinking, then he said, 'Well, I'm not going to drink any more.' Boom! Gone! He said, 'I'm going to get in shape' and he'd start running around Belle Isle. This was in his late 50s and early 60s, and he's running Belle Isle."

His family's medical history was problematic—his dad probably drank excessively, and his mother's blood circulation problems led to amputation of both legs and eventually her death at age 52. Alvina Cunningham's death in January 1948 broke her son's heart, and as he aged he wondered if he had inherited her health problems.

"Bill was really worried the whole time," Eleanor said. "He talked a lot about his mother, that she died at an early age and she'd lost both of her legs, and that's what he grew up with." Cunningham, she said, knew he had to "change everything."

"He was a serious diabetic," said Sister Ellen Gardner. "Any change in his metabolism triggered an overreaction." She believed Cunningham's often over-the-top emotional outbursts were partly caused by "an imbalance in his metabolism. ... It didn't take much because of the diabetes. I wasn't afraid of him. ... I just waited until he got done saying what he needed to say. It took a length of time to make a salad or eat six crackers or time to get something into his system that made him more easygoing. ... I do not think he held grudges. On the other hand, if he jumped on you or gone ballistic or whatever—I've heard people say that it wasn't easy for them to forget. This was a very big person in the eyes of everybody else."

The opening of the Center for Advanced Technologies was coming on fast in 1993. Money had to be raised, teaching staff hired, curriculum designed, reconstruction wrapped up, new computerized machinery installed. He'd not had time to consistently go on his long jogs, and his diet of lots of greasy fats and carbohydrates was catching up to him. His favorite was gobbling up the crispy skin from a roasted turkey.

"Look at how he smoked and drank, and he loved meat; big steak, red, rare meat," Janet Josaitis Denk said. "Scotch and sirloin and a cigar, that was Uncle Bill." During camping trips to property he'd bought with Don and Eleanor Josaitis on the shores of Lake Huron north of Port Huron, he'd insist on cooking over a fire. He devoured the fattest and greasiest bits. "Bill would always cook," Don said. "He would fix bacon and eggs and always take grease from the bacon and pour it all over the toast. He loved steak and he would pour the grease all over the potatoes."

The priest often ate late at night at one of Detroit's best establishments, a friend to many restaurant and saloon owners. By 1993, Cunningham was probably 30 pounds heavier than he had been in the 1980s. Bags sagged under his still-intense brown eyes; he grew a double chin and his long wavy hair was turning grey, if not quite the silver mane his dad was known for. "He had this problem of not eating until seven, eight at night, and then he'd build this huge plate and sit down and watch TV," Don said.

The priest was fatigued, whether he wished to admit it or not. There always was something he had to do most evenings. When it came time for bed, he would read a book on his nightstand or watch a "Star Trek" rerun or some other show before snatching a few hours of sleep. "Cunningham's big thing was to veg out in front of the television," Janet said. Worse, he sometimes analyzed the plots of TV shows out loud *ad nauseam*. "He would go on and on about some lame episode from 'Colombo' like it was 'Beowulf.' 'MacGyver,' he loved 'MacGyver.' … He loved crappy television. Mom would say it's his way of unwinding." They'd be sitting there listening to the priest talk about some television show he was watching, Janet said, then "you'd look over and he'd be snoring, and then you'd get the TV back."

Mary Sullivan said Cunningham "had a terrible diet; he used to eat and drink all through the year and then during Lent he would fast and abstain. That was very hard on his system." During his Lenten fasts, Cunningham would lose weight but then gain it all back—and maybe more—beginning at Easter. "He felt it wasn't doing any damage."

Cunningham was committed to getting a handle on his diabetes and leading a healthier lifestyle. He ran farther distances on different routes. One route was east on Jefferson Avenue from Belle Isle toward the St. Clair Shores beauty shop where Eleanor got her hair done. Don Josaitis would follow the priest as he ran along the lakeshore. "I always called him Will because of will power," said Sister Ellen. "Will was the name they used for his father and when I started using it, he liked it."

Charlie Grenville, the genius behind Focus: HOPE.

29

In God We Trust

ON A BLUSTERY winter day in the early 1980s, Eleanor Josaitis, Charlie Grenville and Tony Campbell walked the two blocks down Oakman Boulevard to Madonna Church to join Father Cunningham in a Mass of desperation. Standing in the sanctuary, the four of them absorbed that day's reading from the Gospel, shared the bread and wine, and prayed that a pending foundation grant would come through to bail out Focus: HOPE.

Later, when they learned that the foundation had rejected their proposal, the group met again to consider payless paydays for employees and possible layoffs. As that meeting wound down, Campbell thought of a simple gesture to end on an upbeat note. He reached in his pocket and pulled out what he had, a Lincoln penny that he handed to Cunningham. "In God We Trust," Campbell said, reciting the nation's motto emblazoned on the coin.

Thereafter, when things got tough at Focus: HOPE, Josaitis or Cunningham would pull out a penny and profess their rock-solid faith that God would provide. Passing a penny symbolized their belief that God would lead them on the right path to help heal the wounds of racism that had plagued Detroit for decades. And, as far as Cunningham and Josaitis were concerned, God was behind their phenomenal success in squeezing every possible dollar from private foundations and government entities to fund Focus: HOPE projects.

Grenville was the hidden genius behind Focus: HOPE. After designing and managing the supplemental food commodity program, he led a development staff that worked countless hours on the complexities of building and maintaining relationships with literally hundreds of people—the folks who made decisions on how to spend public and private dollars. They included program officers at foundations and officials from the highest levels of federal and state governments. Just from 1981 to 1991, 16 major foundations and 47 smaller family foundations had donated $6.3 million to Focus: HOPE's various programs. More than 100 corporations had given $3.7 million in the 1980s. And departments and agencies at the federal, state and local levels had granted $61 million in cash and equipment in that decade. In 1987, even more federal money started rolling in when Congress and the Department of Defense agreed to fund Focus: HOPE's Center for Advanced Technologies at $100 million over 10 years. Focus: HOPE's ambitious budget would top $90 million annually in the mid-1990s.

Focus: HOPE was a showcase for taking positive action to overcome the effects of racism by providing opportunities to the disadvantaged. While some of the various things Focus: HOPE did were charitable in nature, the goal for all of them was advancement of social justice, Grenville said in a 1983 in-house interview on videotape. "The feeding of children is not done here out of a sense of charity and helping the poor. It's done out of a sense of readying a generation of people so that they can realize some justice in their lives. ... All of our projects address in some fashion an injustice."

Grenville and the development department he ran for several years were just as crucial to Focus: HOPE's success as Cunningham's charisma and Josaitis' hospitality. Grenville's skillset was his mastery of a myriad of federal regulations and RFPs [requests for proposals] across several federal departments while writing first-rate proposals that could sail through the choppy waters of government bureaucracy.

Michigan had a powerful Congressional delegation that helped make Cunningham's visions reality. But the state is also blessed to be the home of some of the nation's largest foundations: Kellogg, Mott and Kresge, among them. The Ford Foundation, based in New York City, that was begun by Henry Ford's son Edsel in Michigan also was an important funder. All of them made large grants to Focus: HOPE in response to proposals written by Grenville. "The foundations would listen to Charlie, while the politicos would prefer to have me or Eleanor tell them something," Ken Kudek said. "They always viewed Bill as a visionary, but a dreamer. I think Charlie was viewed as a nuts-and-bolts guy."

Once a funding opportunity was identified, a long application process began. "I presently have a proposal in to the Health and Human Services Department, a pre-application," Grenville said in the 1983 interview. "It had to be 10 pages long. It is one of 1,500 applications. On or about April 10, they will announce which 500 will be allowed to submit a full proposal and out of that 500, they will fund 150."

Grenville's grant proposals had to offer a clear picture of the issue and the practical approach Focus: HOPE was offering to address the need. The organization's record of success was a major component. Once a grant check cleared, deadlines loomed for reports back to the foundations and the government about what was accomplished and how Focus: HOPE used the funds. The reports required extensive data collection and documentation of the impact on the people served.

The pressure on Grenville and his team to produce reports and proposals that would bring enough money in to meet payroll grew substantially over the years. "I do a great deal of the writing at Focus: HOPE," Grenville said during the interview. "I do publications. I do studies. I do reports. I do proposals. I design programs."

"It was a stressful place," said Laura Blyth Poplawski, who began working with Grenville in 1989. "We had to make budget. We were waiting for grant money to make payroll sometimes."

Grenville frequently talked wistfully with colleagues about how the organization grew from a small advocacy group of volunteers into a national model for distributing food commodities to the poor. How they worked to train diverse groups of teenagers to break from the prejudices of their parents and learn to trust each other. How they started a Machinist Training Institute and a Fast Track remedial math and reading program to create opportunities for good-paying jobs for the disadvantaged.

It's interesting that in the one-hour video interview with Carl Bidleman, Grenville smokes three cigarettes and does not mention Cunningham or Josaitis by name. Still, he called Focus: HOPE a "remarkable collection of people … that includes not only the staff people but the volunteers. What defines Focus: HOPE is a willingness to be very practical, to look at situations that have racial implications or have to do with justice, and find our way to a practical resolution. There is a certain character of courage that has to be invoked in a lot of situations."

Grenville "really did present himself to me as the brains behind [Focus: HOPE], and I believed him," Poplawski said. Grenville told her that he, not Cunningham or Josaitis, had written the Focus: HOPE mission statement. Whatever the truth, the three of them appeared to be "very close friends, a cool little triangle of personalities," she said. And they fought like long-term partners who could agree to disagree. "They certainly weren't afraid to argue and loudly," Poplawski said. "Throwing files at each other. Charlie getting very angry at Eleanor, storming upstairs, storming out and smoking." And yet, "most of the time everyone was wonderful."

Paul O'Neill, Josaitis' administrative assistant for about two years, said Grenville's responsibilities included "refining ideas" about innovative programs that would advance the cause of increasing economic opportunities for minorities. "Father had very loose visions," O'Neill said. "They were great visions, but he wasn't a detail man. Charlie would know what details he had put into the proposals. ... Charlie took Father's grand ideas and fleshed them out and gave them bones and muscles and veins. ... It was a lot of pressure."

Grenville's stress must have been increasing, especially after his bout with cancer and strict sobriety. Still, vigorous discussion and debate with Bill and Eleanor, shouting matches, proper etiquette in front of guests —and prayer—had been standard operating procedure at Focus: HOPE from the beginning. "The tension between Charlie, Father Cunningham and Eleanor was very practical," said O'Neill. As they developed the CAT, "Father Cunningham would focus on that Star Trek stuff, the floor color, the doors 'whooshing.' For Charlie, that was all superfluous and distracting to him."

In conversations with colleagues, both Cunningham and Josaitis expressed disappointment that Grenville was still smoking even after surgery for esophageal cancer. Coughing as he came in every morning, Grenville continued researching, writing and revising. Cunningham, who drew a small salary as a priest for the Archdiocese of Detroit and enjoyed free room and board at Madonna, had inherited modest wealth and could afford to donate his time to Focus: HOPE. Grenville, while technically still a priest, received no pay or benefits from the archdiocese and he needed the meager Focus: HOPE paycheck. The nicotine, he seemed to believe, focused and energized his mind for the tough intellectual work.

Joanna Woods, who was running the MTI, said Grenville "was well loved by Eleanor and Father" although "they hated that he smoked. ... Eleanor used to cuss him out across the whole room: 'Put that cigarette out!' They loved him to death— that was evident—but they were mad at him for smoking."

The stress on Grenville increased markedly in the 1990s as Focus: HOPE expanded while still operating with a thin margin between income and expenses. The real killer was the contracts for automotive parts that were supposed to fund Focus: HOPE's for-profit enterprises. Reasons included the fact that when students mastered tasks required for one part they'd move on to other tasks and new students would have to be trained to take over. Error rates were high and manufacturing specs were constantly changing. Most of the contracts turned out to be money-losers.

At about the same time, Focus: HOPE was finding it harder to get large foundations to continue funding programs at the same level as in past years. Cunningham, with Grenville's grant proposal-writing acumen, had won major grants from many of the largest foundations. But foundation directions change and new program officers bring different perspectives about how to stay true to their foundation's mission. "Focus: HOPE fatigue" infected several foundations.

John Burkhardt, a 1968 graduate of Sacred Heart Seminary High School, was a student of Cunningham's, and he had worked at Focus: HOPE for a few summers during college. Burkhardt later became a Kellogg Foundation National Leadership Fellow from 1989 until 1993, when he began an eight-year stint as a program officer for the foundation. By then, Kellogg had given Focus: HOPE tens of thousands of dollars in grants, but by the mid-1990s had rejected most of Cunningham's requests for funding.

Cunningham had "run through—and sometimes run over—many program officers at the Kellogg Foundation, and he had spent out the vast reserves of approval extended to him by some of the board members," Burkhardt said. "Bill was almost always on the lookout for resources, and often badly in need of them. But that was rarely reflected in his approach to funders and, to his credit, he certainly knew that foundations don't respond to need as much to ideas. Honestly, Father Cunningham was convinced to his core that he deserved the support of these foundations because he was doing their work better than they could."

When they were in Battle Creek to meet with Kellogg staff, Cunningham and Josaitis would say hello to Burkhardt. Although his portfolio overseeing leadership development and higher education programs did not include Focus: HOPE, he got a call one day from Josaitis, who wanted insight into why Kellogg's support for Focus: HOPE had stopped. Burkhardt came to discuss ideas that might generate a discussion at Kellogg about a grant.

"We met in the volunteer center and Eleanor got us started, and then left the room to do something else. Bill and I were alone in the room," Burkhardt said. After a short discussion about Kellogg's strategies in Detroit and the importance of finding a "fit" as the basis for a proposal, Burkhardt waited for the new idea from the visionary priest. But Cunningham either chose to ignore what was being said about the Kellogg strategy framework or didn't really want to hear anything from Burkhardt at all. Instead, Cunningham wanted to talk about a building on Oakman Boulevard that he planned to acquire, the nearly empty Yellow Pages building on the other side of the Lodge Freeway. "There was a vacant building, but no apparent new idea beyond the possibilities it represented," Burkhardt said. He surmised that this really wasn't anything new from Cunningham. As Cunningham ventured further into his story of rescuing a building, Burkhardt suggested that the priest "give me the essence of an idea that I can carry back to Battle Creek to make a case for support."

Years later, Burkhardt could not remember what exactly he had said or if perhaps he had crossed some line by insisting on a central ambition for the project, a concept, or a handhold. "I must have used the word 'idea' because he said: 'Idea! Idea! What do you mean idea?'" What followed was a lecture about Detroit, its history, Focus: HOPE's victory over the Automobile Club of Michigan, and how institutions, including the Catholic Church and major foundations, were abandoning the city. Burkhardt, who said he felt like he was once again in Cunningham's high school English Lit class, said he believed he understood most of that, but he still needed a proposal with "a concept, a purpose."

"And he went off again, and the '*purpose* is to bring justice, the *purpose* is to pay something back for our sins.'" Cunningham then went on to praise the "very bright students" in the seminary high school class of 1968, apparently suggesting that Burkhardt might be an exception or at least a drag on the average. He then challenged him in a more personal way: "Why do you think you hold a position like the one you do? Why would you work so hard to get yourself in a position where you can do something, and then not do it?"

"He was kind of going off on me, and Eleanor appears at the door," Burkhardt said. "And she says, 'Bill, why are you talking with him like this? He's come here to visit us. Let's go have lunch.' And Bill said, in words very close to this: 'Eleanor, why do you interrupt me when I'm amusing myself?' And he flashes me a big smile and her a big smile, and we go across the street for lunch," Burkhardt said. "I never resented it and it certainly did not disappoint me at all. It was Repertory Theater and for that scene I was cast in a part—or perhaps I was a prop. Eleanor said 'cut' and we dropped our scripts without another word."

Cunningham was pranking him—or was he? Several years passed before Kellogg made another grant to Focus: HOPE.

Grenville began expressing doubt that he was the right man for the job, so much depended on him. "I remember Charlie saying that he really wasn't a development or grant writer," Campbell said. "He did the best he could. I don't think he regretted doing it. He was thinking somebody else was going to take over and they'd better get a good person."

Beginning in August 1995, Grenville experienced severe lower back pain, extreme fatigue and a swollen right testicle, according to a disability insurance claim he filed on October 1. "No heavy lifting, bending or heavy work," a physician prescribed. "No stressful environments. Complete sedentary limitations. PT is totally debilitated." The life insurance company's approval of the disability claim would come too late for Grenville.

His last day at work was August 29, 1995. On September 5, he was admitted to the University of Michigan Hospital. After stabilizing his condition, doctors told Grenville they would treat him only if he promised to quit smoking. He wouldn't promise to even try to quit, so he was transferred to Sinai Hospital in Detroit. Kudek stopped to see him around the time of Grenville's 54th birthday and "he was already completely jaundiced; I mean, he was yellow."

About two weeks later, Josaitis and grant writer Jim Aho were holding a vigil in Grenville's hospital room when the phone rang. "I remember Cunningham calling and the two of them talking, Bill reminding him—even though Charlie was a former priest— Bill told him, 'You know, you're still a priest and you have to keep that in mind right now.' I guess that was code between a couple of Catholic priests to prepare for his death."

Grenville died the next day, October 23. A memorial service led by Cunningham and Josaitis took place at Madonna on November 2. The Madonna choir and Cunningham's folk singer-friends sang spirituals and "The Battle Hymn of the Republic." Grenville's ashes were buried under a tree on the south side of the Focus: HOPE Resource Center, much of them scattered by a stiff, cold wind that was accented by light snow. His estate amounted to thousands of books he had collected over several decades and a $49,000 life insurance policy paid to the beneficiary, his sister Diane Harter of Westland.

With Grenville's death, Cunningham and Josaitis asked Kudek to take over the development department. It was a crucial appointment, but a more urgent issue was the struggling finance department. Campbell had taken over for a part-time bookkeeper in 1977 to become Focus: HOPE's business manger, and he had risen to finance director with a demanding array of responsibilities that expanded as the organization grew. While earning his master's degree in business administration at the University of Detroit, Campbell's day job was tracking every dollar that passed through the large, unwieldy and complex nonprofit organization that employed 800 people with more than a dozen different funding streams.

While Campbell kept track of the numbers, Cunningham never relinquished any authority over the budget. Focus: HOPE's Board of Directors—commonly known as Friends of Bill or FOBs—had gone years without meeting. "Even if they had a meeting, there wasn't a comprehensive overall budget" for them to review, Campbell said. Cunningham always preferred running the organization without a board of trustees getting in the way. "In the beginning, he asked Dykema Gossett [a law firm] what's the minimum that the board has to do? And they said, they have to appoint you as executive director," Campbell said. Cunningham told them to "write it up so that's all they [board members] do." And for about 25 years, that's basically all Focus: HOPE's board of directors did.

Campbell said auditors from Arthur Andersen sometimes asked for copies of the minutes of board meetings. "We would say there weren't any meetings and they would just note that there weren't any meetings," Campbell said. An operating budget for the entire operation was occasionally created at the behest of some funder or news reporter. If that happened, Campbell and Cunningham would total up the grants approved and grants pending, then work with various department heads to get a best-case scenario for the coming year. Cunningham often had ideas on special projects and someone would guestimate a dollar amount for them. There was no funding yet for many programs to be created or expanded, but the budgets represented Cunningham's vision of what Focus: HOPE could accomplish in a given year. Cunningham didn't show any disappointment when revenues for a particular year fell short of the goal in the budget.[45]

Cunningham trusted Campbell to keep track of the numbers, but he had a firm grasp of the details hidden in the larger picture. Once, Campbell spent a couple of days crunching numbers on a looming deficit for one Focus: HOPE program and then

---

45 *Anyone who took a close look at Crain's Detroit Business's yearly ranking of the area's largest [by budget] nonprofits could see the dichotomy. In December 1994, Focus: HOPE ranked second [behind Wayne Community Living Services] with a 1995 operating budget of $91.2 million, up from $89.7 million the previous year. And yet, 1994 revenue had been just $75.7 million, a $14 million shortfall. In 1996, Crain's ranked Focus: HOPE third largest with an operating budget of $78.7 million even though revenues for 1995 had fallen to $65.2 million, not the $91.2 million "budgeted" the year before. "We didn't spend money that we didn't have," Tony Campbell explained. "So that when the next year came and actual revenue was counted we had a deficit that was much smaller than that gap shown in Crain's. We thought big, but we didn't spend all that money."*

brought his calculations to Cunningham. "I walked up to him with a couple of pieces of paper and he said, 'It's about $50,000, right?' Yeah, it was. Bill would have the budget numbers in his head," Campbell said. Campbell once asked a certified public accountant who had been sent to Focus: HOPE to do court-ordered community service about how they might improve accounting procedures. The accountant didn't think much could be done. "You just don't have enough horses," the CPA said. He took that to mean that the organization did not have enough "competent staff to do it." Nevertheless, Campbell said audits always were "clean."[46]

Kay Bell, an accountant from Birmingham who had been handling the books for Christ Church Cranbrook in Bloomfield Hills, came to work as Focus: HOPE's new controller in January 1996. She was amazed when one of her first duties entailed getting Cunningham to endorse a $10 million check from the Pentagon—the last installment of the $100 million over 10 years the Defense Department had sent to support the CAT. That thrill was soon replaced by dismay as she realized just how complex and discombobulated the finance system was at Focus: HOPE. "It was really hard to tell how they counted income when I got there," Bell said. "Any accounting project is like a jigsaw puzzle. You just need a table big enough to get all the pieces on the table. At Focus: HOPE, I was never getting all the pieces on the table. The Center for Children was a freestanding entity with money coming from the state for childcare. The food program had money from the USDA and it was accounted for differently. The CAT was funded with a federal grant from the Department of Defense."

Bell said the MTI students at the time did not pay tuition and the funding was "piecemeal." Still, teachers, administrators and support staff all had to be paid. At Industry Mall, various

---

46   *Although there never was any suggestion that the Arthur Andersen firm had done anything wrong at Focus: HOPE, it should be noted that in June 2002 the company was convicted of criminal activity for its role in the Enron Energy debacle in Texas. The conviction was overturned a few months later, but the company had gone out of business by then.*

for-profit business entities worked under innumerable contracts to produce auto parts, mostly at a loss. "They weren't tracking that stuff, how many people left the program, who owes us what money, who's chasing the money," Bell said. "Bank reconciliations weren't happening."

Focus: HOPE's weekly payroll then was about 800. "I'd get checks back from the bank and the box would be this long," Bell said stretching her arms out. "How am I supposed to reconcile this?" All the finance department could do was scan the summary of entries from the payroll processing company that recorded how much went into each paycheck, as well as taxes and other deductions. But there was no way to check each one by hand every week.

Inevitably, people began to commit fraud against Focus: HOPE. Bell said she had just started randomly checking checks from the general account that had cleared the bank—checks always signed by Cunningham—when she spotted four or five checks with signatures that looked like a child had scrawled "Father Cunningham" on them. The blank checks were without watermarks and had been created simply to test their new printers. They had been sent for shredding, but were pilfered. Two employees were charged, convicted and sentenced to short prison terms.

Another time someone in shipping and receiving took a box of newly printed checks, slit open the bottom, removed one set and then sealed it up again with clear tape. Several of the checks cleared before someone noticed they weren't in sequence. In another fraud, an employee had carefully and almost imperceptibly changed the amount of his Focus: HOPE paycheck from $137 to $637. "It took us a good long while to find it," Bell said.

Josaitis was hurt by the betrayals. After all, she had scrutinized each and every person hired by Focus: HOPE. Had she missed something when she shook their hands and looked into their eyes? In her orientations with small groups of new hires—always scheduled for Tuesdays at 8 a.m. sharp—Josaitis had impressed most of them with her passion while telling the story of Focus: HOPE. When people she had cleared proved to be untrustworthy, Josaitis reacted with shock, anger and sadness. The betrayal of her trust was more painful than the lost money. "She just went ballistic" when they were victimized by thieves, Bell said.

Kudek, as the new development director, had experience working with state government officials on getting job training funds for the MTI, and he had taken the lead on convincing high-tech companies to donate hardware, software and cash to Focus: HOPE. Kudek built relationships with several tech companies like EDS, Hewlett-Packard and eventually Oracle and Microsoft. But like Cunningham, Kudek was not well versed in how computers actually worked.

Fortunately, a Focus: HOPE colleague was computer savvy— Linda Hanks. Hanks came to Focus: HOPE in 1983 as a data entry processor for the food program and had worked her way up to running the Information Technology department. Focus: HOPE's earliest acquisition was a PRIME computer with two 80-meg drives. "What we ran on that was the food program, the finances and maybe the volunteer data base," Hanks said. "The development department used Wang word processing machines." On the industrial side of Focus: HOPE, they were trying to run software provided by the Automotive Industry Action Group that was developing a standard computer-based process for handling contracts for car parts.

Schmoozing friends among local high-tech companies, Kudek connected with Karen Casman, a regional sales manager for Microsoft. It took several months, but Kudek finally got the attention of Michigan native, Steve Ballmer, executive vice president of Microsoft widely considered as Bill Gates' right hand.[47] Ballmer was raised in Farmington Hills and attended Detroit Country Day High School in Beverly Hills where other notables like comedian Robin Williams, NBA star Chris Webber, and astronomer Paul Kalas were students. Reportedly, Ballmer's mother, Beatrice, had become interested in Cunningham and Focus: HOPE, possibly because it was located within two blocks of Beatrice's childhood home in northwest Detroit. However

---

47   *Ballmer succeeded Gates as CEO in 2000.*

that worked, Ballmer came to Focus: HOPE on April 24, 1996, bringing with him $1.5 million in software and cash for the civil rights organization, reportedly the first large charitable donation made by Microsoft.[48]

During his visit to Focus: HOPE, Ballmer told the *Free Press'* Rachel Konrad that, "I can't think of a better match for Microsoft than this place." A joyful Cunningham told Konrad that partnering with Microsoft was like "riding shotgun down the information superhighway in a super-powered Mustang." He added: "It's a rough but exciting ride. ... As we say here, 'if you don't make a friend of change, change will be your worst enemy.'" At a news conference, Cunningham and Ballmer opened a "toolbox" full of Microsoft products, including BackOffice, Access, Windows95 and Schedule+. Ballmer admitted that there was a bit of self-interest at play in the donation. "The obvious benefit here is that if we can get people to learn about computers with Microsoft software, we'll keep them using Microsoft all their lives," he said. "That's how you keep a business growing."

The Microsoft products were a great help to Focus: HOPE's administration and food program. But the MTI and the CAT were hybrid learning centers that combined education programs ranging from remedial to post-graduate with high-skill and high-tech manufacturing operations involving customers, contracts and production deadlines.

The CAT needed a specialized computer program that could integrate everything in their manufacturing process, from raw materials to finished product. Kudek worked on leaders at Oracle to convince them to consider Focus: HOPE as a partner instead of a customer. Oracle, which wanted to sell their product to Focus: HOPE, eventually came through with a donation of software that was designed for a manufacturing operation.

EDS provided several programmers to assist Hanks' small IT department with implementation, but there were a number of challenges getting the Oracle system to work right. "The

---

48   *Steve Ballmer did not respond to requests for an interview for this book.*

whole thing was scary because most companies would take two years" to integrate a new system, Campbell said. "Cunningham declared we were going to do it in six months. Our team was whoever EDS could spare here and there, a hodgepodge of [Focus: HOPE] technical people to do this, and a deadline of six months." Hanks said that even though the deadline was not realistic, it was typical Cunningham: "That's who Father was. Father was very demanding, and he was very emotional, so he would let you know what he was thinking." Eventually, "we got it to work" but Campbell said most of the software's potential went unused.

Bell said the Oracle software was able to handle the various Focus: HOPE components that included the CAT, the MTI and the for-profit enterprises. However, large amounts of data had to be entered into the system and there were never enough competent people to do the job. One person in each department was trained on the Oracle software, and that person was supposed to train others in the department on skills like data entry. It should have worked but Bell said staffers who were trained on the Oracle system left for better paying jobs in the private sector. "As soon as I would get somebody up to speed on how to do their little piece of it right, they'd get hired by industry at three times the salary," Bell said.

Through a donation, a RolmPhone 400 was installed on Cunningham's desk. The 400, which transmitted data over the telephone lines, was used extensively by the military and defense contractors, so it should have been a natural fit. But Cunningham was disappointed in the technology. He wanted a phone attached to a computer that would automatically show the picture of the person on the other end of the line as well as some personal data about him or her. Of course, such a thing would have required someone pouring large amounts of data into the computer.

Cunningham never became adept at working at a computer. "I don't ever remember him turning it on, never saw him use it," Aho said. "I never saw him turn the chair around, put his hands on the keyboard and face the computer. He had hand-written everything on yellow legal pads, and he had beautiful handwriting."

Campbell said Cunningham didn't want to spend the time learning how to operate a computer, although he respected what they could do and knew that the technology absolutely represented the future. Even so, he was impatient for the kind of Star Trek-like technology he thought Focus: HOPE needed—technology like Skype that would take several more years to develop. "Father's love was autos and motorcycles and he really loved manufacturing; he had an understanding of manufacturing," Hanks said. "I.T. technology—he didn't have the same interest. And it was not easy to learn. It was a frustration for him trying to get the information out."

Top left: Father Cunningham's sermons often included tears, laughter and reminisces of his life as a child and a seminarian.

Top right: Bill and Eleanor pose with kids from the Center for Children in August 1996.

Bottom: Cunningham turns on the charm with Detroit Free Press reporters Dan Shine and Jack Kresnak minutes after announcing he had cancer.

Credits: Elizabeth DeBeliso, Focus: HOPE

30

Who Do You Say I Am?

IN BLACK, WHITE and gold African-print vestments, Father William T. Cunningham stood at the Madonna church ambo on a Sunday in June 1995 as an "Alleluia!" was sung by the choir during the Mass celebrating the 40th anniversary of his ordination to the priesthood. Then, he read from Luke, Chapter 9:

> One day when Jesus was praying in seclusion and his disciples were with him, he put the question to them: 'Who do the crowds say that I am?' 'John the baptizer,' they replied. 'And some say Elijah or one of the other prophets who has returned from the dead.' 'But, you, who do you say I am?' Peter said in reply, 'the Messiah of God.' He strictly forbad them to tell this to no one. The Son of Man, he said, must first endure many sufferings and be rejected by the elders, the high priests and the scribes and be put to death, and then be raised up on the third day. Jesus said to all: 'Who ever wishes to be my follower must deny his very self, take up his cross each day, follow in my

steps. Who ever would save his life will lose it. Who ever loses his life for my sake, will save it.' This is the Gospel of the Lord.

The sermon that followed was typical Cunningham, full of passion, controversial assertions and references to personal relationships. He called St. Paul "probably the most bigoted, most anti-feminist character in the scriptures." But, Cunningham said in that Sunday's reading Paul got it right. "Paul says with such extraordinary clarity that we are all one. He says it because he knows it's not an accomplishment. He knows it's something revealed by God, and therefore something we can hope for."

Dealing with the ups and downs of his diabetes, weary from the burdens of running both Madonna and Focus: HOPE, Father Cunningham grew a bit introspective that year. He began thinking about his legacy, telling Eleanor Josaitis and other colleagues that he did not want buildings or streets named after him, particularly their stretch of Oakman Boulevard.

In 1995, in a speech at Sacred Heart Seminary before a mostly female group about the coming millennium in 2000, Cunningham predicted that someone would want to play "My Way" at his funeral. The Paul Anka song made famous by Frank Sinatra had "the worst lyrics of any song, the damnedest song," Cunningham said. The priest, who had gone with a friend to see Sinatra in Detroit in 1989, said when the familiar musical refrain started in the orchestra, he told the person with him, "I'm going to get up and leave—I'm going to throw up if he sings that song. I got to get out of here." His companion told him that he couldn't just walk out with his Roman collar on—what would it look like? Besides, the tickets cost $100 each. "I says, restrain me, cause I'm getting ready." But Cunningham said Sinatra took the mic and told the crowd that he didn't like the song he was about to sing, but it had made him a lot of money, so he had to do it. Cunningham stayed.

"The dumbest thing in the world," Cunningham said. "If there is a purgatory, then I'm sure to go through it and somebody will sing this song at my funeral. The last thing in the world any of us wants to do is 'our way.'"

In the face of daunting obstacles, the priest could raise everyone's spirits with a story, a joke or a prayer. "When he came to the office to see to things, he always had this beaming smile and no matter how you were feeling, somehow those bad moods would go away," said Patsy McMahon, a former Catholic nun and longtime Focus: HOPE colleague.

Despite the many successes at Focus: HOPE, Cunningham slipped into something of a funk in 1995. He had not been feeling well, and he worried about losing his legs like his mother did. His type 2 diabetes was problematic and scary. And his eyesight seemed to be getting worse, most obviously when he struggled while reading the Gospel during Mass. Seeing how sick Charlie Grenville got, Cunningham had given up the cigars and cut back on his drinking.

A bitter newspaper strike at *The Detroit News* and *Free Press* that began in July 1995 put Cunningham in an awkward position. He was a friend of Neal Shine, then the *Free Press'* publisher, as well as several of the striking journalists. The Detroit Newspaper Guild represented reporters, non-management editors, photographers and other editorial employees at both papers. Most took to the streets with picket signs in solidarity with the other unions. That didn't stop the Detroit Newspaper Agency that published both papers from putting out scaled-back copies of the *Free Press* and *News*, and delivering them. The DNA showed its determination to break the strike by using helicopters to lift bundles of newspapers over crowds of picketers outside its printing plant in Sterling Heights. As the weeks wore on, several journalists broke with the strikers and began crossing the picket line outside the newspaper buildings downtown. Longtime workplace friendships ended acrimoniously. The pain from the strike was widespread and it became obvious to many that the labor dispute would go on for a long time.

A few weeks after the strike began, the Reverend Harry Cook, an Episcopal priest who had previously been a religion writer at the *Free Press*, was asked by someone at the guild to organize a prayer service to heal some of the hurt. Hoping to bring an end to the strike, Cook agreed and asked Cunningham to host it at

Focus: HOPE. So, it was arranged and about 50 people, including Managing Editor Bob McGruder of the *Free Press*, came to the CAT to see if prayer could help. Unlike the sidewalks outside the newspapers where union chants and shouts of "scab!" echoed off downtown skyscrapers, there was a respectful silence outside the CAT, although tension was in the air. Cook relied on Cunningham to offer the prayers.

If people expected Cunningham to give one of his fiery speeches with a ringing challenge to newspaper management and union leaders to stop the nonsense and resolve differences, they were disappointed. "Cunningham was a very cunning guy; he knew how to play it," said Cook, adding that he was a close friend of both the priest and Neal Shine. "He wasn't going to insult Shine. It was so uncharacteristic. You've heard Cunningham thunder. When he got a bone in his teeth, it was just incredible. But all of a sudden, he turned into a typical priest."

Shine was seriously ill at Cottage Hospital in Grosse Pointe after apparently collapsing from stress. Doctors didn't really know what was wrong until Shine's daughter Susan Epp noticed a rash on his back while bathing him and called his personal physician, who had admitting privileges to Henry Ford Hospital. Shine had a severe case of shingles that was affecting his organs and causing him tremendous pain. With the right diagnosis, Shine was given the proper treatment and later returned to work as publisher.

At the prayer service all anyone knew was that Shine was gravely ill, adding to the sadness of the event. As it ended, Cunningham approached the author, then a striking reporter, with tears in his eyes and said, "I don't think Neal's going to make it." I thought Cunningham didn't look that good himself.

A few months later, Cook invited Shine and Cunningham to lunch at the Traffic Jam near Wayne State University. But he didn't tell either that the other also would be there. Cook arrived first and was soon joined by Shine. When Father Cunningham showed up, Shine said, "What the hell is this?" Cook explained that they were the best hope of ending the strike. He pleaded with them to do whatever they could because the city they all loved needed the strike to end.

"It was one of the great disappointments of my life," Cook said. "They almost backed their chairs away from the table, like they didn't want to touch it with a 10-foot pole. It was an uncomfortable lunch. Cunningham said the most disingenuous thing: 'I don't know what I can do about it.' I thought, you built this kingdom, you've shaken down millionaires, you've made gold out of dross, you brought Bush to town."

In August 1995, Joseph Priestly (J.P.) McCarthy died. J.P was the longtime host of a morning news and talk show on WJR-AM, a powerhouse station that most movers and shakers in Detroit listened to. Cunningham was invited to concelebrate the funeral Mass at St. Hugo of the Hills Catholic Church in Bloomfield Hills on August 19, and to give the eulogy. Perhaps mindful of the dignitaries expected to attend and the live television audience on WDIV, Channel 4, Cunningham uncharacteristically prepared for it. He wrote several pages of notes and then placed them on a shelf of the ambo at St. Hugo before Mass began—at least he thought he had. But he couldn't find the notes when he searched for them, a little panic in his eyes, as two cardinals, two governors and hundreds of other powerful people waited. "You won't believe this: all my notes are gone," he said. He turned to St. Hugo's pastor, Monsignor Anthony Tocco, asking "Somebody remove those?"

He began an off-the-cuff sermon saying, "I've never really used notes before." His celebration of McCarthy's life was warm, especially to McCarthy's widow, Judy, their children and grandchildren. But there was none of the "fire in the belly" rhetoric that he was known for. Whatever he'd written down likely would have been better.

A few weeks later, Cunningham was invited to speak to an engineering group at the University of California, San Diego. While there, Cunningham connected with a Focus: HOPE volunteer from the old days, Joanne Cacavelli Johnson, who had moved out west and was running the local office of U.S. Senator Dianne Feinstein. Josaitis called to warn Joanne not to let the priest have more than one glass of wine during the banquet because of his diabetes.

"When he got up to speak he introduced me and explained how we had gone back to the early years of Focus: HOPE," Johnson said. "Bill gave a very strange speech that night. He was very disconnected, kind of rambling all over the place. He wasn't becoming angry. He was becoming frustrated. He was really trying to lay out a program that these engineers should be speaking to and addressing. I kind of looked around the audience and realized there was stony silence. He was not going in the right direction. I told him that I thought the speech was fine, but 'you got carried away on a few points.'"

Later, Johnson told Josaitis that she'd gotten negative feedback on Cunningham's speech. "We thought his diabetes was so out of control that it was impacting his ability to think coherently across a straight line," Johnson said. "I felt really sad that night. I knew something bad was going to happen. But also, I am glad we had that last time together."

Cunningham had lost some of his edge, diminishing his ability to work a room. "It came out that he had diabetes, and his voice was like 50 percent of what it was," folk singer Ron Coden said. "There was a tremor in it. He was thinner."

Somewhat prematurely, news leaked in July that Father Cunningham was working on another big idea: A $19.8 million renovation of the old Yellow Pages building on Oakman into a high-tech hotel and conference center. The 117-room hotel envisioned by Cunningham would be called Tech Villas and allow Focus: HOPE to offer housing for engineers, scholars and foreign dignitaries visiting the CAT. "Hundreds of professionals visit us each year to study how we take urban youth and prepare them to be future engineers," Cunningham told *Detroit News* reporter R.J. King. Cunningham expected approval of $13 million in loans and grants from the federal Department of Housing and Urban Development.

In August 1996, Cunningham was invited back to the University of Michigan Ross School of Business for the annual management seminar. In a 20-minute speech (unusually short by

Cunningham's standards), Cunningham described the history of Focus: HOPE, beginning with the 1967 Detroit civil disturbance: "Out of the violence, tumult, the madness and confusion of that historic revolution, a remnant of us, black and white, from Detroit and its suburbs, of every economic and religious background, joined together for intelligent and practical action." He then went on to discuss the food program that in the past month had supplied a "month's groceries to 42,404 babies, mothers and elderly, and we're celebrating because three years ago we averaged 85,000 a month. Our program became national and has been copied in 21 states."

Cunningham spoke about the MTI and the CAT that he called "a veritable Disneyland, a Star Trekian setting of electronics, making its own electricity with doors, lights and mostly everything electronic, unlike anything else anywhere in the world." He predicted that the MTI would prepare 200 trained machinists to enroll into the CAT as students of engineering. "Risk-taking, imagination, quick access to needed and current information are far more important than memory or practices protected by experience," Cunningham said. "Focus: HOPE engineers cherish the challenge: 'Going boldly where no one has gone before.' With competence in Japanese and German, they will access their global competition and push leadership relentlessly."[49]

Cunningham then, as usual, invited the U-M students and professors to join in his cause. "Please visit Focus: HOPE and know that in this blessed nation our greatest competitive edge remains our rich diversity of race and cultures," he said. CAT students "are to be empirical scientists, grappling daily with new data for ever developing new processes, new designs and new

---

49 *There never were regular classes in the Japanese and German languages at the CAT. There was a six-week introductory course in German at the MTI in the early 1990s that ended when the teacher found another job. Asking students to learn a second language like Japanese while studying the math and science required to be engineers was unrealistic, and Father Cunningham never publicly addressed the discrepancy between his rhetoric and the reality.*

products. In 1995, technology and science grew more in that one year than the accumulated knowledge of science from the beginning of civilization. … You know, when God created us, he made us to his own image and likeness. That is, he created us to be creators. No professional on the face of the earth creates more change, innovates and improves the quality of our lives more, than working engineers. Your destiny is to renew the face of the earth."

As his lifestyle grew healthier that year, a lot of Cunningham's mental acuity returned. And his physical appearance and stamina improved as he kept to an exercise regimen that was mostly jogging, a better diet, and his daily self-administered insulin injections. "My God, he was handsomer than ever," said Donna DiSante. "He looked like a movie star."

On a warm afternoon a few weeks after the U-M speech, Cunningham and Josaitis walked down to the Center for Children and posed with two of the kids for a portrait by photographer Jack Lang. In the photo, Bill and Eleanor are beaming, even glowing with positive energy. And then, seemingly overnight, Cunningham came to work looking jaundiced. "He was just yellow," DiSante said. Don Josaitis, who hadn't seen Cunningham for about three weeks, ran into the priest that September and was surprised at his appearance. He said Cunningham looked fit and trim—except for the jaundice. "The color of your skin is horrible, spooky," Josaitis said he told Cunningham. "He seemed to be very surprised."

Aho said Cunningham woke up one morning, started to shave and realized he was "yellow as squash." He came to a retirement party for Patsy McMahon that day and his skin coloring startled people. "It was very obvious something was wrong," Aho said. "He joked about it. He said something like: 'I woke up this morning and all of a sudden I'm Asian.' He really didn't know what was going on."

Then, Cunningham developed severe stomach pain. On September 22, he called Dr. Cornelius McCole, an ophthalmologist and a longtime friend, to report the pain and also that his skin was slightly yellow and his urine was discolored. McCole urged him to go to Henry Ford Hospital for tests immediately. It was cancer. Under the care of one of the hospital's top cancer specialists, Dr. Robert O'Bryan, Cunningham began a chemotherapy regimen. At least three times a week, Eleanor would drive Cunningham to Henry Ford, drop him off so he could see his doctor and then pick him up an hour later. Every time, they'd go back to the office and go to work. "And then one day, I took him to the doctor and when I went to pick him up, he got in the car and he just said to me, 'Go to Belle Isle,'" Josaitis said. "And I knew something was seriously wrong because whenever we had a very bad day—fighting, or nothing going right—we would go to Belle Isle and pray." They chose a favorite spot, a quiet area at the far eastern tip looking out into Lake St. Clair.

"We drove to Belle isle in absolute silence. We got onto the island, parked in our favorite spot. He said, 'Eleanor, the cancer is worse. They said I have three weeks to live.' I'm just looking at him, not saying a word." As many as 30 minutes went by in silence, she said. Finally, Eleanor pulled out a legal pad to take notes. "OK, Bill," she said. "Tell me what you want me to do."

With practical things to talk about, their emotions were held in check as Cunningham began throwing ideas out. Just then, Josaitis' cell phone chimed. O'Bryan was calling, so she put it on speaker. O'Bryan told them that he had found a doctor in Grosse Pointe who "deals with exactly the same kind of cancer that you have; he's doing a lot of experimental work and you may want to see him," according to Josaitis. "We immediately took down the name and address of this guy and we just jumped on the road, headed to Grosse Pointe," Josaitis said. That doctor, however, thought Cunningham would be better off with a more experienced oncologist—Dr. Vainutis Vaitkevicius, of Harper Hospital's Karmanos Cancer Institute, part of the Detroit Medical Center. An appointment with "Dr. Vee," as he was known, was soon set.

A cancerous tumor was detected near the gall bladder and under the liver, pressing on the nearby bile duct. It is one of the most difficult areas for a surgeon to work, but Cunningham was prepared for whatever was coming. "Bill told me that there was an opportunity, that they were doing experimental things and he liked Dr. Vee very much, and he would be more than happy to be part of" the experiment, Josaitis said. "They could put him in the hospital and do whatever they wanted, do as much research as they wanted."

The following Sunday morning in the Madonna rectory, Sister Cecilia Begin said she was ready to begin their ritual by reading aloud Father John Castelot's column from *The Michigan Catholic* for Cunningham to use as a basis for that day's homily. "This particular Sunday, Father said, 'Cecilia, don't read to me today; I want to tell you something,'" she said. "He had been to the doctor and he said the doctor said he had cancer and he had two weeks to live. Two weeks!" Cunningham told her not to tell anyone yet, that he wasn't ready to speak publicly about his death sentence. "I felt I would just die," Cecilia said. "He went on to Mass and I went on to Mass. I cried all through Mass. They wondered what was wrong with me. They knew he wasn't feeling well, and he had been losing weight. He didn't tell them until another Sunday."

Cunningham called his sister Betty Horning and asked her to bring the family down to Madonna so he could discuss something with them. "We just met and we knew what was going on," Horning's daughter Betty Edwards said. "I was there when the lawyers met and legal papers were written, the will. Power of attorney he gave to mother."

How would Focus: HOPE handle the announcement that they knew would shock many? Shine was called in and suggested that they hold a news conference with Cunningham making the announcement and taking questions from reporters. On October 2, 1996, Cunningham and Josaitis met with a handful of top managers and told them about the cancer, a short time before the news conference that was attended by more than 100 other Focus: HOPE employees.

His eyes moistening, his skin disconcertingly yellow and his voice raspy, Cunningham stood at a podium before the crowd assembled at the CAT. He did not mince words, describing the cancer as "lethal" and "fast-moving." The "best advice" he got from his doctors was that "I could go to bed and be comfortable, watch TV for a while and in about four or five weeks, you'd be attending a funeral. That's not my disposition." Under the fluorescent lighting of the CAT, the yellow in his skin and eyeballs jumped out, and he joked about his jaundice. "I know that I don't look particularly photogenic up here today," he said. A world-renowned specialist would perform a procedure the next morning and he would undergo follow-up therapy. "I've set the course for a fight that should take one-and-a-half to two months," he said. "My life has been a series of miracles. For me, miracles have been like snowflakes."

Cunningham and Josaitis privately had decided that he would have to take a leave of absence from Focus: HOPE. He also would have to resign as pastor of Madonna.

At the news conference, he said he wrestled with the decision to step aside: "I have always asked for direction from God. His will be done. That's always part of the argument against what I believe His will should be. We cut deals all the time." Cunningham said he'd notified Cardinal Adam Maida, then the head of the Archdiocese of Detroit, and Maida had accepted his resignation. Cunningham said Maida promised to send a "good parish servant" to take over Madonna. Cunningham asserted that he wasn't worried about his congregation. "The people of Madonna will tell [the new priest] what he needs to do," he said. "I'm comfortable with their strength, their devotion and their love."

Cunningham's administrative assistant, Sharon Agnew, had taken the day off and was with a granddaughter when she got the news. "I heard it on television and I took off running up there," Agnew said. A *Detroit News* photographer took a picture as she came through the big doors of the CAT, weeping uncontrollably. A reporter asked her who was going to fill Cunningham's shoes. "That was the wrong thing to say to me. Everybody sort of looked at me. I think he knew it was a big mistake. I did cut right in—nobody could ever fill his shoes. ...

"At that time, in his mind he was thinking that they're going to conquer this, because he kept coming to work," Agnew said.

"He came on in even though his coloring was off and went right to his desk. I'm thinking that all of us just knew that with this aggressive treatment that they're going to find the right combination of chemo or whatever and knock it out."

Greg Petty, the pastoral assistant at Madonna, said he admired Cunningham's grit in facing the cancer diagnosis and "the courage it took for him to decide on that aggressive treatment, because you knew it was going to be hell." Cunningham told everyone that he was doing everything his doctors told him to do and that he was feeling better, said Ron Coden, the Jewish folk singer Cunningham always asked to lend his musical talents to Good Friday services at Madonna. "He said, 'I've got so much to do, so much to accomplish, that I can't take a chance of not being able to finish this.' He really did not want to die. He was not afraid of dying but he really wanted to move on," Coden said.

Josaitis told reporters that she was temporarily taking over as executive director of Focus: HOPE, admitting that her skills were different than Cunningham's. "What has made us very successful is we complement one another," she said. "We've worked together over 28 years. We have the same passion when it comes to civil rights. But he is the communicator, the leader, the visionary, the risk-taker. And I'm the organizer." She added: "Nothing is going to change. We know what our goals are. We have never ever lost sight of what our mission is."

Cunningham's illness and decision to step aside stunned Focus: HOPE staffers, led off the local evening news programs and was all over the front page in the morning newspapers. Several reports mentioned Focus: HOPE's penny-sharing custom and pennies began coming in from all over.

During a two-hour procedure, Dr. Rene Peleman inserted an endoscope with a tiny camera on its tip through Cunningham's mouth, stomach and intestines. The doctor injected dye into the liver duct area and took pictures. He also took microscopic samples of tissue for testing and inserted a shunt into the duct to allow bile to drain from the liver into the small intestine. There were no visible signs that cancer had spread from the duct. Liver cancer is more difficult to treat because radiation therapy could destroy the vital organ. There was no miracle yet, but the initial word was positive. "Good news for Cunningham: Cancer in bile duct, not liver," read the front-page headline in *The Detroit News*.

Shine, though, probably knew better. His column about Cunningham published in the *Free Press* on October 14 is among the most poignant pieces he ever wrote: "Years ago, I stopped trying to figure out just what it is that enables Cunningham to succeed, often against the most unbelievable odds, at accomplishing what others with more experience, more help and more resources have failed to do. ... Cunningham has been diagnosed with cancer and faces the most difficult challenge of his life. But those who know him also know he will bring to this new fight those things that have sustained him in all the others: his strong faith in God, hope that has never wavered, an unyielding belief in prayer and its special power, and the certainty that nothing is impossible without the help of those you love."

Father Cunningham and Eleanor Josaitis in October 1996 at his last Walk for Justice.

Credit: Focus: HOPE

31

No Bumps in the Road

WEAKENED BY THE surgery to clear his bile duct, Father Cunningham returned to the Madonna rectory to rest for the war to come. Tissue samples would soon reveal the bad news that the tumor had invaded his liver. He faced several weeks of arduous therapy that included twice-daily visits to the Karmanos Cancer Institute at Harper Hospital for radiation treatments, plus chemotherapy every month.

Cunningham insisted on visiting the Center for Advanced Technologies to let his Focus: HOPE colleagues see him in the flesh. He was driven slowly down Oakman Boulevard and through oversize doors into the CAT. A large crowd of employees, Focus: HOPE volunteers as well as children and staff from nearby Glazer Elementary School, cheered and held up signs with the organization's latest catchphrase, "No Bumps in the Road."

Eleanor Josaitis told *Crain's Detroit Business* reporter Joseph Serwach that Cunningham's leave of absence was temporary and he expected to return to work. "He will be back. There's not going to be a bump in the road," she said.

The *Crain's* piece raised questions about Focus: HOPE's management succession plan, given that Cunningham was 66 and Josaitis was 65. Bob Kunkel, a Ford prototype-planning supervisor who was volunteering at Focus: HOPE, told *Crain's* that it would be a challenge to fill the void left by Cunningham. "I'm just as concerned as anybody about who fills the shoes of a guy of this magnitude," Kunkel said. "Father Cunningham is just one of those guys who electrifies you. He gets your attention. He just makes sense. ... You're just privileged to meet people like that."

The priest was feeling too ill to take many of the calls from friends and parishioners. That Sunday, he made brief appearances at both Masses. "I stayed in the back of the church until Communion, and after Communion I talked to the people for just a moment. I thanked them for their deep affection and their vigil," he told *Michigan Catholic* reporter Robert Delaney. Cunningham had summoned Delaney to the rectory to spread the word about how optimistic he felt facing the cancer.

Cunningham said he had intensified his prayers, not only for healing but also for Focus: HOPE. "I said to the Lord, 'If you're going to intervene to clear up the cancer, you might as well take the sugar diabetes with it, and make me a fully healthy person for the next few years.' ... You know, we all do this bargaining. It might not be the height of spirituality but it's certainly very human. So, I've been telling the Lord that I will certainly struggle to purify my heart, to purify my spirit, and to be a better servant, and to energize myself to work harder on behalf of His Gospel. And, to do the sides of the aisle—to help us lift the Center for Advanced Technologies to a new level. And, to make it possible for young men and women in industrial cities across America to have the opportunity that these metro Detroit kids have."

After the last Mass, Cunningham and parishioners walked slowly down the street to Madonna's Shrine to St. Peregrine, believed to have been one of only two shrines in the country dedicated to the patron saint of cancer patients. They prayed some more. That evening, Cunningham went to Belle Isle alone with one of his dogs to walk. Strangers recognized him, came up to him and told him they were praying for him. "I've never experienced anything quite like the affection and support I'm getting from people of all denominations," Cunningham told Delaney. "The people want me to fight, and I'm certainly going to do that. The doctors are fighting, and I'm supporting them with every ounce of strength I have. And I'm a fighter—I don't expect to lie down and go to sleep."

Despite the odds against survival, Cunningham talked about his plans to acquire the Yellow Pages building, then owned by Ameritech. Focus: HOPE would turn it into "Tech Villas," a multi-use hotel and tech center where scientists, manufacturing engineers and other professionals could "come to live with us for a few months, and then to take back home the spirit of this thing, and apply it to the particular needs and capabilities of their communities." Delany made sure to mention that many people planned to attend the 21st Focus: HOPE Walk for Justice on October 13 as a tribute to the ailing priest.

The night before the Walk, the rectory housekeeper and cook, Mitzi Smith, sautéed a steak with a little butter and onion, then took it to him in his upstairs suite. While she was cleaning up the kitchen, Cunningham called her on the intercom: "What the hell did you do with that steak? Oh, my God, it tastes just like how my father used to make it." The priest had not eaten a decent meal in months, and Smith was happy his appetite had returned. At that morning's Masses at Madonna, Cunningham spoke briefly and told his congregation that diabetes be damned, he'd eaten well the night before. "I had steak and mashed potatoes with butter because my doctors told me not to worry about cholesterol right now, but to concentrate on getting healthy," he told them. "And I had ice cream for dessert!"

The weather for the Walk that day was warm and sunny, and the crowd swelled to a reported 18,000. Dignitaries and politicians, including Mayor Dennis Archer, U.S. Senator Carl Levin, Detroit Police Chief Isaiah McKinnon, future Congresswoman Carolyn Cheeks Kilpatrick and Cardinal Adam Maida, squeezed onto the stage erected in the parking lot across

Oakman Boulevard from the CAT. There was an unspoken agreement that none of them would hog the mic, despite it being an election year. Everyone just wanted to hear Cunningham speak.

Cunningham told the crowd that doctors were doing everything they can so that when he died one day, it would not be from cancer. "I feel your strength every day," said the priest, who was wearing a long-sleeve black Focus: HOPE Walk T-shirt and a white Focus: HOPE baseball cap. "But it's a contest for me to eat, to stay up, to fight."

Cunningham led the marchers for a quarter mile down Oakman to the Madonna Church. He took the elevator to the second-floor balcony. From there, he smiled and waved at the people cheering him as they passed by. Detroit Police Sergeant Daran Carey arranged for Cunningham to get rides on the back of two Harley-Davidson cop bikes, one from the DPD and one from the State Police. "He was happier than hell" to get on the Harleys, Carey said.

The following morning, the radiation regimen began. Dr. Vaitkevicius told Cunningham that the treatment would be painful, but without it the prognosis was certain death. "I told him dying would be the easy way to deal with his cancer," the doctor told Patricia Anstett, the medical writer for the *Free Press*. "He elected to fight very hard. It's a sacrifice for his work. He's an unusually brave man." Despite a series of sophisticated tests, doctors still weren't sure of the exact site of Cunningham's primary tumor. "I can't promise a cure," Vaitkevicius said. "But there's a significant possibility we can prolong his life."

Shortly after starting chemotherapy, Cunningham was sitting in the Madonna parish rectory with Sister Ellen Gardner, talking about the toxic chemicals coursing through his body. "Look at what this chemo has done to my fingers; all my fingernails are turning white," he said. "And, besides that, they told me that now I was going to be able to read people's minds." Sister Ellen, who always thought Cunningham was the most perceptive and instinctive man she'd ever known, replied: "Oh? Well, you're going to be even more intuitive than you are? Let's test that: One word, two syllables, four letters in each syllable." "Bullshit!" he said. "Bingo!" Gardner said.

Folk-singer and Cunningham's favorite Jew, Ron Coden, stopped by to see him one night at the rectory. "He said he wasn't scared about this and he was looking forward to the fight and he was going to lick this thing," Coden said. Cunningham told Coden: "I've been praying to God and I think I should pray to Him like you do with *Fiddler on the Roof*. 'And while You're fixing that, there's the diabetes here.' It was a nonchalant way of talking to God and just showed me how much he enjoyed that piece of material."

Despite the illness and discomfort, Cunningham came in to work every day. His immune system was fragile, so he could not be in crowds and had to limit the time he spent with other people. "People wanted to touch him," Sister Ellen said. "People who knew he was in chemo and knew how vulnerable he was still wanted to touch him. And that was dangerous for him."

Several weeks of daily radiation treatment increased his nausea and sapped his strength. On November 11, he was readmitted to Harper Hospital so he could be fed intravenously. "His spirits are good, but his body is weak," Josaitis told a reporter. "This hospitalization is not really a setback. It's part of the whole treatment. The doctors are not discouraged by this."

Cunningham sent a note that was distributed to Focus: HOPE colleagues and Madonna parishioners: "My doctors express guarded optimism. Within another week or so, we will have more definite information, but it appears that we're beating the cancer." Most believed him, but the biopsy results were not good news. While doctors had hoped that the cancer was confined to the bile duct, tests showed it had invaded his liver, spread to his gall bladder and was pressing against lymph nodes.

Josaitis gave the staff at the Resource Center daily updates as soon as she walked in, always adding: "No bumps in the road." That meant: keep working normally. "It was very hard on her and on everybody," said Ann Slawnik, then Focus: HOPE's community affairs director. "Once they told us what it was, I didn't think he was going to last much longer. ... He looked so bad, he looked so sick. That was hard." Cunningham was allowed to go home to the rectory just before Christmas.

Josaitis often took pen to paper to write her prayers out longhand, almost in a stream-of-consciousness, early in the morning. In a three and a half-page prayer written during Cunningham's illness, Josaitis pleaded with God to show mercy in his hour of need:

> God, please look into my heart today and see and hear all that I want you to know about this man. Know, God, that I love him. Let him, God, pause a moment with me and share a cup of water and a moment's rest before he climbs the next mountain. ... Again God, I ask you to look into my tear filled eyes and understand what I ask you. Know him, love him, bless him and be proud of him. He tries, he fails but he always stands. Know this man of yours, Father William Cunningham.

By December 23, 10 million pennies worth $100,000 had poured into Focus: HOPE. Lemenu went to visit Cunningham and asked what he'd like to say in a thank-you note to everyone who sent in a penny. After dictating the note, Cunningham "just sat there," Lemenu said. The card he produced featured his drawing of a simple snowflake to go with Cunningham's words: "Miracles like snowflakes shower on us. 'In God We Trust' is on every penny. Bless you for your prayers. Your love is my healing."

Martin Luther King Jr. Day was January 20, but Cunningham's surgery was scheduled for the 14th. He might not make it out of the operating room alive. So, on the 13th he videotaped a message that might be his last chance to speak to his colleagues *en masse*. In the video he appears wan, weak and worn out. His face was gaunt and his voice was raspy. And his thoughts didn't always follow one another. He tried to be upbeat, full of confidence and forward-looking. It was not a great performance, but the emotion and sadness in his voice broke the hearts of many who saw it.

Dr. King gave his life. He knew it would be a question

of witnessing with his life before he was finished. We are a paramount civil rights organization in the United States, perhaps the leading. And I'm proud of everyone who participates with us: the managers, the volunteers, the colleagues. Everyone participates. We make mistakes. We don't always take the right direction because there's no blueprint, there's no road map. ... Focus: HOPE is a model for the nation. We just have to make sure that you don't get stagnant, that fresh and new ideas come out of our group. They don't come from on high. They come from the hearts, the spirits, the thinking of each of our colleagues. ... I want your continued prayers. ... After the surgery, I anticipate that I'm going to be in great shape. And, that I'm going to return healthier than ever. And, that I will walk with you colleagues many, many more Walks for Justice. God bless the ... [His last word was inaudible.]

Early the next morning, the surgical team of Dr. Donald Weaver, Harper's chief surgeon, and Dr. Peter Littrup, a specialist in cryosurgery that destroys cancer by freezing its cells, began a nine-hour surgery. Karmanos released a statement to reporters later that day saying that Dr. Weaver "couldn't be more pleased with the outcome." More information would be released after doctors analyze results and confer with Father Cunningham. The following morning, Jim Aho and several other Focus: HOPE colleagues were at the Resource Center waiting for word when Cunningham called and was put on speaker. "You could tell he was very happy to report that the doctor said they had gotten all the cancer," Aho said. "At that point, he had to be pretty sure that he was going to make it."

Doctors were exercising caution, but Josaitis echoed Cunningham's optimism. "When I saw him sitting up in a chair, with that big Irish grin on his face, I knew we were going to make it," she said during a news conference at the hospital. "His faith and all the prayers and pennies from people will get him through this. ...

He's giving orders and absolutely believing he is totally cured of cancer."

Sister Ellen said no one wanted to acknowledge that Cunningham was gravely, even hopelessly, ill. "There was an unspoken conspiracy to support the miracle," Ellen said. "We really, really believed it. We believed that when he got done with this, they would find a way to do liver cancer, to take care of the liver cancer. And so we always spoke in very positive terms. And he did, too."

On April 28, Microsoft chairman Bill Gates came to Detroit bearing gifts of cash and software: $500,000 for the Detroit Public Library, and triple that amount to Focus: HOPE. He did not go to the Focus: HOPE campus that day and did not meet Cunningham. But Gates praised Cunningham and Josaitis when he took the podium at the library: "Even around the nation, Focus: HOPE must come to mind. It's a pretty incredible thing, what's been done there."

At Karmanos, doctors had used all the available high-tech techniques to surgically remove the cancer. But, "almost from the beginning," Vaitkevicius said in an interview, doctors knew that it would be virtually impossible to save Cunningham's life. The cancer "was right in the center of the liver," the oncologist said. "If you catch them very early skilled surgeons can get rid of them." In the weeks after the surgery in January, Vaitkevicius said, "the main thing that impressed me was how concerned he was about Focus: HOPE. And Mrs. Josaitis came every day, sometimes several times a day, to help him. It was obvious that he very heavily relied on her. But there was no question that he was the boss."

Josaitis' task, as suggested by doctors, was to snap him out of his stupor. "Here was the trick I had with the doctors," she said years later. "I would go and he would be very low, down in the dumps, and I would deliberately tell him something that I knew was going to drive him crazy. I would come in and say, 'We're going to close the MTI,' anything that would just rattle his cage. ... He'd tell me what I can do and what I can't do. He'd be typical Bill. But then I would go back at night and it would be the opposite. I would just tell him everything that happened during the day. He would ask me questions, and always give me things he wanted to do."

Sister Cecilia Begin, still volunteering at Madonna and advising Sister Ellen despite her retirement a few years before, also sat with him every day at the hospital. Ellen came about three times a week. The nuns talked with each other about parish matters in his room so Cunningham could hear about what was going on without having to summon the energy to respond.

Although the cancer had apparently been eradicated, a serious infection set in at the site of the surgery, where there was a large hole in Cunningham's liver. "He was hopeful, but not banking on that," Vaitkevicius said. "I presumed that he prayed and other people prayed for him, and he was hoping somehow someone would intervene for him. Unfortunately, miracles don't happen very often."

Madonna parishioner Ollie Burton had been battling cancer as well as multiple sclerosis for several years. Ollie—the wife of Cunningham look-alike Fred Burton, Rosa Parks' driver in Detroit—was hospitalized about the same time as Father Cunningham. Her last chance, too, was experimental surgery with a slim chance of success. By telephone from their respective hospital beds, Ollie and Cunningham prayed together and spoke about their faith in God. "Mom wanted to pray with Father; she wanted to tell him it was going to be OK," said her daughter Freda Burton-Stanfield. "She had so much faith in God. She never cried. She never asked why. She just knew that God was going to take care of her. ... Mom's surgery was one day and Father's surgery was like two days after. The church had a special Mass for my mother and at the same time they were praying for Father Cunningham." Ollie died a few weeks after surgery.

As the weeks wore on, Cunningham's mood became gloomy. "I think he was sad that he was going to leave Focus: HOPE, but never desperate," Vaitkevicius said. "Some people fear, but he never had an expression of fear. He didn't finish it and he felt guilty about it. He was sad. He was never afraid of death. The only fear was what was going to happen to Focus: HOPE. But he had confidence in Eleanor that she would be all right."

On May 5, when it was obvious that Cunningham was not going to survive much longer, arrangements were made for him to return to Oakman Boulevard in a donated van equipped with a wheelchair lift. Josaitis drove the van first down Oakman past utility crews laying high-speed fiber optic wires in the "islands" on the boulevard to connect the Yellow Pages building with the CAT and the rest of the Focus: HOPE campus.

They stopped at Madonna. "We boosted his dogs up into the van so he could see and pet the dogs," Sister Ellen said. Across the street, Machinist Training Institute director Joanna Woods said, hundreds of students from the MTI and the CAT dressed in their dark-blue Focus: HOPE uniforms were lined up on the north side of Oakman Boulevard so they could cheer as he went by. However, "we got word that he was only going to the other side [of Oakman], so I had all the students run to the other side, just this big wave of blue. It really looked like a river, there were so many students," Woods said. "And Father saw that, because he really did want to stop at the MTI side. So, then they came back with this [second] wave of students."

As students lined the street smiling, waving and shouting his name, Josaitis stopped the van in front of the MTI. Cunningham beckoned Woods and Tom Murphy, the retired drill sergeant and Fast Track teacher. "When he talked to me, he held my hand and said, 'Joanna, I don't think I've ever seen anything so beautiful,'" referring to the enthusiastic students. "I think I said to the effect, 'Yeah, Father, this is what we always wanted.' He just smiled and held my hand." Murphy said he told Cunningham: "We're going to keep this going, Father." The priest responded, "That's what I want."

On Sunday May 18, the priest was brought by van back to Madonna so he could be seen by parishioners between the 9 and 11 a.m. Masses. The side doors of the van were opened so people could approach. Greg Petty said he watched as parishioners lined up to see their pastor. "I watched people climb in and out of that van, and they go in with hope and anticipation and come out weeping. Boy that was touchy."

Hospital chaplain Father John Markham, who was also pastor at St. Elizabeth Catholic Church, administered the last rites— now called the sacrament of anointing the sick—about half a dozen times for Cunningham. "One time—he may have been somewhat delirious, I'm not exactly sure—but he said, 'John, do you think the Church is going to survive?' I said, 'Yeah, I think it will.' He had great allegiance to the Catholic Church, but he didn't subscribe to everything that comes out as Roman policy. I don't know of any Catholic that does."

Josaitis said Cunningham was practical in his approach to death, expressing his wishes for the funeral. "We planned who was going to perform services, where it was going to be held, who was going to be the pall bearers, every detail," she said.[50] The priest was adamant about something else. "He turned to me, tears coming down: 'You promise me. You promise me you won't put my name on this boulevard and not on this building.'" Cunningham wanted her to swear she would keep his work at Focus: HOPE alive. "He was looking at me like I had to sign an agreement. It was not going to stop. 'Yes, I promise you I will make your work live on.'"

On a particularly fine spring morning that week, Cunningham asked Dr. Weaver to take him to Belle Isle. "I think it was clear by that time that he wasn't going to make a full and complete recovery from his disease and subsequent treatment," Dr. Weaver said. Weaver pulled his Buick Regal to a door where he met Eleanor and helped Cunningham get into the front seat.

They parked near the Scott Fountain with a spectacular view of downtown. "By then, I can honestly say, we had had dozens of lengthy conversations about life, about living, about God, about all kinds of different subjects, and I think in a sense we had become friends," Weaver said. But now, the priest was quiet

---

50   Josaitis said Cunningham told her, "If anybody is going to write my biography, it's going to be Jack Kresnak." According to her, Cunningham was just trying to protect me from all kinds of stuff. He loved you, Jack, and he just wanted you to do it. You were special, and you knew him."

and reflective. "The trip was about something else, seeing something in the past or probably more importantly seeing something towards the future," Weaver said.

Toward the end, "You couldn't understand a word he was saying," Josaitis said. "You wouldn't even have known him. It was like somebody dug up a body somewhere, just to show you an old skull."

Don Josaitis, who had been in the hospital every morning to help the priest walk back and forth down the hallway, called Eleanor and said, "I can't understand what he's saying." Nearly unconscious and unable to articulate his words clearly, Cunningham was trying to tell Don something. Eleanor rushed to the hospital and finally figured out what Cunningham's words were: "Art Van." "Bill, do you want me to go to Art Van and get the furniture for the cottage?" she asked. He nodded yes. At that point, their jointly owned cottage near Lexington along the Lake Huron shore was just a shell without furniture. Cunningham seemed desperate to go there. "You want Don to get the van and get you to the cottage in the van?" Eleanor asked. Cunningham nodded yes. Clearly, he wanted to die surrounded by nature and not in a sterile hospital room. Josaitis said she told the priest: "Bill, let me just go see if I can talk to the doctor and we can get you out of here."

When Josaitis spoke to the doctor, she said, he started to cry. The doctor—a Doctor Foreman, she said—came into the room and told Cunningham: "Father, I know you want to leave and you want to go up to the cottage, but you have to give me three days." He would die exactly three days later.

On Sunday May 25, someone from Focus: HOPE called Frank Kubik and told him Cunningham was near death. It was time for "a few of the old timers" to come by to say goodbye. "They let you have a few moments alone with him," Kubik said. "I went into the room and I could see him. His eyes were open. He had an oxygen mask on, a clear one. He just looked troubled, that's the word I would use. And somehow, I knew he heard me. His eyes were following me, but he looked troubled."

Carl Bidleman took a red-eye flight from San Francisco and came to the hospital with Lemenu early in the morning. "He was not able to speak, but there was a look. He looked at me and there was like this great sadness in his eyes," Lemenu said. Those who were there, including Cunningham's sister Betty Horning and her family, held hands around his bedside and took turns saying a farewell to the man who had done so much for them. "It was really hard for me to have any words; I was struck dumb," Lemenu said.[51]

Vaitkevicius said he felt a sense of deep loss. "I felt this was a man who had a mission, that accomplished his mission, but not complete satisfaction that there was something else to do. But God decided he wanted to look at him in private." He later explained to *The Michigan Catholic* that Cunningham did not die from the cancer, but from an infection that grew from the hole left in his liver. The infection, which could not be treated effectively by antibiotics, spread to his bloodstream and lungs, resulting in respiratory failure.

Early the next morning—Tuesday, May 27—Josaitis was at Focus: HOPE to greet people as they came in and reassure everyone that there would be "no bumps in the road." She stopped by all seven divisions of the organization to thank and hug everyone. She met with a steady stream of reporters and urged them to remind their readers, viewers or listeners that if they wished to honor Cunningham that they should make a contribution to Focus: HOPE.

The body lay in state continuously at Madonna beginning at 6 p.m. that Thursday until the funeral at 11 a.m. Saturday. Hundreds came to the church despite a steady rain that week. The Detroit Police Department provided an honor guard of two officers around the clock. The casket was completely open so people could see Cunningham laid out in his priestly vestments, as well as his motorcycle boots.

---

51   *Lemenu's grief was compounded knowing that his own dad had died on the same date—May 26—that also was a Memorial Day; the two most important male role models in his life.*

During the funeral service that was broadcast by Detroit's three network-affiliated television stations, Josaitis read a letter from President Bill Clinton calling Cunningham's death a "great loss, not only for his family and friends, but for the people of Detroit ... and the nation. ... He left a legacy of compassion and achievement." Josaitis told the crowd that Cunningham did not want buildings or streets named after him, but he wanted them to carry on. "Now it's our turn, dear friends, to answer the call and say, 'Here we are, and your work will continue.'"

A monsignor from the Chancery had refused permission for Cunningham's folk-singer friends to sing "Carry It On," the unofficial Focus: HOPE anthem, during Mass as inappropriate. They did anyway, after a fashion. Standing in a circle around the open casket, the folkies sang the church-approved "Amazing Grace" but alternated verses with "Carry It On."

Cunningham had asked Father Paul Berg, a longtime professor of philosophy at Sacred Heart Seminary, to do the eulogy. The crowd gave Berg a standing ovation when he called Cunningham "the most beloved and respected person in the city of Detroit." Berg also was applauded when he quoted a seminarian asking, "Why aren't there more priests like Father Cunningham?" Berg gestured to the bishops behind him, suggesting that they should ask themselves the same thing.

Berg talked about accompanying Cunningham to Selma to march with the Rev. Martin Luther King Jr., in 1965, along with the co-founder of Focus: HOPE, Father Jerome Fraser. He listed 17 Focus: HOPE programs to serve the poor and called Cunningham "the visionary, the implementer/accomplisher, the sustainer, the passionate." He was passionate "for the poor, for the good, for the right, for the noble."

The funeral procession included about 80 vehicles escorted by motorcycle cops from Detroit Police, the State Police and at least two sheriff's departments. Burial was in Holy Sepulchre Cemetery in Southfield next to his parents in a modest plot.

On Sunday, a handful of close friends gathered at the Josaitis home. Tony and Mary Campbell, Bidleman and his wife Karen Ciesnicki, Lemenu, Thom Armstead and a few others were there. Someone put in a videotape of the funeral coverage by WDIV, Channel 4, the NBC affiliate. They sipped scotch or wine as they watched. They heard the "color commentator"—Father Walter Ziemba, president of St. Mary's College in Orchard Lake and rector of the seminary there—say that Cunningham "was a man of many virtues and one of them was humility. ... Basically, he was humble." At that, "the room literally exploded with laughter, hoots and hollers," Bidleman said. Someone shouted, "Guess this guy never met Bill!" "We were incredulous," Bidleman said. "Of the many adjectives attributed to Cunningham, 'humble' was never among them."

Lemenu, however, had a more nuanced opinion: "Bill at times wistfully wished that he could be seen as a humble man. I remember him saying it from the pulpit at Madonna. He did have his moments and at the end of his life was profoundly humbled. He did not want to die, and 'surrender' was not in his vocabulary. ... That he could not talk God into giving him more time was, I'm sure, a profound disappointment. I did not hear him say it, but I would bet that in the end he conceded and let God have His way. He was a man of faith, and more humble than even he knew."[52]

---

52   *Of all the tributes written about Cunningham in the weeks following his death, the most poignant was penned by Lemenu. It was published on June 1 in the Detroit Sunday Journal, the newspaper put out by striking newspaper journalists: "Father Bill Cunningham, born Feb. 20, 1930, was the most alive person we'd ever known. This is the place [Madonna]where his baritone voice rang out with challenges. His laughter filled the air with contagious joy. His eyes flamed brighter than the candles one moment; tears flowed freely down his cheeks the next. ... Wanting to believe what Bill taught, that there is information and opportunity in every crisis, I have sent an open letter to the universe. How do I make sense of this? Why, God, have you taken Bill Cunningham away? Perhaps this morning I was given a partial answer. At 10 a.m. I was dropping off Carl [Bidleman] at Madonna Church where he was helping with the funeral arrangements. Standing at the corner bus stop in the pouring rain was an older woman in a long, white dress. Carl and I approached her and discovered that she had made a two-hour journey by foot and several buses to pay her respects to Father*

Cunningham. She discovered that his body was not yet at Madonna. I was intrigued by her, for she remained absolutely cheerful as she embarked on her journey home. Her name is Marie Woods. She's 75 with an infectious laugh and a stubborn disposition. As I was driving her home, she told me that she had a mission to help people even if sometimes they resisted it. ... I asked her if she knew Father Cunningham. She said, 'Do I know Father Cunningham? I know him a long, long time. All the good he do for people. I shook his hand once. Yes, sir, I know him a long time.' I think I get it. Marie and those people embracing in church and telling Cunningham stories are putting the lie to this rumor that he is dead. He's alive in everyone who met him and in those who know him by the stories and the continuation of his work. I can still send him letters, and the Father Cunningham that lives now in me can answer them. Thank you, Bill. But I've got to confess I sure wish I could walk up to you and see those eyes and hear your laugh one more time."

Eleanor Josaitis and Rosa Parks during the first Walk for Justice after
Father Cunningham's death.

Credit: Focus: HOPE

32

The Assembly

TO THE SURPRISE of no one, Eleanor Josaitis was back at work that Monday, two days after Father Cunningham's funeral. Months of running Focus: HOPE while seeing him through rounds of treatments and surgeries had left her fatigued. She deserved a break, but she had vowed before God and Cunningham to keep Focus: HOPE going. And if there was one thing Eleanor knew in her heart about tough challenges, it was get to work.

For many years, decades really, Eleanor followed a morning routine that exemplifies her steadfast faith and tireless search for ways to serve. She'd set her alarm for 5 a.m., but nearly always awoke at 4:45. She'd make her way into the kitchen, start the coffee pot and sit down in her pajamas. Then, for a few minutes she would stop thinking about everything that had to be done that day for Focus: HOPE and surrender to the Almighty. "OK, God, it's your turn," she'd say aloud. She'd listen for God's voice. Then, she'd bring her mind back to her endless list of tasks and run pressing ones by "the Assembly."

The Assembly was her personal board of directors to whom she always turned for advice and intercession. All members happened to be dead, but they were very much alive in Eleanor's spiritual imaginings. Martin Luther King Jr., and Malcolm X were Assembly members, as were Mohandas Gandhi, Golda Meir, Anwar Sadat, and Eleanor Roosevelt, for whom she was named. Senator Philip Hart, who taught her how to deal with Washington, was an esteemed member.

Bill Cunningham was recently inducted. His voice in her mind's ear was freshest. But the Assembly's chairman would always be Dario Bonucchi, the folk music impresario who helped get Focus: HOPE off the ground. "I pray to them often, just my own little thing. 'Hey, Bonucchi! If you're up there, let's get the Assembly helping us and helping Focus: Hope raise money,'" she explained.

Focus: HOPE's board of directors—forced now to start regular meetings—gathered on June 16 and unanimously elected Eleanor to a four-year term as executive director. Her age (65) was a concern, but she knew the operation better than anyone and was passionate about keeping it going. Still, she and the board knew well that Father Cunningham would be a tough act to follow.

Eleanor showed she was in control at a June 24 news conference announcing a $2.6 million contract with the Pentagon to research and develop advanced materials used in military diesel engines. The contract came about largely because of Senator Carl Levin, a senior member of the Armed Services Committee. "This is a moment that Father Cunningham had been waiting for for a long time," Eleanor said. "I'm sorry he can't be with us, but I'm sure in spirit he's with us." People admired how she kept promising to keep Cunningham's vision and work alive.

The still-grieving staff accepted Eleanor's leadership. From his perspective, food program director Frank Kubik said it seemed like Cunningham was still around: "What she did was because of him. It was always what would he think, what would he do, would he approve? He would be happy with this. He would not be happy with that."

Kay Bell, then Focus: HOPE's controller, said Eleanor's demeanor became "a little sterner, a little straighter. ... She put on the armor when she needed to." Bell thought about the responsibility Eleanor was taking on, fully aware that her skillset was different than Cunningham's. "She was never the visionary. She was the manager, the administrator. She did not have that schmooze that was really needed to charm the money out of the trees like Bill did."

Eleanor considered herself the hope for Focus: HOPE, despite internal doubts. She stood tall and confident, retelling over and over the story of how Focus: HOPE began as a response to the deadly and devastating 1967 "rebellion."

But she lacked Cunningham's insight and intuition that nurtured a useful understanding of manufacturing operations. Unlike the priest, who had an ability to convince professionals from multiple disciplines that he knew what he was talking about, Eleanor's knowledge of the complex industrial side of Focus: HOPE was sharply limited. She had professional manufacturers like Lloyd Reuss, Tim Sullivan, Lud Koci and Thom Armstead to rely on. But, none of them, least of all Eleanor, could negotiate an agreement like Cunningham, a notoriously stubborn bargainer.

Eleanor's concerns centered on making the place look neat and tidy, and ensuring that employees were polite, dressed in proper business attire or Focus: HOPE uniforms, and were on time. "She'd come down here at six o'clock in the morning. She'd be here standing at the time clock, making sure that her students were here on time. And if they weren't on time, she'd raise hell with them. She was fully engaged, fully supportive of what Father wanted to do," Sullivan said.

Things settled into a new normalcy and then—to paraphrase an expression frequently used at Focus: HOPE—the crap hit the fan. It was hot and humid on July 2, 1997, with thunderstorms forecast. By 6 p.m. nearly everyone had left the Focus: HOPE campus, including Eleanor. In the Resource Center, four people were still in the building: Kay Bell, Ken Kudek, IT chief Linda Hanks and Mike Montgomery, a fund development officer.

They were standing at windows on the upper mezzanine while a heavy rainstorm and strong winds pounded the Resource Center. Suddenly, Kudek felt his ears pop from a drastic change in air pressure. "Hit the deck!" he yelled. They all ducked under desks as the Resource Center's roof sailed away and rain poured into the building. "When I came out from under the desk, I was standing in a waterfall," Bell said. "Water was everywhere. Most of the roof was gone."

Roofs were gone from other Focus: HOPE buildings, too, including the Center for Children and the CAT. Several homes on Kendall Street were destroyed and nearby Glazer Elementary School was severely damaged. Historically, tornados were rare in Detroit, but in this storm three twisters struck inside city limits, among 13 tornados that raked southeast Michigan that evening.[53] Thankfully, no one was hurt at Focus: HOPE, and the room that contained mainframe computers and telecommunications equipment were safe and dry.

Colleagues and volunteers rushed to the campus to help, searching with flashlights for anything of value that could be salvaged. At dawn, more people came and they worked all week to clean up. Detroit Police Sergeant Daran Carey, who proudly said he was Cunningham's and Josaitis' "personal police officer," showed up and Josaitis put him to work immediately. "Eleanor was picking up everything," Carey said. "I was doing whatever Eleanor told me—move this, move that. I worked harder that night than in my whole 20 years with the police department."

Items were carried down the street to the recently acquired Michigan Bell Telephone Company building (known as the

---

53   *Seven people were killed, including five in Grosse Pointe Farms who were swept into Lake St. Clair along with the gazebo in which they'd taken shelter. The strongest tornado that day was measured as an EF3. The insurance settlement was $18 million—probably a lot less than Cunningham would have negotiated. In what many believed a miracle, a busload of young children from Focus: HOPE's Center for Children that had been on a day trip to Kensington Metro Park near Milford was delayed by two hours when the bus broke down. It had been scheduled to return to Focus: HOPE at 6 p.m., just as the tornado hit.*

Yellow Pages building because of the large sign on its roof) for drying, sorting and filing. Although it survived the tornado, that building was in bad shape. It had been used as a parking garage by Michigan Bell for several years and the little-used front entrance was completely engulfed with pigeon droppings. People came and went through the ground-floor garage and loading dock area. Two floors of offices were cleared and became temporary headquarters of Focus: HOPE. Plans to develop Cunningham's last visionary idea, Tech Villas, in the old building were postponed and eventually cancelled because of the need to repair and regroup all along Oakman Boulevard.

As she had been so many times before when tragedy struck Focus: HOPE, Josaitis was optimistic about the opportunities that arose from challenges. "I think something good will come out of this—a new housing project, a new mall in the neighborhood," Josaitis told the *Free Press* a few days after the storm. "It gives me more determination to make the city and state better. I've seen the riots. I've seen the hate and anger and total frustration. The last four days I've seen every creed and color working together."

Tens of thousands of people and thousands of businesses in southeast Michigan were without power. One bright spot was Focus: HOPE which, despite the damage, had industrial-size generators running on natural gas that powered its campus, even as the surrounding neighborhood endured weeks without electricity. "Everybody said, 'Father's helping us,'" said Tim Sullivan. "Father had everything fully insured to the max and it covered all the things we needed." Sullivan said they could not afford a production shutdown of more than 48 hours and they managed to restart manufacturing operations in two days.

Cunningham's death had resulted in thousands of dollars in donations, but the money was a temporary fix for Focus: HOPE's operating budget that would end the year $9.4 million in the red. Eleanor's never-say-die attitude and talk about the insurance coverage actually stalled cash donations coming in for a few weeks. "The tornado gave us a great way to acknowledge that we needed to raise money," Montgomery said. "Eleanor had bought in. Eleanor understood." Still, she did not want it publicly known that Focus: HOPE was in financial trouble, echoing Cunningham's notion that people would not donate to a nonprofit on the verge of bankruptcy.

Cunningham always was able to miraculously find a source of cash to get through one financial crisis or another. William S. White, the longtime head of the C.S. Mott Foundation, said that he had visited the CAT one day when Cunningham pulled him aside. "We got a little cash flow problem," the priest confided. "It was on a Tuesday, and he needed $400,000 by the end of the week so he could make payroll," White said. "And so, I said, 'OK, you got it!'" It was an easy call, he said, for a man and woman who had a vision. "As far as I'm concerned, Focus: HOPE is one of the most successful organizations anywhere."

Josaitis expected that revenues from the production divisions of Focus: HOPE would rise from $10.6 million (actual) in 1997 to $18.1 million (projected) in 1998. Revenues nearly matched her projections when Focus: HOPE got a $7.1 million contract with General Motors to produce 3.4 liter Dual Overhead Cam (DOHC) manifolds. But there was a dark lining to that silver cloud.

"That contract with GM almost killed us," Kudek said. The contract for work on a new engine "was going to be the savior-contract for the CAT which was losing money." But GM stopped production because the new engine was not selling. "The building is being lit, being heated," Kudek said. "These are CAT candidates that are primarily working these jobs. We can't just turn around and lay them off tomorrow."

Three months later, GM decided it hadn't marketed the new engine well enough so they had Focus: HOPE ramp up production again. Focus: HOPE began churning out thousands of pieces, but GM's supplier of the raw aluminum castings to turn into manifolds sent many that were deceptively defective. Too many air bubbles formed in the metal during cooling, and no one could tell if the piece was flawed until it was machined. "Where the flaw shows up in the manufacturing process could be any place," Kudek said. "It could even be the last step of polishing the face. Now you've got to scrap it." GM credited Focus: HOPE for the cost of the scrapped metal, "but they didn't credit you for the work, the labor, the wear on machine tools, the overhead of heating the plant, the electricity."

Among Focus: HOPE's funders and partners, especially the automotive executives invested in the organization's machinist and engineering training programs, a consensus developed that Josaitis needed a strong manager for the manufacturing operations. They found one in Tim Duperron, who had spent several years at Ford Motor Company as a manufacturing engineer and later plant manager of the company's casting plant in Cleveland.

"The automotive companies were very worried about what was going to happen with the manufacturing activity at Focus: HOPE without Bill," Dupperon said in an interview. "Bill could call on high-horsepower people to help. Eleanor didn't have the same ability."

He began in February 1998 with the title of chief operating officer and he was told, "everybody reports to you." The first thing he did was to ask Josaitis for an organizational chart. "She handed me a phone list," Duperron said. "Here's this list with a couple of hundred names on it. I said, 'Eleanor, do you have an organization chart?' She said, 'Use that.' 'Eleanor, I'm trying to see who reports to me.' [She said] 'Every one of those names in bold reports to you.' There were 36 bold names on that list. I had a 36-to-1 report relationship when I started here." Duperron soon learned that changing the "mom and pop" culture of Focus: HOPE was not going to be easy. "When Father told her 'make my work live on,' I think she took that to mean to keep it exactly the way it is right now."

At the time, Focus: HOPE employed 786 people on its 40-acre campus and had an operating budget of $62.5 million in 1998. The organization claimed 49,000 volunteers helping out on several projects. By August 1998, Duperron developed a list of essential, do-or-die changes to 13 programs and brought it to Josaitis. "I can't get Eleanor to agree on one of them, not one," he said.

Despite the fundraising difficulties, Josaitis scored a major coup when an anonymous donor gave $7 million to Focus: HOPE in 1998 to develop a new high-tech training program. The Information Technology Center (ITC) opened in 1999 as a place to train computer network administrators, systems administrators and data base administrators, Hanks said. That year there was a very high demand for trained IT administrators due to the calendar change to 2000—many feared older computers would be unable to make the adjustment. "People were getting hired before they graduated" from the ITC, Linda Hanks said. Then, the tech bubble burst in 2001. Most companies already had invested in new computers and personnel to handle Y2K, so they stopped hiring.

The $7 million gift to create a new training program was essential to modernize Focus: HOPE's education programs, but it did little to help pay for Focus: HOPE's other projects to assist the needy. In 1999 Dave Egner, who had been named to succeed Gilbert Hudson as president of the Hudson-Webber Foundation, said he was driving on his way to work downtown when he got a call on his cell phone from Montgomery. "I don't think Focus: HOPE's got enough cash to finish the month; it's a mess," Montgomery told Egner. "For some reason Eleanor listens to you."

"I literally hung up with Mike and called El and said, 'I'm going to be driving by your place in about 10 minutes, can I stop in?'" Egner said. They met in the conference room near Josaitis's office and Egner asked her if things were going well in spite of Father's death and the tornado. "Are you OK? Is Focus: HOPE OK?" he kept asking. "After a few minutes of trying to convince me everything was OK, she got angry with me." In previous meetings, "El would always lean over and grab my hand to make a point. At this point, she actually smashed her fist on top of my hand, and said, 'You don't tell the bad part of the story. Nobody will fund you.'"

Egner laid it on the line—she and Focus: HOPE would have to be upfront with the foundation community or risk losing their support. "For the next 90 minutes we entered into a discussion into how the foundation world would walk away if Focus: HOPE was not only showing where the warts were but also having a set of strategies for dealing with them," Egner said. When he asked about how much the Focus: HOPE board could help, Josaitis shook her head no, meaning not much. Cunningham had always told her "to never get a board; they just get in the way and slow you down," she said. "She was trying to pay respect to Father's style at a time of this great transition, and it really put her between a rock and a hard place." Josaitis agreed to bring on new, more powerful people onto Focus: HOPE's board. She also agreed "that if I could get the foundations in the room, she would build the problem-solving strategies," Egner said.

Josaitis and Duperron came to the meeting with the foundation leaders, having done their homework. "They had prepared a terrific summary of where they were, what the gaps were, what they planned to do about it, and then very courageously the areas where they didn't know how to restructure," Egner said. "It was extremely candid and forthright. ... El was El. She got up and did her whole spiel: this is why it matters, this is why we started it, this is why we have to keep it working. She was the spiritual guidance of that place, no question, after Father died."

They talked about an executive succession plan, and Josaitis agreed to develop one. "She was in a different place of understanding and started building the board shortly after the funders came in," Egner said. There was widespread support from the foundations, but he said they never would have responded that way without Josaitis. The foundation heads respected her and wanted her to succeed. And he personally admired Josaitis for how she handled that period with dignity and resolve. "To go from 'you don't tell the bad news' to within weeks presenting credible data with solutions, and then implementing the plan— they turned a corner." Egner said the foundations stepped up to the challenge and agreed to provide support and to meet regularly with Josaitis and her team for three years, a commitment that would stretch into a second three-year period.

The new board approved launching Focus: HOPE's first campaign to draw in donations from well-heeled individuals. Auto company executives involved in the fundraising committee included Jacques Nasser, Ford's president and CEO from 1998-2001; John Barth, a top executive and later CEO of Johnson Controls; Kenneth Way, CEO of the Lear Corporation from 1988 to 2000, and Vern Istock of the National Bank of Detroit, who was chairman of Bank One Corporation from 1999-2000. The goal was $75 million. Those recruited to the board included Jack Litzenberg, a senior program officer at the C.S. Mott Foundation; James Padilla, president of the Ford Motor Company, and William F. Jones Jr., vice president of corporate and financial activities for DaimlerChrysler.

Josaitis and Lloyd Reuss, the former GM president and dean of the CAT, thought that the auto parts business would cover the high costs of running high-quality machinist and engineering programs. But huge operating losses piling up at the CAT and the MTI every day were a drag on the entire organization. "That meant that the earn-money strategy became less and less viable every day," said Montgomery. "At the same time on the government side, the amount of federal money available was generally decreasing. The State of Michigan, beginning in the [John] Engler administration, went from an approach to job training that would fund an organization like Focus: HOPE to training programs that would be for a narrowly defined incentive to move companies to the state: training grants."

Josaitis never actually did much to recruit a successor. Someone on the Focus: HOPE board suggested Keith Cooley, a former senior engineer at GM and director of strategic planning for corporate communications. Cooley was one of GM's top African-American executives. But when he met Eleanor, she told him she wanted to make one thing clear: "I'm not going to retire." Cooley said, "She just wasn't interested in anybody replacing her."

The board hired him anyway in June 2002. "He and Eleanor didn't get along," Duperron said. "Eleanor actually treated him really badly. She was ruthless." Cooley had never met Cunningham. But he understood that "Bill was the idea guy, the big thinker, and Eleanor was the one who actually had to make it materialize," he said.

At an event at the Somerset Mall in Troy to honor Eleanor, Cooley was in the food line with her husband Don. "I said,
'Don, you've got to be awfully proud.'" He responded that he
was. Realizing that Don never seemed to be recognized for the
sacrifice he and his kids had made as his wife devoted herself to
Cunningham and Focus: HOPE, Cooley asked, "What do you
really want out of life?"

"He looked at me, got tears in his eyes, and he said, 'I'd like to
have my wife back.' I said, 'I'll make you a deal. I'll do whatever
I can to give her more time for you,'" Cooley said. Don told him
that if he did pull that off, "I would be forever in your debt."

"Keith didn't really understand the traditions of the organization, how it had been run from the heart, it had been run from
the spirit," said former congressman Bill Brodhead, who was
then a Focus: HOPE board member. "It wasn't a dollars-and-
cents operation. And Father Cunningham's style and Eleanor's
style was: if this is the right thing to do, let's do it and figure out
how to pay for it later," Brodhead said. Josaitis, he said, "was
always very, very optimistic that the Lord will provide. Whereas,
Keith was obviously looking at things from a dollars-and-cents
perspective."

Josaitis resisted every change Cooley attempted. Eventually,
he told the board that he was being "hogtied" by Josaitis: "I can't
make the changes that I think need to be made because Eleanor
is working the way she always worked," according to Brodhead.

Against Eleanor's desires, Focus: HOPE announced in
December 2005 that it was getting out of the manufacturing
business at the CAT, while continuing operations at the MTI
and maintaining the food commodities program, its remedial
education and computer skills training program. After 12 years,
the CAT would end its auto parts business and shift to research
and development work for the Defense Department under much
smaller contracts with the Pentagon. Brodhead said he remembered speaking with Josaitis around that time when she was 72
years old, and commenting that "20 years from now, it is my
hope—and I hope it's your hope—that this organization is here
and it's strong and it's helping people in Detroit; and you're not

going to be here and I'm not going to be here. She said, 'I will be here.' I thought, oh boy! It was hard for her to let go."

In January 2006, the board decided to promote Cooley to CEO and to name Josaitis as "CEO emeritus," as a way to soften the blow. The new board also believed Josaitis had to leave the Resource Center, where she'd worked side-by-side with Cunningham for decades. Some thought she should leave the campus entirely, but Josaitis would have none of that. She agreed to move down the street to a second floor office at the CAT.

Privately, Josaitis was livid, telling Lemenu that a "coup" had been "orchestrated by Keith Cooley [who] manipulated board members systematically to vote against her." Lemenu said Josaitis "was deeply hurt, but she kept saying she had to do what Phil Hart had taught her, and that was to out-class them."

Publicly, Eleanor was as gracious as always, telling reporters that it was an orderly transition to new leadership. "I'm not stepping down," she told one. "I'm stepping up to a new challenge."

In January 2006, Governor Jennifer Granholm named Cooley director of the Department of Labor and Economic Growth. Although Josaitis offered to come back during the hunt for a new CEO, the board told her no and took 18 months to elect one of its own members, William F. Jones Jr., to the position. That pleased her.

Josaitis was diagnosed with breast cancer in late 2008. After many months of treatment, she was declared free of the cancer in 2009. That summer, however, she was at their cottage on Lake Huron sitting in a recliner and reading. When she tried to get up, the pain in her back was excruciating. She thought it was because she'd sat for so long, but the pain was relentless. Several days later she went to her doctor and was diagnosed with cancer in her ovaries and in the lining of her uterus.

There was little hope of a cure. Her health also suffered from frequent twists or falls that left her with a broken hip and spine. She left her desk at Focus: HOPE's CAT for the last time in the fall of 2010. After staying at home for several weeks in a hospital bed set up in the den, she began to move from medical facility to nursing home and, finally, to Angela Hospice in Livonia, where family and friends gathered as her life of service wound down. Noel Tichy a U-M business professor, author and friend of the family, used his frequent-flyer miles to help some of the Josaitis kids and grandchildren come to Michigan to be with her during her final days.

Even while dealing with cancer and her own mortality, Eleanor lay in bed, signing thank-you letters to donors sending money to Focus: HOPE in tribute to her. She worked like that virtually until the hour of her death, 3:45 a.m. on August 9, 2011.

Former Mayor Dennis Archer told the *Free Press* that Eleanor "may have been short in stature, but she was huge in intellect, character, integrity, compassion and desire to give back." *Forbes* magazine called her "Detroit's Mother Theresa."

Senator Carl Levin gave the eulogy at Blessed Sacrament Cathedral, praising both the charismatic priest and the iron-willed housewife: "They saw that underlying many of the problems that they sought to solve was something fundamental: distrust, discrimination and hate. And so at the center of their efforts, they placed a core belief in what they termed 'the dignity and the beauty of every person,' and they worked to heal the wounds of racism and division.

"These were all practical steps, but they were never easy. Eleanor's enemies were as old as humanity, and those enemies put up a fight. Eleanor got hate letters. They just further fueled her resolve. Her offices were firebombed. No cowardly vandal could intimidate her. She said, 'You can deck the SOBs, or you can out-class them.' She chose to out-class them, and she outlasted them."

In 2014, almost exactly three years after her death, Don Josaitis sat in his Dearborn apartment and tried to answer questions about her past, some of them things he'd rather not remember. Why don't you ask her, he told the interviewer, motioning to a black box that sat on a bookshelf containing her ashes. She'd made him promise to scatter the ashes into Lake

Huron from a freighter, the big ships she loved watching pass by on Belle Isle or by the cottage on the lake.

At a swanky fundraiser for Focus: HOPE that year, Don Josaitis walked in to see his wife's face projected onto an oversize screen. At the event, U.S. Attorney General Eric Holder gave a speech in tribute to Focus: HOPE, Father Cunningham and Eleanor Josaitis. "He's talking about her, mentioning her name 100 times, talking about the things she did. And it was just like, gosh, she was really a great person," Don said. "I look back on it, and I think I'm more proud of her now than I was then."

Bibliography

Casey, Genevieve, "The Conscience of Detroit" (Marygrove College Press).

Fine, Sidney, "Violence in the Model City" (University of Michigan Press; reissued as a paperback in 2008 by Michigan State University Press).

Gavrilovich, Peter & McGraw, Bill, "The Detroit Almanac – 300 years of life in the Motor City" (Detroit Free Press)

McGreevy, John T., "Parish Boundaries: The Catholic Encounter with Race in the Twentieth-Century Urban North" (University of Chicago Press).

Spoto, Donald, "Reluctant Saint; the Life of Francis of Assisi" (2002, Viking Compass).

Spreen, Johannes & Holloway, Diane, PhD, "Who Killed Detroit?: Other Cities Beware" (iUniverse, Inc.)

Sugrue, Thomas J, "The Origins of the Urban Crisis – Race and Inequality in postwar Detroit." (1996, Princeton University Press)

Tentler, Leslie Woodcock, "Seasons of Grace: A History of the Catholic Archdiocese of Detroit" (Wayne State University Press.)

Young, Coleman & Lonnie Wheeler, "Hard Stuff – The Autobiography of Mayor Coleman Young." (1994, Viking Penguin)

Acknowledgements

WITHOUT THE GENEROUS help of a wide range of people
this book would not exist. Begin with Eleanor Josaitis who
assigned this task and steadfastly believed that I would finish
it some day. Then to William LeFevre and the rest of the staff
of the Walter P. Reuther Library at Wayne State University
where the Focus: HOPE materials are archived. A special
thanks to Jane Fields, the archivist at Sacred Heart Major
Seminary, Monsignor Ed Baldwin, Roman Godzak, archivist
for the Archdiocese of Detroit, and Ned McGrath, the longtime
communications director for the AOD. Many people shared
documents, pictures and memories of Father Cunningham
with me – thank you all. I am grateful to more than 200 people
who agreed to be interviewed. Laura Blyth Poplawski and
Carol Jachim provided key records and documents. The superb
memories of Thom Armstead and a slew of ex-seminarians
(and spouses) like Tony and Mary Campbell, Jerry Lemenu,
Frank Rashid, Carl Bidleman, Bob Brutell, John Burkhardt
and Mike Chateau were invaluable. Jim Aho, thankfully, had
digitalized many of Focus: HOPE historic photographs before
the 1997 tornado scattered many to the wind. Photographers
Ira Rosenberg and John Collier allowed me to grace this book
with their extraordinary pictures. Elizabeth Horning, Father
Cunningham's sister and her family, were kind and gracious as
they shared stories, as were Don Josaitis and his family. A big
thank-you to Martin (Hoot) McInerney for his early support.
I will always be in debt to Neal Shine for giving me a shot in

journalism, for his feedback on early chapters of this book and for his encouragement. Elmore Leonard reviewed an early chapter and gave me excellent advice on writing and format. Isaiah (Ike) McKinnon, then Detroit Police Chief, provided the investigators' file on the 1978 arson fire at Focus: HOPE. Thanks also to Javan Kienzle who copyedited several early chapters and helped me figure out style points. Tom Ferguson read the manuscript with a copy-editor's eyes and saved me from multiple embarrassments. I also am grateful to Jeffra Rockwell who sent me a copy of the tape of Dr. Martin Luther King Jr.'s sermon at Central Methodist Church during his last visit to Detroit in March 1968. Bill McGraw was always there when I had a question about Detroit history. David Crumm showed me how the book could become reality and guided me to writing a better narrative. Diane Kresnak, the love of my life, was the biggest supporter of all and the most thorough proofreader I could find. Lastly, I am eternally grateful to William F. Jones of Focus: HOPE and the Rev. Faith Fowler of Cass Community Publishing House for bringing it all together.

About the Author

JACK KRESNAK CAPPED a 38-year career as a reporter and editor at the *Detroit Free Press* in December 2007 with a 14-part narrative serial about a murdered foster child named Ricky Holland – the longest series the newspaper had ever published. A month earlier, Kresnak was recognized by the Michigan Supreme Court with a unanimous resolution praising his coverage of children's issues for more than 20 years – the first time a journalist was honored by the high court.

Over two decades covering juvenile justice and child welfare, Kresnak received dozens of awards for his work, including the Casey Center for Families and Children's Medal for Meritorious

Journalism on Behalf of Children, the Child Welfare League of America's Anna Quindlen Award, the Toni House Journalism Award from the America Judicature Society, and the Excellence in Journalism award from the National Association of Child Advocates. He was twice named Journalist of the Year by the metro Detroit chapter of the Society of Professional Journalists. In 2008 he was inducted into the Michigan Journalism Hall of Fame.

Kresnak was named President and CEO of Michigan's Children, a non-profit advocacy organization based in Lansing, in 2008. He retired in 2012 to complete *Hope for the City*, his first book.

Kresnak lives in Livonia, Michigan, with his wife Diane Kresnak. They have three children and nine grandchildren.

CPSIA information can be obtained
at www.ICGtesting.com
Printed in the USA
FFOW02n0050210416
23328FF